# ART FOR SURVIVAL

The Illustrator and the Environment

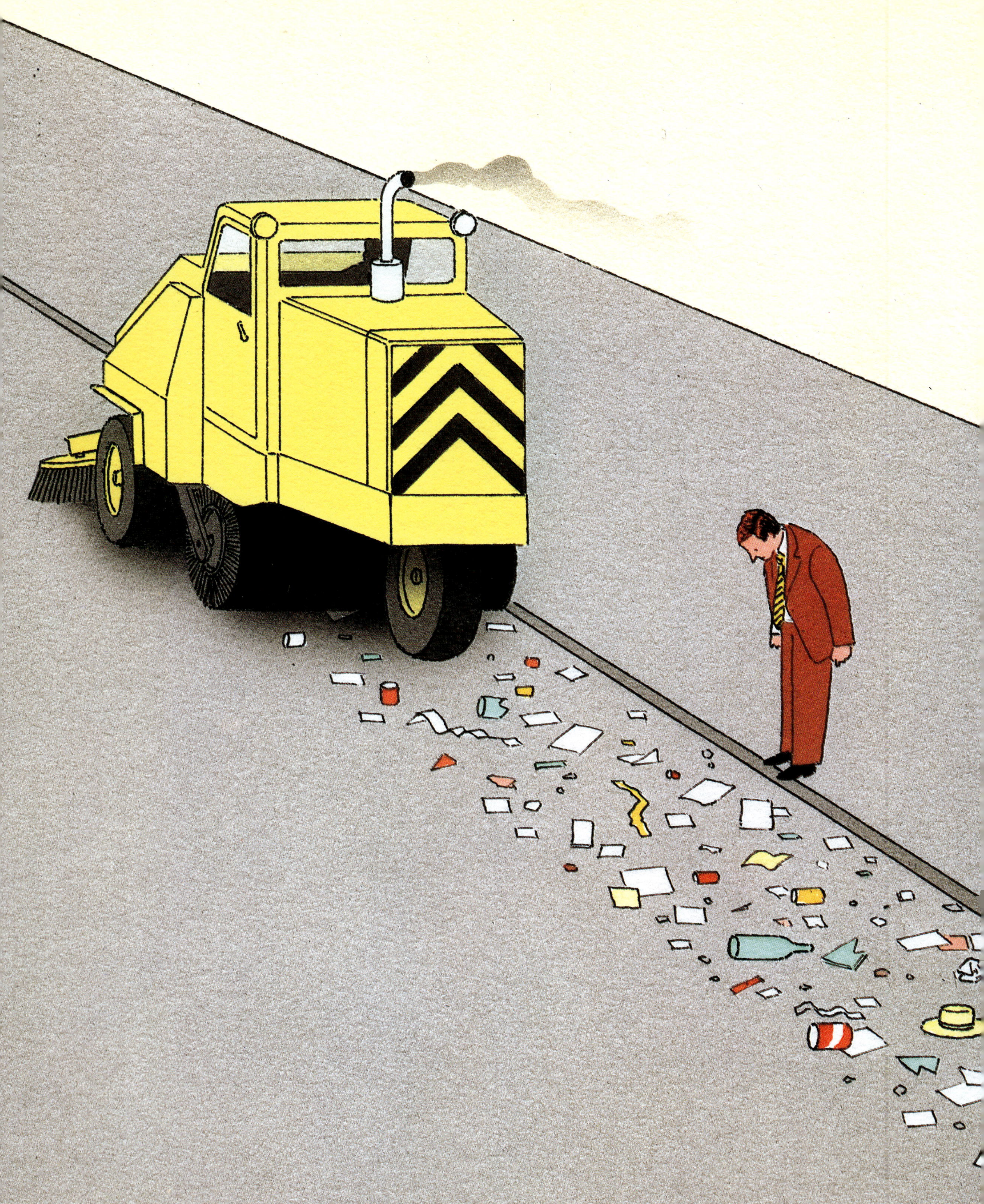

# ART FOR SURVIVAL

The Illustrator and the Environment

Der Illustrator und die Umwelt

L'Illustrateur et l'Environnement

The Illustrator and the Environment exhibition

was sponsored by

The United Nations Environmental Programme

in cooperation with

Earth Island Institute and the Society of Illustrators, Inc.

presented at

The Society of Illustrators Museum of American Illustration

Exhibition curated by Charlotte Bralds

Publisher and Creative Director: B. Martin Pedersen

Editor: Joy Aquilino

Associate Art Director: Randell Pearson

Graphis Press Corp., Zurich (Switzerland)

## GRAPHIS PUBLICATIONS

**GRAPHIS**, THE INTERNATIONAL BI-MONTHLY JOURNAL OF VISUAL COMMUNICATION
**GRAPHIS DESIGN**, THE INTERNATIONAL ANNUAL OF DESIGN AND ILLUSTRATION
**GRAPHIS PHOTO**, THE INTERNATIONAL ANNUAL OF PHOTOGRAPHY
**GRAPHIS POSTER**, THE INTERNATIONAL ANNUAL OF POSTER ART
**GRAPHIS PACKAGING**, AN INTERNATIONAL SURVEY OF PACKAGING DESIGN
**GRAPHIS LETTERHEAD**, AN INTERNATIONAL SURVEY OF LETTERHEAD DESIGN
**GRAPHIS DIAGRAM**, THE GRAPHIC VISUALIZATION OF ABSTRACT, TECHNICAL AND STATISTICAL FACTS AND FUNCTIONS
**GRAPHIS LOGO**, AN INTERNATIONAL SURVEY OF LOGOS
**GRAPHIS PUBLICATION DESIGN**, AN INTERNATIONAL SURVEY OF THE BEST IN MAGAZINE DESIGN
**GRAPHIS ANNUAL REPORTS**, AN INTERNATIONAL COMPILATION OF THE BEST DESIGNED ANNUAL REPORTS
**GRAPHIS CORPORATE IDENTITY**, AN INTERNATIONAL COMPILATION OF THE BEST IN CORPORATE IDENTITY DESIGN

## GRAPHIS PUBLIKATIONEN

**GRAPHIS**, DIE INTERNATIONALE ZWEIMONATSZEITSCHRIFT DER VISUELLEN KOMMUNIKATION
**GRAPHIS DESIGN**, DAS INTERNATIONALE JAHRBUCH ÜBER DESIGN UND ILLUSTRATION
**GRAPHIS PUBLICATION DESIGN**, EINE INTERNATIONALE ZUSAMMENSTELLUNG DES BESTEN ZEITSCHRIFTEN-DESIGNS
**THE GRAPHIC DESIGNER'S GREEN BOOK**, UMWELTANLIEGEN DER DESIGN- UND DRUCKINDUSTRIE, VON ANN CHICK
**THE ILLUSTRATOR AND THE ENVIRONMENT: ART FOR SURVIVAL**, DER KATALOG FÜR EINE AUSSTELLUNG IM RAHMEN DES UMWELT-PROGRAMMS DER UNO, IN ZUSAMMENARBEIT MIT DEM EARTH ISLAND INSTITUTE UND DER SOCIETY OF ILLUSTRATORS, INC.
**GRAPHIS LETTERHEAD**, EIN INTERNATIONALER ÜBERBLICK ÜBER BRIEFPAPIERGESTALTUNG
**GRAPHIS LOGO**, EINE INTERNATIONALE AUSWAHL VON FIRMEN-LOGOS
**GRAPHIS PHOTO**, DAS INTERNATIONALE JAHRBUCH DER PHOTOGRAPHIE
**GRAPHIS POSTER**, DAS INTERNATIONALE JAHRBUCH DER PLAKATKUNST
**GRAPHIS PACKAGING**, EIN INTERNATIONALER ÜBERBLICK ÜBER DIE PACKUNGSGESTALTUNG
**GRAPHIS DIAGRAM**, DIE GRAPHISCHE DARSTELLUNG ABSTRAKTER TECHNISCHER UND STATISTISCHER DATEN UND FAKTEN
**GRAPHIS ANNUAL REPORTS**, EIN INTERNATIONALER ÜBERBLICK ÜBER DIE GESTALTUNG VON JAHRESBERICHTEN
**GRAPHIS CORPORATE IDENTITY**, EINE INTERNATIONALE AUSWAHL DES BESTEN CORPORATE IDENTITY DESIGNS

## PUBLICATIONS GRAPHIS

**GRAPHIS**, LA REVUE BIMESTRIELLE INTERNATIONALE DE LA COMMUNICATION VISUELLE
**GRAPHIS DESIGN**, LE RÉPERTOIRE INTERNATIONAL DE LA COMMUNICATION VISUELLE
**GRAPHIS PUBLICATION DESIGN**, LE RÉPERTOIRE INTERNATIONAL DU DESIGN DE PÉRIODIQUES
**THE GRAPHIC DESIGNER'S GREEN BOOK**, L'INDUSTRIE GRAPHIQUE FACE AUX PROBLÈMES D'ENVIRONNEMENT, PAR ANN CHICK
**THE ILLUSTRATOR AND THE ENVIRONMENT: ART FOR SURVIVAL**, CATALOGUE D'UNE EXPOSITION SPONSORSÉE PAR LE PROGRAMME DES NATIONS-UNIES POUR L'ENVIRONNEMENT, EN COLLABORATION AVEC LE EARTH ISLAND INSTITUTE ET LA SOCIETY OF ILLUSTRATORS, INC.
**GRAPHIS LETTERHEAD**, LE RÉPERTOIRE INTERNATIONAL DU DESIGN DE PAPIER À LETTRES
**GRAPHIS LOGO**, LE RÉPERTOIRE INTERNATIONAL DU LOGO
**GRAPHIS PHOTO**, LE RÉPERTOIRE INTERNATIONAL DE LA PHOTOGRAPHIE
**GRAPHIS POSTER**, LE RÉPERTOIRE INTERNATIONAL DE L'AFFICHE
**GRAPHIS PACKAGING**, LE RÉPERTOIRE INTERNATIONAL DE LA CRÉATION D'EMBALLAGES
**GRAPHIS DIAGRAM**, LE RÉPERTOIRE GRAPHIQUE DE FAITS ET DONNÉES ABSTRAITS, TECHNIQUES ET STATISTIQUES
**GRAPHIS ANNUAL REPORTS**, PANORAMA INTERNATIONAL DU MEILLEUR DESIGN DE RAPPORTS ANNUELS D'ENTREPRISES
**GRAPHIS CORPORATE IDENTITY**, PANORAMA INTERNATIONAL DU MEILLEUR DESIGN D'IDENTITÉ CORPORATE

PUBLICATION NO. 207 (ISBN 3-85709-434-6)


FRONTISPIECE: "STREET SWEEPER" BY GUY BILLOUT, WATERCOLOR AND AIRBRUSH.

PRINTED IN JAPAN BY TOPPAN PRINTING CO., LTD.

# CONTENTS • INHALT • CONTENTU

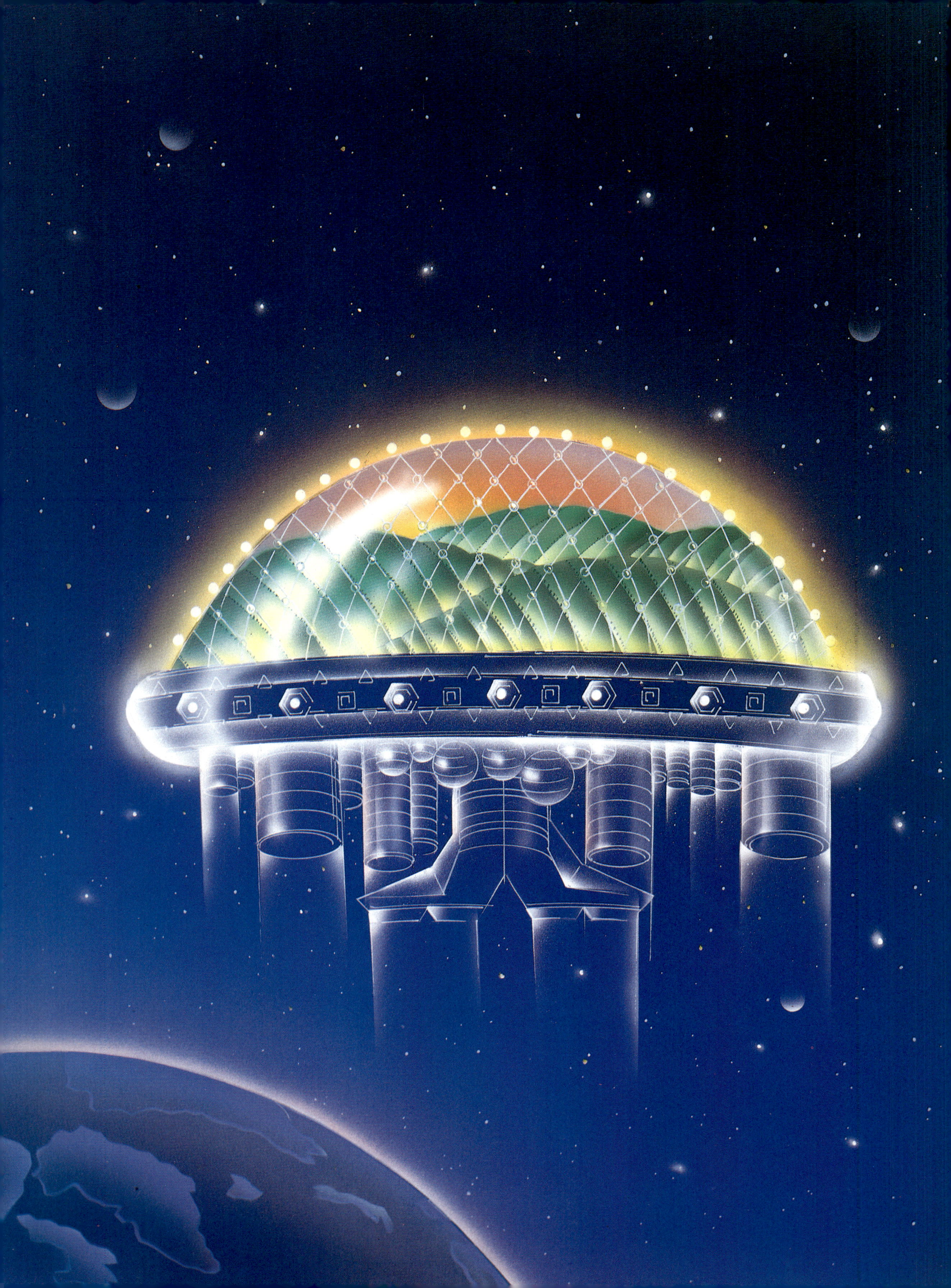

Foreword

## RAY BRADBURY

"FUTURE FARMING" BY CAROL GILLOT, GOUACHE AND AIRBRUSH

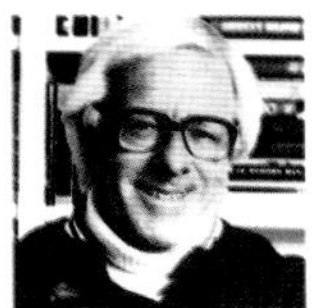

*Vanity, vanity, all is vanity. □ No. For me, anyway: Metaphor, metaphor, all is metaphor. □ That is, if you have an adhesive mind. A mind that can take two objects, large and small, high or low, hot or cold, and stick them together so that they fuse and are never again the same. The adhesion must seem natural, unstrained, and it must not bash the head, kick the shins, or beat the long-dead horse. □ Metaphor. The handle we invent to lift a mammoth, fly the Empire State, or turn a fleet of battleships into a cloud of vinegar-gnats. Metaphor. The idea elevator. Metaphor. The skin around a scatter of islands to turn them into a continent. □ And now, here, metaphors to express a difficult ecological-becoming-political subject. Nothing less than the task of saving the air we breathe, the grass we tread, or the lost cities where we had hoped to find ourselves. □ The problem, as we can see from the art displayed here, is how to shuttle between the ballet step and the bull-ox stampede. Somewhere in between tiptoe-wire-walking on the roof, or falling downstairs in the greenhouse effect, lies a middle ground for ecological influence-peddling. Its territorial imperatives, however, often entice its true believers toward the clenched first, the purple face, and the till-hell-freezes-over outcry. □ My definition of the perfect metaphor is the*

*ghost dandelion become windblown seed. Grey flowers, gone with a breath to recolor the world. □ It follows that if you want to change my mind you must appear not to change it. You must make such a magic trick as will cause me to look here, not there. As in science fiction, you must pretend to scan the future but x-ray the present. The ecological metaphor must gaze into a bronze shield to see Medusa's head, which stands at our near shoulder: 1992. □ Pretense is the heart of metaphor. We must pretend not to be solving a problem. We must act unself-consciously. Then when the problem (air, land, water, beast) is off-guard, solve it with a clean, sidewise, creative blow. □ I made similar metaphors in my novel* Fahrenheit 451*, years ago. I gave future firemen new occupations: burning books, rather than dousing fires. While my readers were preoccupied with the kerosened books, I fed them lessons on how to love libraries. People were so entranced, they hardly noticed I had vaccinated them with Proust, Kipling, Dickinson, and Poe. □ Metaphors must arrive seeming like Hindenburg dirigibles and depart like hares in clover. □ In other words, to say one thing and mean another. All truths worth telling can only be told in reverse or upside down. The stage apron of Hamlet's Elsinore is corpse-strewn, yet its symbolic poetry allows us to walk among the graves without pitfalling in. Such is the gift of metaphor. Everyone dies but the soul exalts in their dying and desires to live. □ Some years ago in a documentary film I saw an elephant killed. I leaped up the aisle to stand in the lobby, weeping. I had never before seen St. Peter's basilica shot and fallen to ruin. Now I had seen just such a terrorist attack on architecture. The two images fused in the moment of destruction. The cathedral and the beast were inseparable. Their bloody dust did not for months settle in the darkness behind my retina. □ So we arrive at metaphors of horror and despair which must be used on occasion because they are so shockingly true. But I would prefer to lead people toward tomorrow with swarms of whales and dolphins like those on a water treatment plant in Redondo Beach, California. The building's murals are so beautiful that you automatically rethink bestial futures. If we see elephants killed too often we may roll over in despair and give up the ghost. I do not wish to kill their blind hunters in order to rebuild Bernini's columns. I wish to swim toward light and air, sky and stars, clean winds and good harvests. I will not refuse the metaphors of destruction, but their use must be limited or our marrow, poisoned, will refuse to rouse us from a failure of will. □ Water striders. The image came to mind as soon as I glanced at the accompanying ecological metaphors. □ To be able to skate on the surface of a concept wihout falling through. □ On summer afternoons in our childhood we often saw, and wished to be, those pond skaters as they left widening calligraphies behind while silently stroking ahead. □ So the finest artists here glide above and not in the surface, which would drown them if they broke the tension. They share the creativity of a midair wirewalker who would topple and fall if for a moment he considered what he was doing. Doing is everything. Thinking about it must come, later. □ It follows then that my favorites among those here assembled are the ones that water-stride ponds without breaking the skin, puncturing the tension, and sinking through. The metaphoric hippo that can shave-skate thin ice. The healthy frog that embodies the sick prince without dying from him. □ Which makes me recall a conversation I had in Rome with Federico Fellini a few years ago. Was it true, I asked, that when he was shooting a film, he never looked at the daily rushes? □ "True," he said. "Why do I refuse to look? Because I don't want to know what I'm doing. I want the film to remain a mystery I must solve each day. If I saw the rushes time and again I would soon grow bored and stale. This way, I provoke my subconscious to give me further gifts." □ It follows then that ecological art, if it isn't careful, will know itself too well, will be self-conscious, if not pontifical. The arrogance of the know-it-all do-gooder can turn off the decent citizen in the marketplace. □ A good picture, as has been said a million times, is worth a thousand words. But a bad picture can cause a thousand imaginary deaths and kill the mind's future. □ I leave you with an image I would suggest to an artist if I were asked to do so. An elephant standing on the altar, surrounded by the marble heavens of St. Peter's with the caption reading: Two of God's Greatest Architectures. For Both: SUPPORT OUR BUILDING FUND. □ To all believers in the future: Off with your logging-boots, on with your ballet slippers.* ■

**RAY BRADBURY**, ONE OF AMERICA'S PREEMINENT WRITERS, HAS PUBLISHED MORE THAN 500 SHORT STORIES, POEMS, NOVELS, AND PLAYS DURING THE LAST 50 YEARS. HIS NOVELS *THE MARTIAN CHRONICLES*, *THE ILLUSTRATED MAN*, AND *FAHRENHEIT 451* ARE ON THE READINGS LISTS IN MOST AMERICAN AND MANY EUROPEAN HIGH SCHOOLS AND UNIVERSITIES. IN RECENT YEARS HE HAS BEEN CREATIVE CONSULTANT IN THE CONSTRUCTION OF SPACESHIP EARTH AT EPCOT, DISNEY WORLD, AND DID SIMILAR WORK ON THE GLENDALE GALLERIA, HORTON PLAZA, IN SAN DIEGO, AND THE WESTSIDE PAVILION IN LOS ANGELES, WITH THE ARCHITECT JON JERDE. HIS NEW BOOK, *YESTERMORROW: POSSIBLE ANSWERS TO IMPOSSIBLE FUTURES*, A SERIES OF ESSAYS ON MALLS, MUSEUMS, WORLD FAIRS, AND HIS WORK FOR DISNEY, WAS PUBLISHED BY CAPRA PRESS IN THE FALL OF 1991. HE IS NOW IN HIS SIXTH YEAR OF WRITING AND PRODUCING "THE RAY BRADBURY TV THEATER" FOR THE USA NETWORK, BASED ON HIS OWN STORIES.

*Eitelkeit, alles ist Eitelkeit. □ Stimmt nicht, für mich wenigstens nicht: Metapher, alles ist Metapher. □ Das heisst, wenn man einen Hang zum Assoziieren hat, einen Kopf, in dem sich zwei Objekte, gross und klein, hoch oder niedrig, heiss oder kalt verbinden, so dass sie verschmelzen und nie mehr sind, was sie waren. Die Verbindung muss natürlich erscheinen, ungezwungen, sie darf nicht im Kopf rumoren, an allen Enden und Ecken zerren. □ Metapher. Das Instrument, das wir erfinden, um ein Mammut in die Höhe zu heben, das Empire State Gebäude fliegen zu lassen oder eine Flotte von Kriegsschiffen in eine Wolke von Stechmücken zu verwandeln. Metapher. Zünder der Idee. Die Haut, die ein paar verstreute Inseln umspannt und aus ihnen einen Kontinent macht. □ Und hier jetzt Metaphern, um ein schwieriges ökologisches und allmählich auch politisches Thema auszudrücken. Es geht um nichts Geringeres als um die Rettung der Luft, die wir zum Atmen brauchen, des Grases, auf dem wir gehen, oder die verlorenen Städte, in denen wir uns zu finden hofften. □ Wie wir anhand der hier gezeigten Kunstwerke feststellen können, ist das Problem, sich zwischen Ballettschritten und dem Getrampel einer Herde Ochsen zurechtzufinden. Zwischen dem Balanceakt auf dem Dach oder dem Fall, geradewegs hinein in den Teibhauseffekt, gibt es eine mittlere Ebene, auf der es um ökologische Einflussnahme geht. Dies ist jedoch auch das ideale Territorium für die Verfechter mit der geballten Faust, dem hochroten Kopf, bereit, «bis ans bittere Ende» zu gehen. □ Meine Definition einer perfekten Metapher ist der verblühte Löwenzahn, dessen Samen in alle Winde getragen werden. Die graue «Pusteblume», mit einem Atemhauch auf den Weg geschickt, um Farbe in die Welt zu bringen. □ Das heisst, wenn ich meine Meinung ändern soll, muss man mich überzeugen, dass ich sie nicht ändere. Mit einem Zaubertrick muss man mich dazu bringen, hierhin zu schauen, nicht dorthin. Wie bei der Science-Fiction, muss man so tun, als zeige man die Zukunft, aber in Wirklichkeit durchleuchtet man die Gegenwart. Die ökologische Metapher muss in ein Bronzeschild schauen, um Medusas Bild zu sehen, 2010 A.D. – und dann schnell Medusas Kopf abschlagen, der ganz nah über unserer Schulter auftaucht: 1992. □ Die erfundene Geschichte ist das Herz der Metapher. Wir müssen so tun, als hätten wir kein Problem zu lösen. Wir müssen unbefangen handeln. Wenn sich das Problem (Luft, Erde, Wasser, Tier) unbeobachtet fühlt, muss man es mit einem sauberen, kreativen Seitenhieb lösen. □ In meinem Roman Fahrenheit 451 benutzte ich vor Jahren ähnliche Metaphern. Ich gab den Feuerwehrleuten der Zukunft neue Beschäftigungen: das Verbrennen von Büchern anstelle der Brandbekämpfung. Während meine Leser sich mit Kerosin übergossenen Büchern befassten, erteilte ich ihnen Lektionen, wie man Bibliotheken lieben lernt. Die Leute waren so abgelenkt, dass sie kaum merkten, wie ich ihnen Proust, Kipling, Dickinson und Poe einimpfte. □ Metaphern müssen wie Luftschiffe daherkommen, um dann wie Hasen im Klee zu verschwinden. □ Anders ausgedrückt, man sagt etwas und meint etwas anderes. Alle Wahrheiten, die es wert sind, ausgesprochen zu werden, lassen sich umgekehrt oder auf dem Kopf darstellen. Auf der Bühne ist Hamlets Helsingør mit Leichen übersäht, doch erlaubt die symbolische Poesie uns, zwischen den Gräbern zu wandeln, ohne hereinzufallen. Das ist die Macht der Metapher. Jeder stirbt, aber die Seele erhebt sich, im Verlangen zu leben. □ Vor einigen Jahren sah ich in einem Dokumentarfilm, wie ein Elefant getötet wird. Ich musste hinaus, um im Foyer zu weinen. Nie zuvor hatte ich die Peterskirche bombardiert und zusammenfallen sehen. Soeben hatte ich einen solch terroristischen Angriff auf die Architektur gesehen. Die beiden Bilder verschmolzen im Moment der Zerstörung. Die Kathedrale und das Tier wurden untrennbar. Noch nach Monaten hatte sich ihr blutiger Staub in der Dunkelheit hinter meiner Netzhaut nicht gesetzt. □ Somit kommen wir zu Metaphern des Grauens und der Verzweiflung, die manchmal eingesetzt werden müssen, weil sie so entsetzlich wahr sind. Ich würde die Menschen lieber mit Walen und Delphinschulen, wie man sie in der Wasseraufbereitungsanlage an der Redondon Beach in Kalifornien antrifft, in die Zukunft führen. Die Wandmalereien an dem Gebäude sind so schön, dass man automatisch über die Zukunft der Tiere nachdenkt. Wenn wir zu häufig sehen müssen, wie Elefanten getötet werden, wenden wir uns schliesslich verzweifelt ab und geben den Geist auf. Ich möchte ihre blinden Jäger nicht töten, um Berninis Säulen wieder aufzubauen. Ich möchte mich zum Licht hin bewegen, zur Luft, zum Himmel und den Sternen, hin zu sauberen Winden und guten Ernten. Ich lehne Metaphern der Zerstörung nicht ab, aber man darf sie nicht zu häufig verwenden, sonst werden wir im Inneren, bereits vergiftet, nicht die Kraft und den Willen finden. □ Wasserläufer. Das Bild kam mir in den Sinn, als ich einen Blick auf die begleitenden ökologischen Metaphern geworfen hatte. □ In der Lage zu sein, auf der Oberfläche eines Konzepts dahinzugleiten, ohne hineinzufallen. □ An den Sommernachmittagen unserer Kindheit schauten wir oft diesen Läufern des Teichs zu oder träumten, selbst die Läufer zu sein, die grosszügige, kalligraphische Spuren zurückliessen, während sie lautlos dahinglitten. □ Die besten Künstler dieser Ausstellung gleiten also über die Oberfläche, nicht auf ihr, denn sie gingen unter, überdehnten sie die Spannung. Sie haben etwas mit dem Künstler auf dem Hochseil gemeinsam, der straucheln und fallen würde, überlegte er einen Moment lang, was er tut. Handeln ist alles, darüber nachdenken muss man – danach. □ Das bedeutet, dass meine Favoriten unter den hier gezeigten Arbeiten jene sind, die über die Teiche gleiten, ohne die Haut aufzureissen und somit die Spannung zu brechen und zu versinken. Das metaphorische Flusspferd, das über dünnes Eis zu gleiten vermag. Der gesunde Frosch, der den kranken Prinzen in sich trägt, ohne daran zugrunde zu gehen. □ Dabei fällt mir eine Unterhaltung ein, die ich vor einigen Jahren mit Federico Fellini in Rom hatte. Stimmt es, fragte ich, dass er beim Drehen eines Filmes nie die tägliche Ausbeute ansähe. □ «Stimmt», sagte er. «Warum? Weil ich nicht wissen will, was ich tue. Ich will, dass der Film ein Rätsel bleibt, das ich jeden Tag von neuem lösen muss. Schaute ich die Aufnahmen immer wieder an, würde ich mich bald langweilen. Durch das Nichthinsehen bringe ich mein Unterbewusstsein dazu, mir weitere Geschenke zu machen.» □ Das heisst, dass ökologische Kunst, wenn sie nicht aufpasst, sich selbst zu gut kennt, sich ihrer selbst bewusst ist, um nicht zu sagen, zu predigen beginnt. Die Arroganz des Allesbesserwissens und Besserhandelns kann dem wohlmeinenden Bürger das Thema verleiden. □ Wie schon unzählige Male gesagt: Ein gutes Bild ist mehr wert als tausend Worte. Ein schlechtes Bild aber kann tausend Tode der Phantasie bedeuten, ihre Zukunft zerstören. □ Ich lasse Sie mit einem Bild zurück, das ich einem Künstler vorschlagen würde, forderte man mich dazu auf: ein Elefant, der auf dem Altar der Peterskirche steht, umgeben von ihren Marmorhimmeln. Die Unterschrift würde lauten: zwei der grossartigsten architektonischen Werke Gottes. Für beide: SPENDET FÜR DIE ERHALTUNG DIESER WERKE. □ An alle, die an die Zukunft glauben: heraus aus den Waldarbeiterstiefeln, hinein in die Ballettschuhe.* ■

**RAY BRADBURY** HAT IN DEN LETZTEN 50 JAHREN ÜBER 500 KURZGESCHICHTEN, GEDICHTE, ROMANE UND THEATERSTÜCKE VERÖFFENTLICHT. SEINE ROMANE *THE MARTIAN CHRONICLES* UND *FAHRENHEIT 451* GEHÖREN ZUR PFLICHTLEKTÜRE DER MEISTEN AMERIKANISCHEN UND ZAHLREICHER EUROPÄISCHER GYMNASIEN UND UNIVERSITÄTEN. IN DEN LETZTEN JAHREN WAR ER BERATER FÜR DIE GESTALTUNG UND KONSTRUKTION DES RAUMSCHIFFES EARTH IN EPCOT, DISNEY WORLD, UND MACHTE ETWAS ÄHNLICHES FÜR DIE GLENDALE GALLERIA, HORTON PLAZA IN SAN DIEGO UND DEN WESTSIDE PAVILION IN LOS ANGELES MIT DEM ARCHITEKTEN JON JERDE. SEIN NEUES BUCH *YESTERMORROW: POSSIBLE ANSWERS TO IMPOSSIBLE FUTURES* (GESTERNMORGEN: MÖGLICHE ANTWORTEN AUF EINE UNMÖGLICHE ZUKUNFT), EINE REIHE VON ESSAYS ÜBER GESCHÄFTSZENTREN, MUSEEN, WELTAUSSTELLUNGEN UND SEINE ARBEIT FÜR DISNEY, IST BEI CAPRA PRESS IM HERBST 1991 ERSCHIENEN. SEIT SECHS JAHREN SCHREIBT UND PRODUZIERT ER AUF DER BASIS SEINER EIGENEN GESCHICHTEN FÜR THE RAY BRADBURY TV THEATER DES TV-PROGRAMMS USA NETWORK.

*Vanité, vanité, tout est vanité. □ Et puis non. Pour moi, tout est métaphore. □ Cela veut dire avoir un esprit associatif. Un esprit qui peut mettre en relation deux objets, grands ou petits, hauts ou bas, chauds ou froids, et les combiner de manière à ce qu'ils se fondent et ne soient plus les mêmes qu'auparavant. Ce processus doit se faire naturellement, sans contrainte. Inutile de se creuser la cervelle ou de courir de droite et de gauche! □ La métaphore. L'instrument que nous avons inventé pour soulever un mammouth, faire planer l'Empire State Building ou transformer une flotte de navires de guerre en nuage de drosophiles. La métaphore, ce détonateur d'idées. La métaphore! La membrane qui enveloppe quelques îles éparpillées et fait d'elles un continent. □ Et maintenant, ces métaphores qui servent à exprimer un thème écologique difficile, qui devient de plus en plus politique. Rien de moins que de protéger l'air dont nous avons besoin pour respirer, de l'herbe sur laquelle nous marchons ou ces villes perdues dans lesquelles nous avions espéré nous retrouver. □ Comme nous pouvons le constater à l'appui des œuvres présentées ici, le problème, c'est de savoir s'orienter au milieu de ces petits pas de danse et du sauve-qui-peut du troupeau. Entre jouer les funambules ou tomber, victimes de l'effet de serre, il existe une voie moyenne, un terrain sur lequel l'influence de l'écologie peut se développer. Cependant, c'est aussi le terrain idéal des défenseurs aux poings serrés, les têtes chaudes, les jusqu'aux-boutistes qui savent ameuter l'opinion. □ Ma définition de la métaphore parfaite serait le pissenlit fané dont les graines sont semées à tout vent. Des fleurs grises à aigrette qui, d'un souffle, s'en vont redonner des couleurs au monde. □ Cela veut dire que si vous voulez changer mon opinion, vous devez faire comme si de rien n'était. Il faudrait un tour de magie pour m'amener à voir ceci, et non cela. Comme dans la science-fiction, il faut faire comme si l'on montrait le futur, alors que c'est la réalité qu'on passe au crible. La métaphore écologique doit regarder dans un bouclier de bronze pour voir la tête de Méduse, l'an 2010. Puis trancher rapidement cette autre tête de Méduse qui apparaît juste derrière notre épaule: 1992. □ Le prétexte est au cœur de la métaphore. Nous devons faire comme s'il n'y avait aucun problème à résoudre. Nous devons agir avec naturel. C'est en abordant tous ces problèmes (l'air, la terre, l'eau, les animaux) sans en avoir l'air que l'on réussira à donner en douce le coup d'élan décisif.* □ *J'ai utilisé de telles métaphores il y a bien des années dans mon roman, Fahrenheit 451. J'avais alors assigné de nouvelles activités aux pompiers: brûler des livres plutôt que d'éteindre les incendies. Tandis que le lecteur se préoccupait de livres arrosés de kérozène, je lui apprenais à aimer les bibliothèques. Les gens étaient tellement distraits que c'est à peine s'ils remarquaient que je leur avais injecté du Proust, du Kipling, du Dickinson ou du Poe.* □ *Les métaphores devraient être aussi aériennes que les dirigeables, et bondir comme des lièvres dans un champ de trèfle.* □ *En d'autres termes, il faut dire une chose tout en pensant à une autre. Toutes les vérités qui sont bonnes à dire peuvent être présentées à l'envers ou sens dessus dessous. Elseneur, où se joue Hamlet, est couvert de cadavres, et pourtant sa poésie symbolique nous permet de marcher parmi les tombes sans trébucher. C'est toute la force de la métaphore. Tout le monde meurt, mais l'âme s'élève dans le désir de vivre.* □ *Voici quelques années, dans un film documentaire, j'ai vu comment on tuait un éléphant. J'ai quitté précipitamment la salle pour aller pleurer dans l'entrée du cinéma. Jamais auparavant je n'avais assisté au bombardement de la cathédrale St-Pierre et à son écroulement. Je n'avais jamais vu non plus une telle attaque terroriste contre l'architecture. L'image de la cathédrale et celle de l'animal se superposaient dans mon esprit. Il fallut des mois pour que leur sanglante poussière ne retombe dans l'obscurité de ma rétine.* □ *Nous en arrivons ainsi aux métaphores de l'horreur et du désespoir qui doivent être utilisées parfois parce qu'elles sont si terriblement réelles. Mais j'aimerais mieux préparer les gens au futur avec des troupeaux de baleines ou de dauphins comme ceux qui sont élevés à Redondo Beach en Californie. Les peintures murales sur les bâtiments sont tellement belles que l'on se met immédiatement à réfléchir à l'avenir des animaux. Si l'on devait regarder un peu plus souvent comment les éléphants sont abattus, on se détournerait avec dégoût et on rendrait l'âme. Je n'ai nullement l'intention de tuer leurs chasseurs aveugles et de reconstruire les colonnes de Bernini. Je préfère me tourner vers la lumière, vers l'air, le ciel et les étoiles, les bons vents et les saines récoltes. Je ne refuse pas les métaphores de la destruction mais nous ne devons pas en abuser, sinon nous ne trouverons plus en nous la force et la volonté nécessaires, nous serons déjà empoisonnés.* □ *Des araignées d'eau. C'est l'image qui m'est venue à l'esprit dès le premier coup d'œil à ces métaphores écologiques.* □ *Etre capable de naviguer à la surface d'un concept, sans tomber.* □ *Les après-midi d'été de notre enfance, nous avons souvent eu l'occasion d'admirer – ou rêvé d'être nous-mêmes – ces araignées d'eau qui évoluaient sur les étangs, développant derrière eux les traces d'une calligraphie, tout en continuant d'avancer en silence.* □ *Il s'ensuit que mes favoris parmi les travaux exposés sont ceux qui savent évoluer sur les étangs sans briser la tension ni sombrer. Ils sont comme ces funambules sur la corde raide qui perdraient l'équilibre et tomberaient s'ils réfléchissaient un seul instant à ce qu'ils sont en train de faire. L'action est tout. Après seulement, on peut y réfléchir.* □ *Il s'ensuit que mes favoris parmi les travaux exposés sont ceux qui glissent sur les étangs sans une éraflure, c'est-à-dire sans briser la tension et sombrer. Comme la vigoureuse grenouille qui porte en elle le prince maladif, sans en être affectée.* □ *Ceci me rappelle une conversation que j'ai eue à Rome voici quelques années avec Federico Fellini. Est-ce vrai qu'il ne regarde jamais les essais de la journée lorsqu'il tourne un film?* □ *«C'est vrai, je refuse de les regarder», m'a-t-il répondu. Et pourquoi donc? «Parce que je ne veux pas savoir ce que je fais. Je veux que le film reste un mystère que je dois résoudre chaque jour. Si je voyais les essais de temps à autre, je m'ennuierais très vite et je perdrais toute fraîcheur. En procédant ainsi, j'incite mon subconscient à me faire de nouveaux cadeaux.»* □ *Cela veut dire que l'art écologique, s'il n'y prend garde, se connaîtra trop bien, sera conscient de soi, sinon pontifiant. L'arrogance de ceux-qui-savent-tout-mieux-que-tout-le-monde peut rebuter le bourgeois le mieux intentionné.* □ *On l'a déjà dit des milliers de fois: une bonne peinture a plus de valeur que des milliers de mots. Mais une mauvaise image peut causer mille morts imaginaires, elle peut détruire l'avenir de l'esprit.* □ *Je vous laisse avec une image que je suggérerais à un artiste s'il me le demandait. Un éléphant debout sur l'autel de la cathédrale St-Pierre, entouré de ciels de marbre, avec ce titre en-dessous: «Deux des plus grandes œuvres architecturales de Dieu». Et cette inscription pour les deux: «Veuillez cotiser pour la conservation de ces œuvres.»* □ *A tous ceux qui croient au futur: quittons nos bottes de bûcherons et enfilons nos chaussons de danse.* ■

**RAY BRADBURY** A PUBLIÉ PLUS DE 500 NOUVELLES, POÈMES, ROMANS ET PIÈCES DE THÉATRE AU COURS DES 50 DERNIÈRES ANNÉES. SES ROMANS *THE MARTIAN CHRONICLES* ET *FAHRENHEIT 451* SONT AU PROGRAMME DE NOMBREUSES ÉCOLES ET UNIVERSITÉS AMÉRICAINES ET DE QUELQUES AUTRES EN EUROPE. RÉCEMMENT, IL A TRAVAILLÉ COMME CONSULTANT EN DESIGN LORS DE LA CONSTRUCTION DU VAISSEAU SPATIAL EARTH À EPCOT, POUR DISNEY WORLD, AINSI QUE POUR LA GLENDALE GALLERIA, HORTON PLAZA À SAN DIEGO ET LE WESTSIDE PAVILION À LOS ANGELES, EN COLLABORATION AVEC L'ARCHITECTE JON JERDE. SON NOUVEAU LIVRE, *YESTERMORROW – POSSIBLE ANSWERS TO IMPOSSIBLE FUTURES*, UNE SÉRIE D'ESSAIS SUR LA POSTE, LES MUSÉES, LES FOIRES UNIVERSELLES ET SON TRAVAIL AU PRÈS DE DISNEY, VIENT DE SORTIR AUX EDITIONS CAPRA PRESS. DEPUIS SIX ANS, IL ÉCRIT LES SCÉNARIOS DE THE RAY BRADBURY TV THEATER, UNE ÉMISSION BASÉE SUR SES PROPRES RÉCITS QU'IL PRODUIT POUR LES CHAINES AMÉRICAINES.

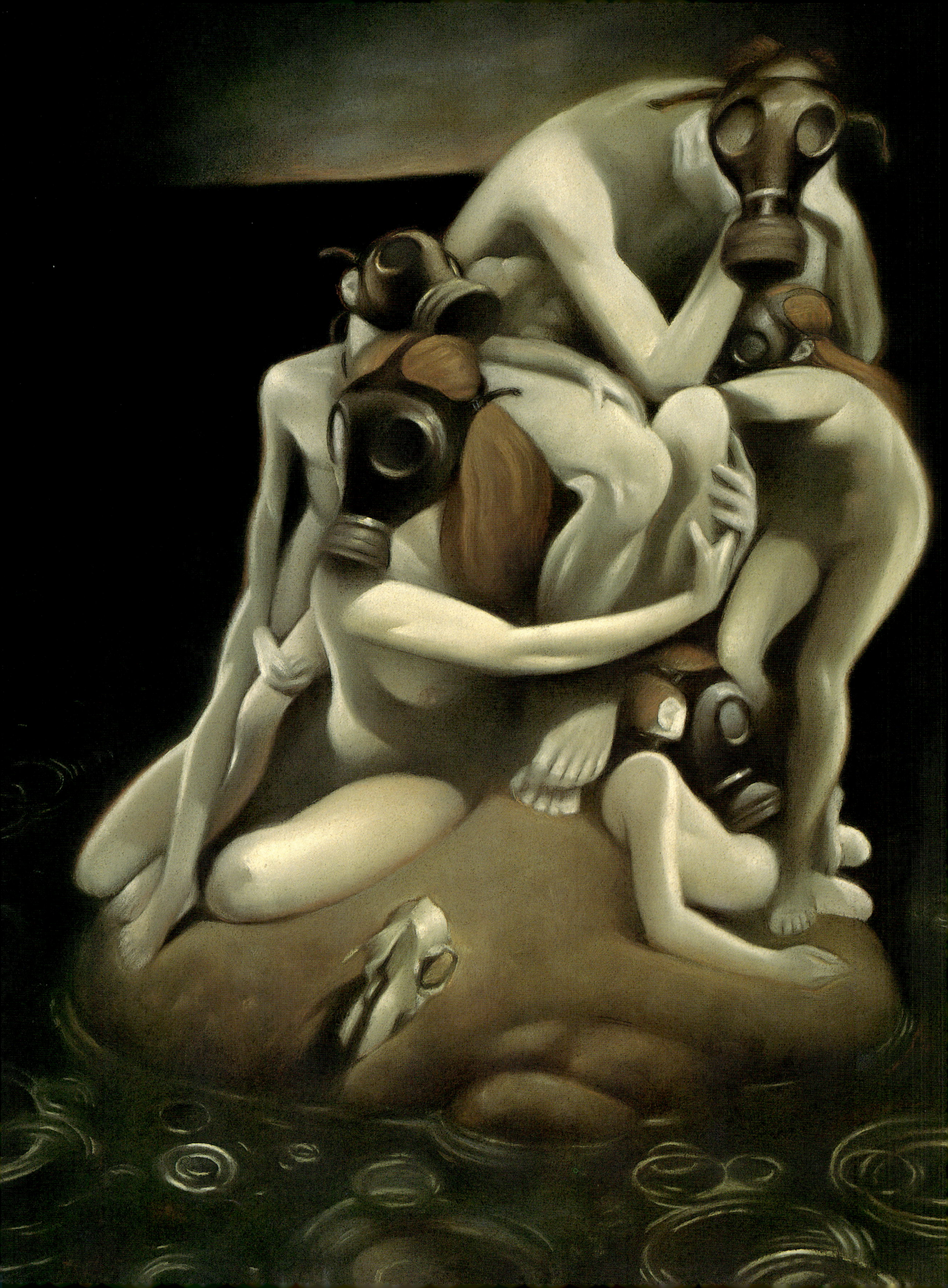

FOREWORD

## NOEL BROWN

"EARTH ISLAND" BY GARY KELLEY, PASTEL ON PAPER

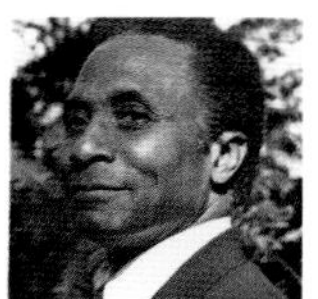

*The environmental issues now facing our world are unprecedented in human experience. We are obligated to rethink many of industrial civilization's technologies and their "benefits" before we reach the point of no return. □ Fortunately, people are beginning to drive the process of change, demanding accountability from both corporate and public arenas, where leaders are asked to answer questions about environmental policy. The vision of a better, healthier world lives on. □ On an individual level, the making of art can infuse this vision with passion. In October 1990, the United Nations Environmental Programme (UNEP) sponsored an exhibition of artwork, the theme of which has become the title for this companion book:* Art for Survival: The Illustrator and the Environment. *This exhibition represented a unique and impressive collection, and received wide critical acclaim. UNEP's sponsorship reinforces its commitment to use the medium of art to convey the urgent messages of our ailing planet and the need for a greater sense of compassion and caring. Through the works exhibited, the artists have communicated this with great power and passion. □ Service to the earth is the greatest service we could perform—a service to life, a service to ourselves.* ■

**NOEL BROWN** IS THE REGIONAL DIRECTOR, UNITED NATIONS ENVIRONMENTAL PROGRAMME, NORTH AMERICA, AND SPECIAL REPRESENTATIVE OF THE EXECUTIVE DIRECTOR. BEFORE HIS APPOINTMENT AS HEAD OF UNEP NORTH AMERICA, HE WAS POLITICAL AFFAIRS OFFICER IN THE DEPARTMENT OF POLITICAL AND SECURITY COUNCIL AFFAIRS. HE HAS REPRESENTED THE UNITED NATIONS ENVIRONMENTAL PROGRAMME AT SUCH CONFERENCES AS THE UNITED NATIONS CONFERENCE ON HABITAT AND HUMAN SETTLEMENTS IN VANCOUVER, 1976; THE UNITED NATIONS CONFERENCE ON SCIENCE AND TECHNOLOGY IN VIENNA, 1979; THE UNITED NATIONS CONFERENCE ON THE LAW OF THE SEA IN GENEVA, 1980; AND THE CONFERENCE OF PLENIPOTENTIARIES ON THE PROTOCAL ON CHLOROFLUOROCARBONS TO THE VIENNA CONVENTION FOR THE PROTECTION OF THE OZONE LAYER IN MONTREAL, 1987. DR. BROWN HAS A PH.D. IN INTERNATIONAL LAW AND RELATIONS FROM YALE, AN M.A. IN INTERNATIONAL LAW AND ORGANIZATION FROM GEORGETOWN, AND A B.A. IN POLITICAL SCIENCE AND ECONOMICS FROM SEATTLE. DR. BROWN IS A JAMAICAN CITIZEN.

*Die gegenwärtigen Umweltprobleme sind etwas bisher Unbekanntes für den Menschen. Im nächsten Jahrzehnt werden alle Kräfte in allen Bereichen der Gesellschaft mobilisiert werden müssen, um die Zerstörung der Umwelt aufzuhalten. Wir sind gezwungen, viele technische Errungenschaften der industriellen Zivilisation und ihre «Vorzüge» neu zu überdenken, bevor alles zu spät ist. □ Glücklicherweise reagieren die Menschen, sie organisieren sich, leiten den Prozess der Veränderung ein. Sie verlangen Rechenschaft, und zwar sowohl in industriellen wie in öffentlichen Bereichen. Umweltbewusstsein und die Vision einer besseren, gesunderen Welt haben sich durchgesetzt. □ Mit Hilfe der Kunst kann der Einzelne dieser Vision Ausdruck verleihen. Im Oktober 1990 fand unter der Schirmherrschaft der UNEP (Umweltprogramm der UNO) eine Ausstellung statt, deren Thema auch der Titel dieses begleitenden Buches ist:* Art for Survival: The Illustrator and the Environment *(«Kunst für das Überleben: Der Illustrator und die Umwelt»). Sie erntete bei der Kritik grosses Lob. Die Schirmherrschaft der UNEP ist ein Zeichen der Entschlossenheit dieser Organisation, die dringenden Belange unseres geschundenen Planeten und das erforderliche Umdenken und Handeln mit Hilfe der Kunst darzustellen. Die Künstler haben dies mit grosser Kraft und Leidenschaft in ihren Werken getan. □ Im Dienste der Erde zu arbeiten war der grösste Dienst, den wir – dem Leben und uns selbst – erweisen konnten.* ■

**NOEL BROWN** IST DER DISTRIKTSDIREKTOR DES UMWELTPROGRAMMS (UNEP) DER UNO FÜR NORDAMERIKA. DAVOR WAR ER BEAUFTRAGTER FÜR POLITISCHE ANGELEGENHEITEN IM DEPARTMENT OF POLITICAL AND SECURITY COUNCIL AFFAIRS. ER HAT DAS UN-UMWELTPROGRAMM BEI VERSCHIEDENEN KONFERENZEN VERTRETEN, DARUNTER BEI DER UN-KONFERENZ ÜBER LEBENSRAUM UND MENSCHLICHE SIEDLUNGEN 1976 IN VANCOUVER, DER UN-KONFERENZ ZUM SCHUTZ DER MEERE 1980 IN GENF UND DER 1987 IN MONTREAL STATTGEFUNDENEN KONFERENZ ÜBER DIE WIENER KONVENTION ZUM SCHUTZ DER OZONSCHICHT. DR. BROWN PROMOVIERTE AN DER YALE-UNIVERSITÄT IM BEREICH INTERNATIONALES RECHT UND INTERNATIONALE BEZIEHUNGEN, IST MA FÜR INTERNATIONALES RECHT UND ORGANISATION (UNIVERSITÄT GEORGETOWN) UND BA FÜR POLITISCHE WISSENSCHAFT UND WIRTSCHAFT (UNIVERSITÄT VON SEATTLE). DR. BROWN IST BÜRGER VON JAMAIKA.

*Les questions d'environnement auxquelles nous sommes confrontées sont sans exemple dans l'histoire de l'humanité. Au cours des dix prochaines années, toutes les forces de la société devront se mobiliser si nous voulons éviter la destruction totale de notre milieu naturel. Il nous faut reconsidérer les acquis technologiques de la civilisation industrielle et ses «avantages» avant qu'il ne soit trop tard.* □ *Fort heureusement, des gens ont commencé à réagir et à s'organiser, véritables initiateurs d'un processus de changement. Ils font appel à la responsabilité du secteur industriel comme du secteur public, demandant aux dirigeants de répondre sérieusement aux questions concernant la politique de l'environnement. Cette prise de conscience écologique et l'espérance d'un monde meilleur, moins pollué, gagnent du terrain.* □ *Au niveau individuel, seul l'art est en mesure d'exprimer cette nouvelle vision. En octobre 1990 a eu lieu aux Etats-Unis une exposition itinérante sponsorisée par l'UNEP (Programme pour l'environnement des Nations-Unies), dont le sujet: Art for Survival: The Illustrator and the Environment («L'art au service de la survie: l'illustrateur et l'environnement») a fourni le titre de ce livre. Cette exposition présentait un ensemble d'œuvres unique, impressionnant et elle a recueilli les louanges unanimes de la critique. Le patronage de l'UNEP est un signe de la détermination de cette organisation à informer de l'urgence des problèmes de notre planète malade et nous amener à changer notre manière de penser. C'est ce que les artistes ont fait avec talent et passion.* □ *Travailler au service de la Terre serait le plus grand service que nous puissions rendre – à la Vie et à nous-même.* ■

**NOEL BROWN** EST DIRECTEUR RÉGIONAL DE L'UNEP (PROGRAMME DES NATIONS-UNIES POUR L'ENVIRONNEMENT) EN AMÉRIQUE DU NORD ET ENVOYÉ SPÉCIAL DU DIRECTEUR. AVANT D'ÊTRE NOMMÉ À CE POSTE, IL ÉTAIT FONCTIONNAIRE CHARGÉ DES AFFAIRES POLITIQUES AU DEPARTEMENT OF POLITICAL AND SECURITY COUNCIL AFFAIRS. IL REPRÉSENTAIT L'UNEP LORS DE LA CONFÉRENCE SUR L'HABITAT HUMAIN À VANCOUVER EN 1976, LA CONFÉRENCE DE L'ONU SUR LA SCIENCE ET LA TECHNOLOGIE À VIENNE EN 1979 ET CELLE SUR LE DROIT DE LA MER À GENÈVE EN 1980, LA CONFÉRENCE DES PLÉNIPOTENTIAIRES DE LA CONVENTION DE VIENNE SUR LA PROTECTION DE LA COUCHE D'OZONE À PROPOS DU PROTOCOLE SUR LES CHLOROFLUOROCARBONES À MONTRÉAL EN 1937. CITOYEN JAMAICAIN, NOEL J. BROWN EST DOCTEUR EN DROIT ET RELATIONS INTERNATIONALES DE L'UNIVERSITÉ DE YALE, TITULAIRE D'UNE MAITRISE EN DROIT INTERNATIONAL ET ORGANISATION DE L'UNIVERSITÉ DE GEORGETOWN ET LICENCIÉ ES SCIENCES POLITIQUES ET ÉCONOMIQUES DE L'UNIVERSITÉ DE SEATTLE.

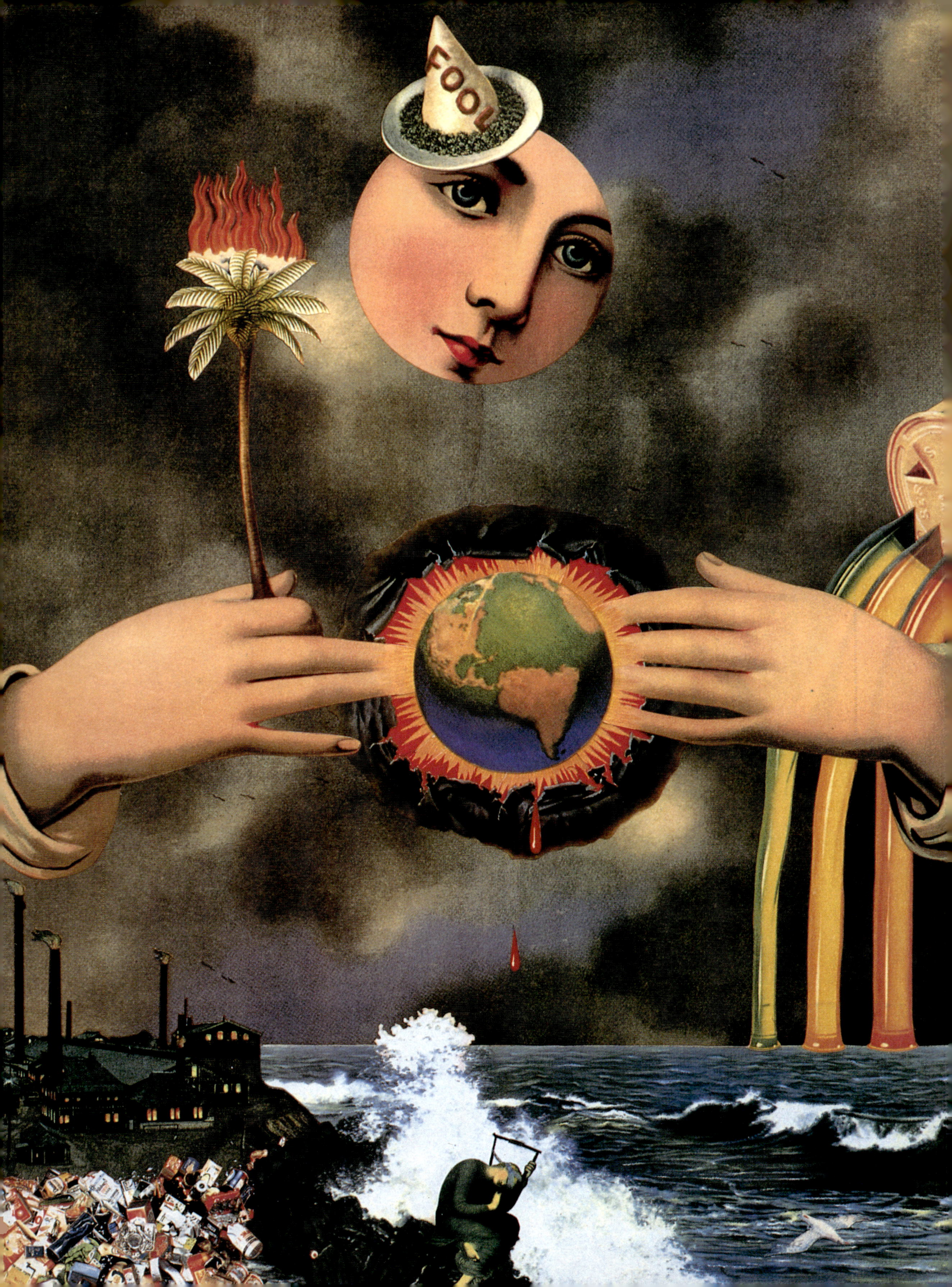
FOOL

FOREWORD

# TOM CRUISE

UNTITLED BY JOHN CRAIG, LASER COPY COLLAGE

*"The force that through the green fuse drives the flower*
*Drives my green age"*
*Dylan Thomas*

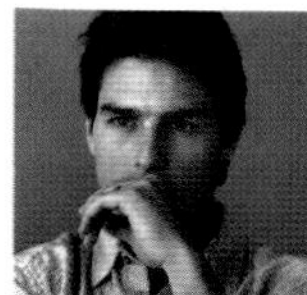

*An artist instills in his or her work an energy, an élan vital, that acts as the vehicle for his or her message and sustains the quality of communication. Gerard Manley Hopkins called it "instress"; Luke Skywalker called it "the Force." There are many names for it, but regardless of what it is called at no time in human history has this energy been more needed than now.* □ *Leading environmental experts estimate that the ecosystems of our planet have perhaps a ten-year window of opportunity, where irreparable harm to the earth's ecology may be averted. We stand on the edge between incredible opportunity and unthinkable destruction.* □ *The hole in the ozone is three times the size of the United States. The world's rainforests are being burned at the rate of a football field a second, causing the extinction of scores of species each week. Nearly six billion tons of carbon dioxide are spewed into the atmosphere each year—the planet is heating up. In the United States we dump over ten billion pounds of toxins into our environment every year, threatening our oceans and coastlines. The very quality of life—and the health of our children—is under siege.* □ *Thus far, governments, scientists, environmental groups, and concerned individuals have been unable to stem the tide of environmental decay. This*

*is the time of the artist. Historically, artists have led society. Their dreams and visions have always helped to shape our future realities. With the environmental challenge we face, this becomes an awesome responsibility and a unique opportunity.* □ *This challenge must be taken up. The ability to reach out to, confront, and communicate with people rests with the artist. Artistic messages in divergent media strike out at, move, and bring people to action. They depict the problems and evoke the solutions. Whether the messages are repugnant, abhorrent, hopeful, or utopian, if they elicit an emotional response or involvement they will help to establish successful communication with the environment.* □ *The illustrations presented in this collection break new ground both for the artists and the environments they depict. The images make us look, think, and care. They communicate. Cherish them: They will inspire you. One would hope that they will, in turn, inspire other artists. As art moves, so will society. Artists hold in their grasp the energy to reestablish man's communication with the environment. As this communication improves, so will the care that leads to positive change. We can dream of a better world. We can make a difference.* ■

*"A culture is only as great as its*
*dreams, and its dreams are dreamed by artists."*
*L. Ron Hubbard*

**TOM CRUISE'S** DEEP COMMITMENT TO THE ENVIRONMENT WAS HEIGHTENED IN 1989 AFTER WITNESSING THE UNCONTROLLED DESTRUCTION OF THE AMAZON RAINFORESTS. SHORTLY THEREAFTER, HE WAS INSTRUMENTAL IN THE IMPLEMENTATION OF RECYCLING PROGRAMS IN THE HOLLYWOOD STUDIOS. HE HOSTED A GATHERING IN WASHINGTON, D.C., TO FORGE NEW DIALOGUES AMONG SCIENTISTS, ENVIRONMENTALISTS, AND INDUSTRY AND WORLD LEADERS IN ORDER TO ARRIVE AT REAL-LIFE SOLUTIONS TO PRESSING ENVIRONMENTAL PROBLEMS. TOM'S ESSAY, "I CAN'T SEE THE FOREST IF THERE ARE NO TREES," APPEARS IN THE ENVIRONMENTAL ANTHOLOGY *HEAVEN IS UNDER OUR FEET* BY DON HENLEY AND DAVID MARSH. DEVOTED TO THE ENVIRONMENTAL EDUCATION OF YOUTH, TOM ALSO CONTRIBUTED TO THE CREATION AND NATIONAL DISTRIBUTION OF "CRY OUT," AN ENVIRONMENTAL BOOKLET FOR CHILDREN. □ TOM CRUISE MADE HIS FILM DEBUT IN 1981 AND HAS TWELVE FILMS TO HIS CREDIT. HE IS THE RECIPIENT OF SEVERAL AWARDS AND HONORS, AMONG THEM THE GOLDEN GLOBE AWARD, THE PEOPLE'S CHOICE AWARD, AND THE PRESTIGIOUS 1991 AMERICAN CINEMA AWARD FOR DISTINGUISHED ACHIEVEMENT IN FILM. ■

*«Die Kraft, die grün die Blumen wachsen lässt,*
*durchtreibt die grünen Jahre meines Lebens.»*
*Dylan Thomas*

*Der Künstler lässt in seine Arbeit eine besondere Kraft einfliessen, einen Elan vital, der Träger seiner Botschaft ist und ihre Wirkung ausmacht. Gerard Manley Hopkins nannte es «instress»; Luke Skywalker nannte es «the Force». Es gibt viele Bezeichnungen dafür, aber egal, wie man es nent, noch nie seit Menschengedenken war diese Kraft so nötig wie heute.* □ *Führende Umweltexperten schätzen, dass uns noch höchstens zehn Jahre bleiben, um irreparable Schäden, die der Ökologie unsers Planeten zugefügt werden, abzuwenden. Wenn das nicht gelingt, wird es zu spät sein. Wir stehen auf Messersschneide zwischen unglaublichen Möglichkeiten und unvorstellbarer Zerstörung.* □ *Das Ozonloch über der Arktis ist dreimal grösser als die Vereinigten Staaten. Pro Sekunde wird ein Stück Regenwald in der Grösse eines Fussballfeldes verbrannt, was zur Folge hat, dass jede Woche Hunderte von Tierarten aussterben. Nahezu sechs Milliarden Tonnen Kohlendioxid werden jedes Jahr in die Atmosphäre abgelassen – die Ursache für die Erwärmung des Planeten. In den Vereinigten Staaten werden jährlich fast 4,5 Milliarden Kilo Giftstoffe deponiert, die unsere Ozeane und Küsten gefährden. Die eigentliche Lebensqualität – und die Gesundheit unserer Kinder – steht auf dem Spiel.* □ *Bis jetzt ist es Regierungen, Wissenschaftlern, Umweltschutzgruppen und anderen umweltbewussten Personen nicht gelungen, die Welle der Umweltzerstörung aufzuhalten. Der Zeitpunkt für den Künstler ist gekommen, auf seine Weise einzugreifen. Historisch gesehen, sind Künstler die Führer der Gesellschaft. Ihre Träume und Visionen haben dazu beigetragen, unsere Realitäten von morgen zu formen. Die Lösung unserer Umweltprobleme wird zu einer immensen Verantwortung und einmaligen Gelegenheit.* □ *Diese Herausforderung muss angenommen werden. Der Künstler hat die Fähigkeit, die Menschen zu erreichen, sie zu konfrontieren und mit ihnen zu kommunizieren. Übermittelt durch die verschiedensten Medien, vermag die Botschaft des Künstlers aufzurütteln, sie bewegt und veranlasst die Menschen zu handeln. Probleme werden aufgezeigt, Lösungen vorgeschlagen. Ob die Botschaften widerlich, abscheulich, hoffnungsvoll oder utopisch sind, spielt keine Rolle. Solange sie eine emotionale Regung oder ein Engagement hervorrufen, tragen sie zur Auseinandersetzung mit der Umwelt bei.* □ *Die Illustrationen in dieser Sammlung eröffnen neue Perspektiven, sowohl für den Künstler als auch für die von ihm dargestellte Umwelt. Die Bilder zwingen zum Hinsehen, zum Nachdenken und zur Anteilnahme. Sie übermitteln eine Botschaft! Nehmen Sie sie in sich auf: Die Bilder werden Sie inspirieren. Hoffentlich werden sie auch andere Künstler inspirieren. Wenn sich etwas in der Kunst bewegt, bewegt sch auch etwas in der Gesellschaft. Der Künstler hat die Kraft, die Auseinandersetzung der Menschheit mit den*

*Umweltproblemen neu zu beleben. Wenn das gelingt, wird das neue Bewusstsein zu einer positiven Veränderung führen. Wir können einfach nur von einer besseren Welt träumen – oder wir können die Veränderung selbst in die Hand nehmen.* ■

*«Eine Kultur ist nur so gut wie ihre Träume,*
*und ihre Träume werden von Künstlern geträumt.»*
*L. Ron Hubbard*

SEIT **TOM CRUISE** 1989 ZEUGE DER WILLKÜRLICHEN ZERSTÖRUNG DER REGENWÄLDER DES AMAZONAS WURDE, SETZT ER SICH MIT GROSSEM ENGAGEMENT FÜR DIE UMWELT EIN. KURZ NACH DIESEM ERLEBNIS WURDEN MIT SEINER HILFE RECYCLING-PROGRAMME IN DEN HOLLYWOOD-STUDIOS DURCHGESETZT. ER WAS GASTGEBER EINER KONFERENZ IN WASHINGTON, D.C., DEREN ZIEL ES WAR, DURCH GESPRÄCHE ZWISCHEN WISSENSCHAFTLERN, GRÜNEN UND FÜHRUNGSKRÄFTEN AUS INDUSTRIE, WIRTSCHAFT UND POLITIK REALISTISCHE LÖSUNGEN FÜR DIE DRINGENDSTEN UMWELTPROBLEME ZU FINDEN. CRUISE' AUFSATZ «ICH KANN DEN WALD NICHT SEHEN, WENN ES KEINE BÄUME GIBT» IST IN DER FÜR DIE ERZIEHUNG DER JUGEND BESTIMMEN UMWELT-ANTHOLOGIE *HEAVEN IS UNDER OUR FEET* («DER HIMMEL BEFINDET SICH UNTER UNSEREN FÜSSEN») VON DON HENLEY UND DAVID MARSH ABGEDRUCKT. TOM CRUISE WAR AUCH AN DER HERSTELLUNG UND DEM NATIONALEN VERTRIEB EINER UMWELTBROSCHÜRE FÜR KINDER, «CRY OUT», BETEILIGT. □ DIE FILMKARRIERE VON TOM CRUISE BEGANN 1981. INZWISCHEN HAT ER 12 FILME GEMACHT UND VERSCHIEDENE PREISE UND AUSZEICHNUNGEN ERHALTEN, U.A. DEN GOLDEN GLOBE AWARD, DEN PEOPLE'S CHOICE AWARD (PUBLIKUMSPREIS) SOWIE 1991 DEN BEGEHRTEN AMERICAN CINEMA AWARD FOR DISTINGUISHED ACHIEVEMENT IN FILM (AMERIKANISCHER KINOPREIS FÜR BESONDERE LEISTUNGEN IM FILM). ■

*«La force qui jaillit de la tige fait croître la fleur*
*Anime mes vertes années.»*
*Dylan Thomas*

*L'artiste met dans son œuvre une énergie, un élan vital qui sous-tend le message et influe sur la qualité de la communication. Les poètes lui ont donné les noms les plus divers,Gerard Manley Hopkins l'appelait son «instress», Luke Skywalker «la Force». Toujours est-il que jamais encore l'humanité n'aura eu tant besoin de cette énergie. □ Les principaux experts en matière d'environnement estiment que nous disposons tout au plus de dix ans pour remédier à la situation, pour empêcher que ne soient infligés à notre écosystème des dommages incalculables, pour agir avant qu'ils ne soient irréversibles. Nous sommes face à cette alternative: saisir cette ultime chance ou aller vers des destructions aux conséquences inimaginables. □ Le trou dans la couche d'ozone est trois fois plus grand que la surface des Etats-Unis. Chaque seconde, une étendue de forêt tropicale de la grandeur d'un terrain de football est brûlée, ce qui entraîne l'extinction de centaines d'espèces animales chaque semaine. Presque 6 milliards de tonnes de dioxyde de carbone sont rejetées dans l'atmosphère chaque année, d'où le réchauffement de la planète. Aux Etats-Unis, chaque année, presque 4,5 milliards de kg de produits toxiques sont déposés dans notre environnement, menaçant nos océans et les zones côtières. Il en va de la qualité de la vie en soi, et qui plus est de la santé de nos enfants. □ Jusqu'à présent, les gouvernements, les scientifiques, les associations de protection de l'environnement et tous ceux qui se préoccupent d'écologie n'ont pas réussi à stopper cette vague de destruction. Voici venu le moment pour l'artiste d'intervenir. Historiquement, les artistes ont toujours joué un rôle de guides dans la société. Ce sont leurs rêves et leurs visions qui ont permis d'inventer l'avenir. Face aux problèmes de l'environnement, l'artiste est investi d'une immense responsabilité et jouit là d'une occasion unique. □ Il lui faut relever ce défi. L'artiste a la capacité de toucher un public, de l'affronter et de communiquer avec lui. Transmis par les médias les plus divers, le message de l'artiste provoque, il dérange et incite les gens à agir. Il met en lumière des problèmes et suggère des solutions. Que le message soit rebutant, voire repoussant, prometteur ou utopique, peu importe. S'il suscite une réaction émotionnelle ou un engagement, il fait avancer le débat. □ Les illustrations de ce volume ouvrent de nouvelles perspectives aussi bien aux artistes qu'à l'environnement qu'ils représentent. Les images nous obligent à regarder, à penser et à nous inquiéter. Elles transmettent un message. Imprégnez-vous-en: elles vous inspireront. Espérons qu'à leur tour, elles inspirent d'autres artistes. Si quelque chose bouge dans l'art, quelque chose bougera aussi dans la société. Les artistes ont l'énergie nécessaire pour rétablir le contact entre l'homme et son environnement. Si l'on y parvient, une telle prise de conscience devrait amener des changements positifs. Nous pouvons rêver d'un monde meilleur - mais nous pouvons aussi y contribuer.* ■

*«La grandeur d'une culture se mesure à*
*ses rêves, et ses rêves sont les rêves des artistes.»*
*L. Ron Hubbard*

DEPUIS QU'IL A ÉTÉ TÉMOIN DE LA DESTRUCTION SAUVAGE DE LA FORÊT AMAZONIENNE, EN 1989, **TOM CRUISE** S'EST ENGAGÉ RÉSOLUMENT POUR LA PROTECTION DE L'ENVIRONNEMENT. PEU APRÈS, IL A CONTRIBUÉ À LA MISE EN PLACE D'UN PROGRAMME DE RECYCLAGE DANS LES STUDIOS DE HOLLYWOOD. IL A ORGANISÉ UNE CONFÉRENCE À WASHINGTON, D.C., DONT L'OBJECTIF ÉTAIT DE TROUVER, AU MOYEN DE DISCUSSIONS ENTRE SCIENTIFIQUES, ÉCOLOGISTES ET DIRIGEANTS DE L'INDUSTRIES, DE L'ÉCONOMIE ET DE LA POLITIQUE, DES SOLUTIONS RÉALISTES AUX PROBLÈMES LES PLUS URGENTS DE L'ENVIRONNEMENT. L'ESSAI DE TOM CRUISE INTITULÉ «JE NE PEUX PAS VOIR LA FORÊT S'IL N'Y A PAS D'ARBRES» A ÉTÉ PUBLIÉ DANS L'ANTHOLOGIE DE DON HENLEY ET DAVID MARSH, *HEAVEN IS UNDER OUR FEET* («LE CIEL EST SOUS NOS PIEDS»), UN OUVRAGE QUI A POUR BUT D'ÉDUQUER LA JEUNESSE AUX PROBLÈMES DE L'ENVIRONNEMENT. TOM CRUISE A ÉGALEMENT PARTICIPÉ À LA CRÉATION ET À LA DISTRIBUTION DE *CRY OUT*, UNE BROCHURE POUR LES ENFANTS SUR L'ENVIRONNEMENT. □ LA CARRIÈRE CINÉMATOGRAPHIQUE DE TOM CRUISE A DÉBUTÉ EN 1981. DEPUIS, IL A TOURNÉ 12 FILMS ET REÇU DIVERS PRIX ET DISTINCTIONS, NOTAMMENT LE GOLDEN GLOBE AWARD, LE PEOPLE'S CHOICE AWARD (GRAND PRIX DU PUBLIC), AINSI QUE LE FAMEUX AMERICAN CINEMA AWARD FOR DISTINGUISHED ACHIEVEMENT IN FILM (GRAND PRIX DU CINÉMA POUR SON ŒUVRE CINÉ-

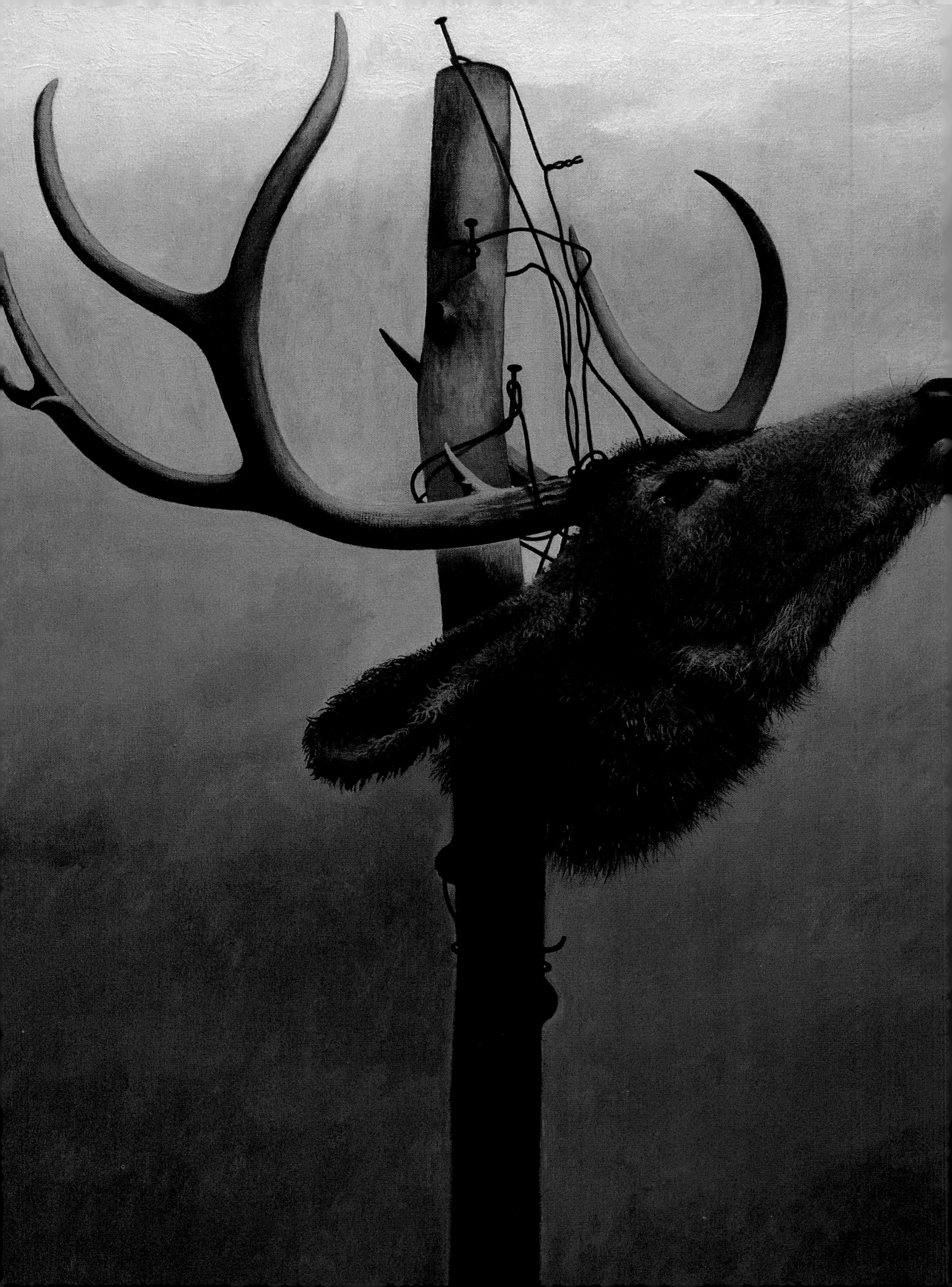

FOREWORD

## WENDELL MINOR

"LAST CALL" BY WENDELL MINOR, ACRYLIC ON CANVAS

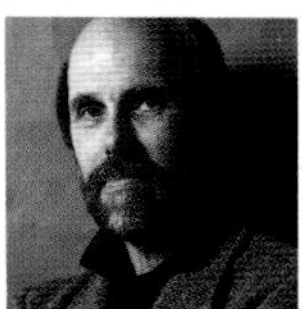

*Every year, 95 million people are added to the earth's population, and the demands we place on our earth increase proportionately. The need for us to understand how we can better utilize and conserve our resources has become a matter of urgency.* □ *Visual images communicate important messages with far more immediacy than the written word.* □ *The illustrator's craft communicates visual images to millions of viewers around the world every day in various print media. For the most part, however, the ideas communicated by these images are not those of the illustrator, but of others. It is rare for an illustrator to be able to communicate directly his or her personal feelings to an audience.* □ *The Illustrator and the Environment Exhibition afforded 150 of the world's most accomplished illustrators to set forth their personal views about the state of our world and environment.* □ *The pages of this book testify to the fact that each artist has his or her own very personal perspective about environmental issues.* □ *These images are powerful and compelling. They deliver a message to the viewer that words cannot.* □ *It is the illustrator's desire that these images elicit an emotional response from the viewer that will change the way they see the world, and hopefully inspire some to become more active in effecting change for a better world.* □ *As president of the Society of*

*Illustrators, it had long been my goal to chair an exhibition that would allow illustrators a forum to express their views on the environment.* □ *The Society of Illustrators was indeed fortunate to have had the talents of Charlotte Bralds as organizer and curator of the exhibition along with the full support and financial backing of the United Nations Environmental Programme, and its regional director, Dr. Noel Brown.* □ *The Illustrator and the Environment Exhibition also helped raise funds for Earth Island Institute. The Institute was founded by David R. Brower in 1982 as a nonprofit organization to develop innovative projects for conservation, preservation, and restoration of the global environment.* □ *The Society of Illustrators, founded in 1901 as a nonprofit organization, was established to actively educate the general public about the world of illustration. The Society's role as educator, through its exhibitions, historic permanent collections, and student scholarship program, has achieved prominence in the public eye.* □ *It is our hope that The Illustrator and the Environment Exhibition has helped the field of illustration contribute to our social and ecological consciousness.* □ *I would like to thank all those who helped make the exhibition and this book possible.* ■

**WENDELL MINOR** IS WELL KNOWN IN THE PUBLISHING INDUSTRY FOR THE PAINTINGS HE HAS DONE FOR SEVERAL CHILDREN'S BOOKS AND FOR THE JACKETS OF MANY BESTSELLING NOVELS. MR. MINOR HAS RECEIVED OVER 200 AWARDS FROM EVERY MAJOR GRAPHICS COMPETITION, INCLUDING A SILVER MEDAL FROM THE SOCIETY OF ILLUSTRATORS AND A SILVER MEDAL FROM THE NEW YORK ART DIRECTORS CLUB. HE HAS BEEN FEATURED IN ARTICLES IN *PRINT* MAGAZINE, *AMERICAN ARTIST*, AND *GRAPHIC DESIGN USA*. MR. MINOR HAS HAD NUMEROUS SOLO EXHIBITIONS, AND HIS WORK CAN BE FOUND IN THE PERMANENT COLLECTIONS OF THE ILLINOIS STATE MUSEUM, NASA, US AIR FORCE, LIBRARY OF CONGRESS, MUSEUM OF AMERICAN ILLUSTRATION, US COAST GUARD, AND USO. HE IS A MEMBER OF THE BOARD OF DIRECTORS OF THE SOCIETY OF ILLUSTRATORS AND SERVED AS THE SOCIETY'S PRESIDENT FROM 1989 TO 1991.

*Jedes Jahr nimmt die Weltbevölkerung um 95 Millionen Menschen zu, und es wird entsprechend mehr von der Erde gefordert. Es wird allerhöchste Zeit, dass wir lernen, unsere Ressourcen besser zu nutzen und zu bewahren.* □ *Bilder vermitteln dringende Botschaften viel direkter als das geschriebene Wort.* □ *Mit Hilfe der verschiedenen Printmedien erreicht der Illustrator mit seinen Bildern täglich Millionen von Menschen in aller Welt. In den meisten Fällen jedoch vermittelt er nicht die eigenen Ideen, Gefühle und Gedanken, sondern die anderer Leute.* □ *Die Ausstellung «Der Illustrator und die Umwelt» gab 150 der besten Illustratoren Gelegenheit, ihren persönlichen Gefühlen über den Zustand der Welt, der Umwelt, Ausdruck zu verleihen.* □ *Auf den Seiten des Katalogs wird deutlich, dass jeder Künstler eine eigene, sehr persönliche Perspektive der Umweltprobleme hat.* □ *Die Bilder sind stark und ergreifend. Sie vermittein dem Betrachter eine Botschaft auf eine Art, wie Worte es nicht vermögen.* □ *Die Illustratoren wollen mit diesen Bildern emotionelle Reaktionen hervorrufen, ihre Sicht der Welt verändern und vielleicht einige dazu bringen, sich aktiv für Veränderungen zugunsten einer besseren Welt einzusetzen.* □ *Als Präsident der Society of Illustrators hatte ich schon lange den Wunsch, den Illustratoren mit einer Ausstellung ein Forum zu bieten, damit sie auf ihre Weise zu den Umweltproblemen Stellung nehmen können. □ Die Society of Illustrators hatte das Glück, Charlotte Bralds als Organisatorin und Kuratorin der Ausstellung zu gewinnen und vom United Nations Environment Programme und dem regionalen Direktor, Dr. Noel Brown, auch in finanzieller Hinsicht volle Unterstützung zu bekommen. □ Die Ausstellung «Der Illustrator und die Umwelt» brachte sogar Geld für das Earth Island Institute ein! Dieses Institut wurde 1982 von David R. Brower als Nonprofit-Unternehmen gegründet, mit dem Ziel, innovative internationale Projekte für die Erhaltung und Wiederherstellung der Umwelt zu entwickeln. □ Die Society of Illustrators wurde 1901 als Nonprofit-Organisation mit der Absicht gegründet, die Illustration der Öffentlichkeit näherzubringen. Durch Ausstellungen, die historischen permanenten Sammlungen und das Stipendienprogramm für Studenten ist es dieser Institution gelungen, eine Bildungsrolle im öffentlichen Leben zu spielen und Anerkennung bei breiten Kreisen der Bevölkerung zu finden. □ Wir hoffen, dass die Illustrationen durch die Ausstellung «Der Illustrator und die Umwelt» dazu beigetragen haben, das soziale und ökologische Bewusstsein zu stärken. □ Ich danke allen, die die Ausstellung und den Katalog ermöglicht haben.* ■

**WENDELL MINOR** HAT SICH DURCH SEINE BILDER FÜR MEHRERE KINDERBÜCHER UND SEINE UMSCHLÄGE FÜR VIELE ERFOLGREICHE ROMANE IN DER VERLAGSBRANCHE EINEN NAMEN GEMACHT. ER HAT ÜBER 200 AUSZEICHNUNGEN BEI DEN WICHTIGEN GRAPHIKDESIGN-WETTBEWERBEN ERHALTEN, DARUNTER SILBERMEDAILLEN DER SOCIETY OF ILLUSTRATORS DES NEW YORK ART DIRECTORS CLUB. ARTIKEL ÜBER IHN SIND IN *PRINT* MAGAZINE, *AMERICAN ARTIST* UND *GRAPHIC DESIGN USA* ERSCHIENEN. SEINE ARBEITEN WURDEN IN ZAHLREICHEN EINZELAUSSTELLUNGEN GEZEIGT UND SIND IN DEN SAMMLUNGEN DES LANDESMUSEUMS VON ILLINOIS, DER NASA, DER US-LUFTWAFFE, DER KONGRESSBIBLIOTHEK, DES MUSEUM OF AMERICAN ILLUSTRATION, DER US-KÜSTENWACHE UND DER UNITED SERVICE ORGANISATION VERTRETEN. ER IST IM VORSTAND DER SOCIETY OF ILLUSTRATORS UND AMTIERTE VON 1989 UND 1991 ALS DEREN PRÄSIDENT.

*Chaque année, la population mondiale s'accroît de 95 millions d'habitants et ce que nous exigeons de la Terre augmente proportionnellement. Il est d'extrême urgence que nous comprenions comment mieux utiliser les ressources de la planète et les preserver. □ Les images visuelles communiquent des messages importants de manière plus immédiate que l'écrit. Grâce au talent des illustrateurs, des images visuelles sont chaque jour transmises à des millions de spectateurs dans le monde, au travers des imprimés les plus divers. Cependant, la plupart du temps, les idées communiquées par ces images ne sont pas celles de l'illustrateur lui-même. Il est rare que ce dernier puisse exprimer au public ses sentiments personnels. □ L'exposition «L'illustrateur et l'environnement» offrait l'occasion à 150 des meilleurs illustrateurs du monde entier de faire connaître leur point de vue personnel sur l'état de ce monde et de l'environnement. □ Les pages de ce livre témoignent du fait que chaque artiste a une perspective personnelle propre en ce qui concerne les questions écologiques. □ Ces images sont puissantes et elles en imposent. Elles délivrent au spectateur un massage que les mots ne sauraient transmettre. □ Tout illustrateur désire que ses images suscitent une réponse émotionnelle de la part du spectateur, qui transformera sa vision du monde et, espérons-le, l'incitera à devenir plus actif, à opérer des changements en vue d'un monde meilleur. □ En tant que président de la Society of Illustrators, il y a longtemps que je souhaitais présenter une exposition qui offre aux illustrateurs un forum pour exprimer leurs opinions au sujet de l'environnement. □ La Society of Illustrators a eu la chance de bénéficier pour cette occasion des talents d'organisatrice de Charlotte Bralds, conjugués à l'appui et au soutien financier du Programme des Nations-Unies pour l'Environnement, et notamment de son directeur régional, Dr. Noel Brown. □ L'exposition «L'illustrateur et l'environnement» a également aidé à récolter des fonds pour le Earth Island Institute. Cet institut a été fondé en 1982 par David R. Brower: organisation à but non lucratif, elle développe des projets innovateurs en matière de conservation, sauvegarde et restauration de l'environnement global. □ Elle aussi organisation à but non lucratif fondée en 1901, la Society of Illustrators, a été crée pour faire connaître au public le monde de l'illustration. Grâce à des expositions, des collections permanentes historiques et des programmes d'études, cette société a acquis auprès du public une excellente réputation pour son rôle éducatif. □ Nous espérons que cette manifestation aura fourni à la branche de l'illustration l'occasion de contribuer à une prise de conscience sociale et écologique. J'aimerais ici remercier tous ceux qui ont aidé à réaliser cette exposition et ce livre.* ■

**WENDELL MINOR** EST CÉLÈBRE DANS LE MONDE DE L'ÉDITION POUR AVOIR ILLUSTRÉ PLUSIEURS LIVRES D'ENFANTS ET RÉALISÉ LES COUVERTURES DE NOMBREUX BEST-SELLERS. IL A REÇU PLUS DE 200 PRIX LORS DE GRANDS CONCOURS D'ART GRAPHIQUE, NOTAMMENT LES MÉDAILLES D'ARGENT DE LA SOCIETY OF ILLUSTRATORS ET DU ART DIRECTORS CLUB DE NEW YORK. IL A FAIT L'OBJET D'ARTICLES DANS *PRINT* MAGAZINE, *AMERICAN ARTIST* ET *GRAPHIC DESIGN USA*. WENDELL MINOR A FAIT DE NOMBREUSES EXPOSITIONS PERSONNELLES ET SON ŒUVRE EST REPRÉSENTÉ DANS LES COLLECTIONS PERMANENTES DE L'ILLINOIS STATE MUSEUM, DE LA NASA, DE L'US AIR FORCE, DE LA BIBLIOTHEQUE DU CONGRES, DU MUSÉE DE L'ILLUSTRATION AMÉRICAINE, DE L'US COAST GUARD, ETC. IL EST MEMBRE DU COMITÉ DIRECTEUR DE LA SOCIETY OF ILLUSTRATORS, DONT IL A ÉTÉ LE PRÉSIDENT DE 1989 À 1991.

IN MEMORY OF RICHARD HESS

1934–1991

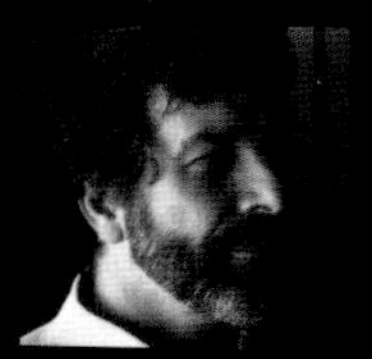

AND TO THOSE WHO,

INSPIRED BY THE BEAUTY OF THE EARTH,

ARE IMPELLED TO ACT

ART, ARTIST'S COMMENTS, AND EARTH FACTS

BILDER, KOMMENTARE DER KÜNSTLER, UND UMWELTFAK

ILLUSTRATION, COMMENTAIRES DES ARTISTES, ET DON

THE NATURAL RESOURCES DEFENSE COUNCIL HAS A DEPARTMENT WHICH DEALS SOLELY WITH URBAN ENVIRONMENTAL CONCERNS; IT HELPS COMMUNITIES FIGHT SELFISH DEVELOPMENT THROUGHOUT THE NATION.

........................

EINE ABTEILUNG DES NATURAL RESOURCES DEFENSE COUNCIL BEFASST SICH AUSSCHLIESSLICH MIT URBANEN UMWELTPROBLEMEN; SIE HILFT DEN GEMEINDEN IM GANZEN LAND, SICH GEGEN RÜCKSICHTSLOSE PROJEKTE ZU WEHREN.

........................

UN DÉPARTEMENT DU NATURAL RESOURCES DEFENSE COUNCIL SE CONSACRE EXCLUSIVEMENT À L'ENVIRONNEMENT URBAIN. IL FOURNIT SON APPUI AUX MUNICIPALITÉS DÉSIRANT S'OPPOSER À DESPROJETS IRRESPONSABLES.

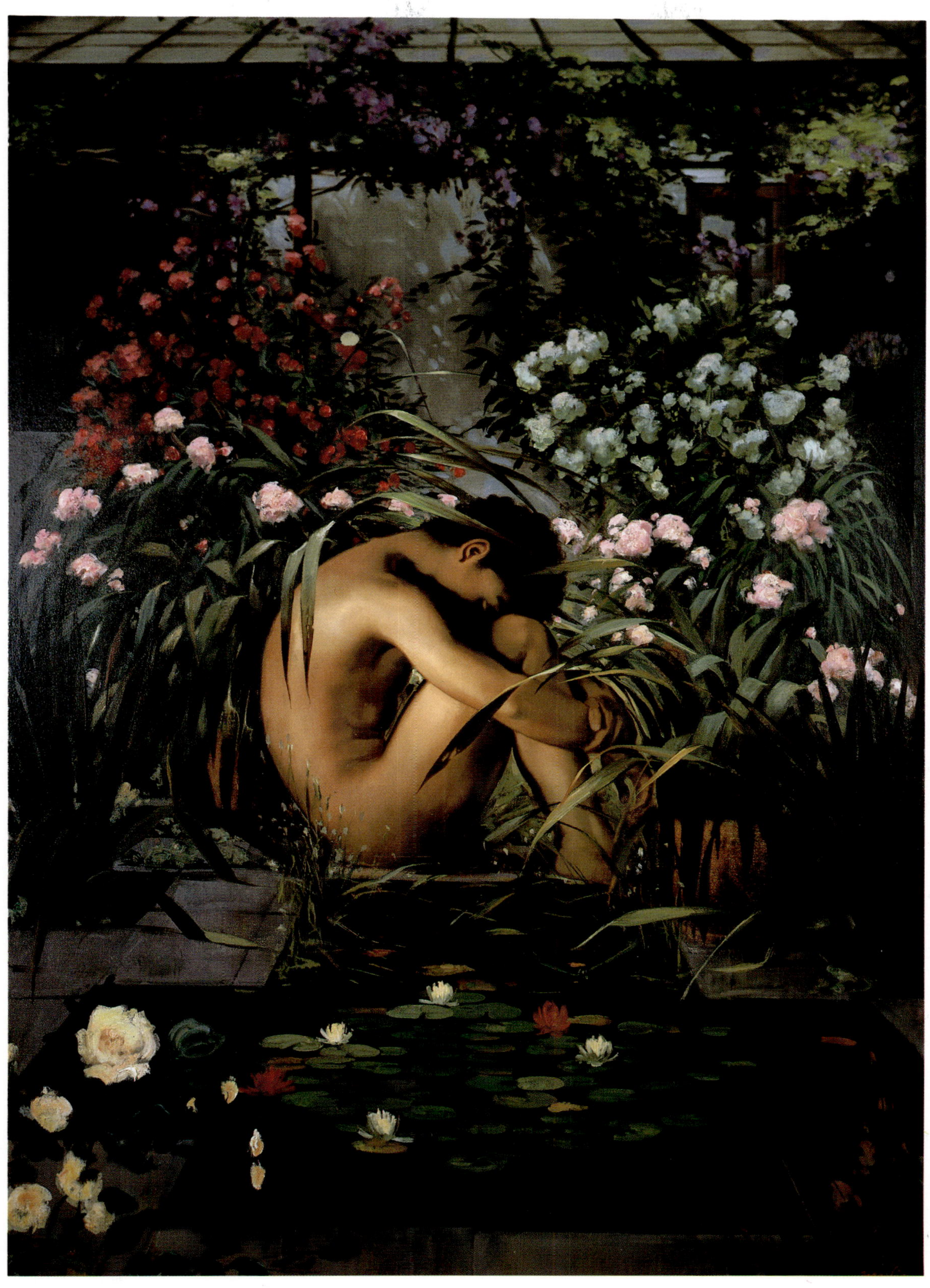

**NUDE BY A CROSS-SHAPED POND**

DANIEL MAFFIA

*OIL ON CANVAS*

"MAN'S LINK TO NATURE IS PHYSICAL AND SPIRITUAL."

IN THE WESTERN HEMISPHERE, POPULATIONS OF MANY FOREST AND MIGRATORY SHOREBIRDS ARE DECLINING AS MUCH AS 60 TO 80 PERCENT IN SOME CASES.

........................

IN DER WESTLICHEN HEMISPHÄRE VERRINGERT SICH DIE POPULATION VON WALDVÖGELN UND ZUGVÖGELN IN MANCHEN FÄLLEN BIS ZU 60 PROZENT.

........................

DANS L'HÉMISPHÈRE OUEST, LE NOMBRE D'OISEAUX DES BOIS ET D'OISEAUX MIGRATEURS EST TOMBÉ DANS CERTAINS CAS DE 60 À 80%.

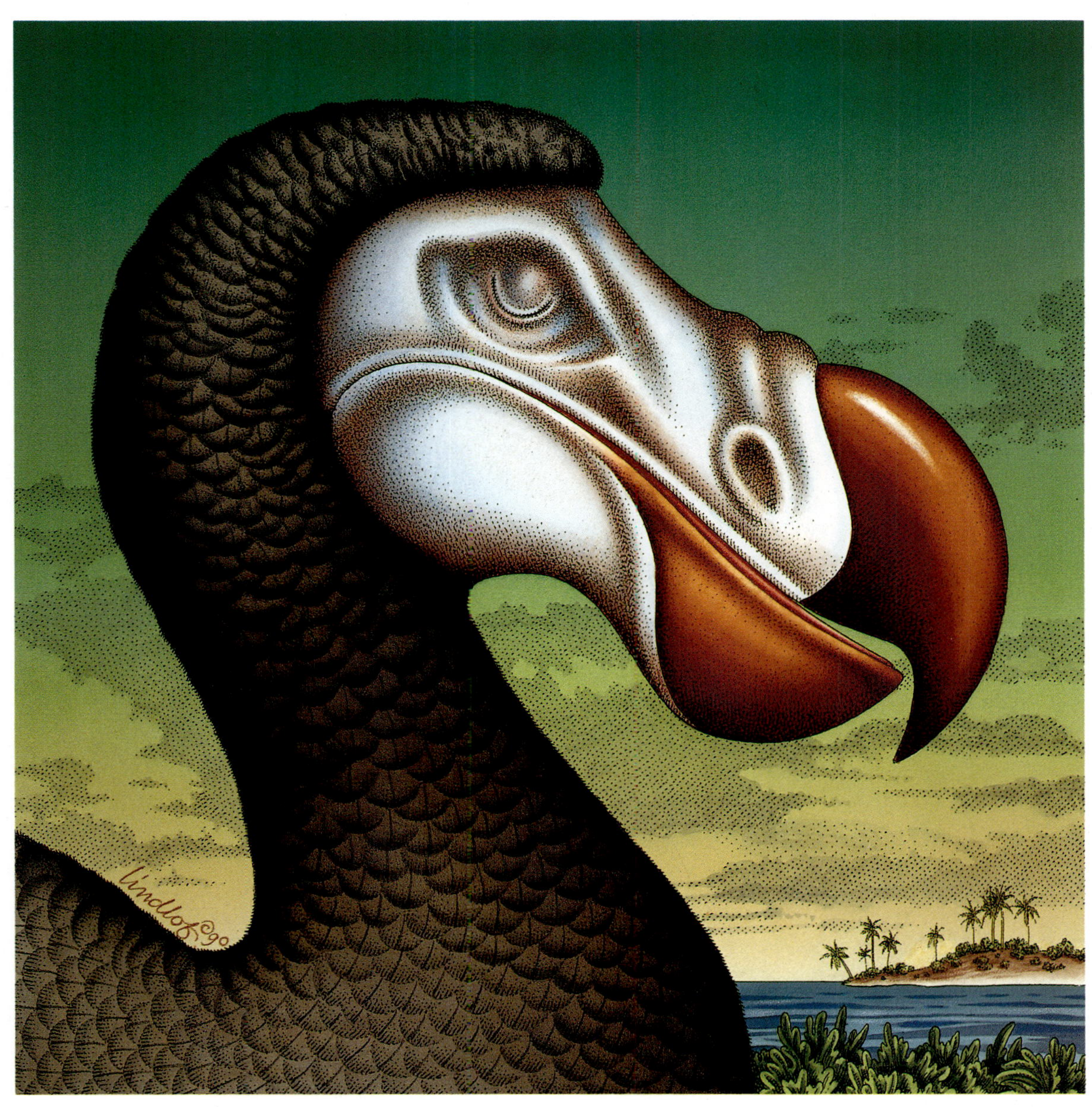


**AS DEAD AS THE DODO**

Ed Lindlof

*India ink and Rotring Artists Color*

"Negative effects upon other species and the environment by the activities of man began much earlier than the Industrial Revolution. The last dodo died in 1681."

ABOUT 10 PERCENT OF ALL
RIVERS MAY BE DESCRIBED AS
HEAVILY POLLUTED.

........................

GEGEN 10 PROZENT ALLER
FLÜSSE MÜSSEN ALS SCHWER
VERSEUCHT BEZEICHNET WERDEN.

........................

ENVIRON 10% DE TOUTES
LES RIVIÈRES PEUVENT
ÊTRE CONSIDÉRÉES COMME
GRAVEMENT POLLUÉES.

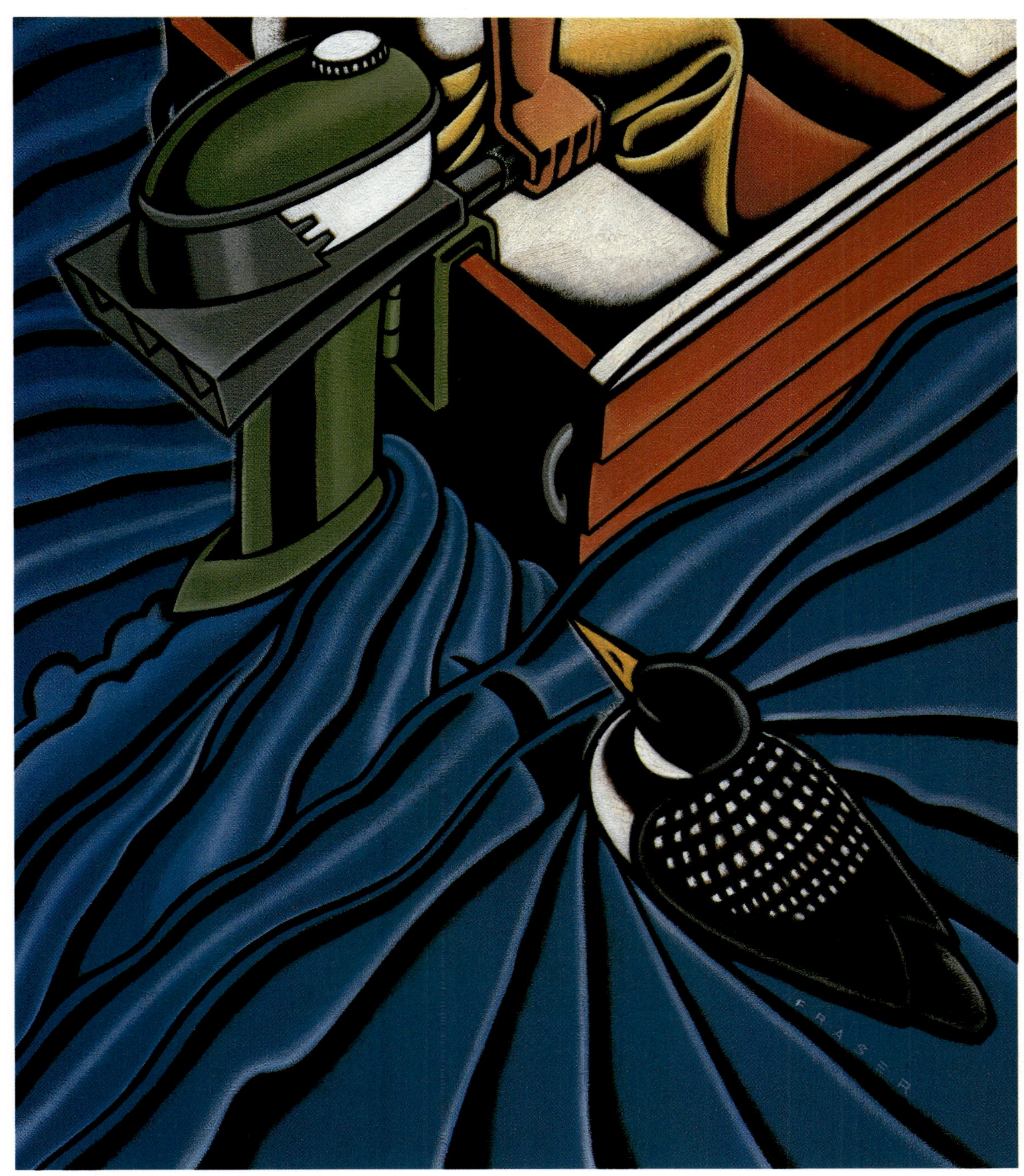


**WAKE**

Douglas Fraser

*Alkyds on paper*

"As the human race moves through the environmentthe effects are seen. Nature and humanity seem to take perpendicular paths. When collisions do occur, nature comes out the loser."

MORE THAN 22.5 BILLION POUNDS OF HAZARDOUS WASTE WERE RELEASED OR DISPOSED OF BY INDUSTRY IN THE UNITED STATES IN 1987.

........................

ÜBER 10 MILLIONEN TONNEN GEFÄHRLICHER ABFALLSTOFFE WURDEN 1987 VON DER INDUSTRIE IN DEN USA AUSGESTOSSEN BZW. DEPONIERT.

........................

PLUS DE 10 MILLIONS DE TONNES DE DÉCHETS DANGEREUX ONT ÉTÉ PRODUITES OU ENTREPOSÉES PAR LES ENTREPRISES AMÉRICAINES EN 1987.

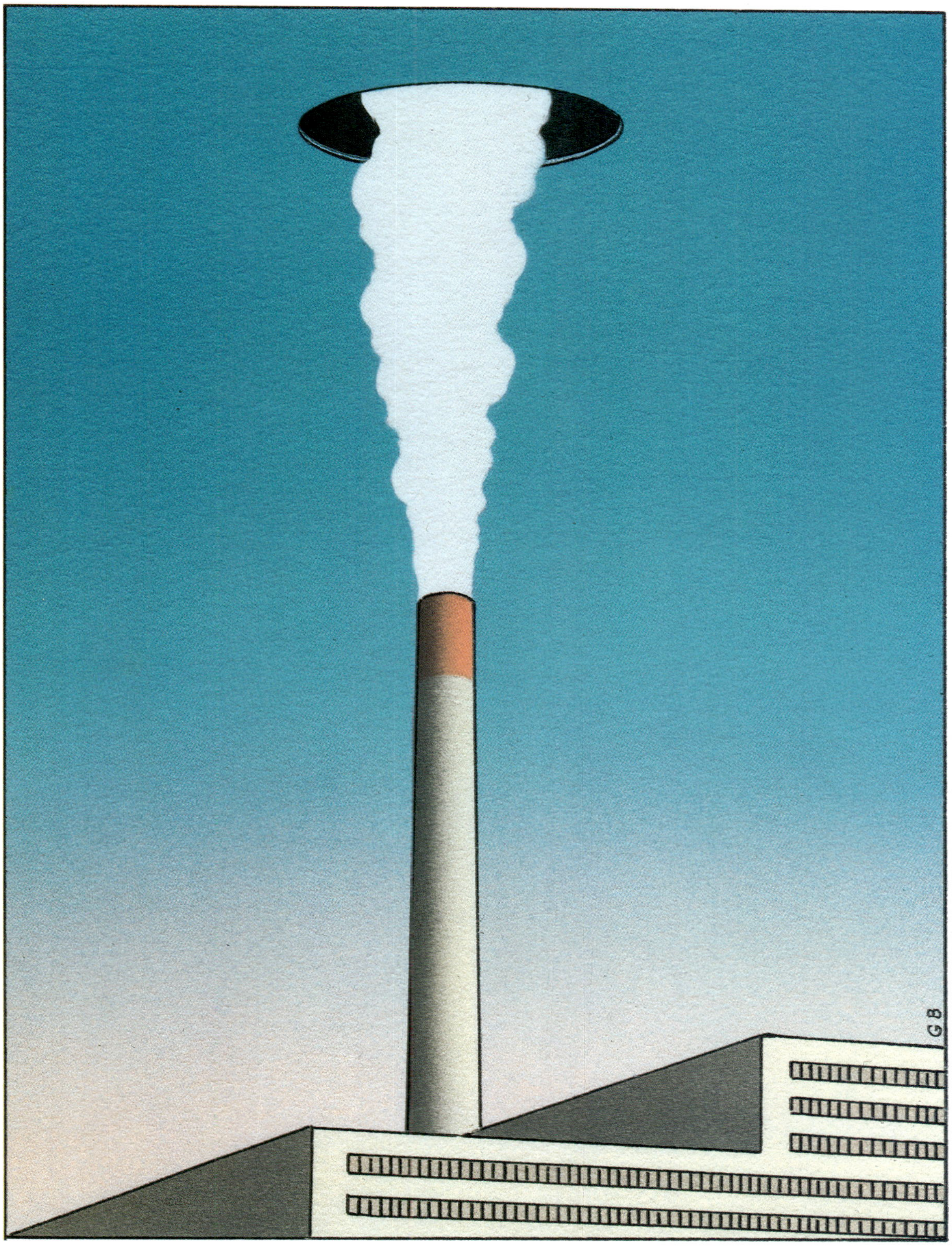

**HOLE IN THE SKY**

Guy Billout

*Watercolor and airbrush*

IT HAS BEEN ESTIMATED
THAT AT LEAST 13 MILLION
CHILDREN WOULD DIE IN 1980
FROM CONTAMINATED WATER.
ACUTE DIARRHEAL DISEASE ALONE
NOW CAUSES SOME 4 MILLION
DEATHS IN CHILDREN.

...........................

DIE GESAMTE ANZAHL DER
BLAUWALE UND BUCKELWALE IST
VON URSPRÜNGLICH 200 000 BZW.
50 000 AUF NUR 15 000 BZW.
3000 ZURÜCKGEGANGEN.

...........................

ON ESTIME QUE 13 MILLIONS
D'ENFANTS AU MOINS SONT
MORTS EN 1980 À CAUSE DE LA
POLLUTION DE L'EAU. QUATRE
MILLIONS D'ENFANTS MEURENT
AUJOURD'HUI DES SUITES
DE DIARRHÉES.

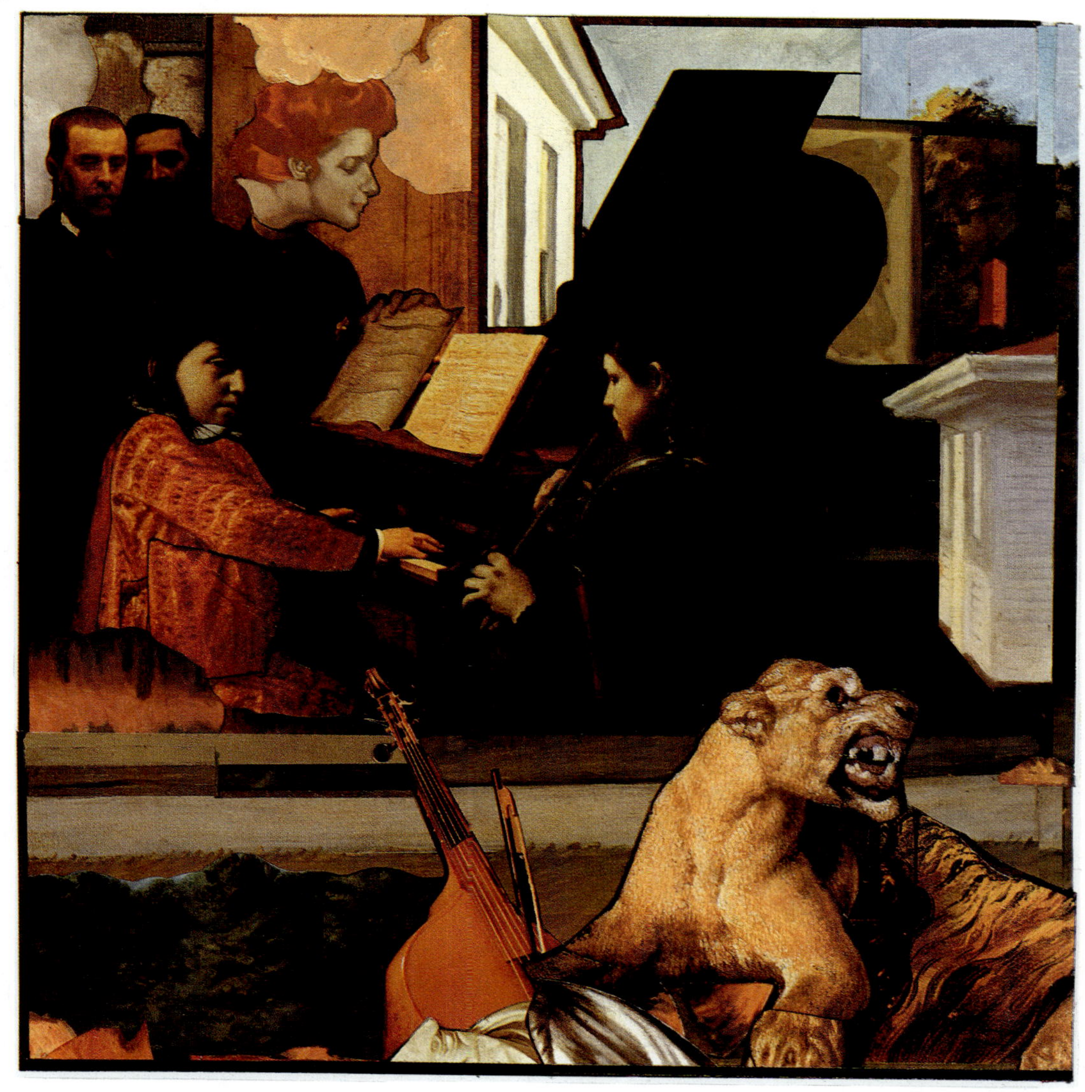

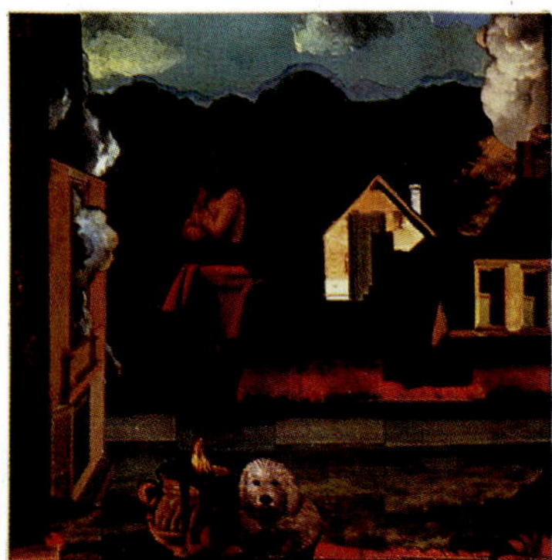

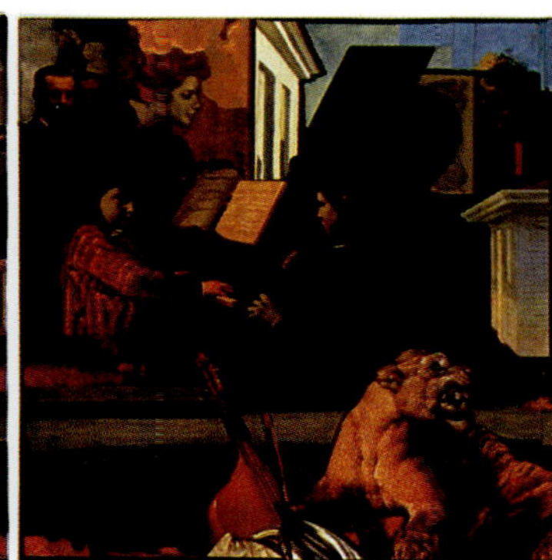

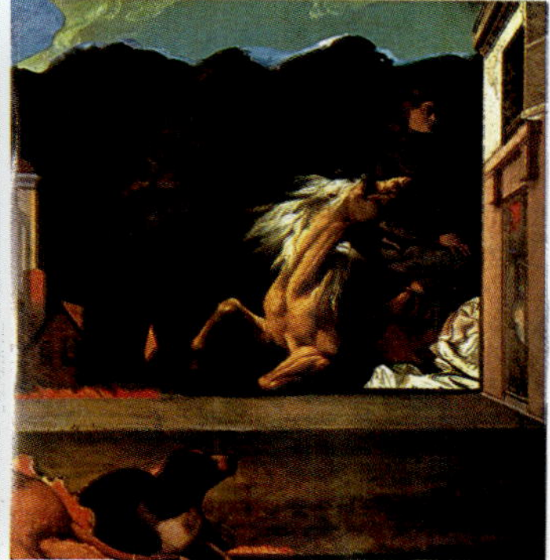

## FIRESIGN TRILOGY

CAROL WALD

*COLLAGE*

"CHILDREN HERE ARE THE OBSERVERS OF REALITY, AS WELL AS THE HARBINGERS OF MYTH. THEY ARE THE INHERITORS OF OUR CULTURE AND ITS ILLS. CHILDREN ARE SEEN AS BEING COMFORTABLE WITH ANIMALS BUT TENSE AMONG HUMAN BEINGS. THEY LINGER IN ROOMS AND IN DOORWAYS, WATCHING ADULTS WHO ARE BUST WITH THEIR PREOCCUPATIONS. THE CHILDREN SEEM OFF AND ALONE IN THEIR NIGHTMARES. HERE, THE CHILD'S PLAYTHING IS NOT A TOY BUT THE VERY SUBSTANCE OF BEING."

MORE THAN TWO-THIRDS OF THE WORLD'S POPULATION LIVE WITHIN 80 KILOMETERS OF A COAST. THE OCEANS COVER 70 PERCENT OF THE EARTH AND THE COASTAL ZONES HAVE THE HIGHEST BIOLOGICAL PRODUCTIVITY.

..........................

MEHR ALS ZWEI DRITTEL DER WELTBEVÖLKERUNG LEBEN NICHT WEITER ALS 80 KM VON EINER KÜSTE ENTFERNT. DIE OZEANE MACHEN 70 PROZENT DER ERDOBERFLÄCHE AUS, UND DIE KÜSTEN SIND BIOLOGISCH AM PRODUKTIVSTEN.

..........................

PLUS DES DEUX TIERS DE LA POPULATION MONDIALE VIVENT À ENVIRON 80 KM D'UNE CÔTE. LES OCÉANS COUVRENT 70% DE LA SURFACE DE LA TERRE ET LES RÉGIONS CÔTIÈRES SONT BIOLOGIQUEMENT LES PLUS RICHES.

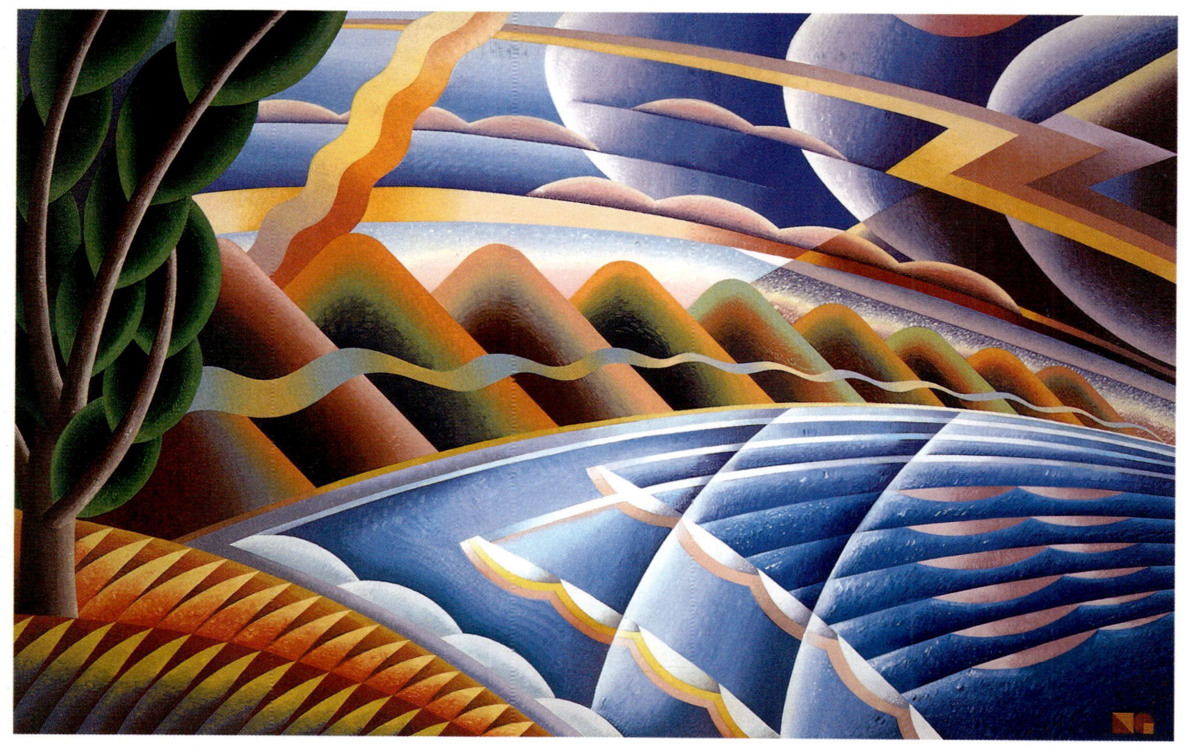

**ISLAND COAST**

NICHOLAS GAETANO

*OIL ON CANVAS*

"THE PAINTING REPRESENTS MY AWE OF THIS MAGICAL THING WE CALL EARTH: A SYNTHESIS OF WONDROUS MOMENTS AND INFINITE POSSIBILITIES. THE PURITY OF COLOR AND CLARITY OF DESIGN BECKON TO MAN FOR ROMANCE AND A DEEPER UNDERSTANDING OF THE BALANCE AND UNITY OF LIFE."

THE EPA ESTIMATES THAT
467,000 TONS OF TOBACCO ARE
BURNED INDOORS EACH YEAR. THIS
THREAT TO NONSMOKERS COULD
INCREASE THEIR RISK OF LUNG
CANCER BY 30 PERCENT.

.........................

ES WIRD GESCHÄTZT, DASS
JÄHRLICH 467 000 TONNEN TABAK
GERAUCHT WERDEN, WODURCH SICH
FÜR NICHTRAUCHER DAS RISIKO
VON LUNGENKREBS DURCH DAS
PASSIVE MITRAUCHEN UM 30
PROZENT ERHÖHT.

.........................

ON ESTIME QUE
CHAQUE ANNÉE, LES FUMEURS
CONSOMMENT 467 000 TONNES DE
TABAC, MENAÇANT LA SANTÉ
DES NON-FUMEURS: LE TABAGISME
PASSIF FAIT AUGMENTER LE RISQUE
DE CANCER DU POUMON
DE 30%.

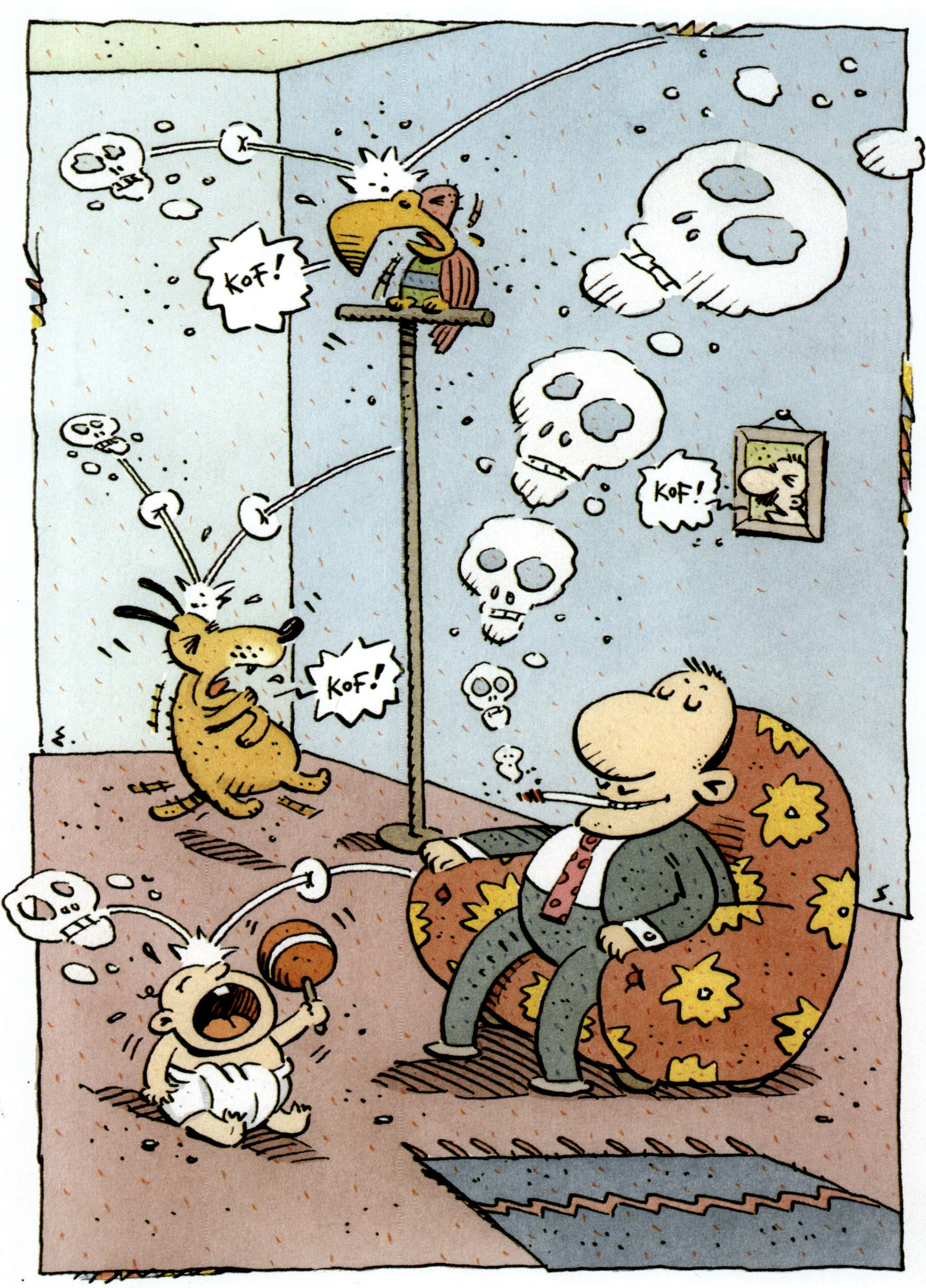


**PASSIVE SMOKING**

ELWOOD H. SMITH

*INDIA INK, WATERCOLOR, AND COLORED PENCIL*

"I TRIED TO SHOW, IN A GRAPHIC BUT HUMOROUS WAY, THE HARMFUL EFFECTS OF PASSIVE SMOKING TO ACCOMPANY AN ARTICLE EXPLORING ITS DANGERS."

RECYCLING ONE TON OF
PAPER INSTEAD OF PRODUCING IT
FROM VIRGIN WOOD RESULTS IN
74 PERCENT LESS AIRPOLLUTION
AND 35 PERCENT LESS
WATER POLLUTION, SAVES TWELVE
PULP TREES, REDUCES SOLID
WASTES GOING TO LANDFILLS, AND
CREATES FIVE TIMES MORE JOBS.

. . . . . . . . . . . . . . . . . . . . . . . . .

WENN MAN EINE TONNE
PAPIER WIEDERVERARBEITET STATT
NEU HERSTELLT, ERZIELT MAN 74 %
WENIGER LUFTVERSCHMUTZUNG
UND 35% WENIGER WASSERVER
SCHMUTZUNG, WÄHREND FÜNF
ARBEITSPLÄTZE
GESCHAFFENWERDEN.

. . . . . . . . . . . . . . . . . . . . . . . . .

RECYCLER UNE TONNE DE
PAPIER AU LIEU DE LA FABRIQUER
PERMET DE DIMINUER LA
POLLUTION DE L'AIR DE 74%,
CELLE DE L'EAU DE 35%, ET DE
CRÉER CINQ FOIS PLUS D'EMPLOIS.

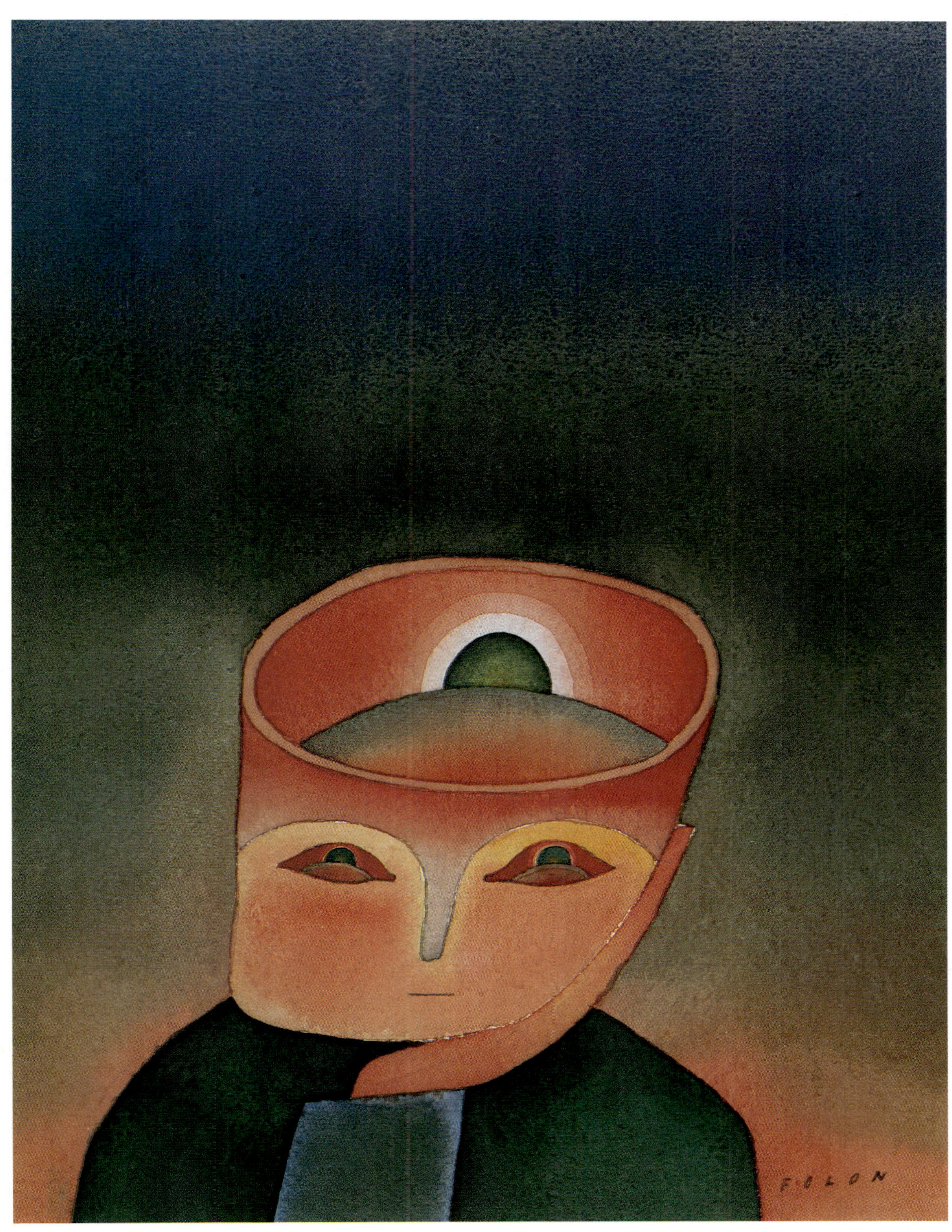


**GREENWAY**

Jean-Michel Folon

*Watercolor on paper*

"The watercolors of my illustration show hope—that 'green' suns are rising in our eyes and thoughts. The person in the image is simply each one of us. We are all responsible for remembering the essential: that each of us is, first and foremost, a center of life, a center of birth for the green suns."

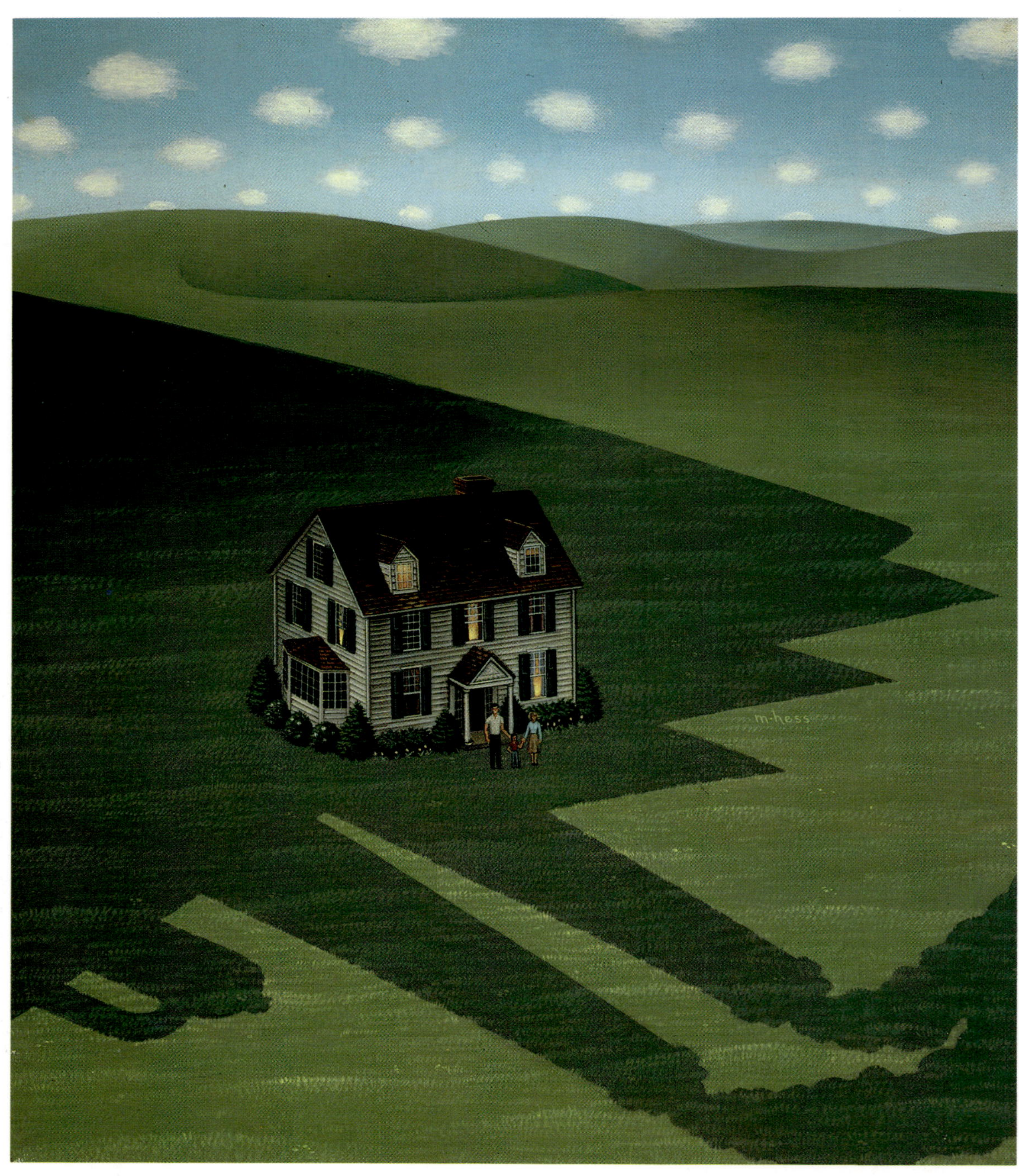


**LIVING IN THE SHADOW OF INDUSTRY**

MARK HESS

*OIL ON CANVAS*

"IN REACHING FOR A BETTER, MORE COMFORTABLE, AND PRODUCTIVE LIFE, WE EXPOSE OURSELVES TO DANGER AND RISKS DEEMED ACCEPTABLE IN RELATIONSHIP TO THEIR BENEFITS. INDUSTRY, IN THIS PAINTING, IS A METAPHOR FOR ALL THE WELL-INTENTIONED DECISIONS MADE EVERY DAY THAT EFFECT OUR ENVIRONMENT, HEALTH, AND WELL-BEING."

IT TAKES 394 POUNDS OF COAL TO PROVIDE ENERGY FOR ONE 100-WATT INCANDESCENT BULB TO BURN FOR 12 HOURS A DAY FOR ONE YEAR. THE SAME COAL WILL MEANWHILE BE EMITTING 936 POUNDS OF CARBON DIOXIDE AND 7.8 POUNDS OF SULPHUR DIOXIDE INTO OUR ATMOSPHERE.

...........................

179 KG KOHLE WERDEN VERBRAUCHT, WENN EINE 100-WATT-GLÜHBIRNE IM JAHR 12 STUNDEN PRO TAG BRENNT. DIE GLEICHE MENGE KOHLE GIBT 425 KG KOHLENDIOXID UND 3,5 KILO SCHWEFELDIOXID IN DIE ATMOSPHÄRE AB.

...........................

L'ÉNERGIE DÉPENSÉE PAR UNE AMPOULE DE 100 W BRÛLANT 12 HEURES PAR JOUR PENDANT UN AN REPRÉSENTE 179 KG DE CHARBON. CETTE MÊME QUANTITÉ DE CHARBON PRODUIRAIT DANS L'INTERVALLE ENVIRON 425 KG DE DIOXYDE DE CARBONE ET 3,538 KG DE DIOXYDE DE SOUFRE.

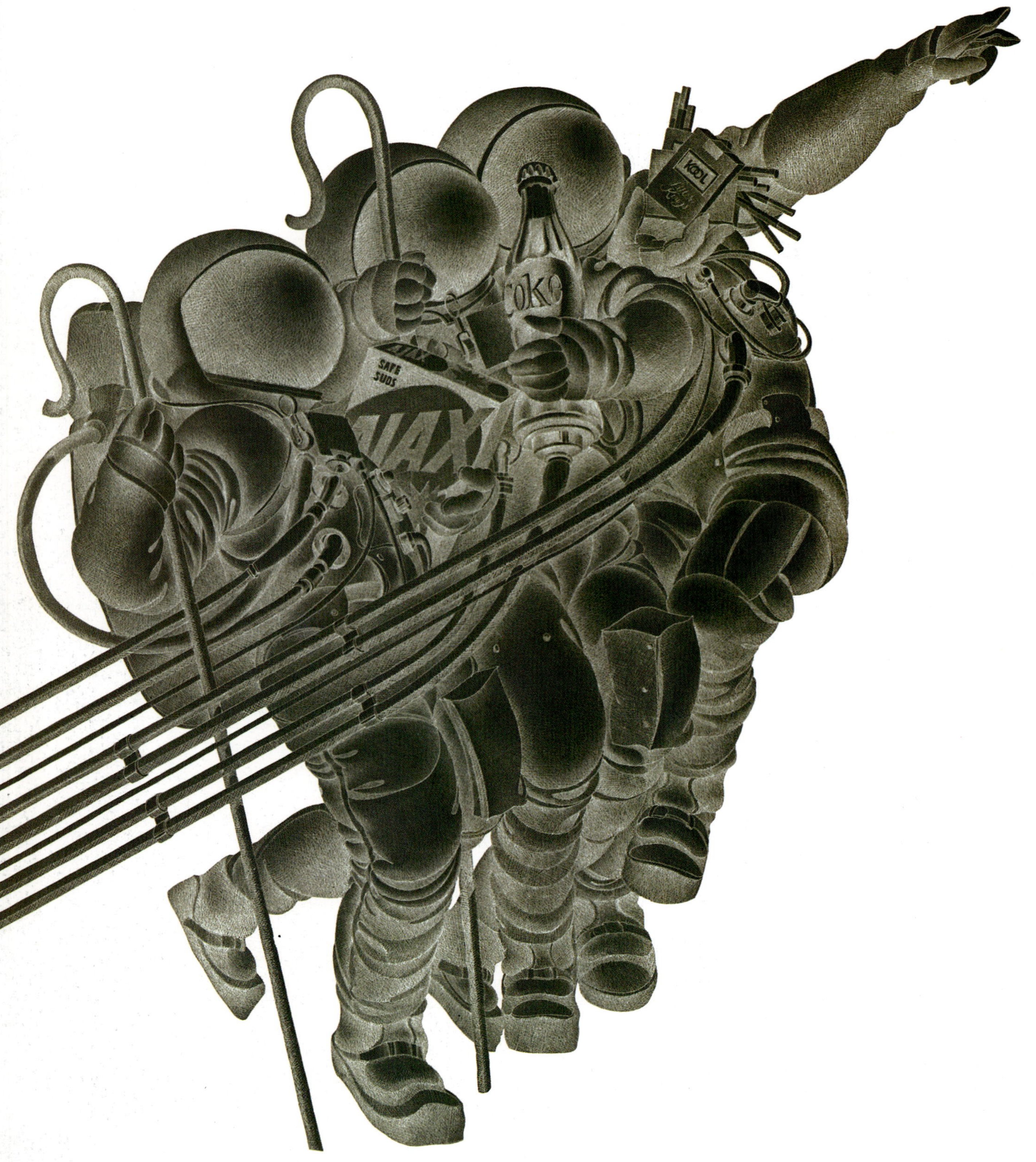


**THEY CAME BEARING GIFTS**

Charles Santore

*Graphite pencil and black paint*

"The science of man often takes on the intensity of religious fervor in its quest for technological perfection—often leaving disasters in its wake. To quote an old proverb: 'The road to hell is paved with good intentions'—or heaven for that matter."

EVEN THOUGH THE EPA REQUIRES THAT RESULTING ASH FROM INCINERATION BE TESTED AND DISPOSED OF AS A HAZARDOUS MATERIAL, MOST OF THE ASH ENDS UP IN OUR LANDFILLS WHERE IT POLLUTES OUR ECOSYSTEM.

........................

OBGLEICH GEMÄSS DER US-UMWELTBEHÖRDE ASCHE UNTERSUCHT UND ALS GEFÄHRLICHES MATERIAL ENTSORGT WERDEN MUSS, LANDET SIE MEISTENS AUF DEPONIEN UND VERSEUCHT DADURCH DAS ÖKOSYSTEM.

........................

BIEN QUE L'ON DEMANDE QUE LES CENDRES D'INCINÉRATION SOIENT ANALYSÉES ET CONSIDÉRÉES COMME POTENTIELLEMENT DANGEREUSES, ELLES FINISSENT POUR LA PLUPART DANS DES DÉCHARGES, POLLUANT NOTRE ÉCOSYSTÈME.

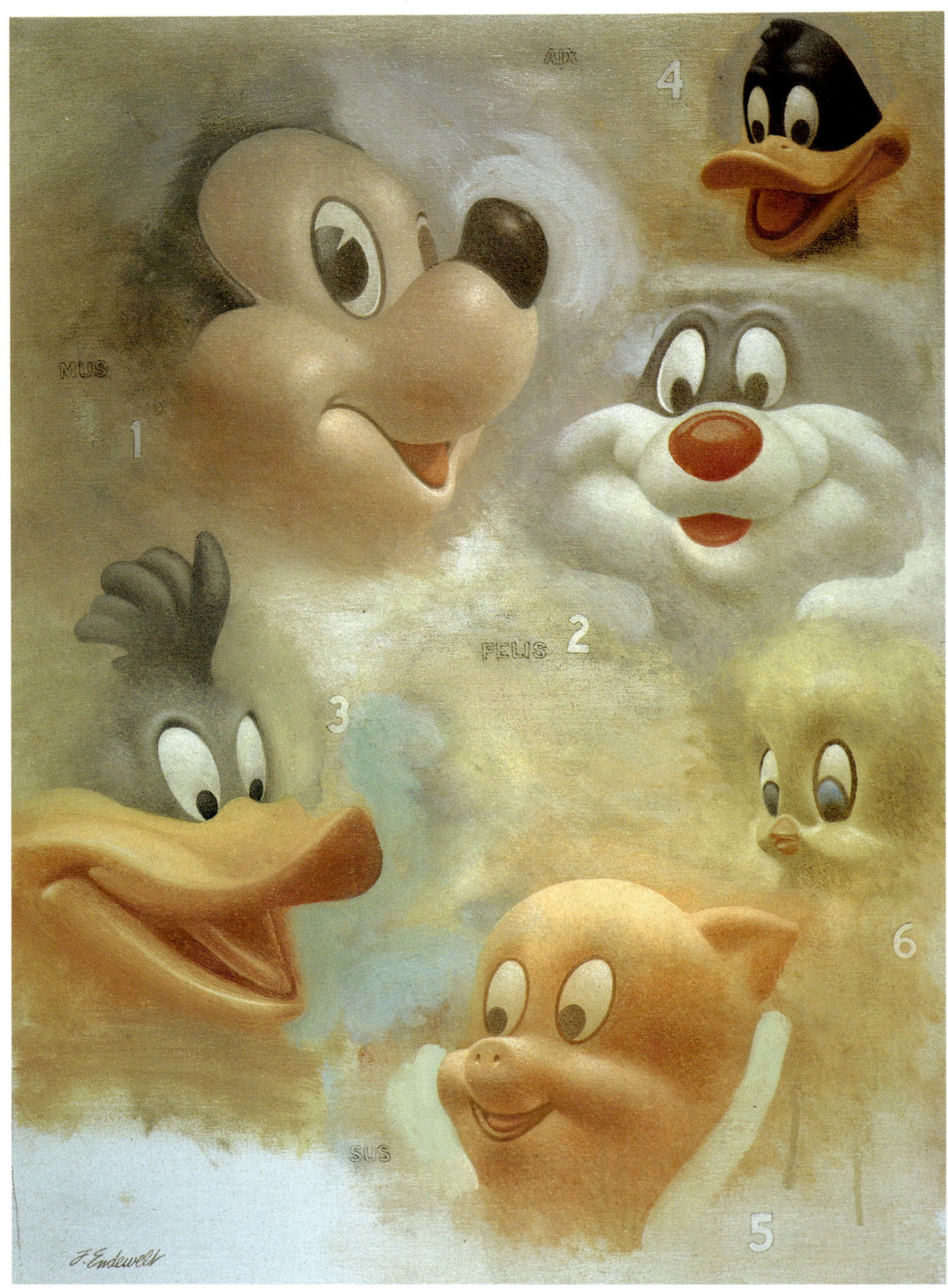


**THE FUTURE OF BIOLOGICAL DIVERSITY**

JACK ENDEWELT

*OIL ON LINEN*

"I CHOSE TO STUDY ANIMALS THAT WE HAVE NEVER TRIED TO KILL."

HABITAT DESTRUCTION BY HUMAN ACTIVITIES, PARTICULARLY IN THE TROPICS, IS THE PRIMARY CAUSE FOR EXTINCTION AND THE WORLDWIDE LOSS OF BIOLOGICAL DIVERSITY.

.........................

DIE ZERSTÖRUNG VON LEBENSRAUM IST DER HAUPTGRUND FÜR DEN VERLUST BIOLOGISCHER VIELFALT.

.........................

LA DESTRUCTION DE L'ESPACE VITAL EST LA PREMIÈRE CAUSE DE LA PERTE DE LA DIVERSITÉ BIOLOGIQUE.

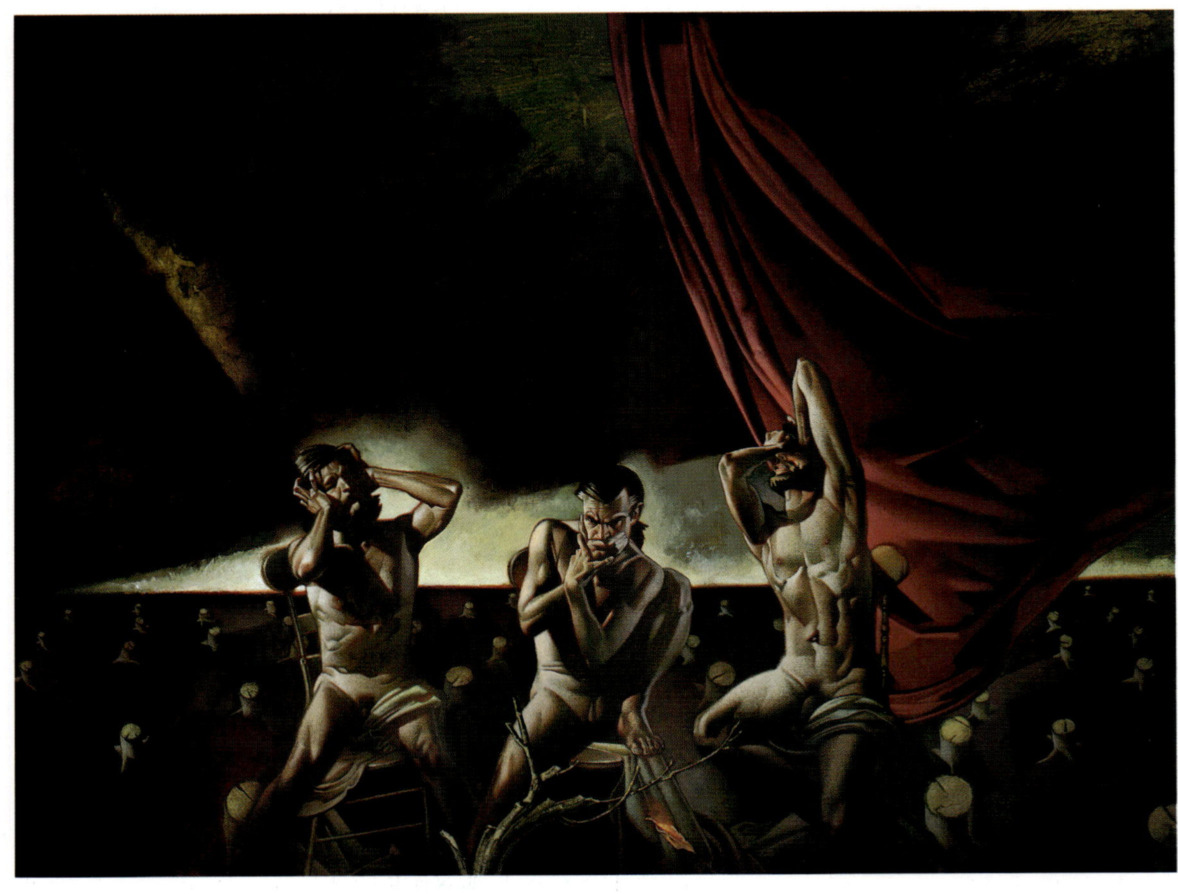

## The Last Leaf

Robert Rodriguez

*Gouache, acrylics, and Prismacolor on canvas*

"This rather apocalyptic scene shows three men gathered to witness the death of the last leaf of the last tree on earth. Their anguished poses—hear no evil, speak no evil, see no evil—symbolize mankind at this point today. And maybe a little over-dramatically, the final curtain comes down."

THE DESTRUCTION OF THE FOREST IS CAUSING THE EXTINCTION OF THE ANIMALS WITHIN IT. GREEN LEAVES NOT ONLY FEED AND HOUSE ANIMALS BUT ALSO ABSORB CARBON DIOXIDE AND EMIT OXYGEN DURING PHOTOSYNTHESIS.

..........................

DIE ZERSTÖRUNG DER WÄLDER VERURSACHT DAS AUSSTERBEN SEINER BEWOHNER. GRÜNE BLÄTTER DIENEN DEN TIEREN NICHT NUR ALS NAHRUNG UND UNTERSCHLUPF, SONDERN ABSORBIEREN AUCH KOHLENDIOXID UND VERSORGEN UNSERE LUFT MIT SAUERSTOFF WÄHREND DER PHOTOSYNTHESE.

..........................

LA DESTRUCTION DES FORÊTS ENTRAÎNE L'EXTINCTION DES ESPÈCES QUI Y HABITENT. NON SEULEMENT LE FEUILLAGE NOURRIT ET ABRITE LES ANIMAUX, IL ABSORBE AUSSI LE DIOXYDE DE CARBONE ET PRODUIT DE L'OXYGÈNE AU COURS DE LA PHOTOSYNTHÈSE.

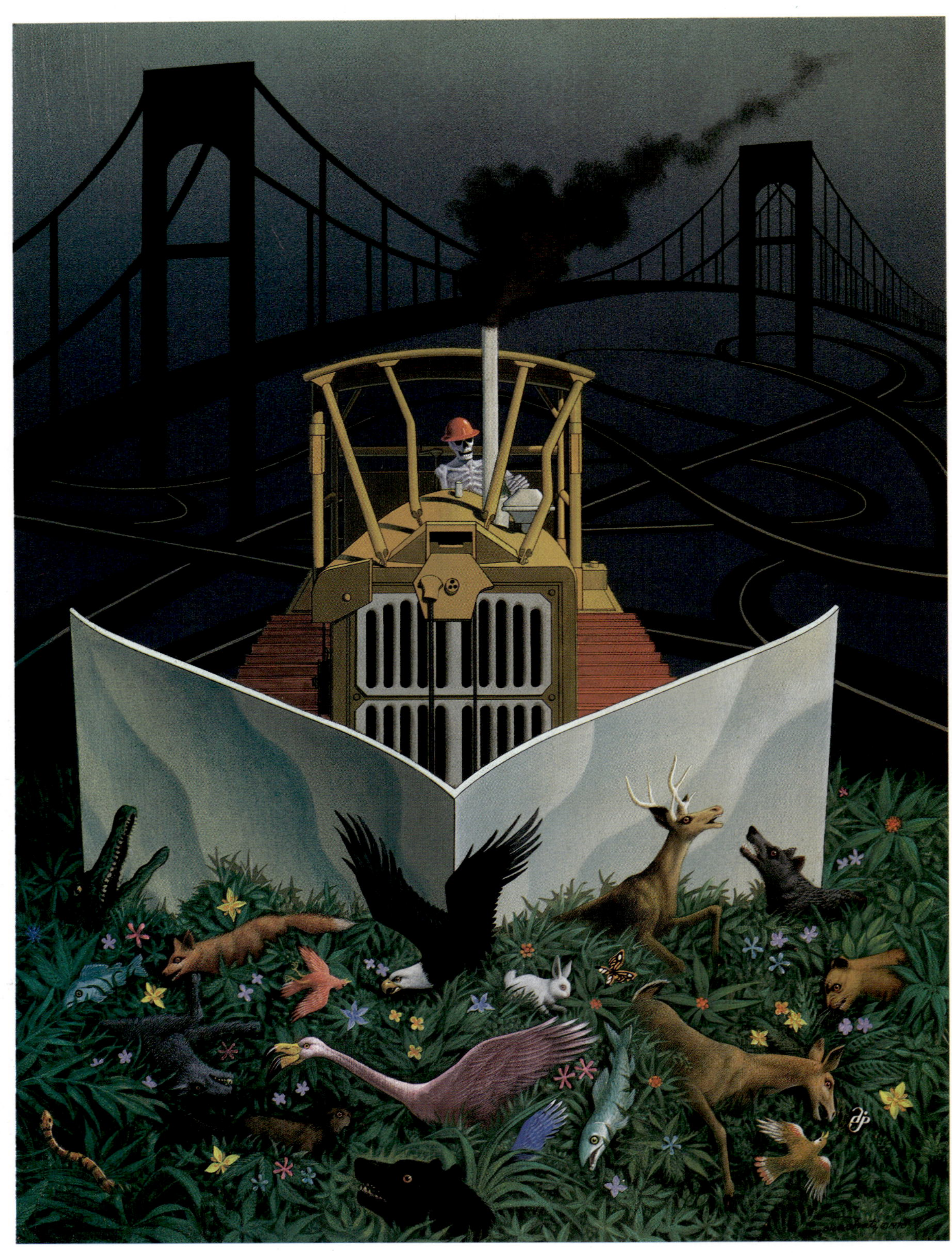

**AMERICA THE RAPED**

Don Ivan Punchatz

*Acrylic on watercolor board*

"This painting was originally commissioned for the cover of the book, *America the Raped*, by the author, Gene Marine. I developed the concept to interpret the main theme of the book: the wanton destruction of Earth's natural environment to satisfy the blind greed of profit-motivated 'engineering mentalities.'"

ONE TO TWO MILLION
SPECIES OF PLANTS AND ANIMALS
ARE THREATENED WITH EXTINCTION
AS A RESULT OF OUR FAILURE TO
ADEQUATELY PROTECT AND
PRESERVE OUR NATURAL
ENVIRONMENT.

..........................

EIN BIS ZWEI MILLIONEN
ARTEN VON PFLANZEN UND TIEREN
SIND VOM AUSSTERBEN BEDROHT,
WEIL WIR UNSERE NATÜRLICHE
UMWELT NICHT AUSREICHEND
GESCHÜTZT UND ERHALTEN HABEN.

..........................

UN À DEUX MILLIONS
D'ESPÈCES DE PLANTES SONT
MENACÉES D'EXTINCTION PARCE
QUE NOUS AVONS ÉTÉ INCAPABLES
DE PROTÉGER EFFICACEMENT
ET DE PRÉSERVER NOTRE
ENVIRONNEMENT NATUREL.

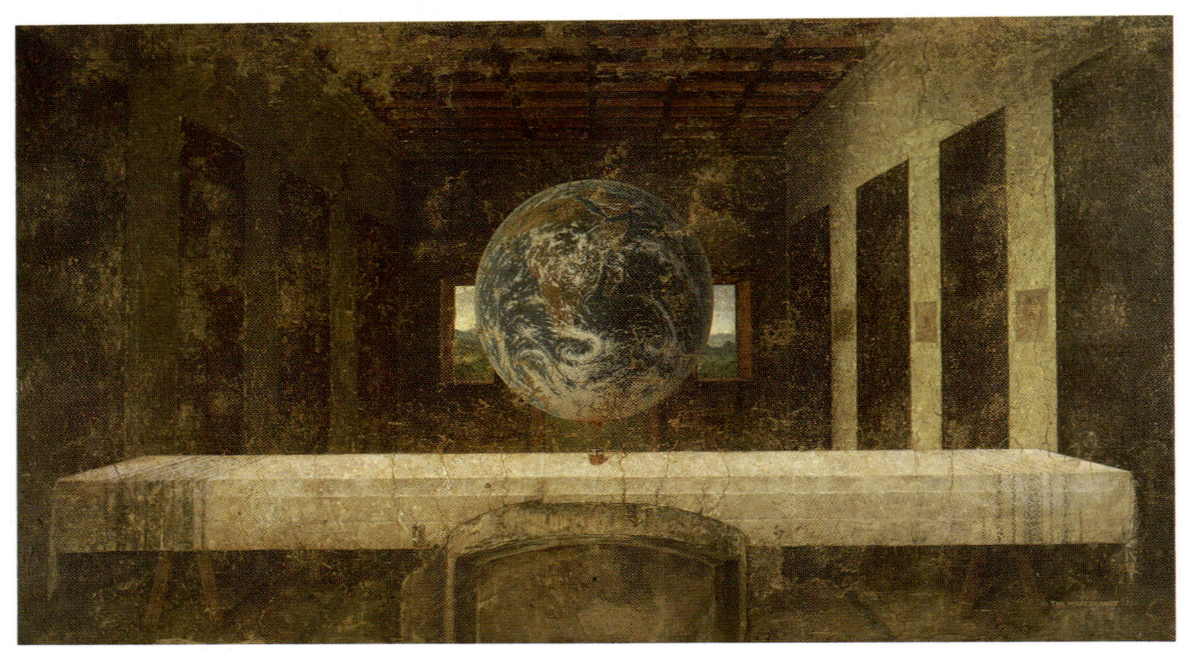

**STUDY IN EARTHTONES #1**
**(THE BLEEDING EARTH)**

TIM HILDEBRANDT

*ACRYLIC ON MASONITE*

"ANY GREAT WORK OF ART THAT IS DETERIORATING IS WORTHY OF RESTORATION. WHAT GREATER WORK IS THERE THAN OUR HOME, THE EARTH?"

A BABY BORN IN A
DEVELOPING COUNTRY IS TEN
TIMES MORE LIKELY TO DIE BEFORE
ITS FIRST BIRTHDAY THAN ONE
BORN IN AN INDUSTRIAL ONE.

..........................

IN EINEM ENTWICKLUNGSLAND
IST DIE WAHRSCHEINLICHKEIT,
DASS EIN NEUGEBORENES
SEINEN ERSTEN GEBURTSTAG NICHT
ERLEBT, ZEHNMAL SO GROSS WIE
IN EINEM INDUSTRIELAND.

..........................

UN ENFANT NÉ DANS UN PAYS
EN VOIE DE DÉVELOPPEMENT A DIX
FOIS MOINS DE CHANCES DE
SURVIVRE JUSQU'À SON PREMIER
ANNIVERSAIRE QUE CELUI D'UN
PAYS INDUSTRIEL.

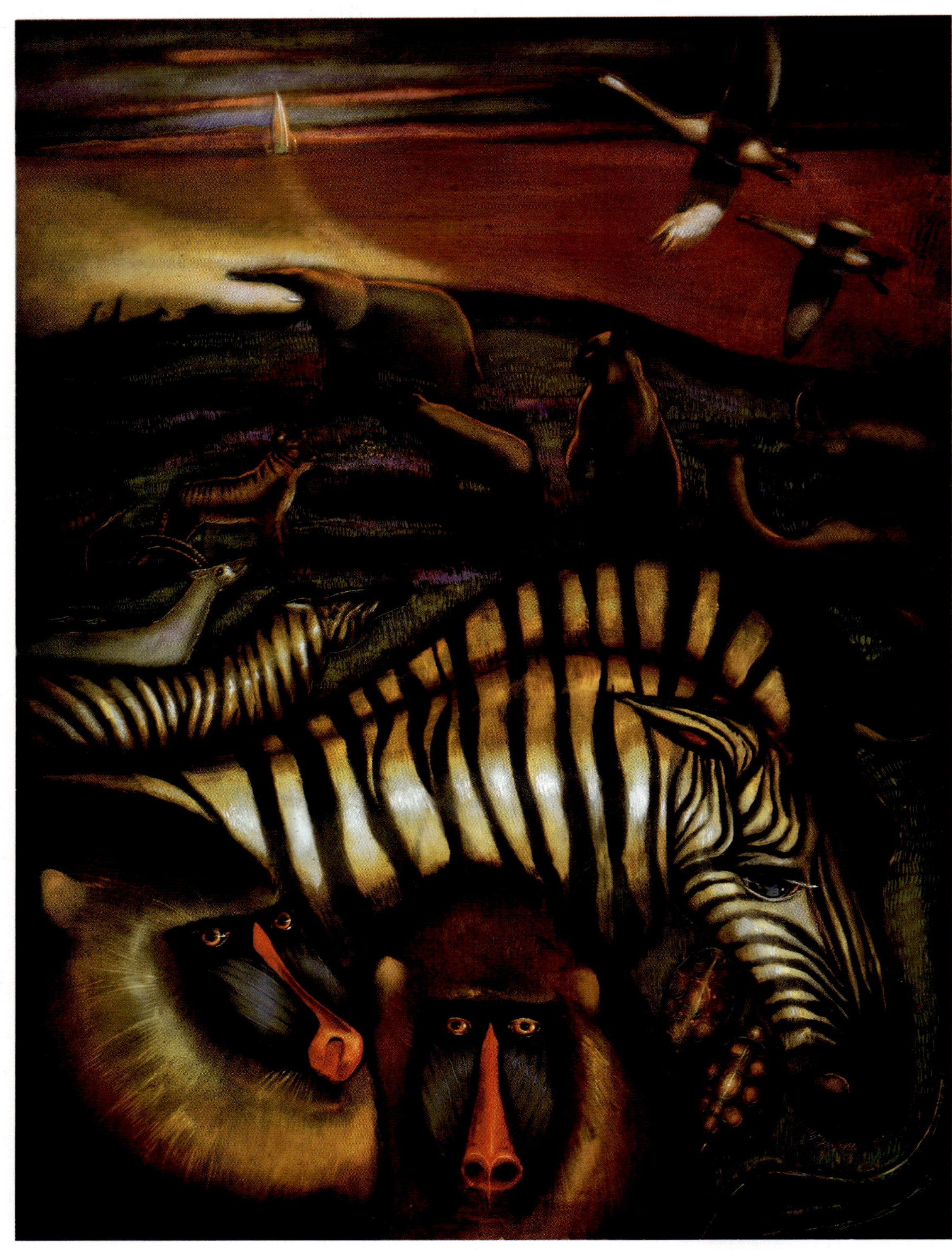

**SECOND ARK**

Deborah Healy

*Oil on canvas*

"I've always had profound feelings for those creatures affected by our use/misuse of the environment. Most recently, the act of environmental terrorism in the Persian Gulf—and its impact on thousands of marine creatures and migratory birds—has deeply affected me. My painting is of animals leaving the earth vacating 'spaceship earth.'"

OF SOME 20,000 PLANT SPECIES ORIGINALLY FOUND IN THE UNITED STATES, 90 SPECIES ARE EXTINCT AND 11 PERCENT (2,040) ARE ENDANGERED OR THREATENED.

........................

VON 20,000 PFLANZENARTEN, DIE MAN URSPRÜNGLICH IN DEN USA KANNTE, SIND 90 ARTEN VERSCHWUNDEN UND 11 PROZENT (2040) SIND VOM AUSSTERBEN BEDROHT.

........................

DES QUELQUES 20,000 ESPÈCES DE PLANTES QUI SE TROUVAIENT AUX ÉTATS-UNIS, 90 ONT DISPARU ET 2040 (11%) SONT EN VOIE D'EXTINCTION OU MENACÉES.

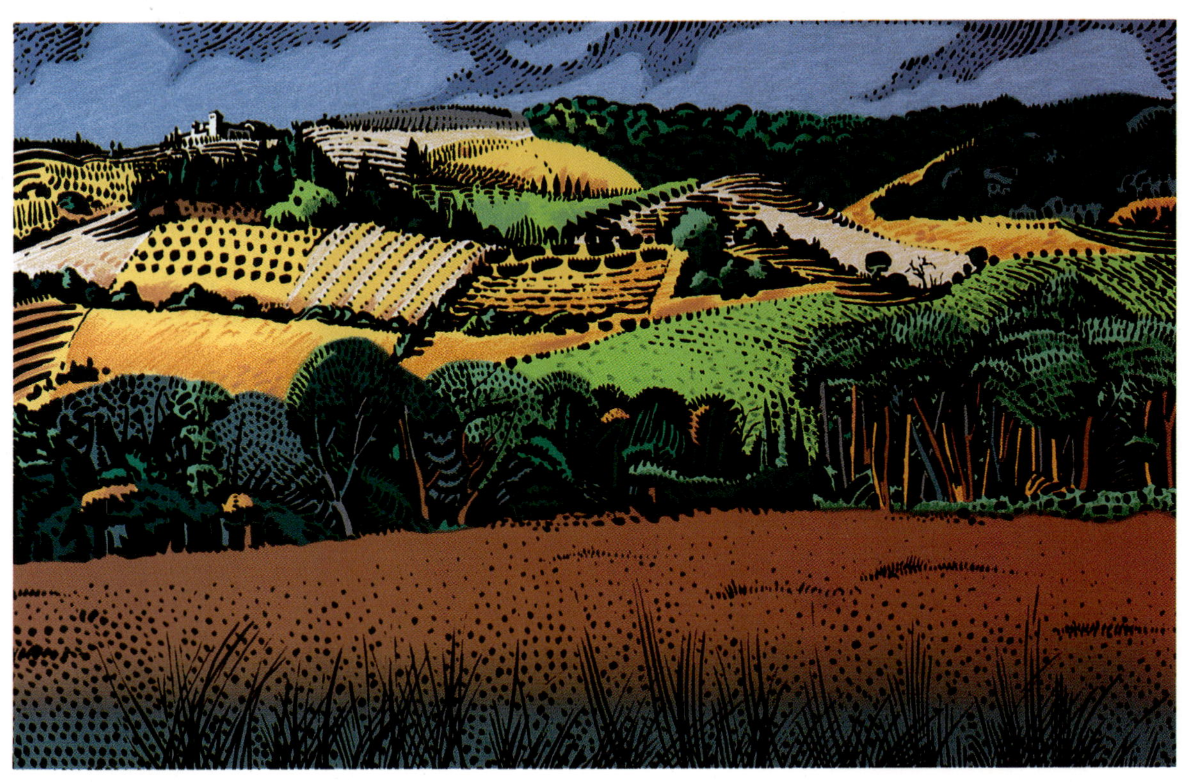

## TUSCANY

Milton Glaser

*Silkscreen*

"The idea was to show the extraordinary and threatened beauty that exists in the world. The landscapes around Tuscany show that all is not yet lost."

HUNDREDS OF FAMILIES
HAD TO BE EVACUATED FROM LOVE
CANAL, U.S., AND LEKKERKERK,
THE NETHERLANDS, AFTER HOMES
HAD BEEN BUILT OVER DUMPS
CONTAINING TOXIC WASTE.

HUNDERTE VON FAMILIEN
MUSSTEN AUS DEN HÄUSERN AM
LOVE CANAL, USA, UND IN
LEKKERKERK IN DEN NIEDERLANDEN
EVAKUIERT WERDEN, WEIL DIE
GEBÄUDE AUF GIFTDEPONIEN
GEBAUT WAREN.

DES CENTAINES DE
FAMILLES ONT DÛ ÊTRE ÉVACUÉES À
LOVE CANAL, AUX USA, ET À
LEKKERKERK, AUX PAYS-BAS,
PARCE QUE LEUR MAISON AVAIT
ÉTÉ CONSTRUITE SUR DES
ANCIENNES DÉCHARGES DE
PRODUITS TOXIQUES.

THE EARTH'S CARRYING CAPACITY, A MEASURE OF RESOURCES, IS BURDENED NOT ONLY BY THE DEMANDS OF 5 BILLION PEOPLE BUT ALSO BY FOOD REQUIREMENTS OF 4 BILLION CATTLE, SHEEP, PIGS, GOATS, AND OTHER LIVESTOCK. OVERGRAZING BY LIVESTOCK CAUSES DESERTIFICATION AND CLEARING LAND FOR CATTLE RANCHING CAUSES DEFORESTATION.

..........................

DIE BELASTBARKEIT DER ERDE HÄNGT VON IHREN RESSOURCEN AB BZW. NICHT NUR VON DEREN BEANSPRUCHUNG DURCH 5 MILLIARDEN MENSCHEN, SONDERN AUCH DURCH DEN FUTTERBEDARF VON 4 MILLIARDEN NUTZTIEREN. ÜBERMÄSSIGE ABGRASUNG VERURSACHT VERWÜSTUNG, UND RODUNG FÜR WEIDELAND VERURSACHT ENTWALDUNG.

..........................

LES CAPACITÉS DE LA TERRE DÉPENDENT DE SES RESSOURCES NATURELLES, MISES À CONTRIBUTION PAR LES EXIGENCES DE 5 MILLIARDS D'HABITANTS MAIS AUSSI PAR LESBESOINS EN NOURRITURE DE 4 MILLIARDS DE TÊTES DE BÉTAIL. L'ÉLEVAGE INTENSIF ENTRAÎNE LA DÉSERTIFICATION ET L'ESSARTAGE DES TERRES EST CAUSE DE DÉFORESTATION.

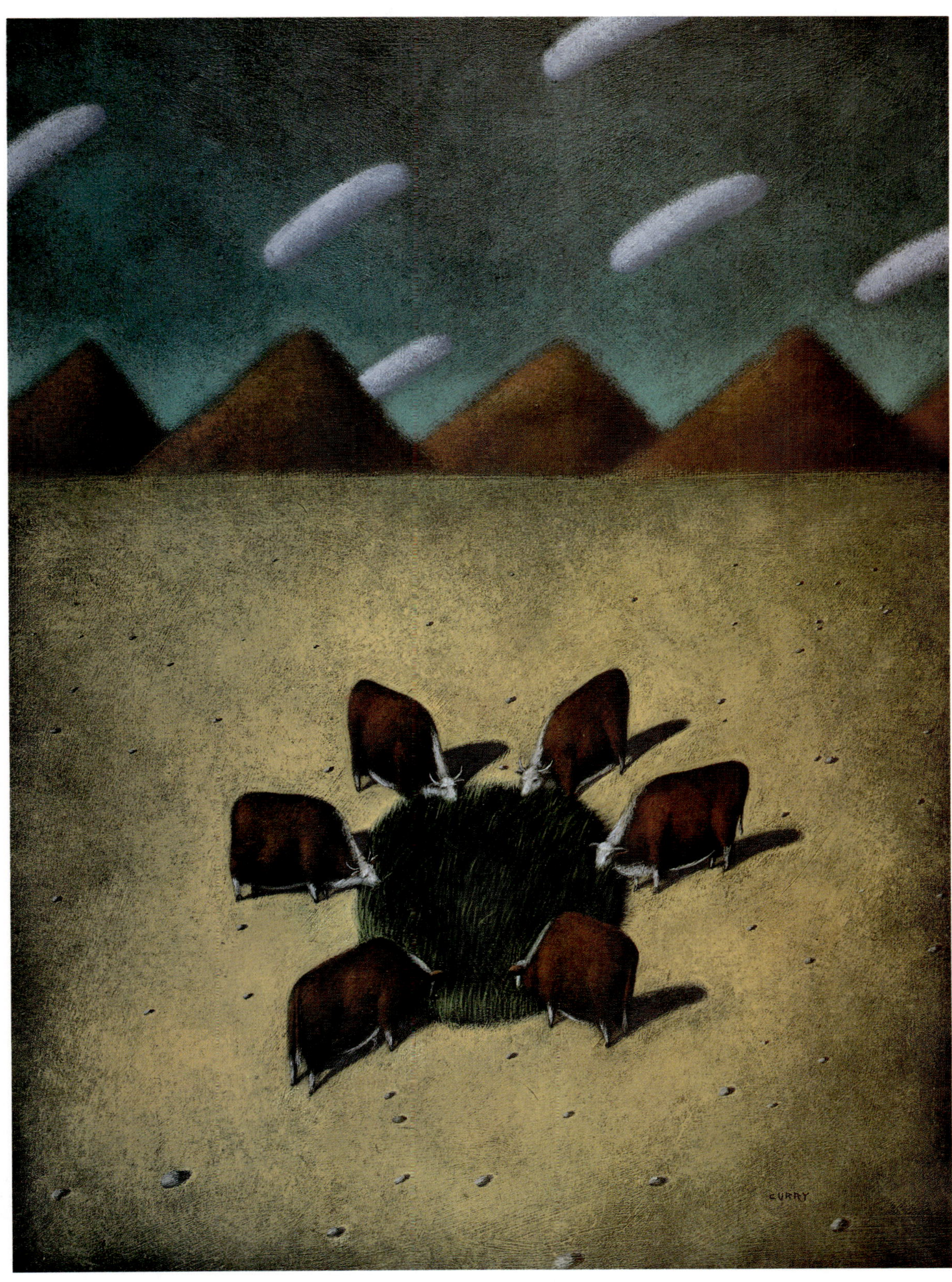


**A PUBLIC BEEF**

TOM CURRY

*ACRYLIC ON BOARD*

"THE ABUSE AND OVERGRAZING OF LARGE AREAS OF PUBL C LAND IS CHANGING THE ONCE ROLLING, GRASSY PLAINS TO VAST WASTELAND- DESERTS. THIS IS AN AREA OF ENVIRONMENTAL DETERIORATION OFTEN OVERLOOKED."

IT HAS BEEN ESTIMATED
THAT BETWEEN 450 AND 750
MILLION PEOPLE ARE SERIOUSLY
MALNOURISHED.

..........................

GEMÄSS SCHÄTZUNG
GEHÖREN WELTWEIT 450 BIS
750 MILLIONEN MENSCHEN ZU DEN
ERNSTLICH UNTERERNÄHRTEN,
DEREN KÖRPERLICHE
ABWEHRKRÄFTE GEGEN
INFEKTIONSKRANKHEITEN
GESCHWÄCHT SIND.

..........................

ON ESTIME QUE DANS
LE MONDE 450 À 750 MILLIONS DE
GENS SONT SOUS-ALIMENTÉS
ET QUE LEUR ORGANISME AFFAIBLI
N'EST PAS EN MESURE DE SE
DÉFENDRE CONTRE LES INFECTIONS.

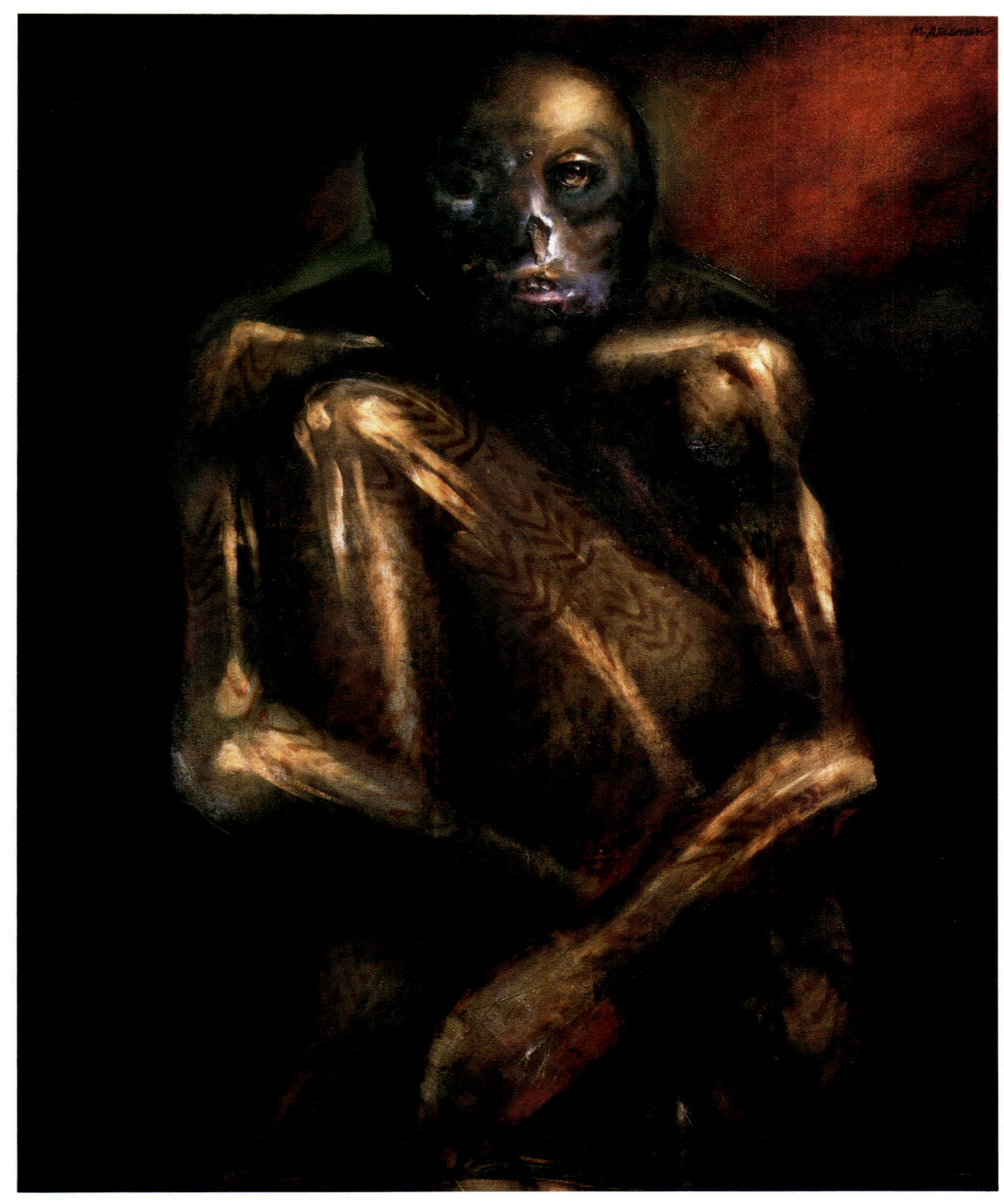

**STARVATION**

Marshall Arisman

*Oil on canvas*

"We are a violent species. Our daily lives are surrounded by an ever-increasing number of tragic losses in all living things. One of the most brutal examples has been directed at ourselves. Starvation, in a world that has the capacity to feed itself, is indeed the beginning of a brave new world."

THE GREATEST VARIETY OF SPECIES EXISTS IN THE TROPICAL DEVELOPING NATIONS, WHICH LACK THE FINANCIAL AND TECHNOLOGICAL RESOURCES TO CONSERVE AND PROTECT THEIR BIOLOGICAL DIVERSITY.

..........................

DIE GRÖSSTE VIELFALT DER ARTEN EXISTIERT IN DEN TROPISCHEN LÄNDERN, DIE KEINE AUSREICHENDEN FINANZIELLEN UND TECHNOLOGISCHEN MITTEL HABEN, UM DIESE VIELFALT ZU SCHÜTZEN UND ZU ERHALTEN.

..........................

ON TROUVE LA PLUS GRANDE VARIÉTÉ D'ESPÈCES DANS LES PAYS TROPICAUX QUI N'ONT PAS LES MOYENS FINANCIERS ET TECHNOLOGIQUES POUR PROTÉGER LEURS RICHESSES NATURELLES.

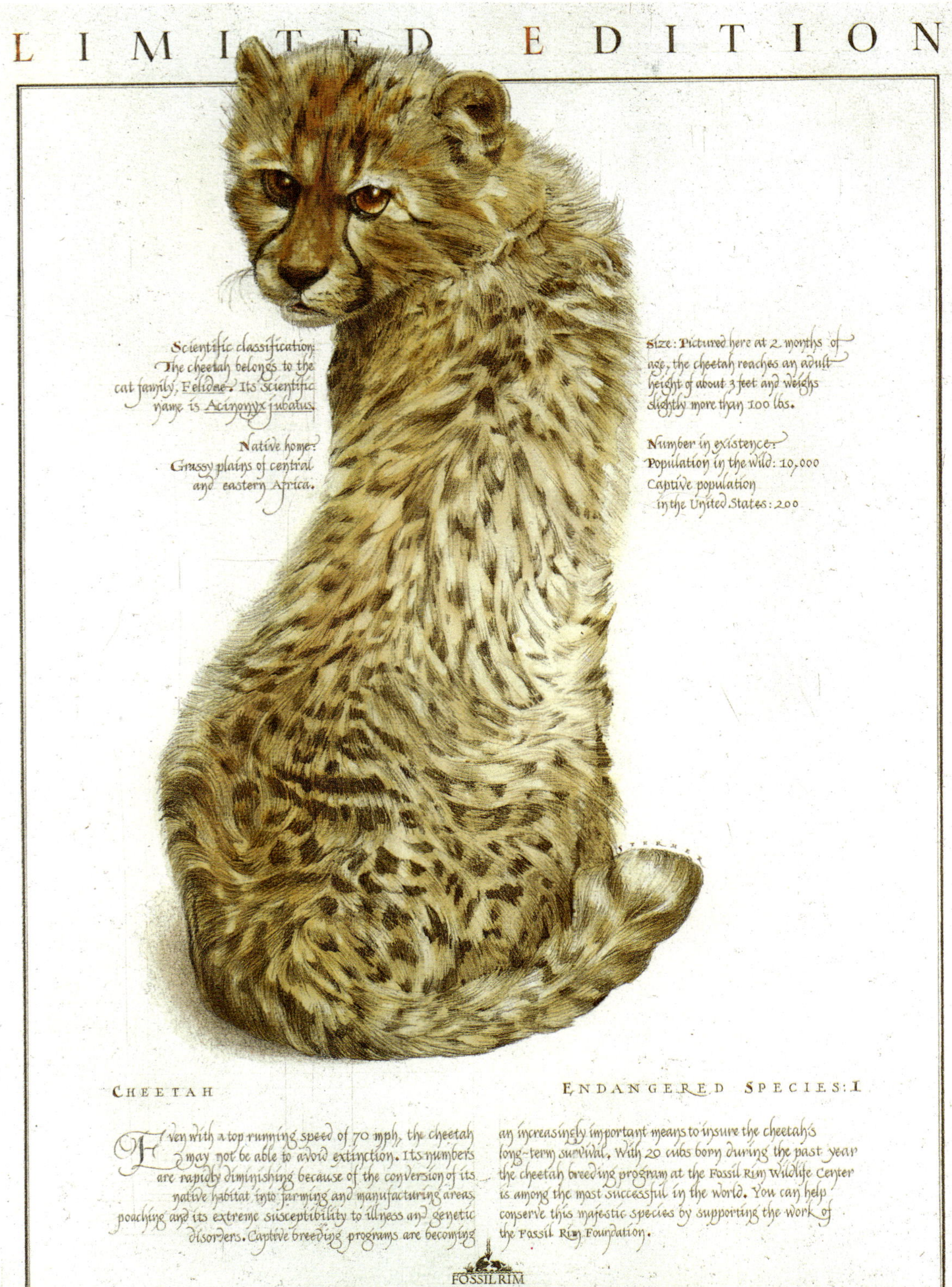


**LIMITED EDITION: CHEETAH**

DUGALD STERMER

*PENCIL AND WATERCOLOR ON ARCHES PAPER*

"THIS WAS DESIGNED AS A POSTER, SPONSORED BY FOSSIL RIM ANIMAL PARK, TO PORTRAY MAINLY TO CHILDREN THE SITUATION FACING MANY ENDANGERED CREATURES THROUGHOUT THE WORLD."

RECYCLING REDUCES
SOLID WASTE AND OIL USE. EACH
TON OF RECYCLED PAPER SAVES
MORE THAN 3 CUBIC YARDS
OF LANDFILL SPACE AND SAVES
380 GALLONS OF OIL.

...........................

DURCH WIEDERVERARBEITUNG
WERDEN FESTSTOFFABFÄLLE
UND DER ÖLVERBRAUCH
REDUZIERT. JEDE TONNE
UMWELTPAPIER SPART MEHR
ALS ZWEI KUBIKMETER
ABFALL UND MEHR ALS
1500 LITER ÖL.

...........................

LE RECYCLAGE PERMET DE
RÉDUIRE LA QUANTITÉ DE DÉCHETS
SOLIDES ET LA CONSOMMATION
D'HUILE. CHAQUE TONNE
DE PAPIER RECYCLÉ REPRÉSENTE
UNE ÉCONOMIE DE PLUS DE 2
MÈTRES CUBES D'ORDURES ET PLUS
DE 1500 LITRES D'HUILE.

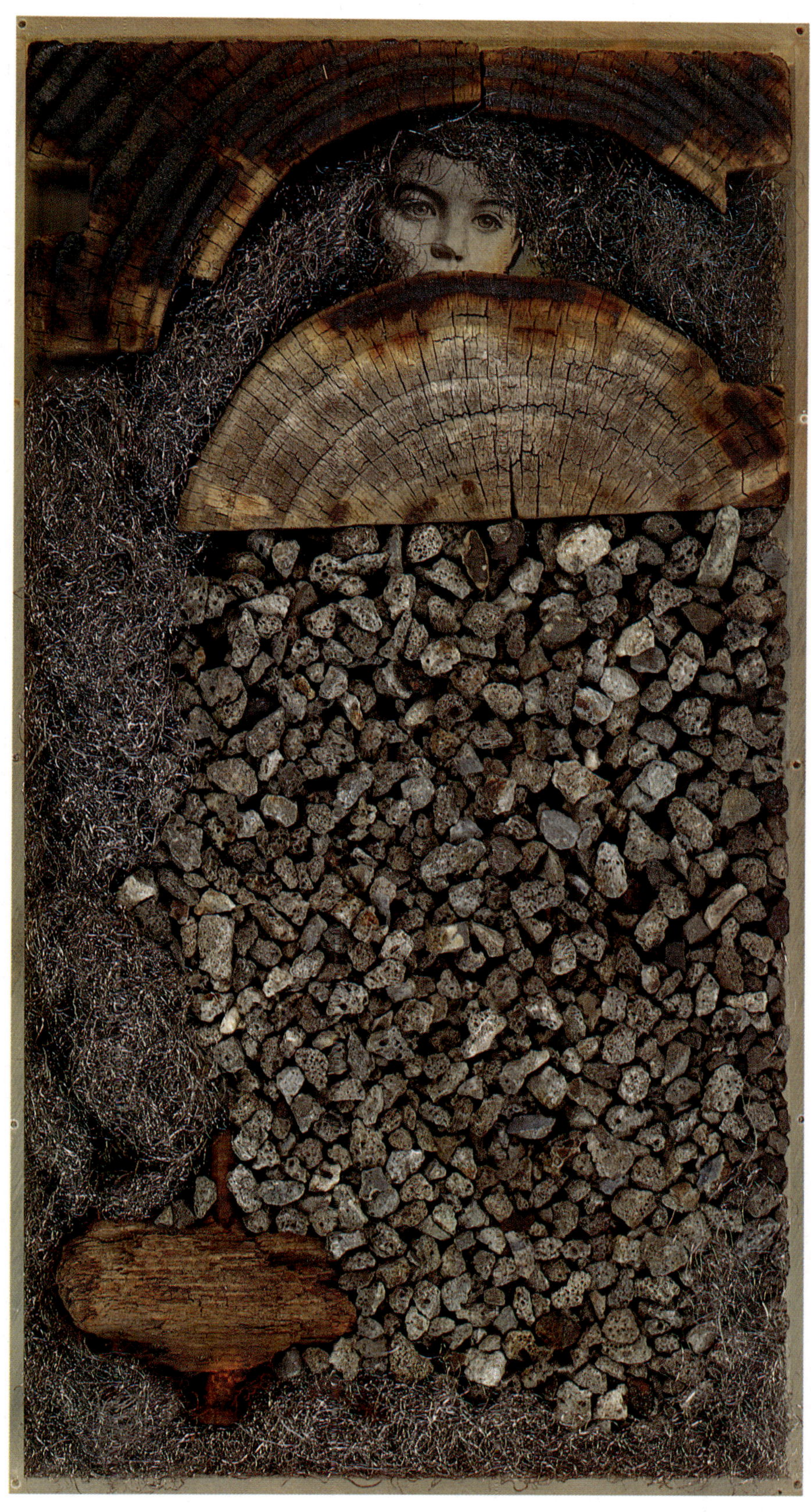

**URBAN RAINBOW**

Joan Hall

*Mixed media assemblage*

"In a world where cities are full of concrete and pollution, and nature becomes more and more obscured, it is still possible to see the rainbow."

IN DECEMBER, 1984, A LEAK OF TOXIC GAS FROM THE UNION CARBIDE PLANT IN BHOPAL, INDIA, KILLED 2,500 PEOPLE, INJURED 150,000, AND CAUSED THE EVACUATION OF 200,000 FROM THE TOWN. IT WAS THE WORST INDUSTRIAL ACCIDENT ON RECORD.

..........................

IM DEZEMBER 1984 WURDEN DURCH DEN AUSTRITT VON GIFTGAS DER UNION CARBIDE-ANLAGE IN BHOPAL, INDIEN, 2500 MENSCHEN GETÖTET, 150 000 VERLETZT UND 200 000 MUSSTEN AUS DER STADT EVAKUIERT WERDEN.

..........................

EN DÉCEMBRE 1984, À BHOPAL, EN INDE, UNE FUITE DE GAZ TOXIQUE PROVENANT DE L'USINE UNION CARBIDE A CAUSÉ LA MORT DE 2500 PERSONNES, BLESSÉ 150 000 AUTRES ET ENTRAÎNÉ L'ÉVACUATION DE 200 000 PERSONNES.

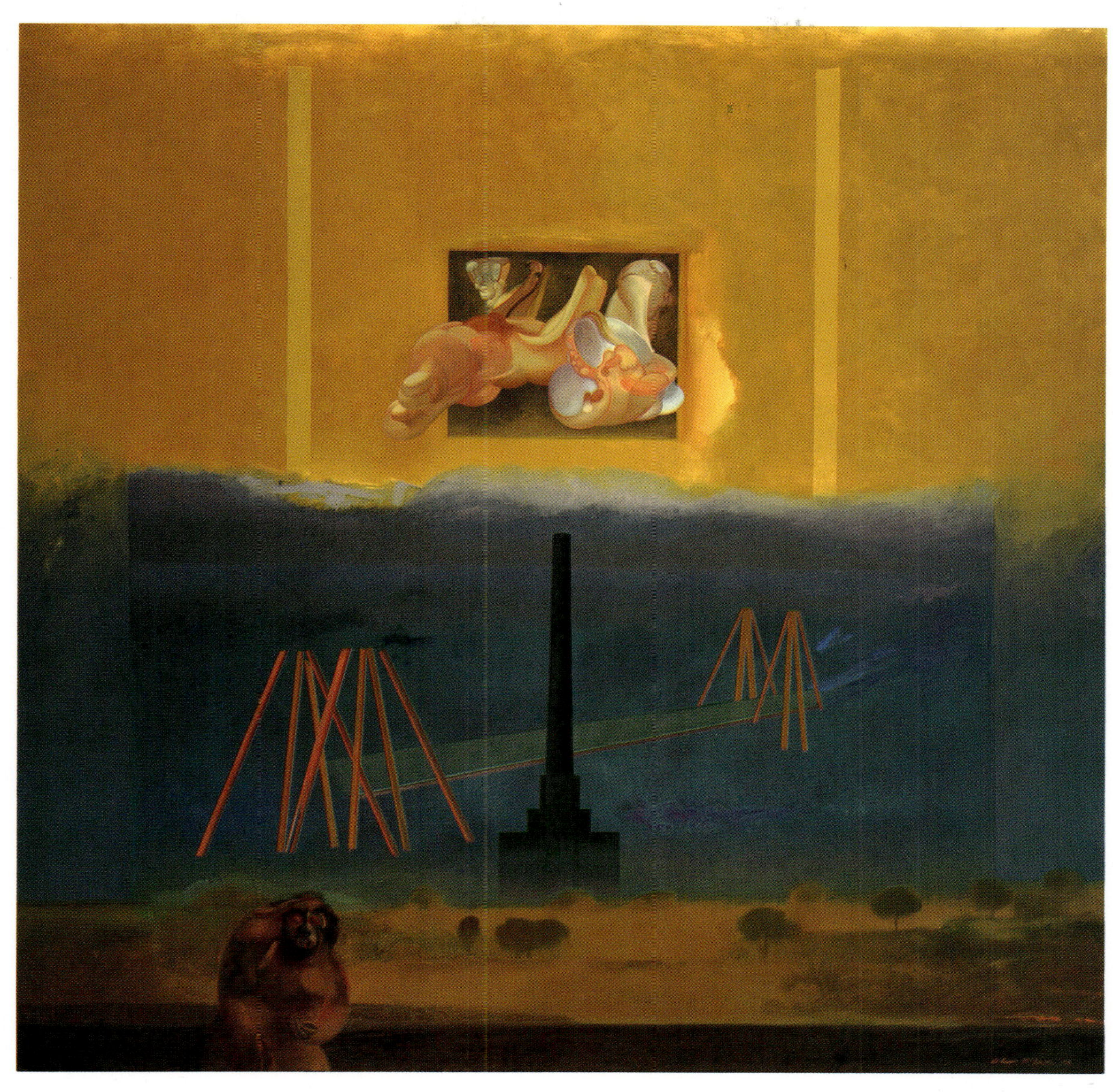

**FUTURE HAZARDS**

Wilson McLean

*Oil on canvas*

INDUSTRIAL COUNTRIES THAT ARE IN THE PROCESS OF DEVELOPMENT USE ENERGY AND RESOURCES AND PRODUCE WASTE IN WAYS THAT ARE CAUSING IRREVERSABLE ENVIRONMENTAL DAMAGE.

..........................

INDUSTRIELÄNDER, DIE SICH IN DER ENTWICKLUNG BEFINDEN, VERBRAUCHEN ENERGIE UND BODENSCHÄTZE UND PRODUZIEREN SOVIEL ABFALL, DASS DIE UMWELTSCHÄDEN NICHT WIEDERGUTZUMACHEN SIND.

..........................

LES PAYS INDUSTRIELS QUI SONT EN PLEIN DÉVELOPPEMENT UTILISENT L'ÉNERGIE ET LES RESSOURCES NATURELLES; ILS PRODUISENT TANT DE DÉCHETS QU'ILS CAUSENT DES DOMMAGES IRRÉVERSIBLES À L'ENVIRONNEMENT.

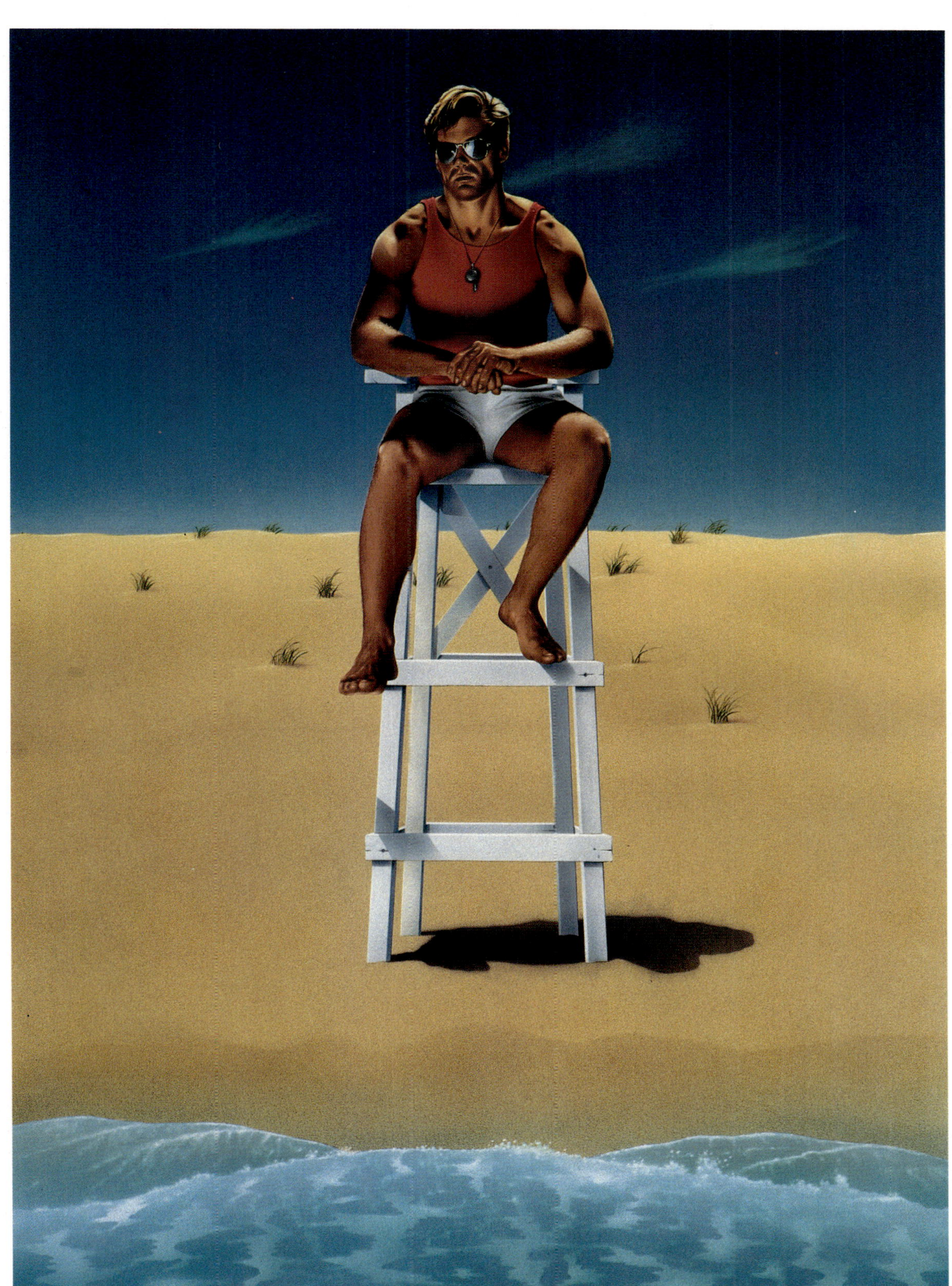

**LIFEGUARD**

JEFFREY WALKER

*AIRBRUSH WITH DYES*

"WHY DO WE HAVE TO BE TOLD TO KEEP OUR AIR CLEAN AND OUR WATERS CLEAR? WHAT WILL HAVE TO HAPPEN BEFORE OUR FOLLY LEAVES NOTHING WORTH LIVING FOR?"

EACH YEAR AN AREA OF THE RAINFOREST THE SIZE OF NEW YORK STATE VANISHES FOREVER. IF THIS PACE CONTINUES, MOST OF THE RAINFOREST WILL BE GONE BY THE END OF THE CENTURY.

........................

JEDES JAHR VERSCHWINDET EIN TEIL DES REGENWALDES IN DER GRÖSSE DES STAATES NEW YORK FÜR IMMER.

........................

CHAQUE ANNÉE, UNE SURFACE DE FORÊT TROPICALE DE LA TAILLE DE L'ÉTAT DE NEW YORK DISPARAÎT.

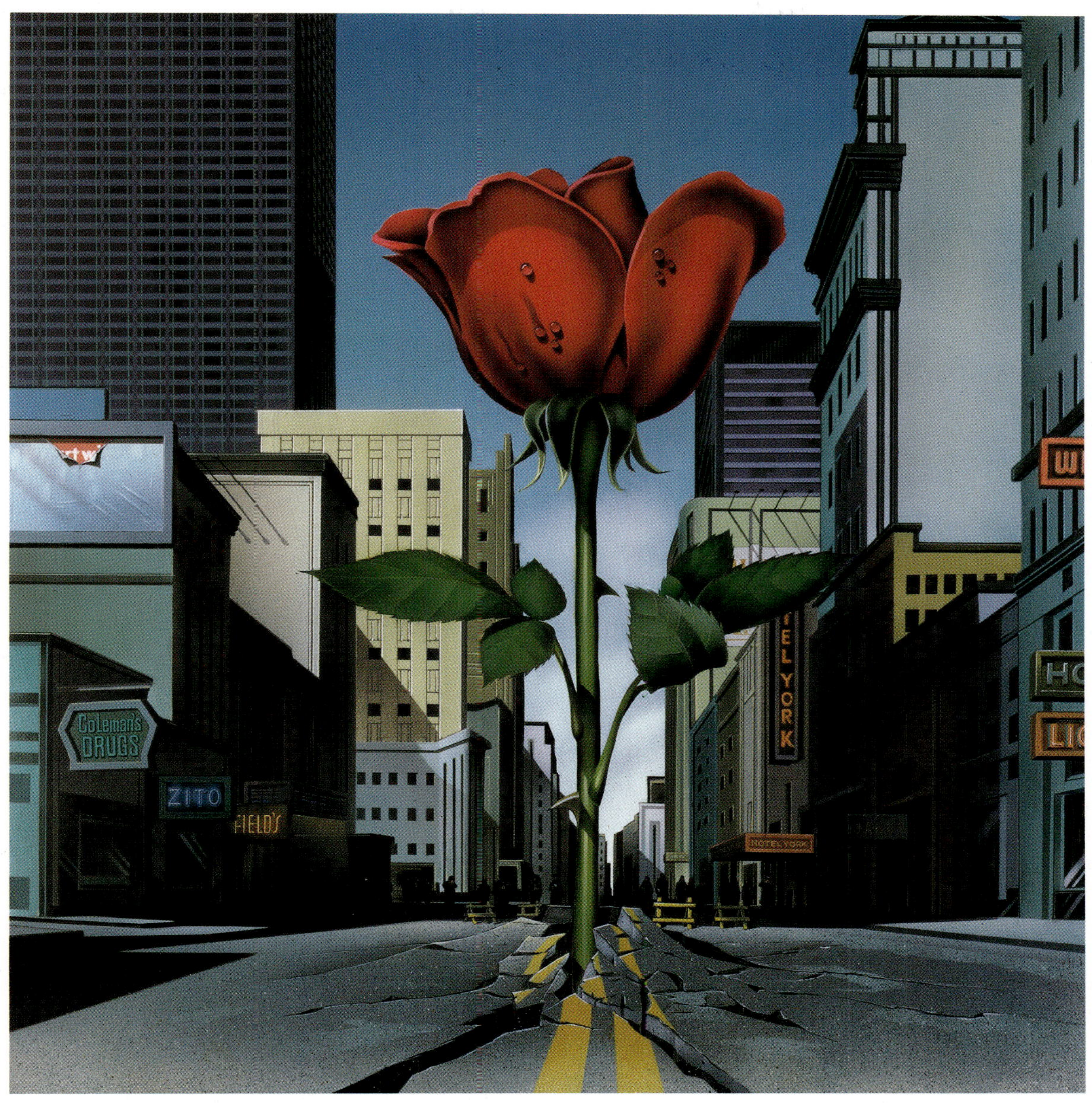


**STRONGER THAN EVER**

ANDY ZITO

*ACRYLIC*

"THE ROSE BREAKING THFOUGH THE GROUND ACTS AS A SYMBOL OF NATURE BECOMING STRONG AGAIN AS OUR NEW PRIORITY."

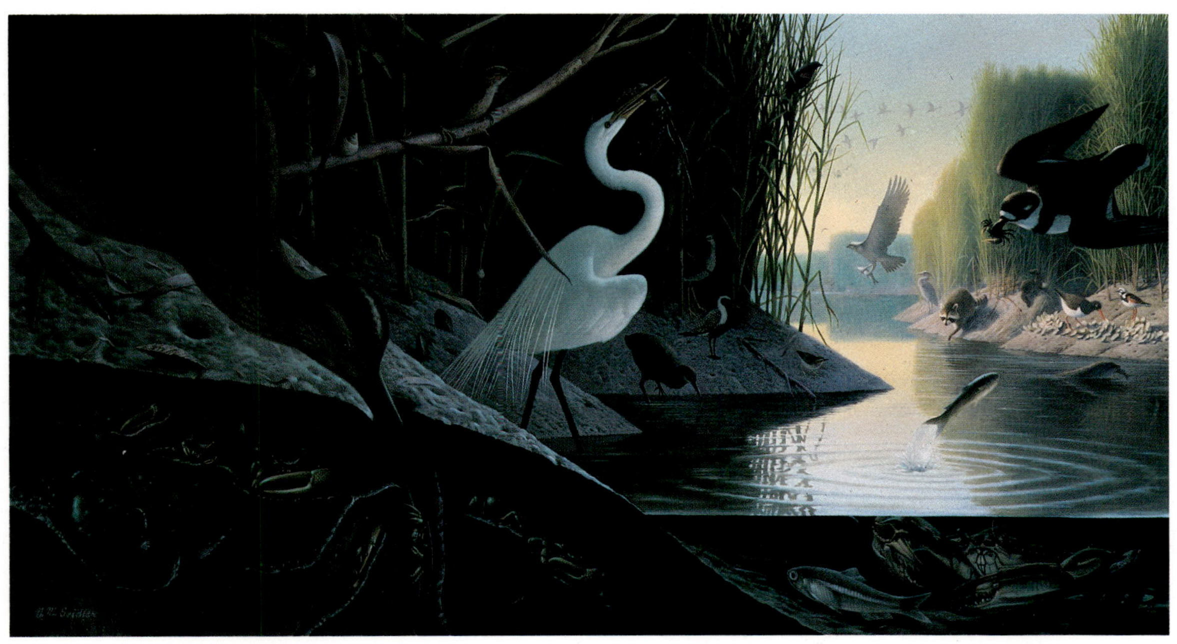

## SALT MARSH, LOW TIDE

NED M. SEIDLER

*OIL ON CANVAS*

"COARDGRASS FORESTS RECHARGED TWICE DAILY BY THE TIDES ARE THE FOUNDATION OF A DELICATELY BALANCED FOOD CHAIN AND RANK AMONG THE MOST ORGANICALLY PRODUCTIVE AREAS ON EARTH. IS IT TOO LATE TO SAVE THEM?"

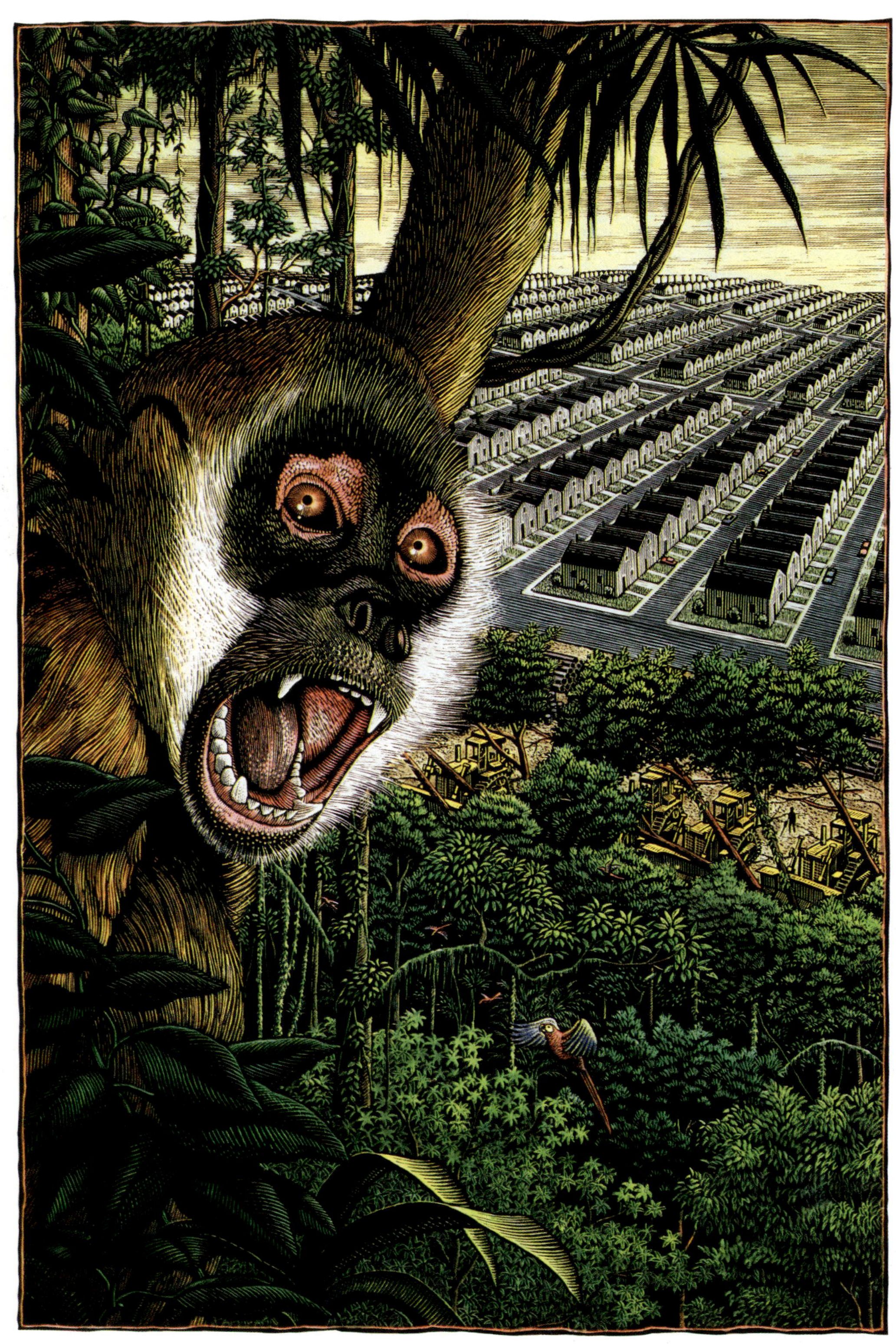

**THE SPREADING STAIN**

Douglas B. Smith

*Scratchboard and watercolor*

"On the surface, this piece would seem to be about deforestation and endangered species. Beyond that it concerns what I see as an underlying cause of all environmental crises, human population growth. If we cannot check our profligate growth, our very success as a species will also be our ultimate downfall."

THE DESTRUCTION OF THE RAINFORESTS HAS ALSO CAUSED CULTURAL EXTINCTION: THE POPULATION OF INDIGENOUS INDIANS HAS FALLEN FROM AN ESTIMATED 6-9 MILLION TO FEWER THAN 200,000. IN THE LAST CENTURY, 87 UNIQUE TRIBES HAVE BEEN EXTERMINATED IN BRAZIL ALONE.

.........................

DIE ZERSTÖRUNG DER REGENWÄLDER HAT AUCH DAS AUSSTERBEN VON KULTUREN VERURSACHT: DIE BEVÖLKERUNG DER EINGEBORENEN INDIANER SANK VON GESCHÄTZTEN 6-9 MILLIONEN AUF UNTER 200 000. IM LETZTEN JAHRHUNDERT WURDEN ALLEIN IN BRASILIEN 87 STÄMME AUSGELÖSCHT.

.........................

LA DESTRUCTION DE LA FORÊT TROPICALE A ÉTÉ LA CAUSE DE LA DISPARITION DE NOMBREUSES CULTURES. LA POPULATION DES INDIENS D'AMAZONIE EST TOMBÉE DE 6-9 MILLIONS À UN PEU MOINS DE 200 000. AU COURS DE CE SIÈCLE, 87 TRIBUS ONT ÉTÉ EXTERMINÉES AU BRÉSIL.

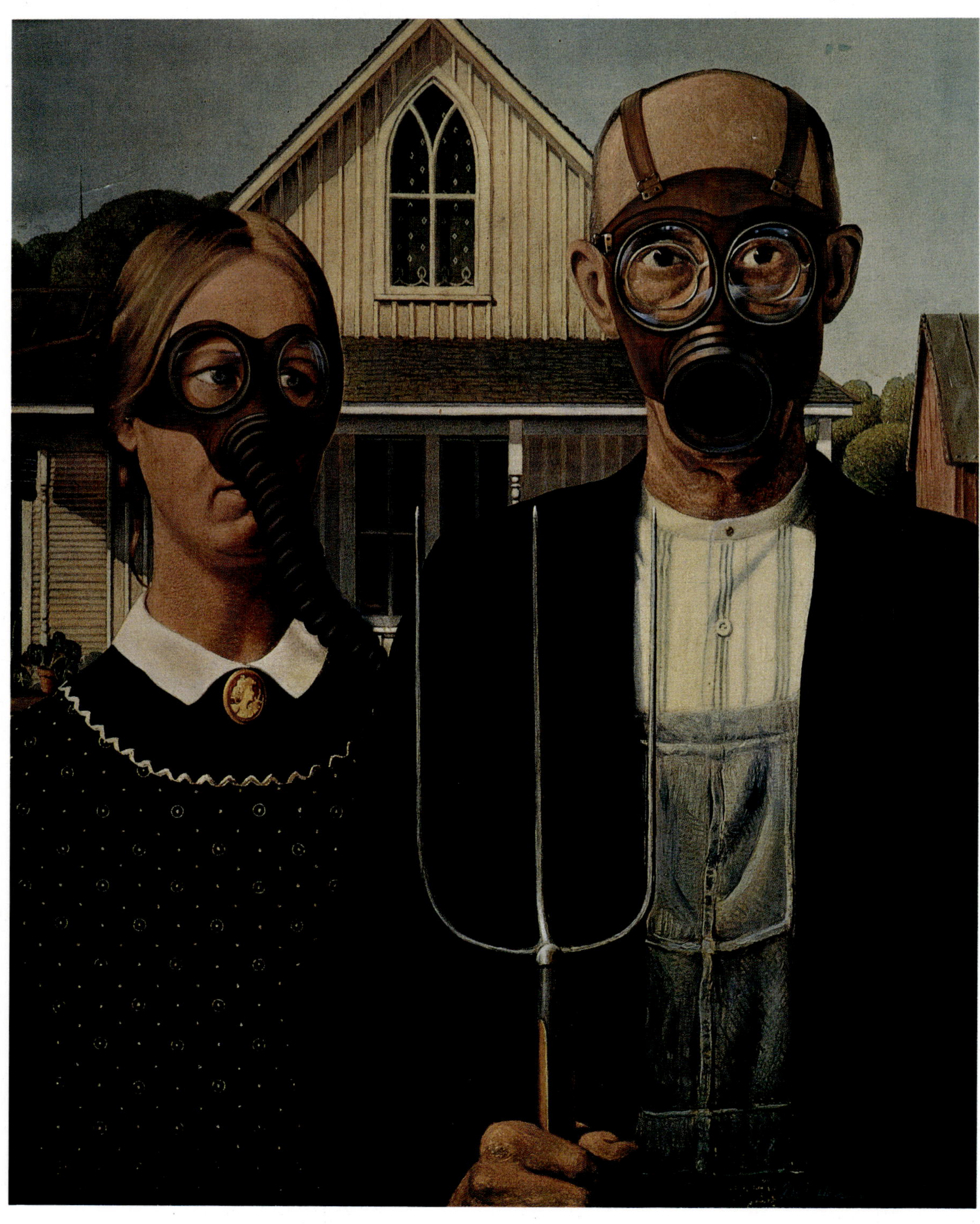

**AMERICAN GOTHIC AIR POLLUTION**

Richard Hess
(Original by Grant Wood)
*Acrylic*

"I selected the best known of American paintings to dramatize what was to become an acute American problem."

THE EARTH'S OZONE LAYER
IS BEING UNNATURALLY REDUCED
PARTLY AS A RESULT OF THE 6
BILLION TONS OF CARBON DIOXIDE
PER YEAR THAT HUMANS ADD
TO OUR ATMOSPHERE.

..........................

DIE OZONSCHICHT DER
ERDE WIRD ZUM TEIL DURCH DIE
6 MILLIARDEN TONNEN
KOHLENDIOXID ZERSTÖRT, DIE
DER MENSCH JEDES JAHR IN DIE
ATMOSPHÄRE SCHICKT.

..........................

LA DIMINUTION DE LA
COUCHE D'OZONE EST EN PARTIE
DUE AUX 6 MILLIARDS DE TONNES
DE DIOXYDE DE CARBONE QUI SONT
REJETÉES CHAQUE ANNÉE
DANS L'ATMOSPHÈRE.

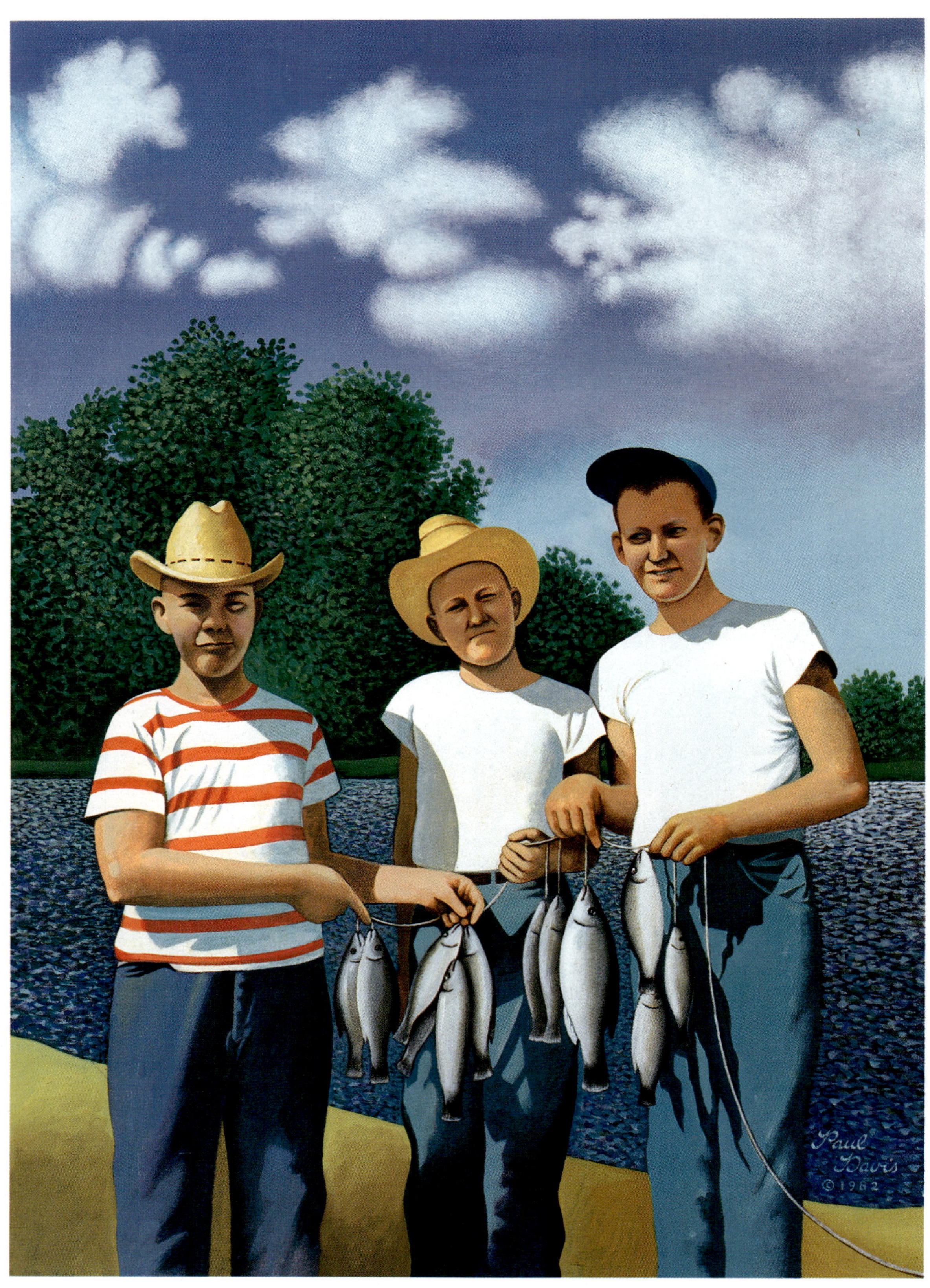


**PETE, STAN, AND ME**

PAUL DAVIS

*ACRYLIC ON CANVAS*

"WHEN WE WENT FISHING IN OKLAHOMA AROUND 1950, THE WATERS WERE STILL CLEAN ENOUGH TO DRINK. IT WAS AN INNOCENT TIME."

THE ACIDITY OF PRECIPITATION HAS QUADRUPLED IN THE NORTHEASTERN U.S. SINCE 1900, PARALLELING INCREASED EMISSIONS OF SULPHUR DIOXIDE AND NITROGEN OXIDES.

..........................

DER SÄUREGEHALT DER NIEDERSCHLÄGE HAT SICH IM NORDOSTEN DER USA SEIT 1900 VERVIERFACHT, ENTSPRECHEND GESTIEGEN SIND DIE EMISSIONEN VON SCHWEFELDIOXID UND STICKSTOFFOXID.

..........................

DEPUIS 1900, L'ACIDITÉ DES PLUIES A QUADRUPLÉ AU NORD-EST DES ÉTATS-UNIS. LES ÉMISSIONS DE DIOXYDE DE SOUFRE ET D'OXYDES D'AZOTE ONT AUGMENTÉ DANS DES PROPORTIONS IDENTIQUES.

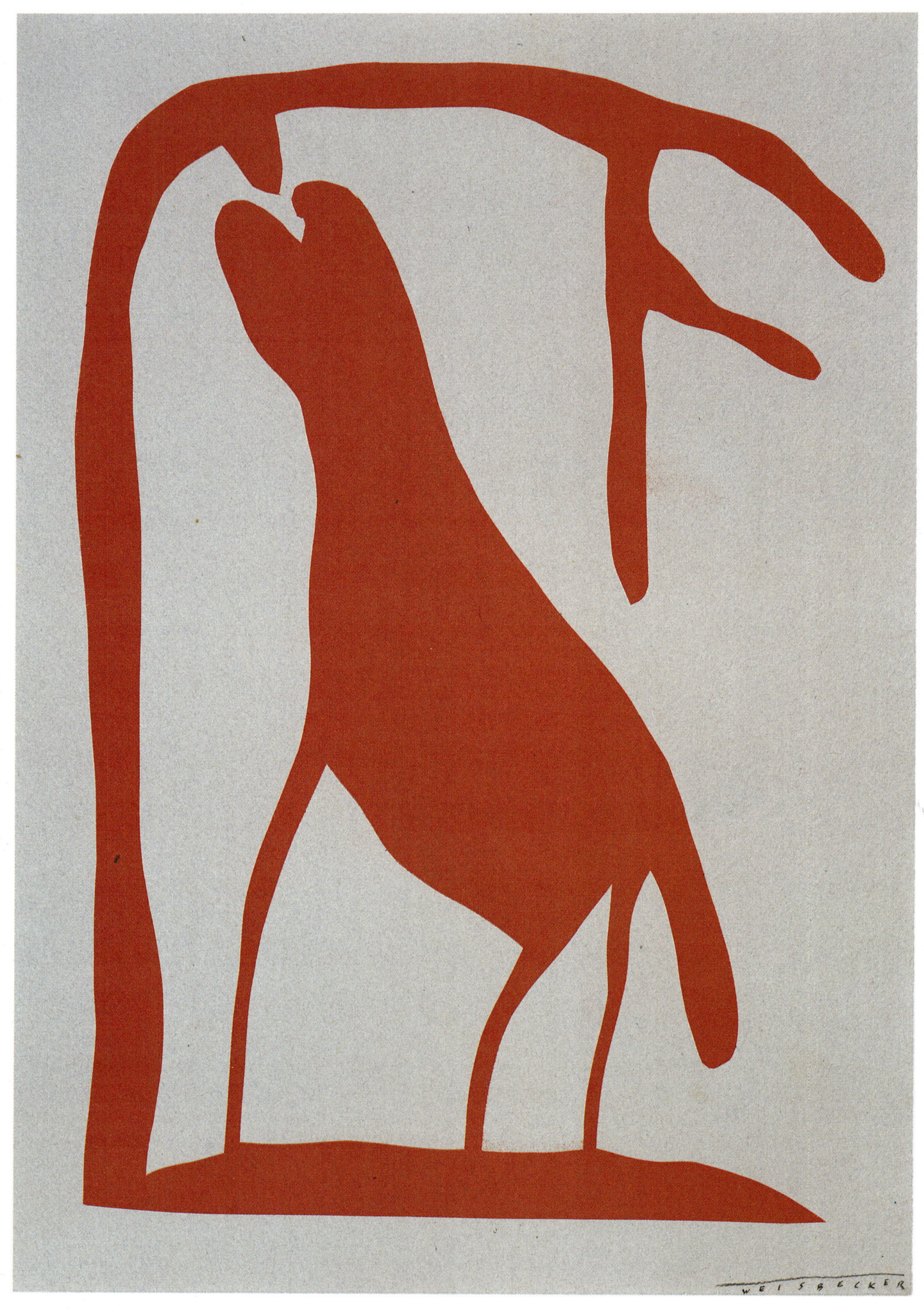


**ENDANGERED SPECIES**

PHILIPPE WEISBECKER

*SILKSCREEN*

IT IS ESTIMATED THAT WE COULD LOSE 10 PERCENT OF THE WORLD'S SPECIES BY THE END OF THE 20TH CENTURY.

.........................

MAN SCHÄTZT, DASS GEGEN ENDE DIESES JAHRHUNDERTS 10 PROZENT DER TIERARTEN AUSGESTORBEN SEIN KÖNNTEN.

.........................

SELON LES ESTIMATIONS, 10% DES ESPÈCES ANIMALES AURONT DISPARU À LA FINDU SIÈCLE.

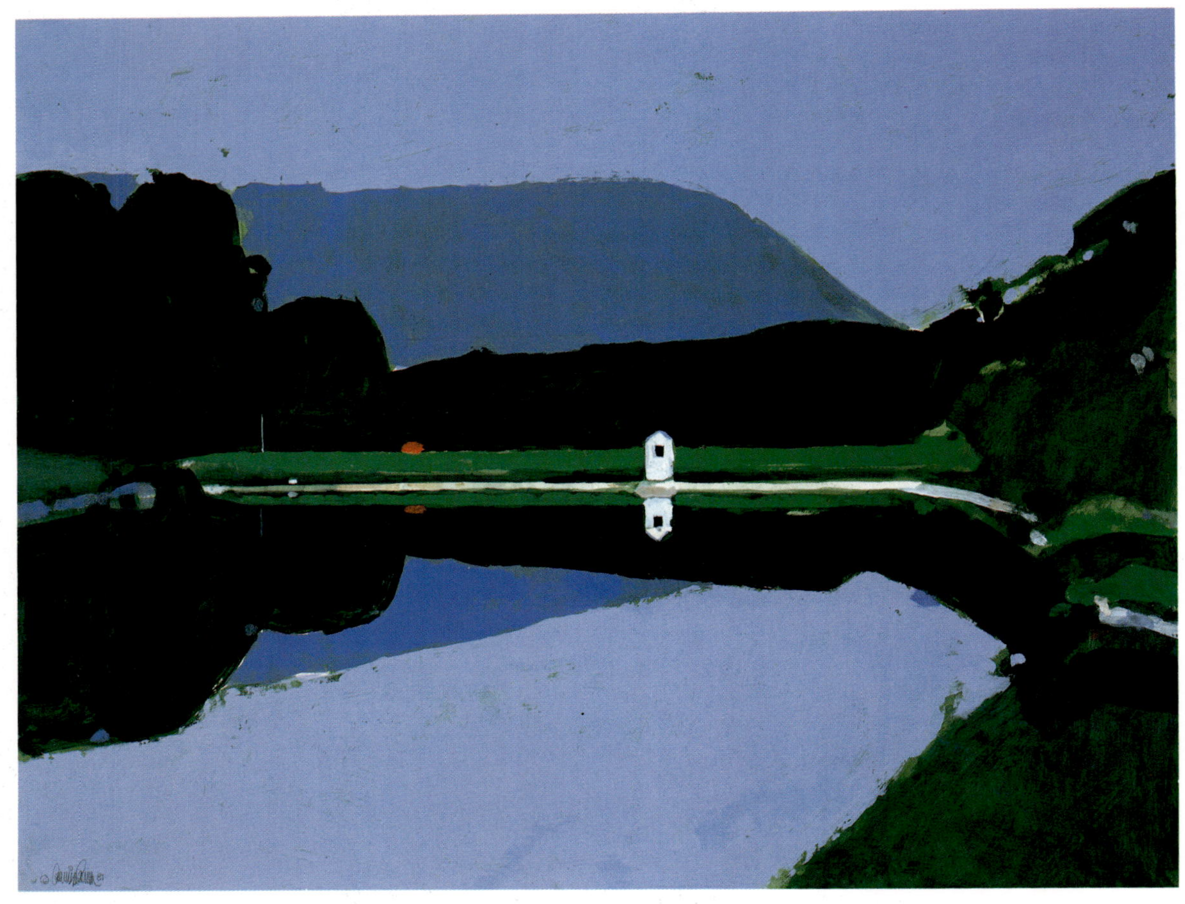

**KENT RESERVOIR**

Robert M. Cunningham

*Acrylic on paper*

"I chose the old reservoir near my home as the subject of this piece because I have always liked it. I believe we are all becoming aware of the necessity of protecting our water sources. We have no choice."

THE AVERAGE RESIDENT
OF THE U.S. CONSUMES MORE
THAN 70 TIMES AS MUCH WATER
EVERY YEAR AS THE AVERAGE
RESIDENT OF GHANA.

..........................

IN DEN USA WIRD IM
DURCHSCHNITT 70 MAL MEHR
WASSER VERBRAUCHT ALS
IN GHANA.

..........................

UN HABITANT DES
ÉTATS-UNIS CONSOMME 70
FOIS PLUS D'EAU QU'UN HABITANT
DU GHÂNA.

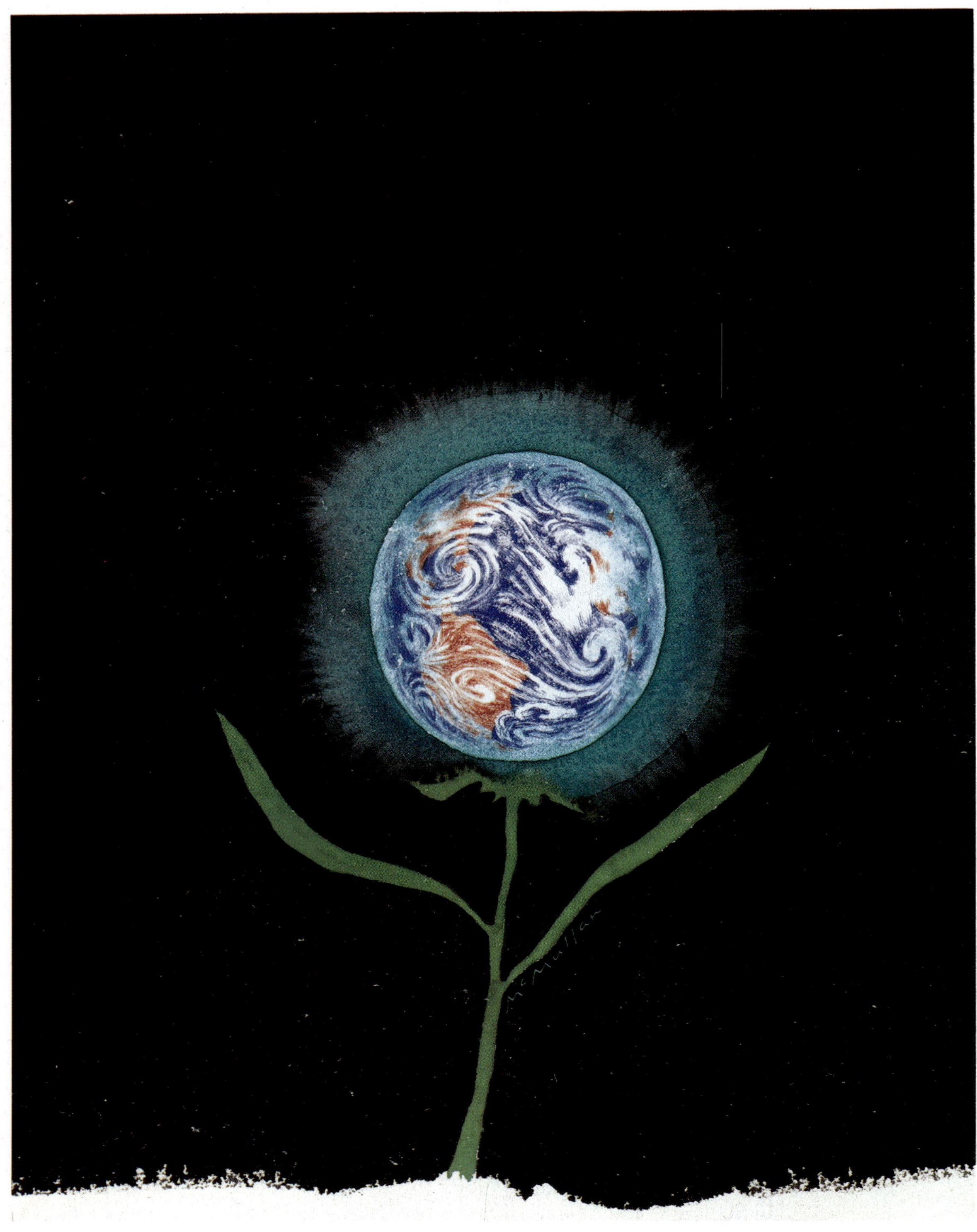

**DANDELION**

JAMES McMULLAN

*WATERCOLOR*

"THE PLANET EARTH AS A FRAGILE PLANET."

EVERY CHEMICAL IS A POTENTIAL HAZARD TO OUR ENVIRONMENT IF WRONGLY USED OR RELEASED IN LARGE QUANTITIES BY ACCIDENT. MORE THAN 7 MILLION CHEMICALS ARE NOW KNOWN. SOME 80,000 ARE IN COMMON USE TODAY AND ABOUT 1,000 NEW CHEMICALS ARE ENTERED INTO COMMERCIAL USE EACH YEAR.

---

JEDE CHEMIKALIE STELLT EINE POTENTIELLE BEDROHUNG DER UMWELT DAR, WENN SIE FALSCH VERWENDET ODER DURCH EINEN UNFALL IN GROSSEN MENGEN FREIGESETZT WIRD. MEHR ALS 7 MILLIONEN CHEMIKALIEN SIND HEUTE BEKANNT. 80 000 WERDEN ALLGEMEIN EINGESETZT UND GEGEN 1000 NEUE CHEMIKALIEN KOMMEN JEDES JAHR IN DEN HANDEL.

---

MAL UTILISÉ OU ACCIDENTELLEMENT LIBÉRÉ DANS L'ATMOSPHÈRE, TOUT PRODUIT CHIMIQUE CONSTITUE UN DANGER POTENTIEL POUR L'ENVIRONNEMENT. ON EN CONNAÎT PLUS DE 7 MILLIONS. QUELQUES 8000 SONT COURAMMENT UTILISÉS ET PLUS DE 1000 NOUVEAUX PRODUITS CHIMIQUES SONT COMMERCIALISÉS CHAQUE ANNÉE.

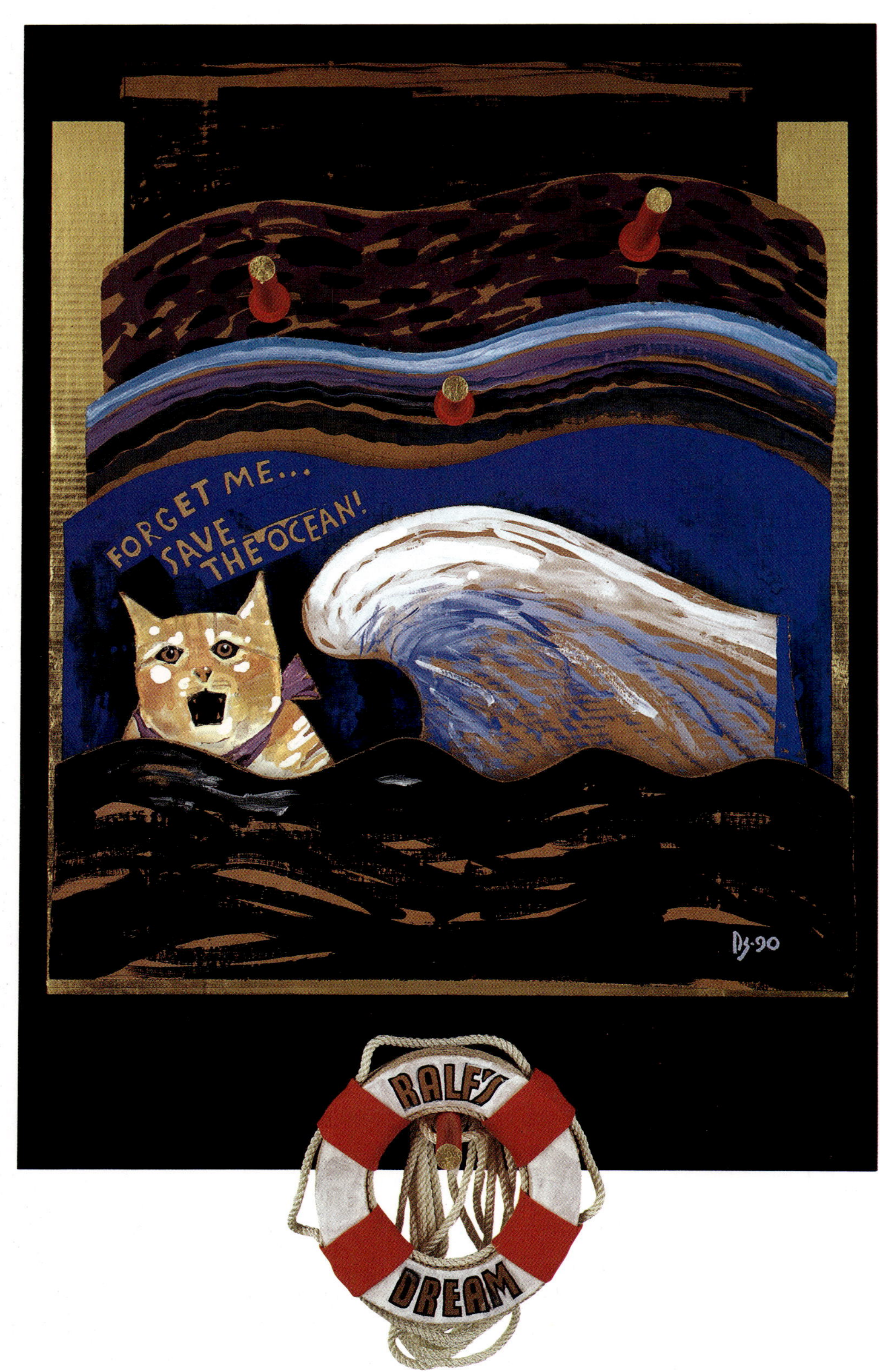


**RALF'S DREAM**

Doug Johnson

*Gouache and gold leaf on corrugated board with found objects*

"Ralf is extraordinarily brave and cares very deeply."

ABOUT FOUR-FIFTHS OF MARINE POLLUTION COMES FROM LAND SEWAGE, INDUSTRIAL WASTE, AND AGRICULTURAL RUN-OFF. THE REST COMES FROM COASTAL MINING, ENERGY PRODUCTION, AND OCEANGOING VESSELS, ESPECIALLY OIL TANKERS.

...........................

GEGEN 4/5 DER MEERESVERSCHMUTZUNG IST AUF KLÄRANLAGEN, INDUSTRIEABFÄLLE UND ABWÄSSER DER LANDWIRTSCHAFT ZURÜCKZUFÜHREN, 1/5 AUF DEN ABBAU VON KÜSTEN, STROMERZEUGUNG UND SCHIFFE, VOR ALLEM ÖLTANKER.

...........................

ENVIRON 4/5 DE LA POLLUTION DES MERS PROVIENT DES EAUX D'ÉGOUT, DES DÉCHETS INDUSTRIELS ET DES EAUX RÉSIDUAIRES DE L'AGRICULTURE, 1/5 DE L'EXPLOITATION DES CÔTES, DE LA PRODUCTION D'ÉNERGIE ET DES BATEAUX.

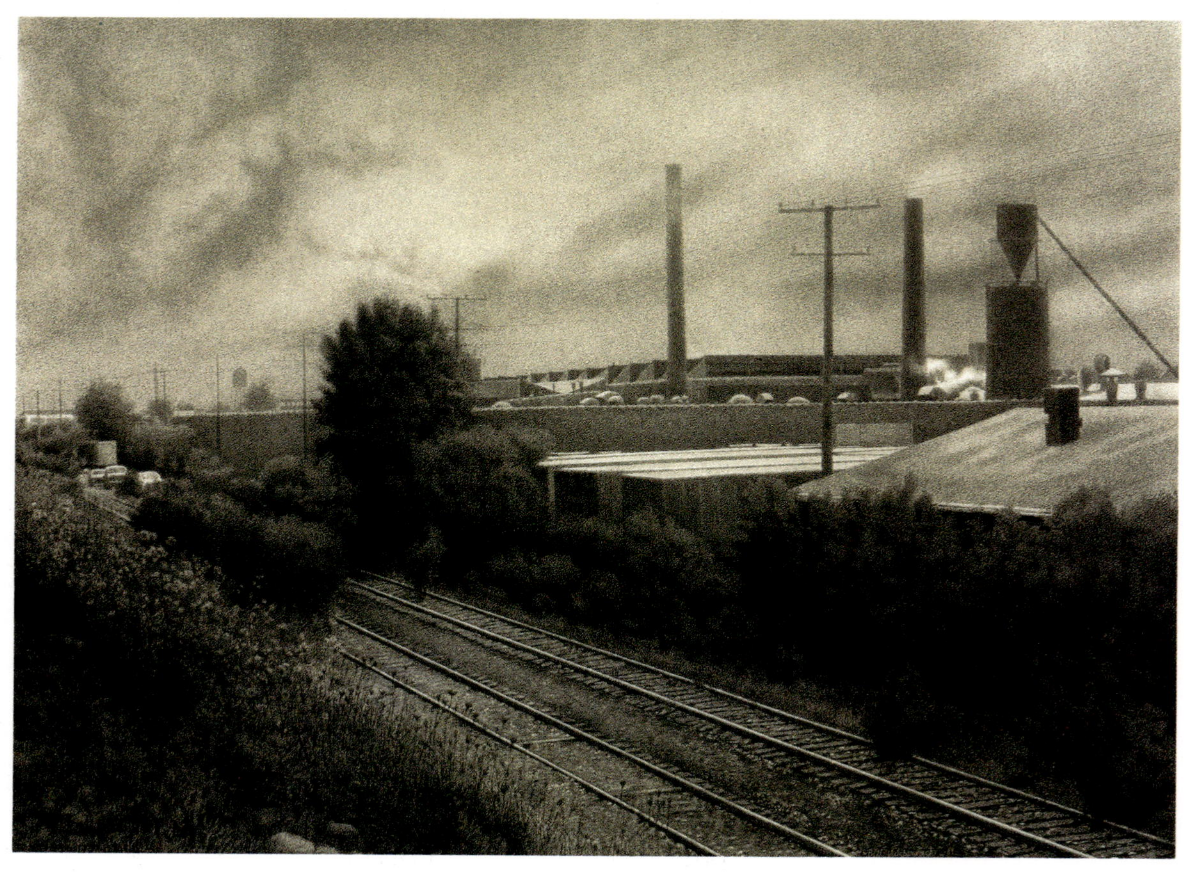

**RAILS ALONG THE BRICKYARD**

BILL VUKSANOVICH

*PENCIL ON PAPER*

"THROUGH THIS DRAWING I WANTED TO DEPICT HOW INDUSTRY IS ENCROACHING ON NATURE. NOW IS THE TIME FOR US TO DEAL WITH NATURE RESPECTFULLY AND USE IT WISELY. EVEN NATURE HAS ITS LIMITS."

WASTES ARE GENERATED
AT EVERY STAGE IN OUR USE OF
MATERIALS. TOTAL U.S. PER
CAPITA WASTE GENERATION
IS TWICE THAT OF ANY
OTHER COUNTRY.

.........................

JEGLICHE VERWENDUNG
EINES MATERIALS VERURSACHT
ABFALL. IN DEN USA IST DER PRO
KOPF PRODUZIERTE ABFALL
DOPPELT SO HOCH WIE IN JEDEM
ANDEREN LAND.

.........................

TOUTE UTILISATION D'UN
MATÉRIAU PRODUIT DES DÉCHETS.
AUX USA, LA QUANTITÉ DE DÉCHETS
PAR TÊTE D'HABITANT EST DEUX
FOIS PLUS ÉLEVÉE QUE DANS LES
AUTRES PAYS.

TWO-THIRDS OF THE WORLD'S 1.8 BILLION CITY DWELLERS BREATHE AIR THAT CONTAINS DANGEROUS LEVELS OF SULPHUR DIOXIDE AND DUST. THESE POLLUTANTS ALSO DRIFT BEYOND URBAN AREAS INTO THE NATURAL ENVIRONMENT.

........................

ZWEI DRITTEL DER 1,8 MILLIARDEN MENSCHEN, DIE IN STÄDTEN WOHNEN, ATMEN LUFT MIT GEFÄHRLICH HOHEN ANTEILEN AN SCHWEFELDIOXID UND STAUB.

........................

DEUX TIERS DES 1,8 MILLIARDS DE PERSONNES QUI HABITENT DANS LES VILLES RESPIRENT UN AIR QUI CONTIENT DES QUANTITÉS DANGEREUSES DE DIOXYDE DE SOUFRE.

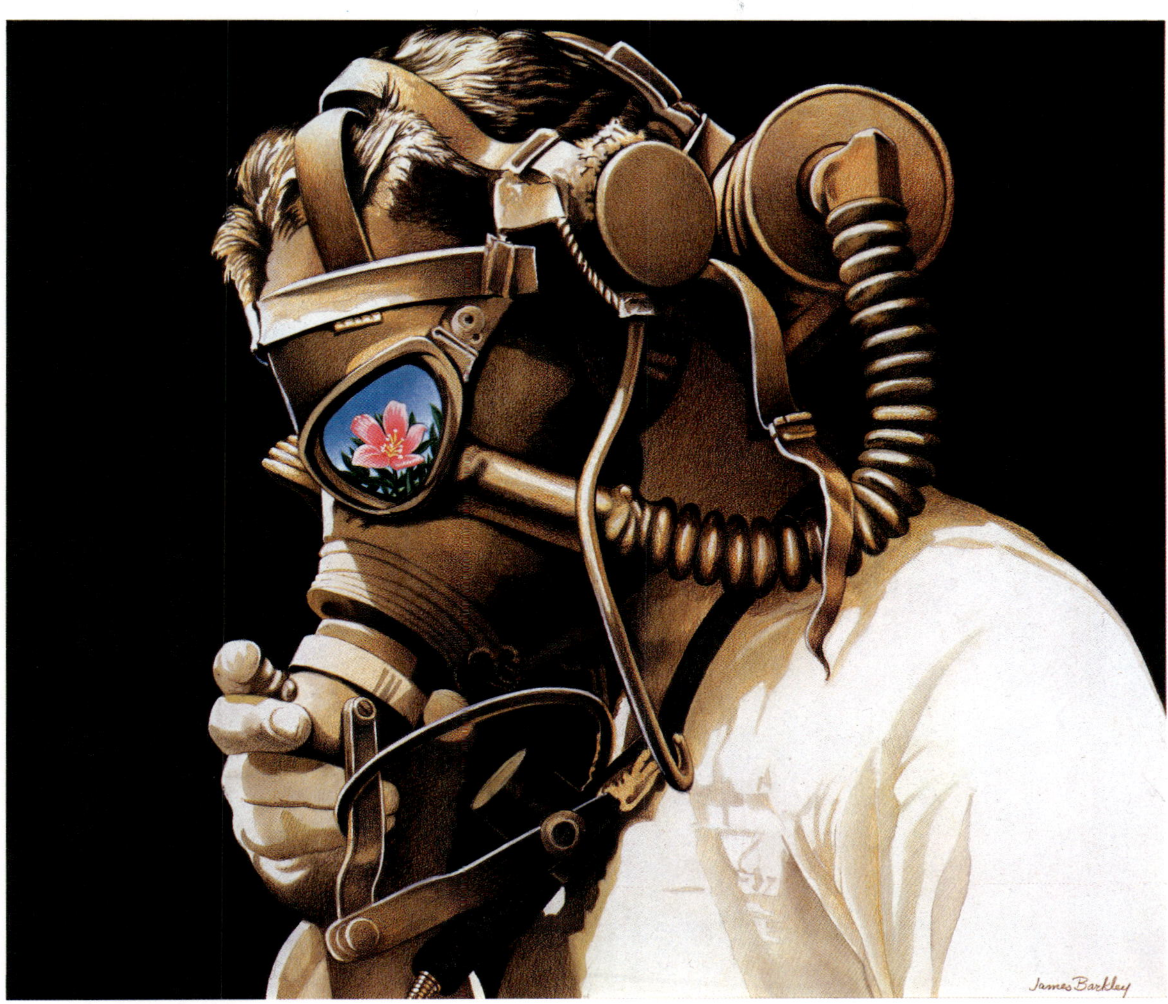


**WHERE HAS ALL THE AIR GONE?**

JAMES BARKLEY

*ACRYLIC*

"THE GAS MASK HAS A VISUAL CONNOTATION ASSOCIATED WITH EVIL, POLLUTION, AND FEAR. USING THIS SYMBOL AND THE JUXTAPOSITION OF A BEAUTIFUL FLOWER IN THE EYE OF THE MASK SETS UP A CONTRADICTION OF VALUES."

ONE THOUSAND NEW PRODUCTS BASED ON GENETICALLY ENGINEERED MICRO-ORGANISMS ARE EXPECTED BY THE YEAR 2000 WITH AN ESTIMATED MARKET VALUE OF $50 BILLION.

IM JAHRE 2000 ERWARTET MAN 1000 NEUE PRODUKTE AUF DER BASIS VON GENMANIPULIERTEN MIKRO-ORGANISMEN. IHR MARKTWERT: 50 MILLIARDEN DOLLAR.

EN L'AN 2000, MILLE NOUVEAUX PRODUITS PROVIENDRONT DE LA MANIPULATION GÉNÉTIQUE DE MICRO-ORGANISMES. CE MARCHÉ REPRÉSENTE 50 MILLIARDS DE DOLLARS.

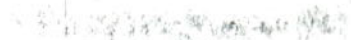

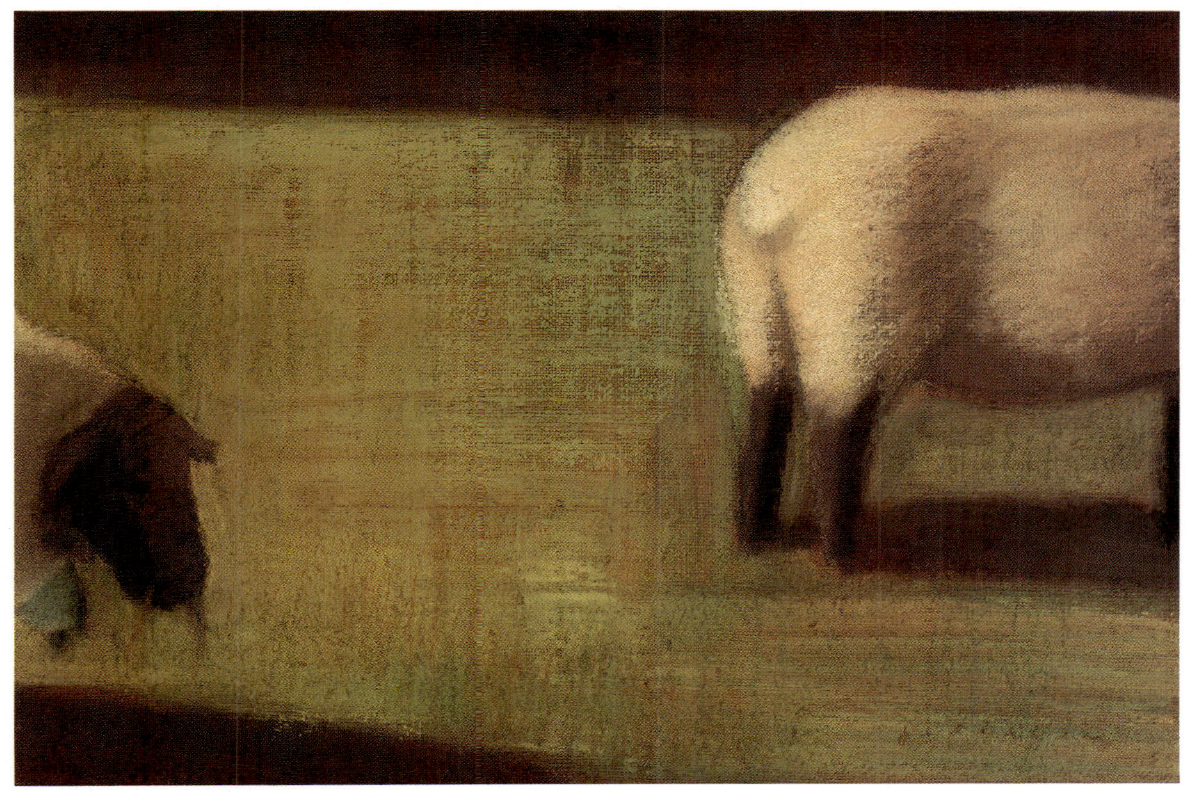

**PINK SHEEP**

JUDY PEDERSEN

*PASTEL*

"AS INDIVIDUALS WE MUST BE CAUTIOUS ABOUT WHAT WE ALLOW BIG CORPORATIONS TO FORCE ON THE UNITED STATES IN THE INTEREST OF HIGHER FOOD PRODUCTION."

THOUSANDS OF ACRES OF WOODLANDS ALL ACROSS THE UNITED STATES HAVE BEEN STRIPPED FROM ACID RAIN DUE TO THE 25 MILLION TONS OF SULPHUR DIOXIDE THAT WE PUMP INTO THE AIR ANNUALLY.

. . . . . . . . . . . . . . . . . . . . . . . . .

MEHRERE TAUSEND HEKTAR WALD WURDEN IN DEN VEREINIGTEN STAATEN DURCH SAUREN REGEN ZERSTÖRT, EIN ERGEBNIS DER 25 MILLIONEN TONNEN SCHWEFELDIOXID, DIE WIR JÄHRLICH IN DIE LUFT ABLASSEN.

. . . . . . . . . . . . . . . . . . . . . . . . .

AUX ÉTATS-UNIS, PLUSIEURS MILLIERS D'HECTARES DE FORÊT ONT ÉTÉ DÉTRUITS PAR LES PLUIES ACIDES RÉSULTANT DES 25 MILLIONS DE TONNES DE DIOXYDE DE SOUFRE QUE NOUS REJETONS CHAQUE ANNÉE DANS L'ATMOSPHÈRE.

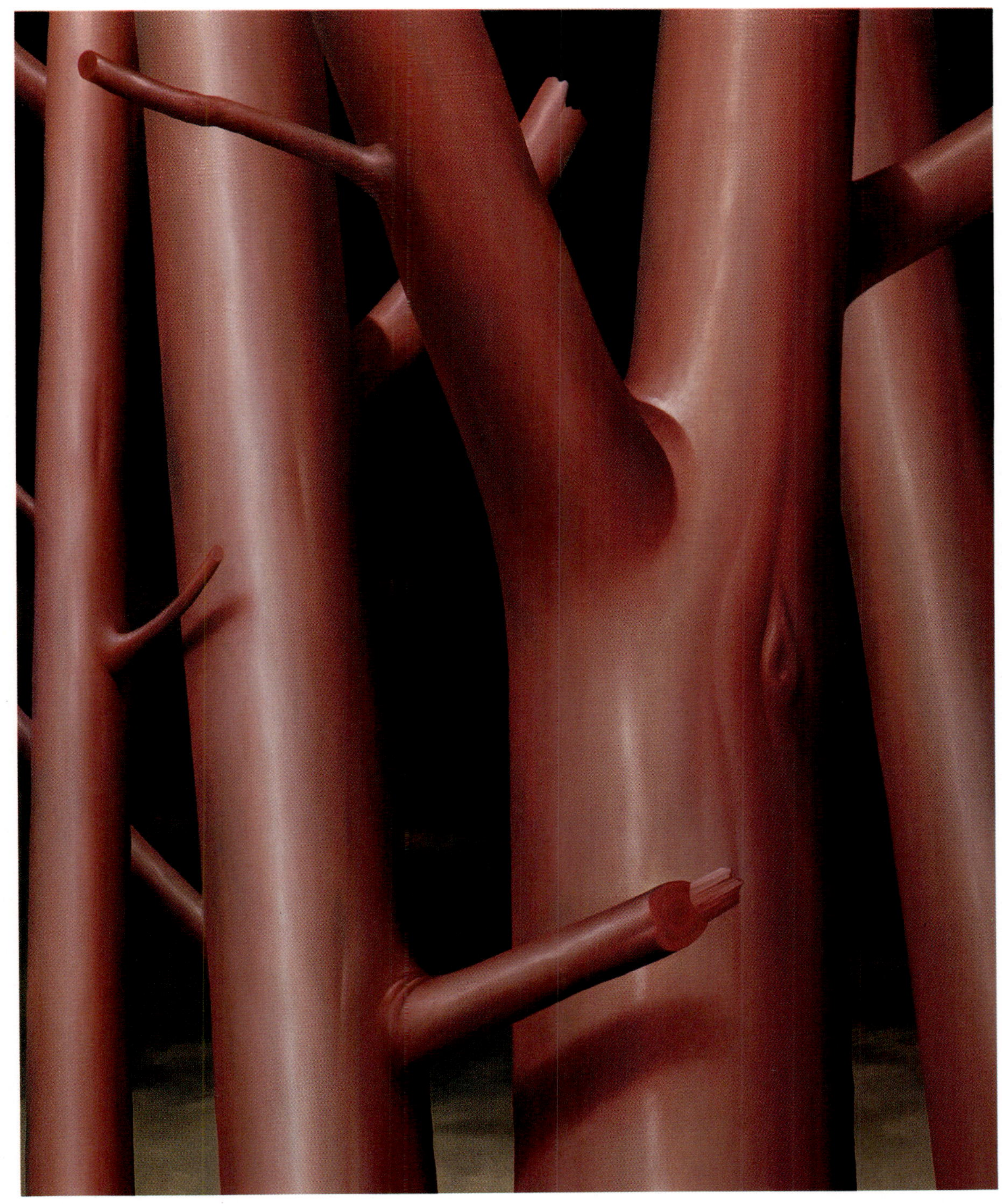

**FLAYED CRABAPPLE**

ROBERT GOLDSTROM

*OIL ON CANVAS*

THE BISON ARE ALSO A
LIVING EXAMPLE OF
A NOW-FLOURISHING SPECIES
SAVED BY PROTECTION
AND CONSERVATION.

..........................

DER BISON IST EIN BEISPIEL
FÜR EINE ART, DIE
GERETTET WERDEN KONNTE UND
SICH JETZT WIEDER VERMEHRT.

..........................

LE BISON FOURNIT L'EXEMPLE
D'UNE ESPÈCE QUI A PU
ÊTRE SAUVÉE ET QUI SE MULTIPLIE.

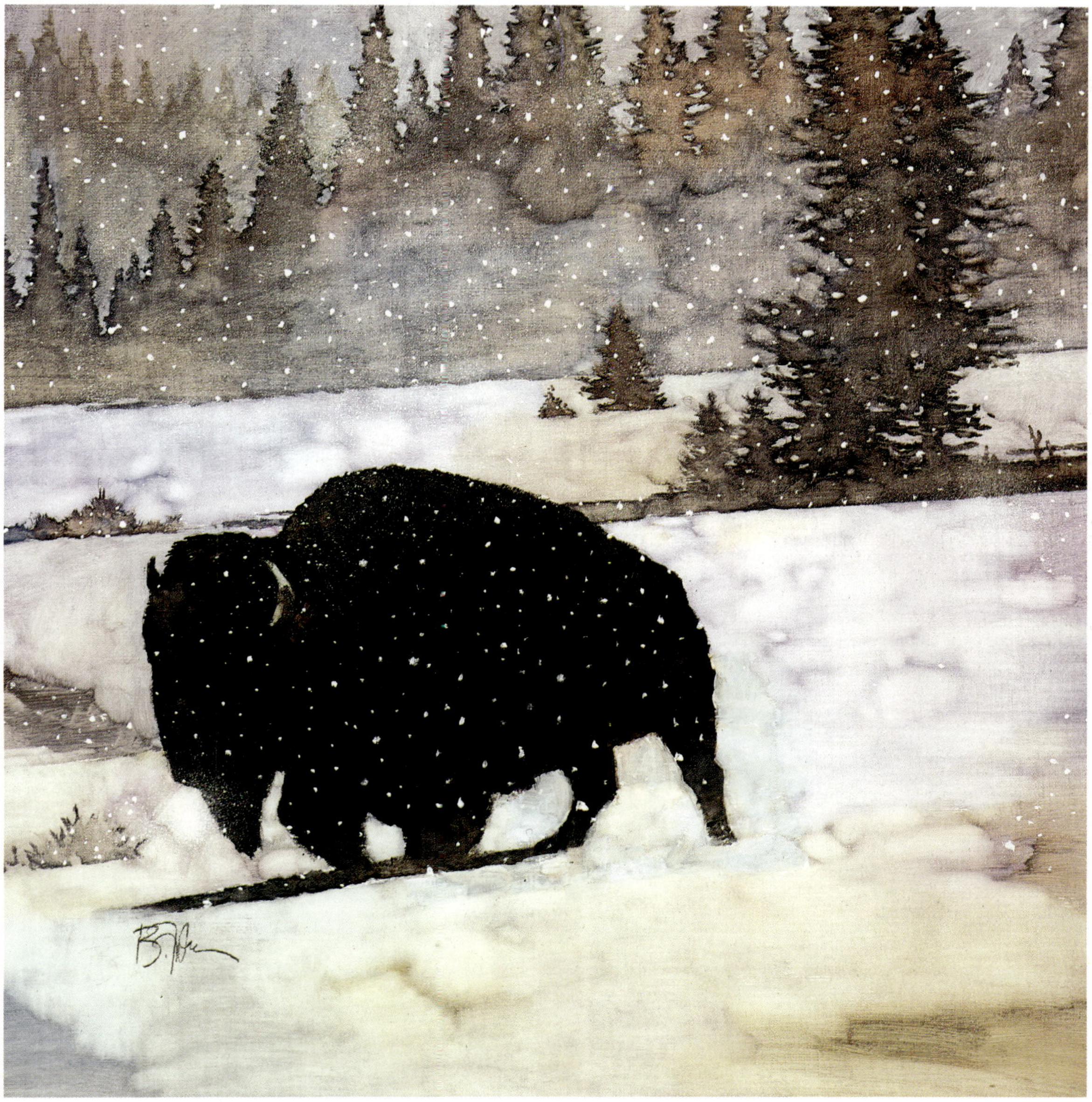

**SURVIVOR**

BART J. FORBES

*OIL ON CANVAS*

"THE BISON IS A LIV NG EXAMPLE OF A MAGNIFICENT SPECIES DRIVEN ALMOST TO EXTINCTION ONLY A FEW YEARS AGO."

THOUSANDS OF TONS OF U.S.
AND EUROPEAN WASTES HAVE BEEN
SHIPPED TO AFRICA AND THE
MIDDLE EAST. MANY ILLEGAL
DUMPINGS HAVE OCCURRED AT
UNREPORTED SITES.

..........................

DIE USA UND EUROPA
SCHICKTEN MEHRERE 1000 TONNEN
ABFALL NACH AFRIKA UND IN DEN
MITTLEREN OSTEN. EINE MENGE
DAVON LANDETE AUF
ILLEGALEN DEPONIEN.

..........................

LES ÉTATS-UNIS ET
L'EUROPE ONT EXPORTÉ EN
AFRIQUE ET AU MOYEN-ORIENT DES
MILLIERS DE TONNES
DE DÉCHETS. DE NOMBREUSES
DÉCHARGES ONT
ÉTÉ INSTALLÉES ILLÉGALEMENT.

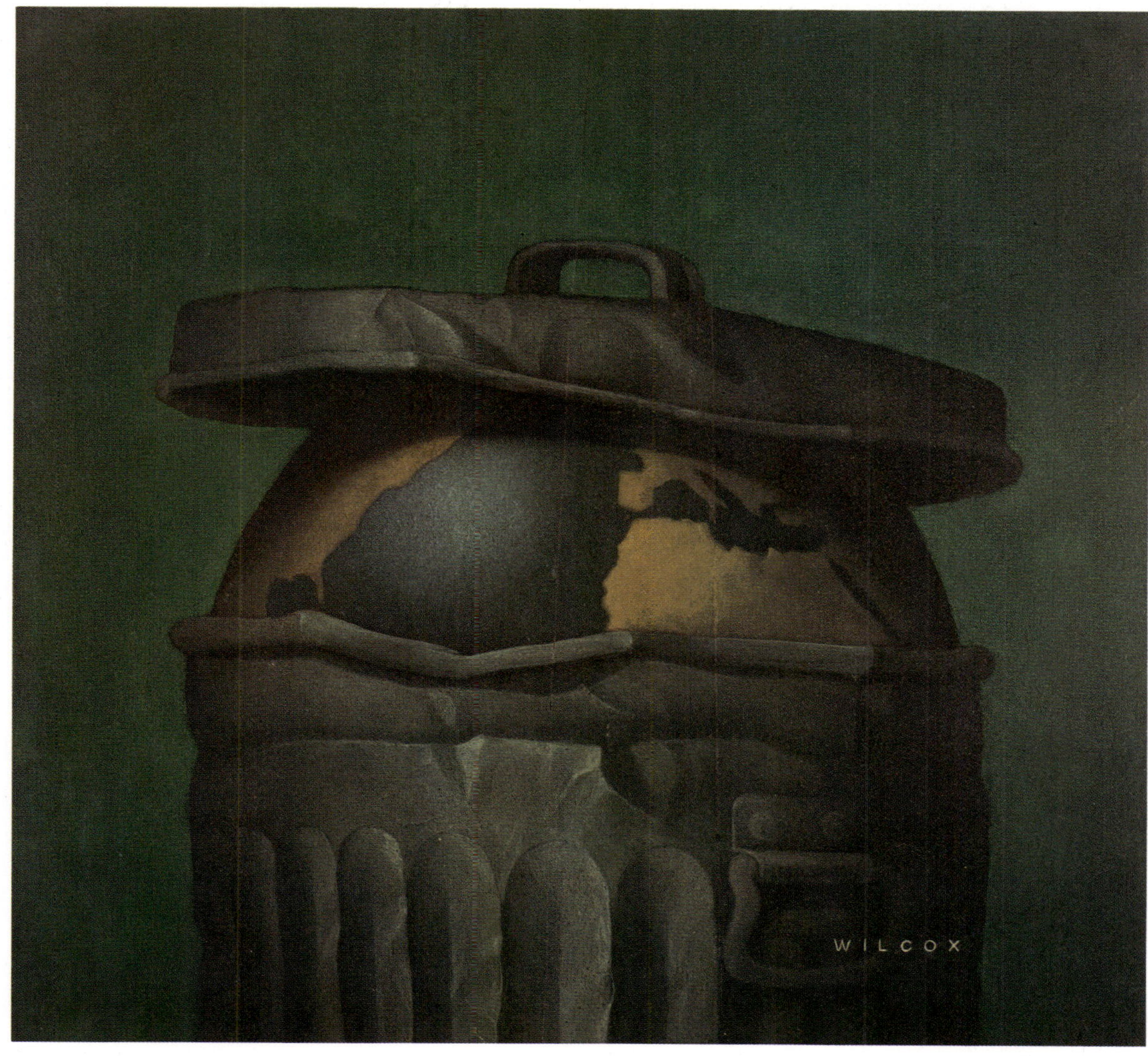


**DON'T TRASH IT**

DAVID WILCOX

*OIL ON CANVAS*

"A WARNING OF WHAT MAY HAPPEN IN THE FUTURE
IF WE CONTINUE AT OUR PRESENT."

IN GERMANY, THE NETHERLANDS, DENMARK, AND SPAIN, MORE THAN 20 PERCENT OF BIRD SPECIES AND OVER 40 PERCENT OF MAMMALIAN SPECIES ARE CLASSIFIED AS THREATENED.

..........................

IN DEUTSCHLAND, DEN NIEDERLANDEN, DÄNEMARK UND SPANIEN GELTEN ÜBER 20 PROZENT DER VOGELARTEN UND ÜBER 40 PROZENT DER SÄUGETIERE ALS BEDROHT.

..........................

EN ALLEMAGNE, AUX PAYS-BAS, AU DANEMARK ET EN ESPAGNE, ON CONSIDÈRE QUE PLUS DE 20% DES OISEAUX ET PLUS DE 40% DES MAMMIFÈRES SONT MENACÉS.

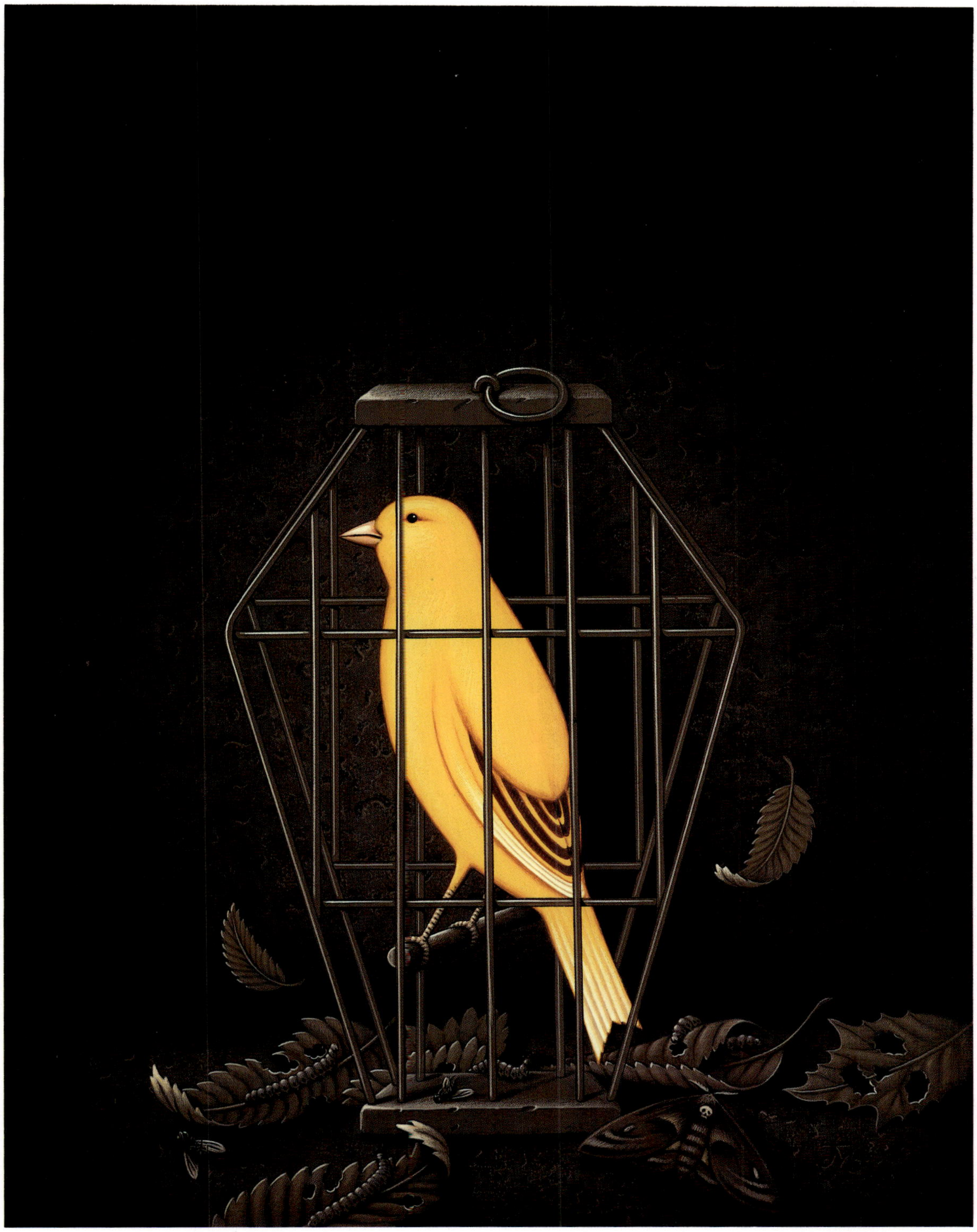

**DEATH IS A LONELY BUSINESS**

JAMES MARSH

*ACRYLIC ON CANVAS BOARD*

"THE CONTRAST BETWEEN LIFE AND DEATH; THE CAGE EMPHASIZES THE POINT."

THE AMOUNT OF RURAL ACREAGE
AFFECTED BY SERIOUS
DESERTIFICATION ROSE FROM 57
MILLION IN 1977 TO
135 MILLION IN 1984.

..........................

DIE SCHWERE VERWÜSTUNG DES
ACKERLANDS IST VON 23
MILLIONEN HEKTAR 1977 AUF
MEHR ALS DAS DOPPELTE IM JAHRE
1984 GESTIEGEN.

..........................

LA DÉSERTIFICATION DES
TERRES AGRICOLES EST PASSÉE DE
23 MILLIONS D'HA EN 1977 À
PLUS DU DOUBLE EN 1984.

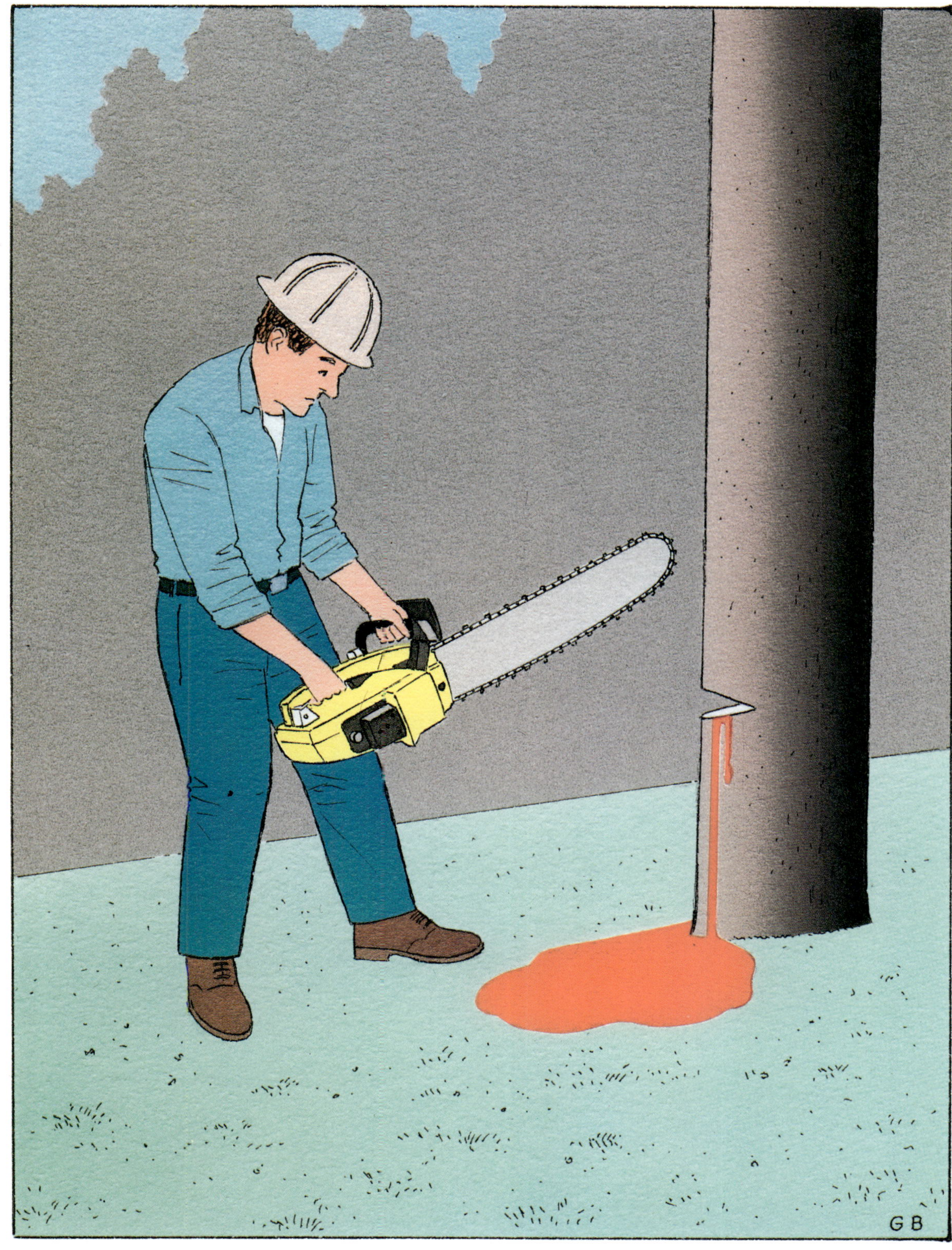


**BLEEDING TREE**

GUY BILLOUT

*WATERCOLOR AND AIRBRUSH*

AMERICANS PLY THEIR
GARDENS, LAWNS AND TREES WITH
270 MILLION POUNDS OF
PESTICIDE EVERY YEAR.

..........................

JEDES JAHR VERBRAUCHEN
DIE AMERIKANER 120 000 TONNEN
PESTIZIDE FÜR IHRE GÄRTEN,
RASEN UND BÄUME.

..........................

LES AMÉRICAINS DÉVERSENT
120 000 TONNES DE PESTICIDES
PAR AN SUR LEURS JARDINS ET
SUR LEURS ARBRES.

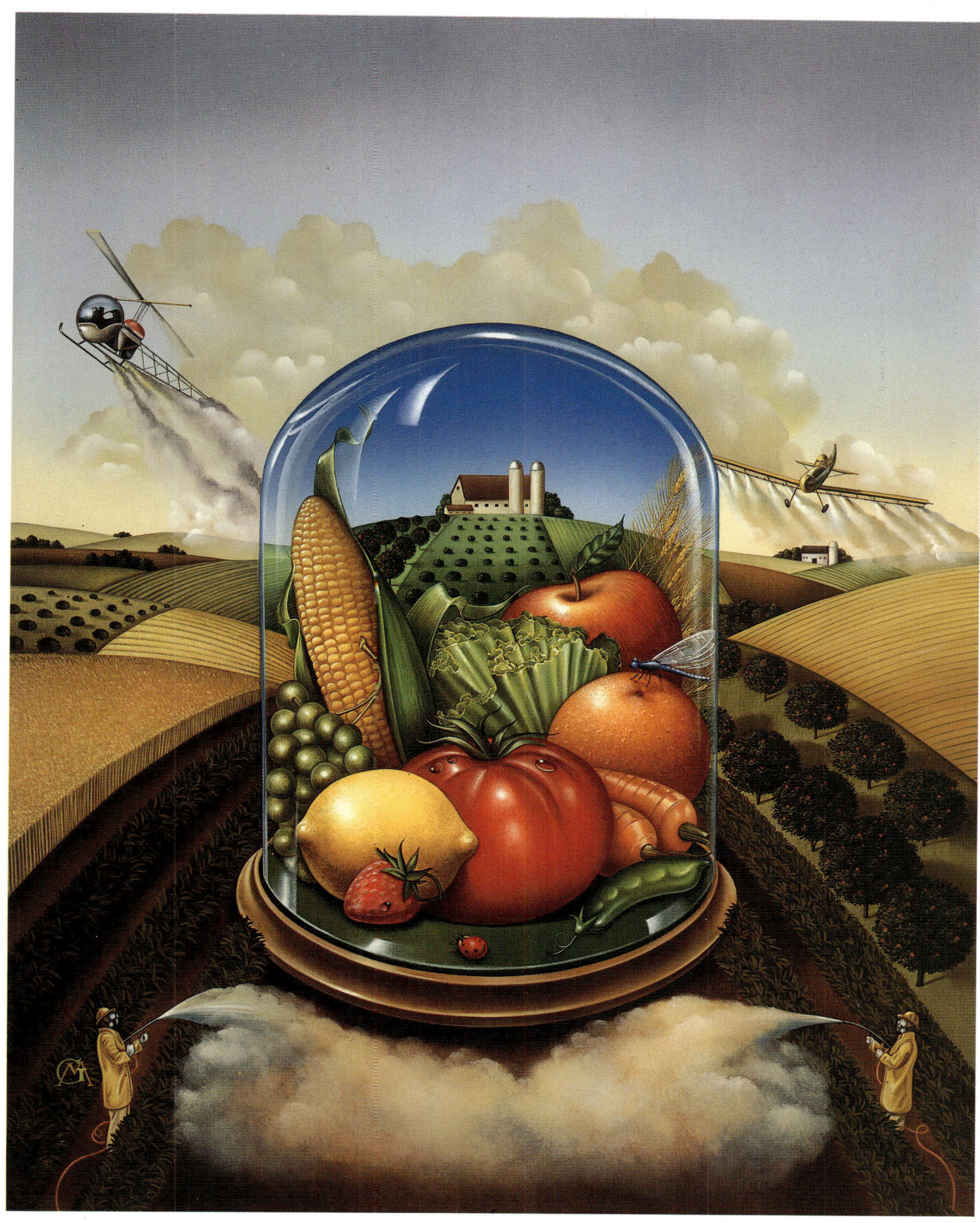

**AMERICA GROWS SAFER FOOD**

CHERYL GRIESBACH AND STANLEY MARTUCCI

*OIL ON MASONITE*

"THIS IS AN ILLUSTRATION FOR AN ARTICLE ON THE NATION'S FARMERS TACKLING THE PESTICIDE CRISIS, AND A COVER FOR *GOOD HEALTH* MAGAZINE."

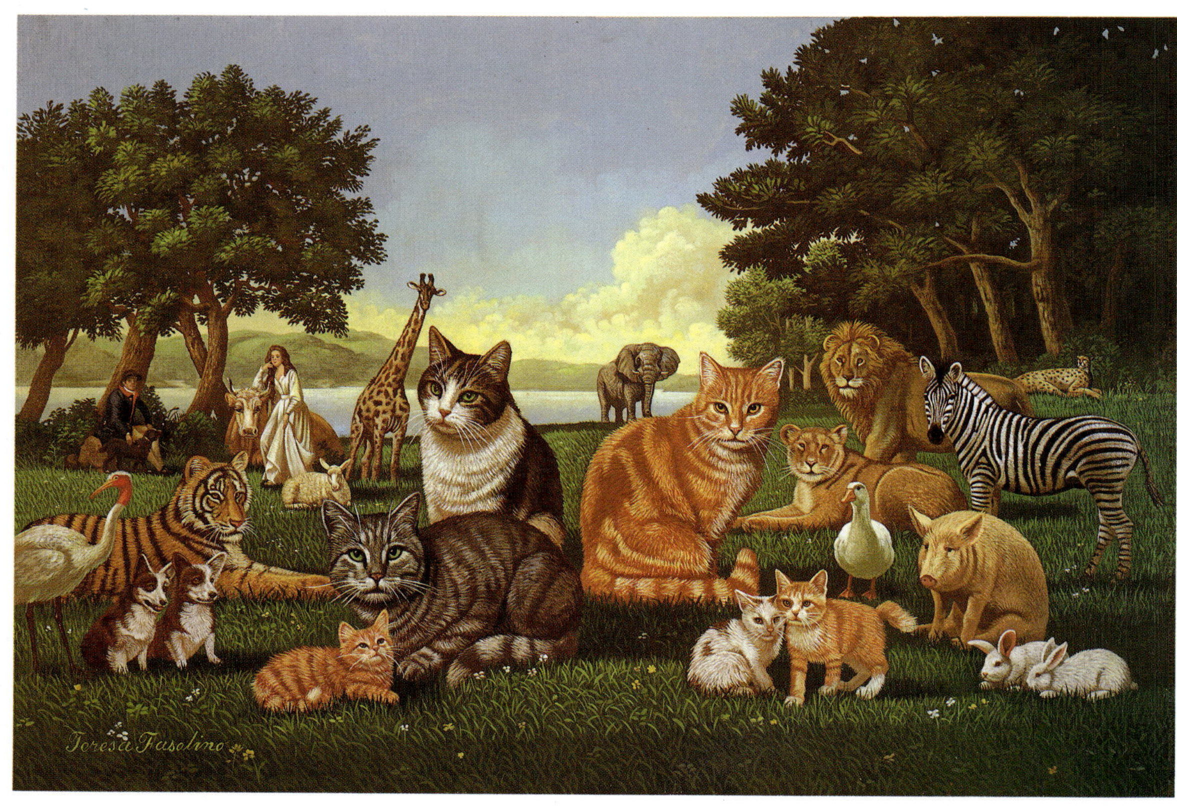


**ENDANGERED KINGDOM**

Teresa Fasolino

*Acrylic*

"The peaceable kingdom symbolizes man living inharmony with nature. Today the peaceable kingdom has become an endangered on where we can lose our most magnificent wildlife, leaving us with only our domesticated friends."

AFRICAN RHINOS DECLINED IN NUMBER FROM 15,000 IN 1980 TO LESS THAN 7,500 IN 1985, WHILE THE SOUTHERN WHITE RHINO POPULATION HAS DROPPED FROM 1,000 TO LESS THAN 15.

..........................

ZWISCHEN 1980 UND 1985 REDUZIERTEN SICH DIE AFRIKA-NISCHEN NASHÖRNER VON 15 000 UM MEHR ALS DIE HÄLFTE; DIE WEISSEN NASHÖRNER VON 1000 AUF WENIGER ALS 15.

..........................

LE NOMBRE DES RHINOCÉROS AFRICAINS EST PASSÉ DE 15 000 EN 1980 À MOINS DE 7500 EN 1985, LE RHINOCÉROS BLANC DE 1000 À MOINS DE 15.

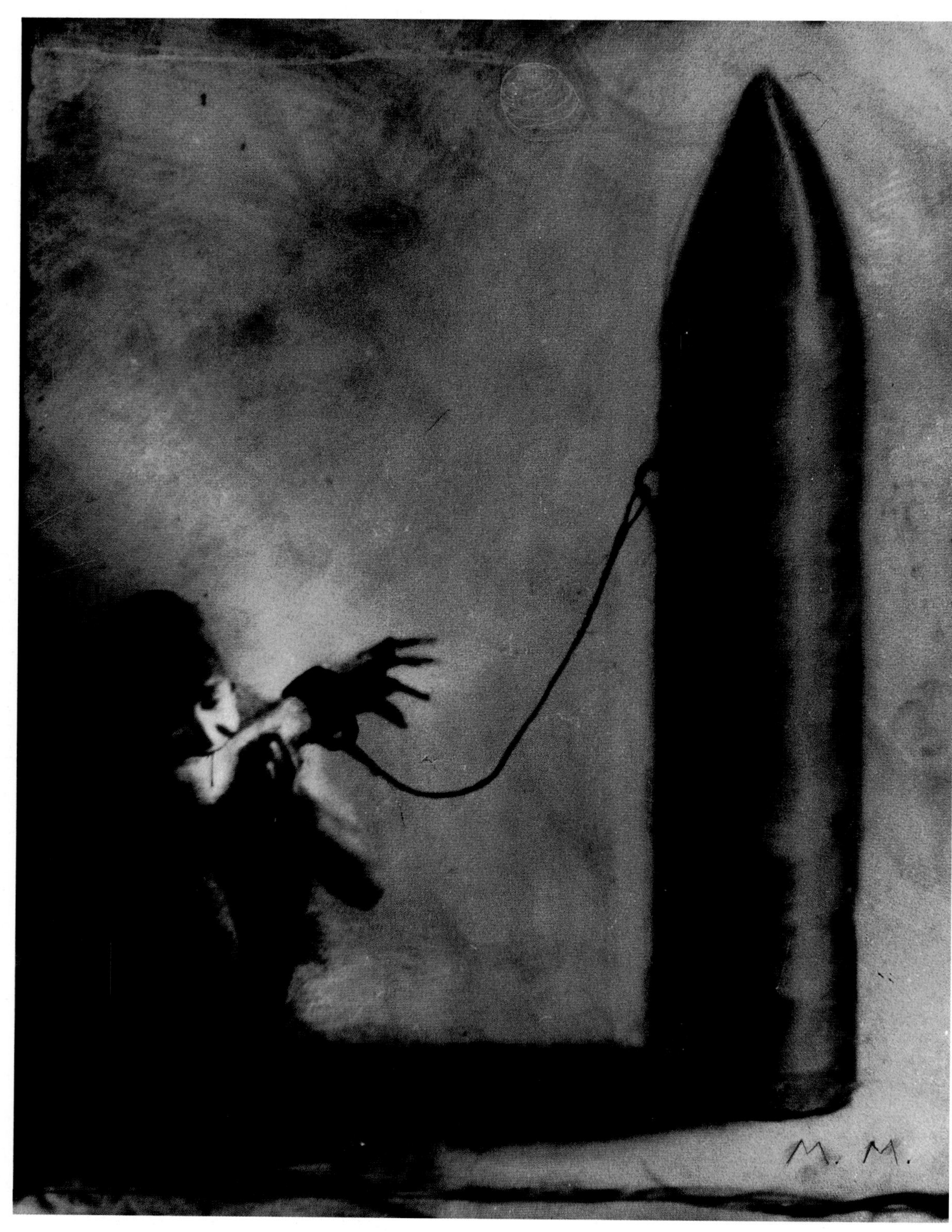


**UNTITLED**

MATT MAHURIN

*PHOTOGRAPH*

DEVELOPMENT LOANS WERE USED TO FINANCE A NUCLEAR POWER PLANT IN THE PHILIPPINES. IT WAS BUILT NEAR A VOLCANO AND, AS A RESULT, CANNOT OPERATE. IT COSTS THE FILIPINO PEOPLE $500,000 IN INTEREST.

..........................

ENTWICKLUNGSGELDER WURDEN AUF DEN PHILIPPINEN FÜR EIN ATOMKRAFTWERK VERWENDET. ES STEHT IN DER NÄHE EINES VULKANS UND KANN NICHT IN BETRIEB GENOMMEN WERDEN. ES KOSTET $ 500 000 AN ZINSEN.

..........................

AUX PHILIPPINES, DES FONDS D'AIDE AU DÉVELOPPEMENT ONT SERVI À FINANCER UNE CENTRALE NUCLÉAIRE. CONSTRUITE PRÈS D'UN VOLCAN, ELLE N'A PU ÊTRE MISE EN SERVICE. LE PEUPLE PAIE LES $ 500 000 D'INTÉRÊTS.

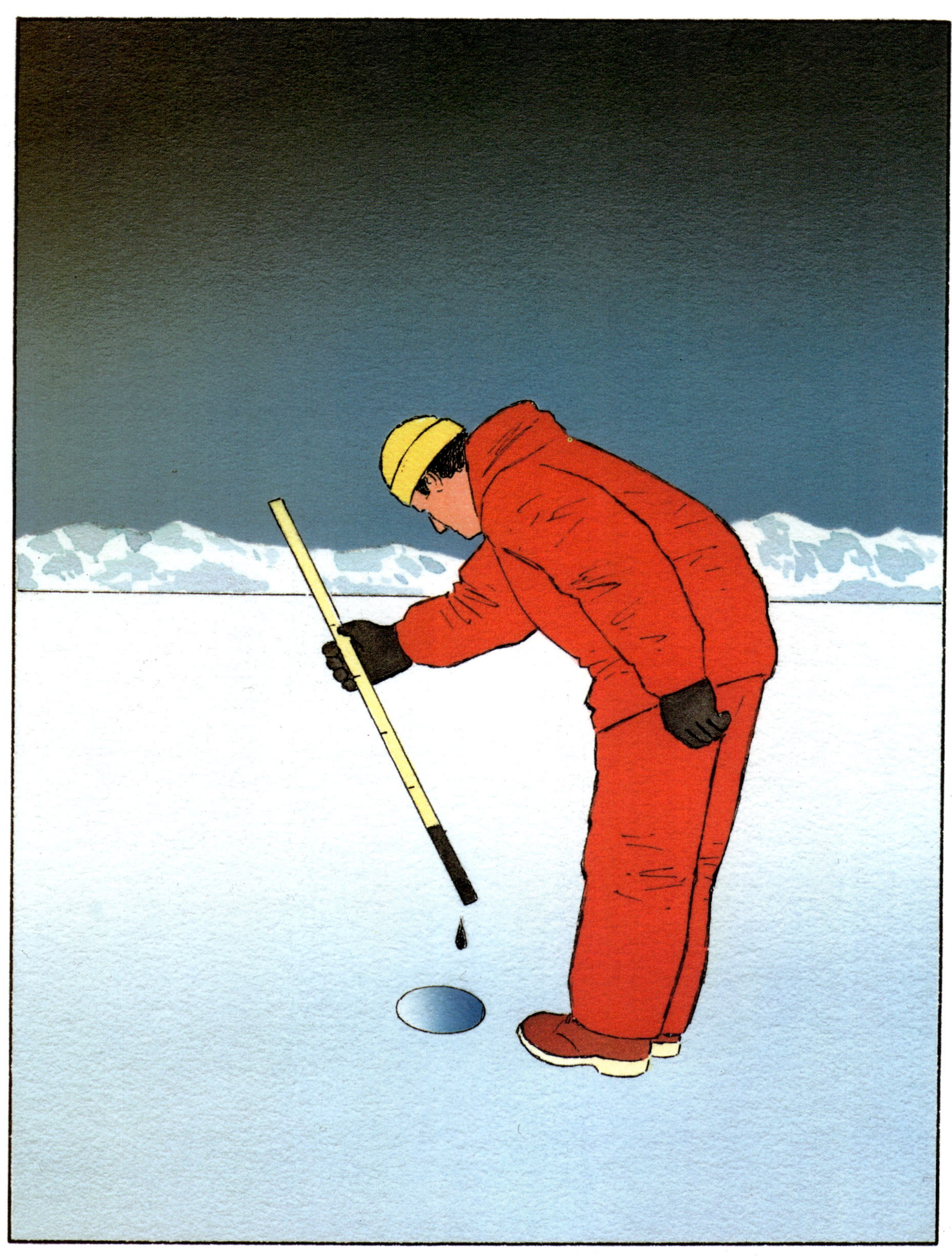

**OIL UNDER THE ICE**

Guy Billout

*Watercolor and airbrush*

SOME 5 MILLION
TONS A YEAR OF THE WORLD'S
TOTAL ANNUAL OIL PRODUCTION,
OR MORE THAN ONE GRAM PER 100
SQUARE METERS OF THE
OCEAN'S SURFACE, ENDS UP
IN THE OCEAN.

..........................

GEGEN 5 MILLIONEN TONNEN
DER JÄHRLICHEN ÖL-FÖRDERMENGE
DER WELT ODER MEHR ALS EIN
GRAMM PRO 100 QUADRATMETER
DER MEERESOBERFLÄCHE
GEHEN INS MEER.

..........................

QUELQUES 5 MILLIONS
DE TONNES DE LA PRODUCTION
MONDIALE ANNUELLE DE PÉTROLE
FINISSENT DANS L'OCÉAN.
CELA REPRÉSENTE PLUS D'UN
GRAMME POUR 100 M2 DE
SURFACE D'EAU.

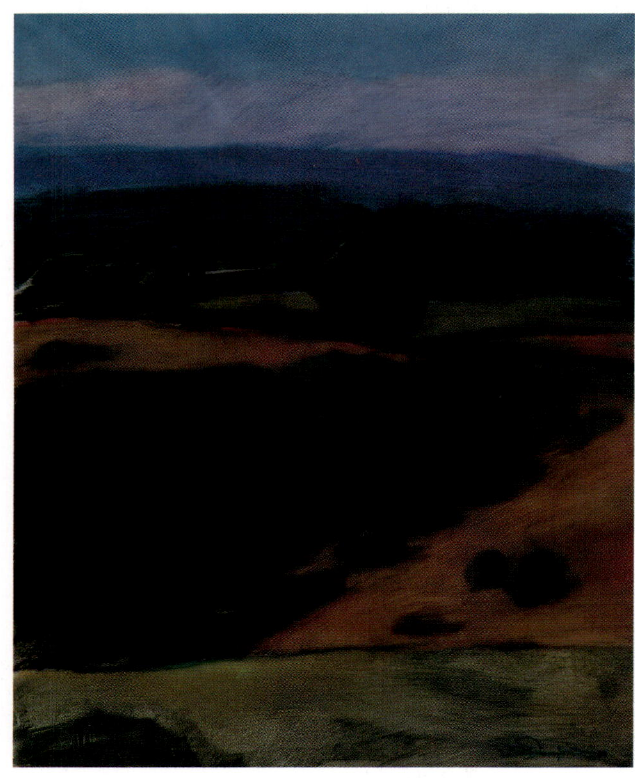

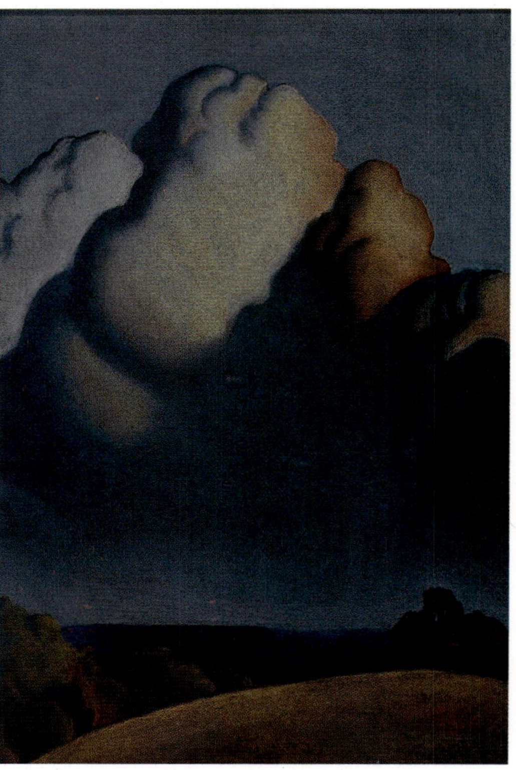

## MISSOURI LANDSCAPE

Mark English

*Oil on canvas*

"Simply a landscape of my particular environment—near Kearney, Missouri."

## FROM AN ARTIST WHO NEVER DOES ENVIRONMENTS

Bill Nelson

*Pastel*

EACH YEAR AMERICANS APPLY
HALF A BILLION POUNDS
OF CHEMICAL FERTILIZER TO THE
EARTH AND ITS PRODUCE.

.........................

JEDES JAHR VERWENDEN
DIE AMERIKANER ÜBER 200 000
TONNEN AN CHEMISCHEN
DÜNGEMITTELN.

.........................

CHAQUE ANNÉE,
LES AMÉRICAINS UTILISENT
ENVIRON 227 000 TONNES
D'ENGRAIS CHIMIQUES.

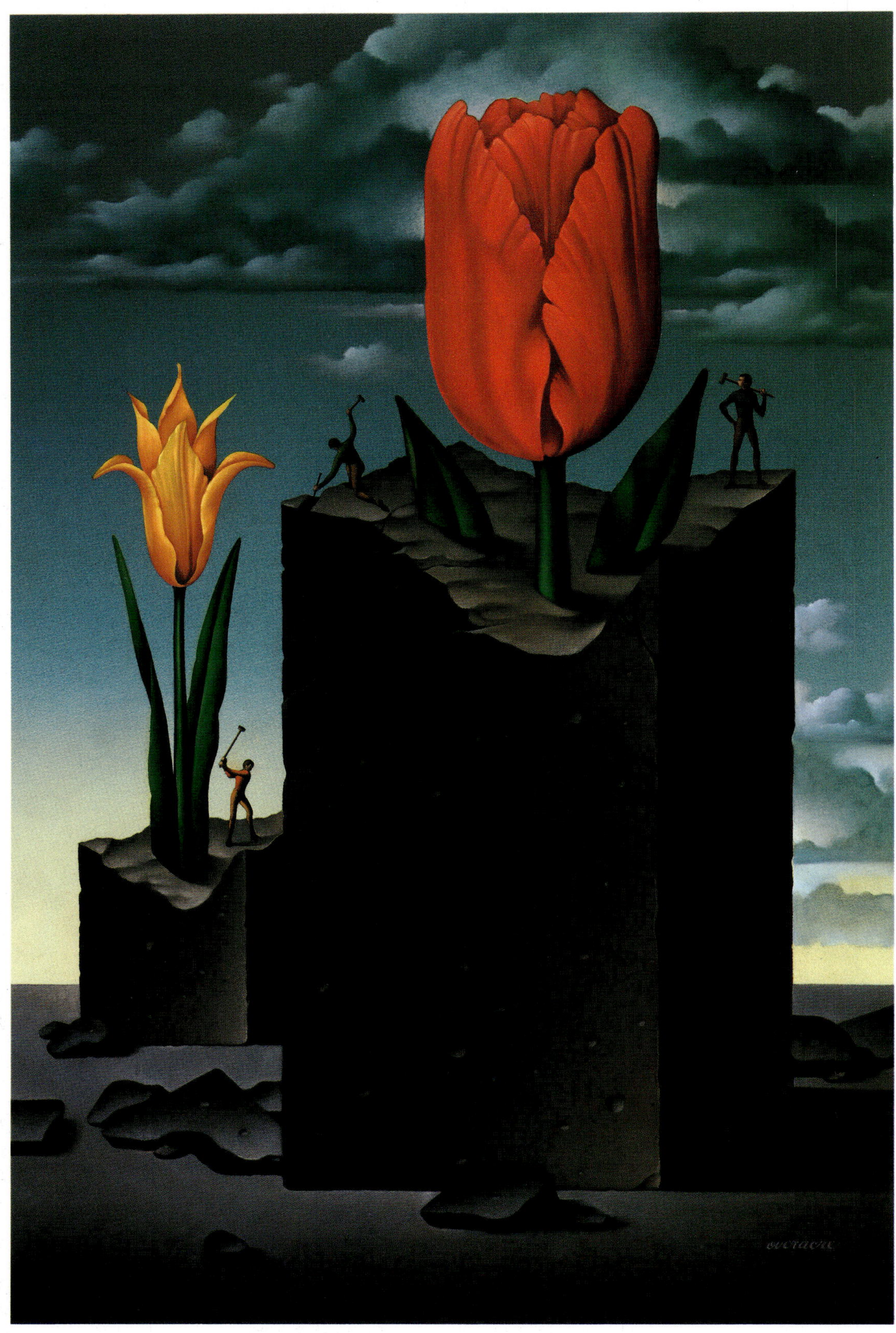

**MONOLITHS/FLOWERS**

Gary Overacre

*Oil on canvas*

"Restoring our environment in the years to come will be a formidable task—one that will require global resolve."

TROPICAL RAINFORESTS
MAKE UP 2 PERCENT OF THE
EARTH'S SURFACE AND ARE
INHABITED BY OVER HALF THE
WORLD'S WILD PLANT, ANIMAL,
AND INSECT SPECIES. RAINFORESTS
ARE CURRENTLY DISAPPEARING
AT A RATE OF 50 ACRES
PER MINUTE.

DIE TROPISCHEN
REGENWÄLDER BEDECKEN
ZWEI PROZENT DER
ERDOBERFLÄCHE; HIER WACHSEN
UND LEBEN ÜBER DIE HÄLFTE ALLER
WILDEN PFLANZEN, TIERE UND
INSEKTENARTEN.
DIESE WÄLDER SCHWINDEN
UM 2 HA PRO MINUTE.

LES FORÊTS TROPICALES
COUVRENT 2% DE LA SURFACE DE
LA TERRE ET ELLES HÉBERGENT
PLUS DE LA MOITIÉ DES ESPÈCES
ANIMALES ET VÉGÉTALES.
ELLES SONT EN TRAIN DE
DISPARAÎTRE, À RAISON DE 2
HA À LA MINUTE.

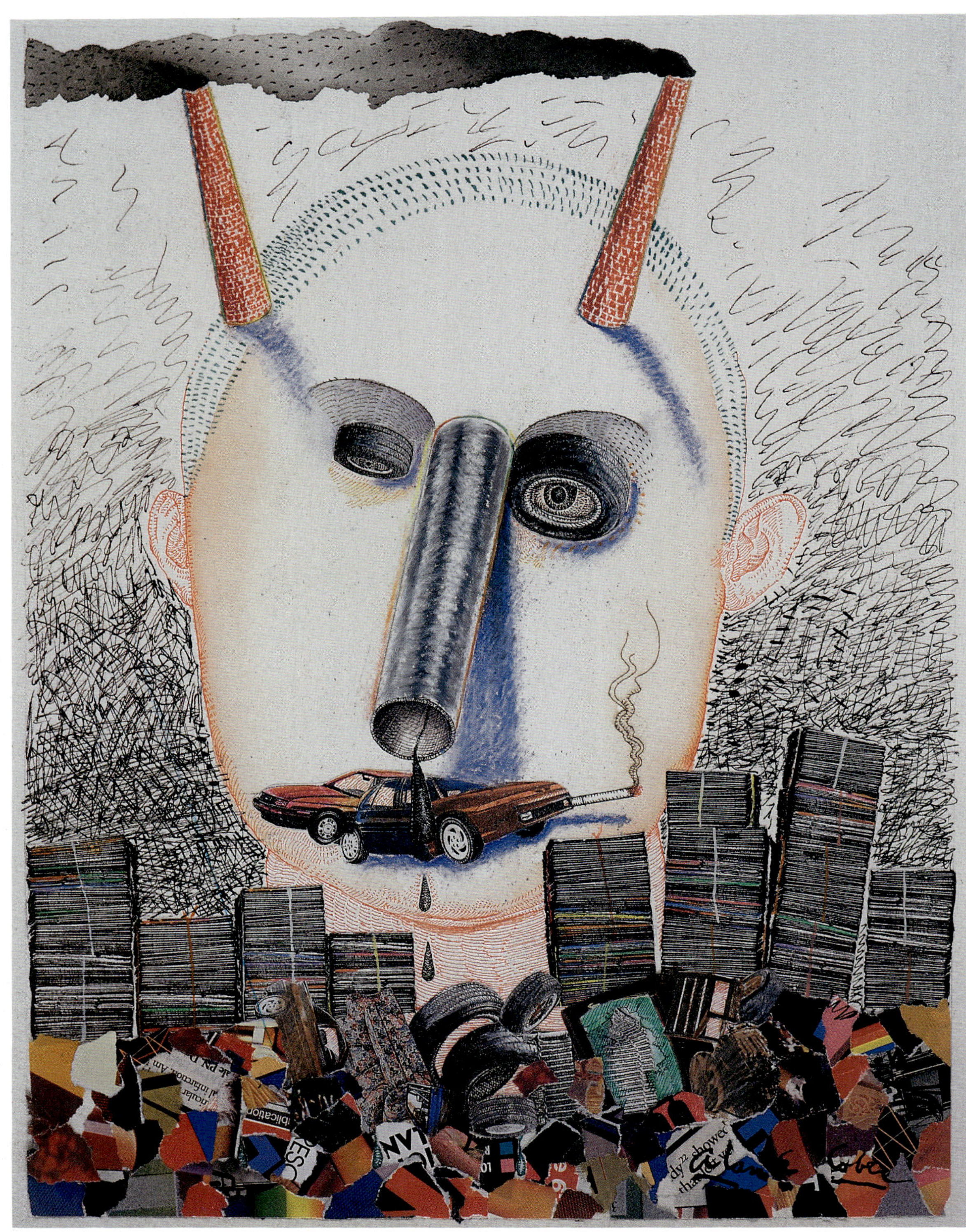

## TAKING OUT AMERICA'S TRASH

ALAN E. COBER

*INK, WATERCOLOR, PRISMACOLOR, COLLAGE*

"IN THE LAST 20 YEARS I'VE HAD THE OPPORTUNITY TO WORK ON SUBJECTS RELATED TO THE ENVIRONMENT. WHAT WE EAT AND BREATHE AND WHAT WE WASTE IS INCREDIBLE. WHERE DOES THIS STUFF GO? WE COVER IT UP AND IT MAY LOOK OKAY—BUT IN MANY CASES WE END UP LIVING ON IT AND DRINKING IT. WHAT ARE WE GOING TO DO WITH ALL THIS STUFF?"

THE ENVIRONMENTAL PROTECTION AGENCY ESTIMATES THAT 80 PERCENT OF THE LANDFILLS NOW IN OPERATION WILL REACH CAPACITY AND CLOSE WITHIN 20 YEARS.

........................

80 PROZENT DER JETZT BENUTZTEN DEPONIEN WERDEN IN 20 JAHREN GEFÜLLT SEIN UND STILLGELEGT WERDEN.

........................

DANS 20 ANS, 80% DES DÉCHARGES AURONT ATTEINT LEUR CAPACITÉ MAXIMUM ET DEVRONT ÊTRE FERMÉES.

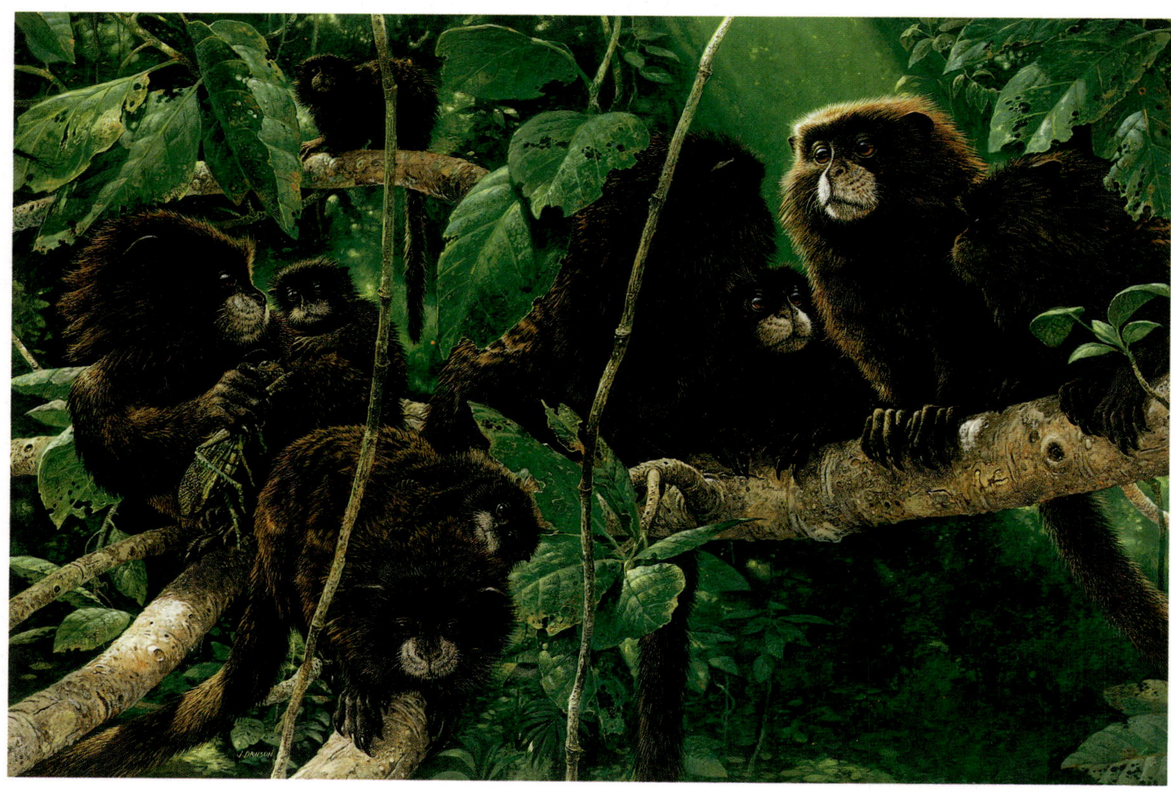

## SADDLE-BACK TAMARIN

John Dawson

"The Saddle-back Tamarin is not on anyone's official 'endangered species' list, but their home—the tropical rainforest of South America—is disappearing. When the home forest disappears, so will the monkey and all natural life. Then lists won't mean much."

ANIMAL SPECIES THAT
NORMALLY MIGRATE IN THE FACE
OF DANGEROUS OR CHANGING
ECOSYSTEMS WILL NOW
HAVE A HARD TIME FINDING A
NEW HABITAT DUE TO THE HUMAN
OBSTACLES OF CITIES, ROADS,
AND FARMLANDS AND THE FACT
THAT WE HAVE DESTROYED
MOST POTENTIAL HABITATS.

.........................

TIERARTEN, DIE
NORMALERWEISE BEI
GEFÄHRLICHEN ODER SICH
VERÄNDERNDEN ÖKOSYSTEMEN
WEITERZIEHEN, WERDEN ES SCHWER
HABEN, NEUEN LEBENSRAUM ZU
FINDEN. DURCH STÄDTE, STRASSEN
UND ACKERLAND HAT DER MENSCH
EINEN GROSSEN TEIL IHRES
POTENTIELLEN LEBENSRAUMS
ZERSTÖRT.

.........................

LES ESPÈCES ANIMALES
QUI ÉMIGRENT EN CAS DE DANGER
OU DE TRANSFORMATION DES
ÉCOSYSTÈMES AURONT DE PLUS
EN PLUS DE DIFFICULTÉS
À TROUVER DE NOUVEAUX
ESPACES VITAUX. L'EXPANSION
DES VILLES, DES ROUTES
ET DES CULTURES ONT CONTRIBUÉ
À LES DÉTRUIRE.

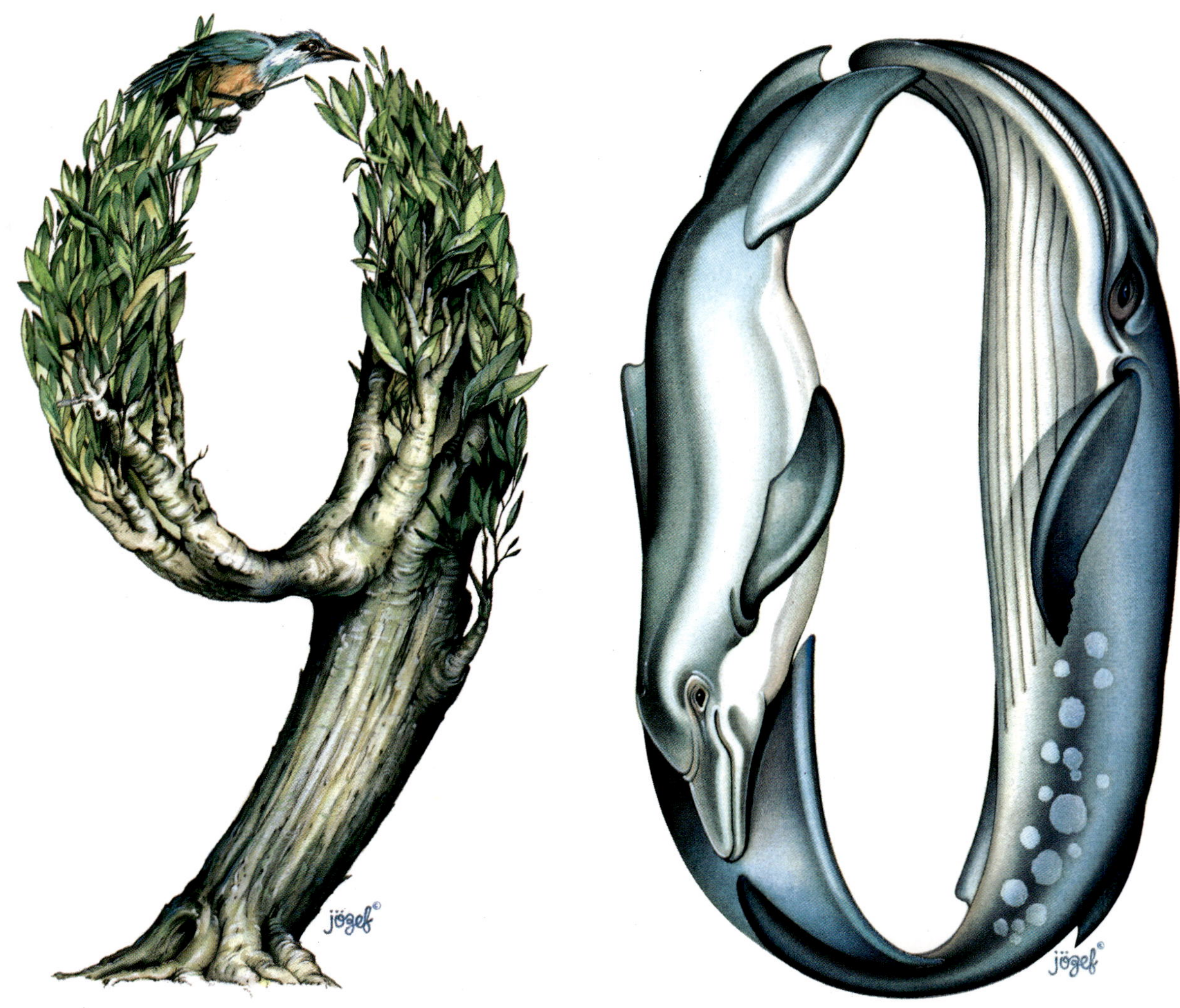


**90**

JÖZEF SUMICHRAST

*TRANSPARENT DYE*

"THE 9 IS MADE FROM A TREE AND BIRD FROM THE TROPICAL RAINFOREST IN SOUTH AMERICA. THE 0 IS MADE FROM A DOLPHIN AND A WHALE. THE "90" SHOWS TODAY'S CONCERN FOR THE LAND, SEA, AND AIR."

EVERY YEAR ON
SEPTEMBER 23, THE CENTER
FOR MARINE CONSERVATION
SPONSORS A NATIONAL
THREE-HOUR BEACH CLEAN-UP.
AROUND THE NATION, VOLUNTEERS
RETRIEVED 2 MILLION POUNDS OF
DEBRIS THIS PAST YEAR.

...........................

JEDES JAHR AM 23.
SEPTEMBER ORGANISIERT DAS US
ZENTRUM FÜR MEERESSCHUTZ EINE
DREISTÜNDIGE STRANDSÄUBERUNG.
LANDESWEIT SAMMELTEN DIE
FREIWILLIGEN LETZTES JAHR RUND
900 000 KG ABFALL.

...........................

CHAQUE ANNÉE, LE 23
SEPTEMBRE, LE CENTRE DE
PROTECTION DES OCÉANS AUX USA
SPONSORISE UNE ACTION
NATIONALE DE NETTOYAGE DES
PLAGES. CETTE ANNÉE, LES
VOLONTAIRES ONT RAMASSÉ
900 000 KG DE DÉTRITUS.

THE EARTH IS ESTIMATED TO BE
4.5 BILLION YEARS OLD AND
HUMANS HAVE INHABITED IT
FOR ONLY 2 OR 3 MILLION YEARS.
ONLY IN THE PAST 200 YEARS
HAVE WE BEGUN TO AFFECT
OUR ENVIRONMENT WITH
A SERIOUS IMPACT.

.........................

MAN SCHÄTZT, DASS DIE
ERDE 4,5 MILLIARDEN JAHRE ALT
IST. DEN MENSCHEN GIBT ES SEIT 2
BIS 3 MILLIONEN JAHREN, UND
ERST IN DEN LETZTEN 200 JAHREN
HABEN WIR BEGONNEN, DER
UMWELT ERNSTHAFTE SCHÄDEN
ZUZUFÜGEN.

.........................

ON ESTIME QUE LA TERRE A 4,5
MILLIARDS D'ANNÉES; L'HOMME Y
HABITE SEULEMENT DEPUIS 2
OU 3 MILLIONS D'ANNÉES. C'EST
AU COURS DES 200 DERNIÈRES
ANNÉES QUE NOUS AVONS
COMMENCÉ À DÉTRUIRE
L'ENVIRONNEMENT.

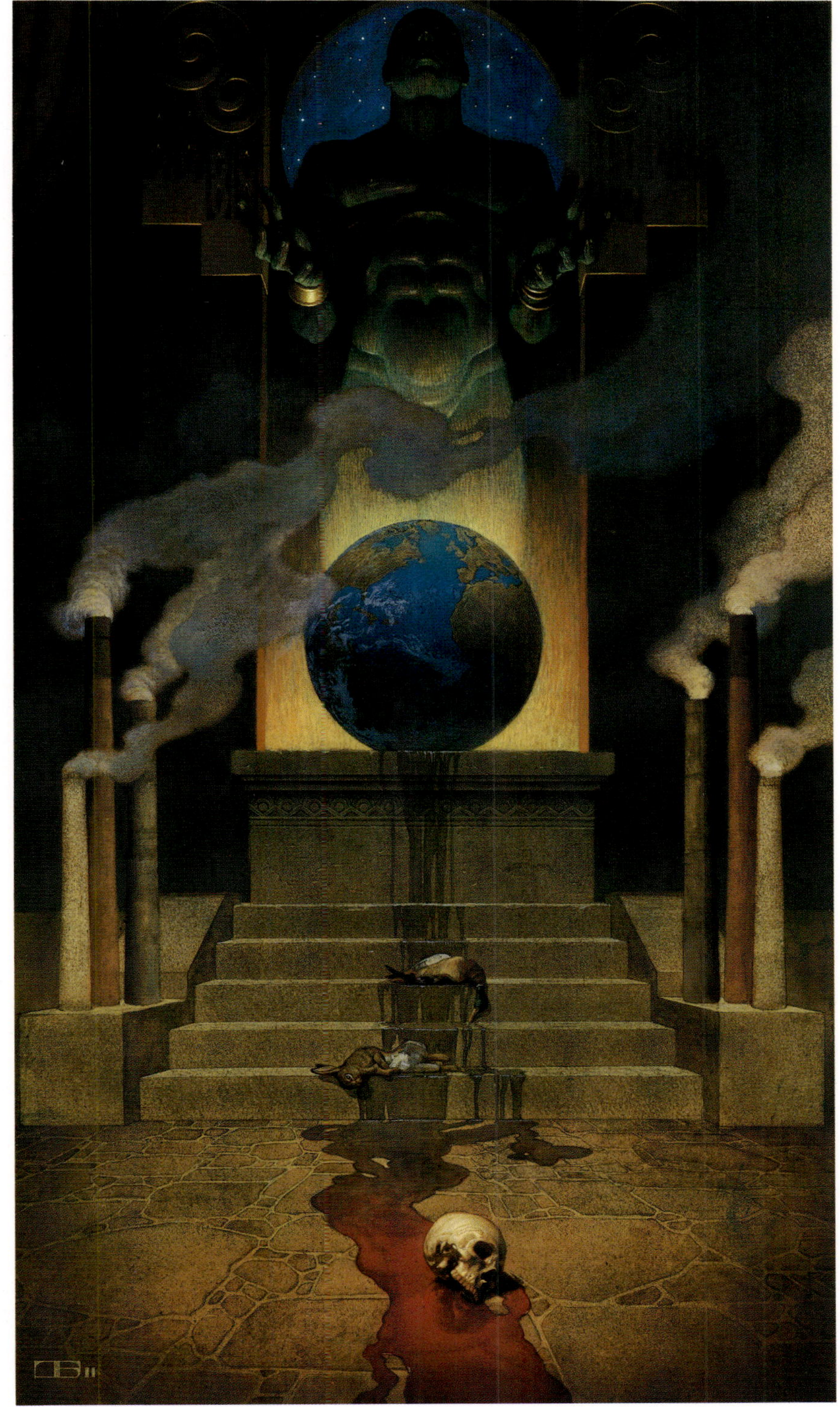

**THE SACRIFICE**

THOMAS BLACKSHEAR

*MIXED MEDIA*

"THE ILLUSTRATION DEPICTS THE WORLD ON A SACRIFICIAL ALTAR, BEING OFFERED TO THE POWERS OF MAN IN THE FORM OF AN IDOLATROUS BRONZE STATUE. THE OUTSTRETCHED HANDS REPRESENT MAN'S GREED AND THE DISSATISFACTION WHICH CAUSES HIM TO CONSTANTLY WANT MORE. GOLDEN WRISTBANDS STAND FOR THE WEALTH MAN IS FOREVER TRYING TO OBTAIN... EVEN AT THE EXPENSE OF THE EARTH."

THE INCREASE OF CARBON DIOXIDE AND OTHER HEAT-ABSORBING GASES IN OUR ATMOSPHERE ARE ALREADY RAISING GLOBAL TEMPERATURES, ALTERING WEATHER PATTERNS, WORSENING STORMS, DISRUPTING AGRICULTURE, AND DESTROYING NATURAL SYSTEMS.

........................

DAS ANSTEIGEN VON SCHWEFELDIOXID UND ANDEREN WÄRMEABSORBIERENDEN GASEN VERURSACHT U.A. EINE ERWÄRMUNG, KLIMAVERÄNDERUNGEN, STÄRKERE STÜRME UND SCHÄDEN IN DER LANDWIRTSCHAFT.

........................

LA PRODUCTION ACCRUE DE DIOXYDE DE CARBONE ET D'AUTRES GAZ ABSORBANT LA CHALEUR PROVOQUE UN RÉCHAUFFEMENT DE LA TERRE, PERTURBE LE CLIMAT ET CAUSE DE SÉRIEUX DOMMAGES DANS L'AGRICULTURE.

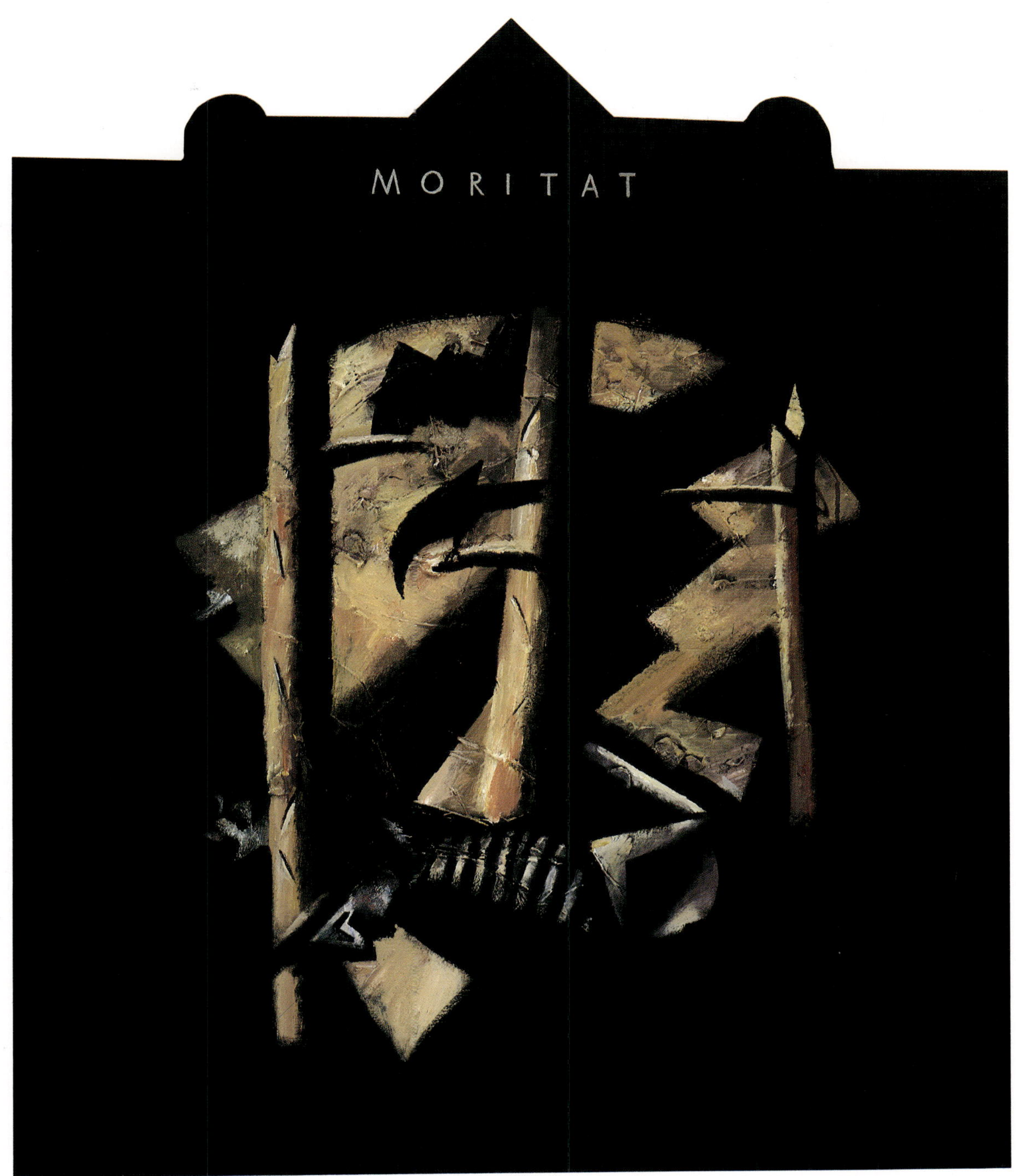


**MORITAT**

John Howard

*Mixed media/acrylic on canvas*

"Painting on a base of beach detritus from outside my studio in Long Island, the image is of a desolated landscape of bare branches and bare bones arranged in the format of a smiling skull. It is a 'deathsong' to the inevitability of the world's apparent chosen path. Set in the frame of a tombstone, it is an epitaph."

AS A RESULT OF FUEL WOOD DEMAND, DELHI LOST 60 PERCENT OF ITS SURROUNDING FOREST COVER WITHIN A DECADE.

.........................

60% DES WALDGEBIETES UM DEHLI GINGEN WEGEN DES BRENNHOLZBEDARFS INNERHALB EINER DEKADE VERLOREN.

.........................

EN 10 ANS, 60% DES FORÊTS DE DEHLI ONT ÉTÉ DÉTRUITES POUR COUVRIR LA DEMANDE EN BOIS DE CHAUFFAGE.

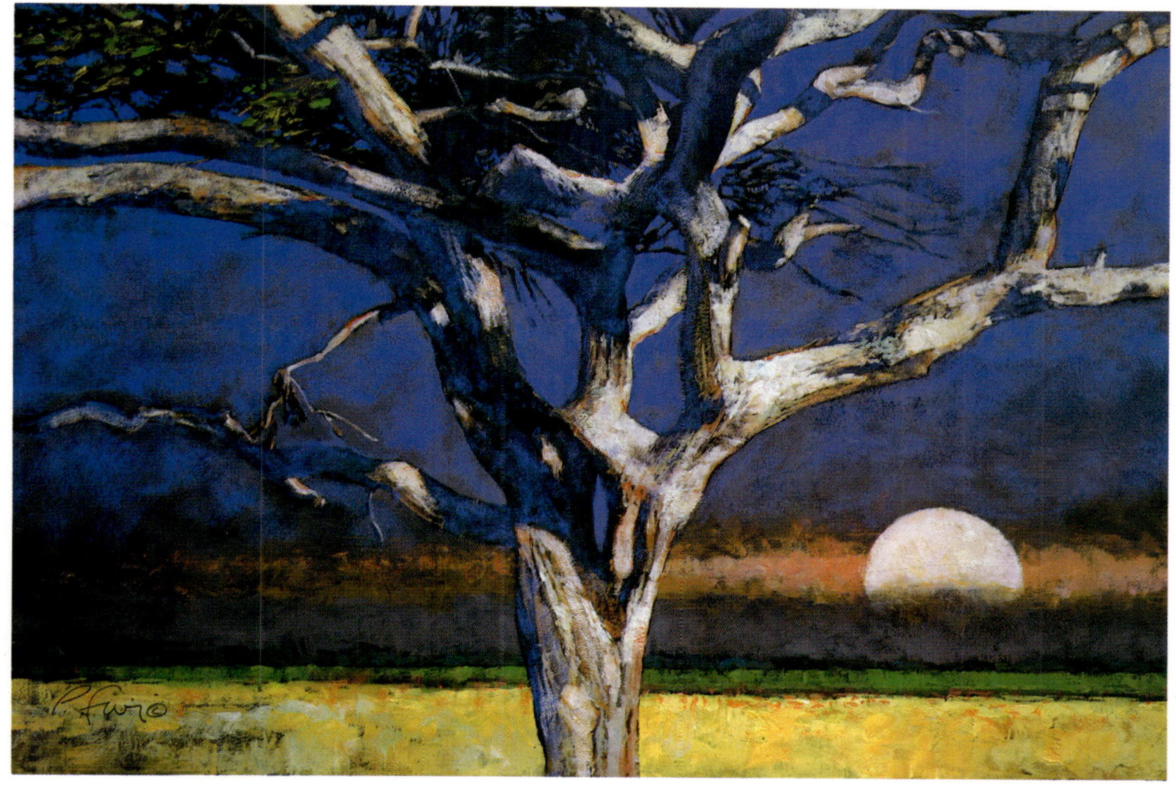

**AFRICAN MOONRISE**

PETER FIORE

"THE TREE AND THE MOON, FOR ME, ARE SYMBOLS OF LIFE AND TIME ETERNAL."

DEFORESTATION OF THE RAINFOREST WILL REDUCE RAINFALL IN THE REGION BY 25 PERCENT, INCREASING THE AVERAGE TEMPERATURE BY 5 DEGREES FAHRENHEIT.

.........................

DURCH DIE ABHOLZUNG DES REGENWALDES WIRD IN DER REGION 25 PROZENT WENIGER REGEN FALLEN UND DIE DURCHSCHNITTSTEMPERATUR UM 2 GRAD CELSIUS STEIGEN.

.........................

LE DÉBOISEMENT DE LA FORÊT AMAZONIENNE RÉDUIRA LA PLUVIOSITÉ DE LA RÉGION DE 25%, FAISANT CROÎTRE LA TEMPÉRATURE MOYENNE DE 5 DEGRÉS FAHRENHEIT.

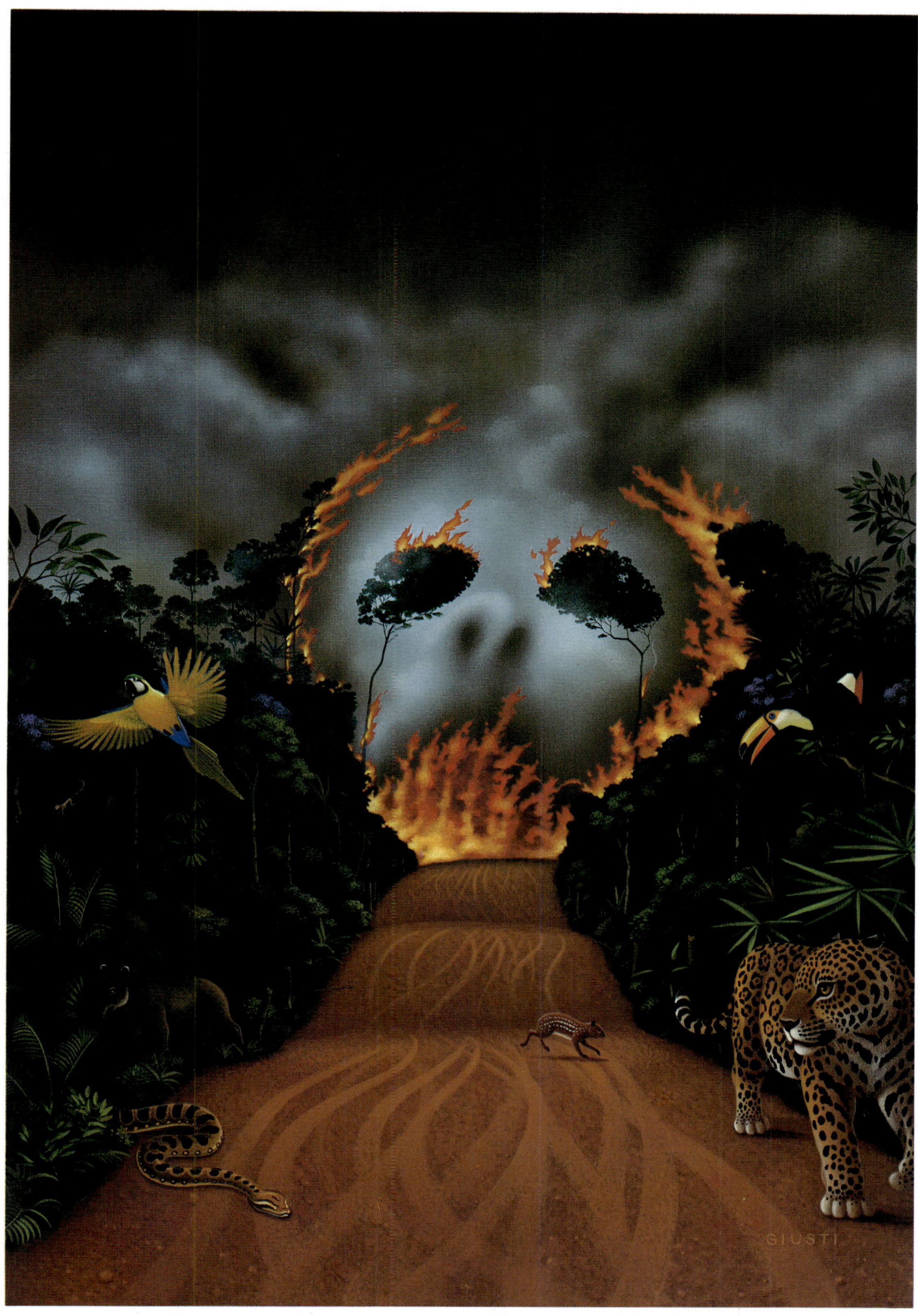


**TORCHING THE AMAZON**

Fobert Giusti

*Acrylic on canvas*

*Reprinted with permission of Time, Inc.*

"*Torching the Amazon* depicts the devastation and loss of jungle habita⁻ due to fire as a means of forest clearing in preparation for development."

5.5 BILLION TONS OF CARBON WERE ADDED TO THE ATMOSPHERE IN 1988 THROUGH FOSSIL FUEL COMBUSTION AND ANOTHER 2.5 BILLION TONS THROUGH DEFORESTATION.

.........................

1988 LIESSEN DIE MENSCHEN 5,5 MILLIARDEN TONNEN KOHLENWASSERSTOFF DURCH DIE VERBRENNUNG FOSSILER BRENNSTOFFE IN DIE ATMOSPHÄRE UND WEITERE 2,5 MILLIARDEN TONNEN DURCH ABHOLZUNGEN.

.........................

EN 1988, L'HUMANITÉ A REJETÉ DANS L'ATMOSPHÈRE 5,5 MILLIARDS DE TONNES DE CARBONE PROVENANT DE LA COMBUSTION D'HYDROCARBURES ET 2,5 MILLIARDS DE TONNES À CAUSE DE LA DÉFORESTATION.

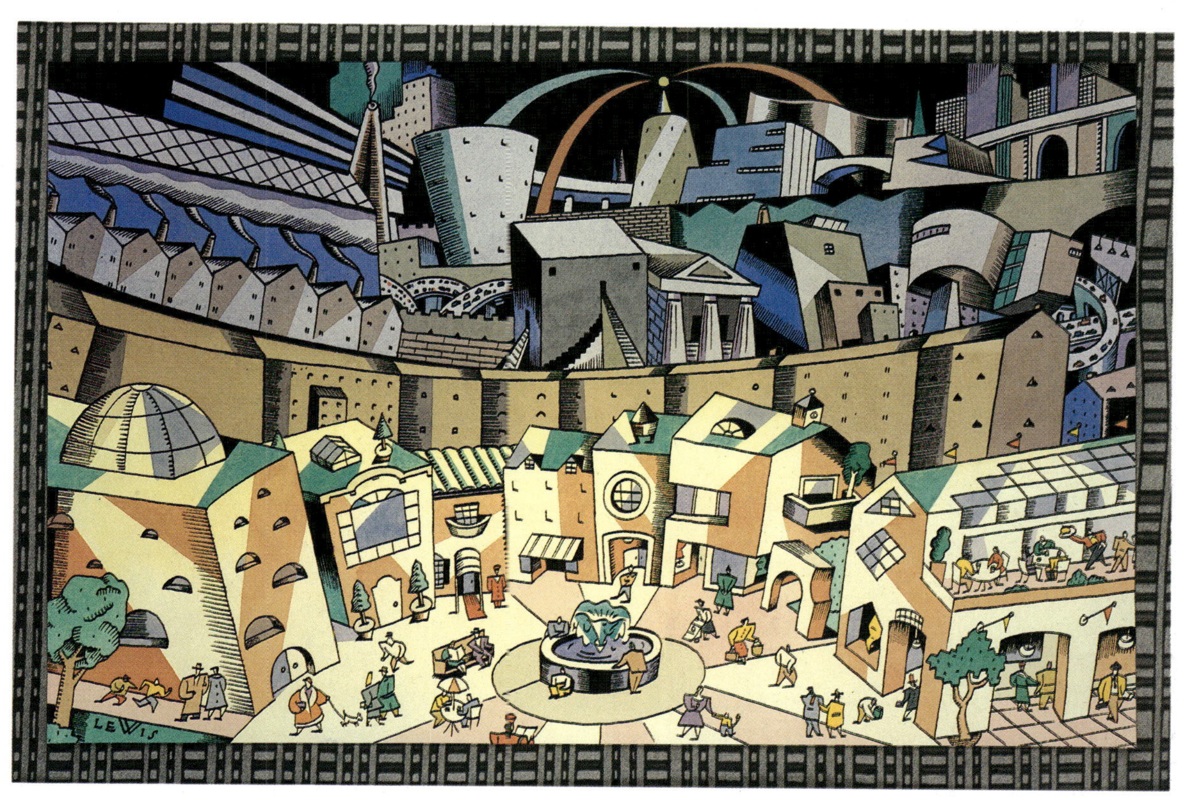


**THE BUILDING AS AN INVITATION**

TIM LEWIS

*WATERCOLOR*

"VITAL ATTENTION IS REQUIRED TO CITIES AS WELL AS RAINFORESTS."

THE AVERAGE AMERICAN
CAR EMITS ITS OWN WEIGHT IN
CARBON INTO THE ATMOSPHERE
EACH YEAR.

..........................

DER KOHLENWASSERSTOFFAUSSTOSS
EINES DURCHSCHNITTLICHEN
AUTOS IN DEN USA PRO
JAHR ENTSPRICHT SEINEMGE WICHT.

..........................

CHAQUE ANNÉE, UNE
VOITURE AMÉRICAINE REJETTE EN
MOYENNE SON POIDS DE CARBONE
DANS L'ATMOSPHÈRE.

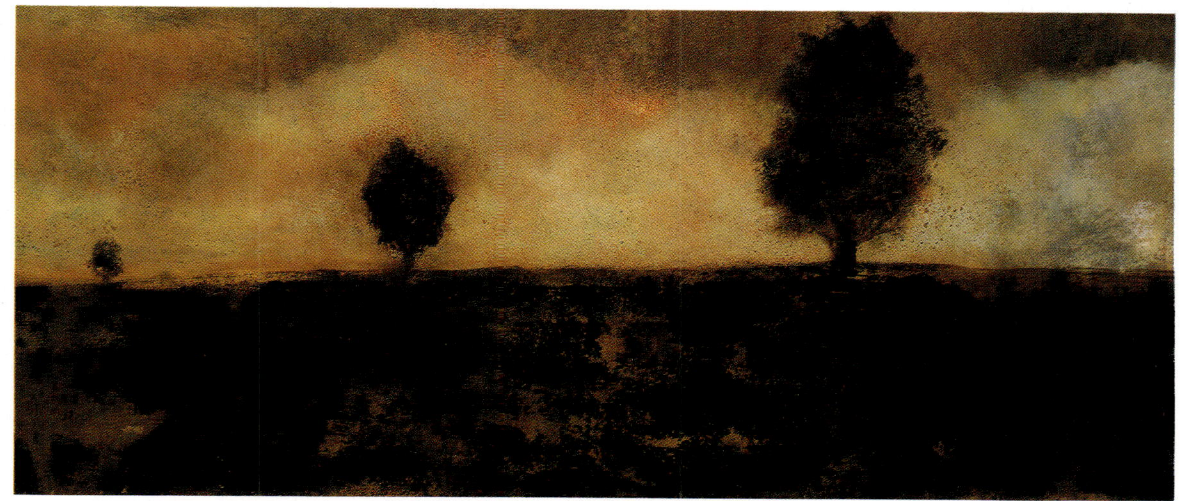

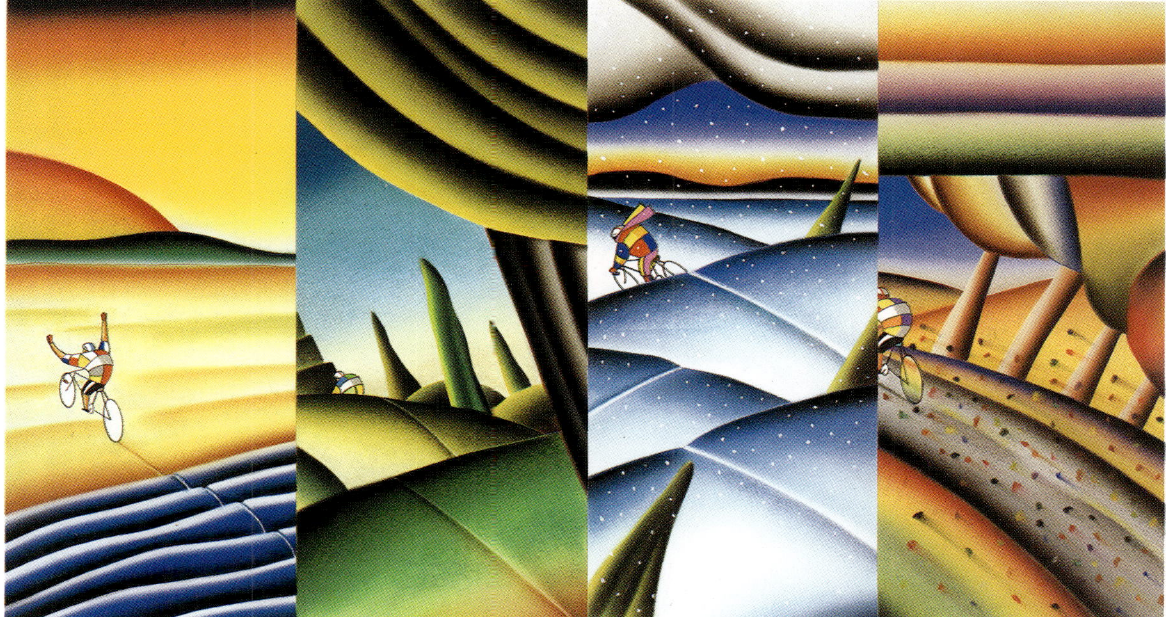

**UNTITLED**

Mark Penberthy

*Oil on gessoed paper*

**SEASONS**

Kurt A. Vargo

*Mixed media*

"The artwork addresses the viable possibilities of cycling as a partial solution to ozone pollution. It's a nontoxic and healthy way for a rider to enjoy his/her environment."

DESTRUCTION OF THE FORESTS HAS TRIGGERED WIDESPREAD FLOODING AND LOSS OF VALUABLE TOPSOIL RESULTING IN SPECIES EXTINCTION, GLOBAL WARMING, AND A DROP IN WORLD FOOD PRODUCTION.

..........................

DIE ZERSTÖRUNG DER WÄLDER HAT ZU ÜBERSCHWEMMUNGEN UND ZUM VERLUST WERTVOLLER ACKERKRUME GEFÜHRT. DIE FOLGEN SIND DAS AUSSTERBEN EINIGER ARTEN, GLOBALE ERWÄRMUNG UND WENIGER NAHRUNG IN DER WELT.

..........................

LA DESTRUCTION DES FORÊTS A PROVOQUÉ DES INONDATIONS ET L'ÉROSION DES SOLS. CELA A ENTRAÎNÉ L'EXTINCTION DE CERTAINES ESPÈCES, UN RÉCHAUFFEMENT GLOBAL DE LA TERRE ET UNE BAISSE DE PRODUCTION DE NOURRITURE.

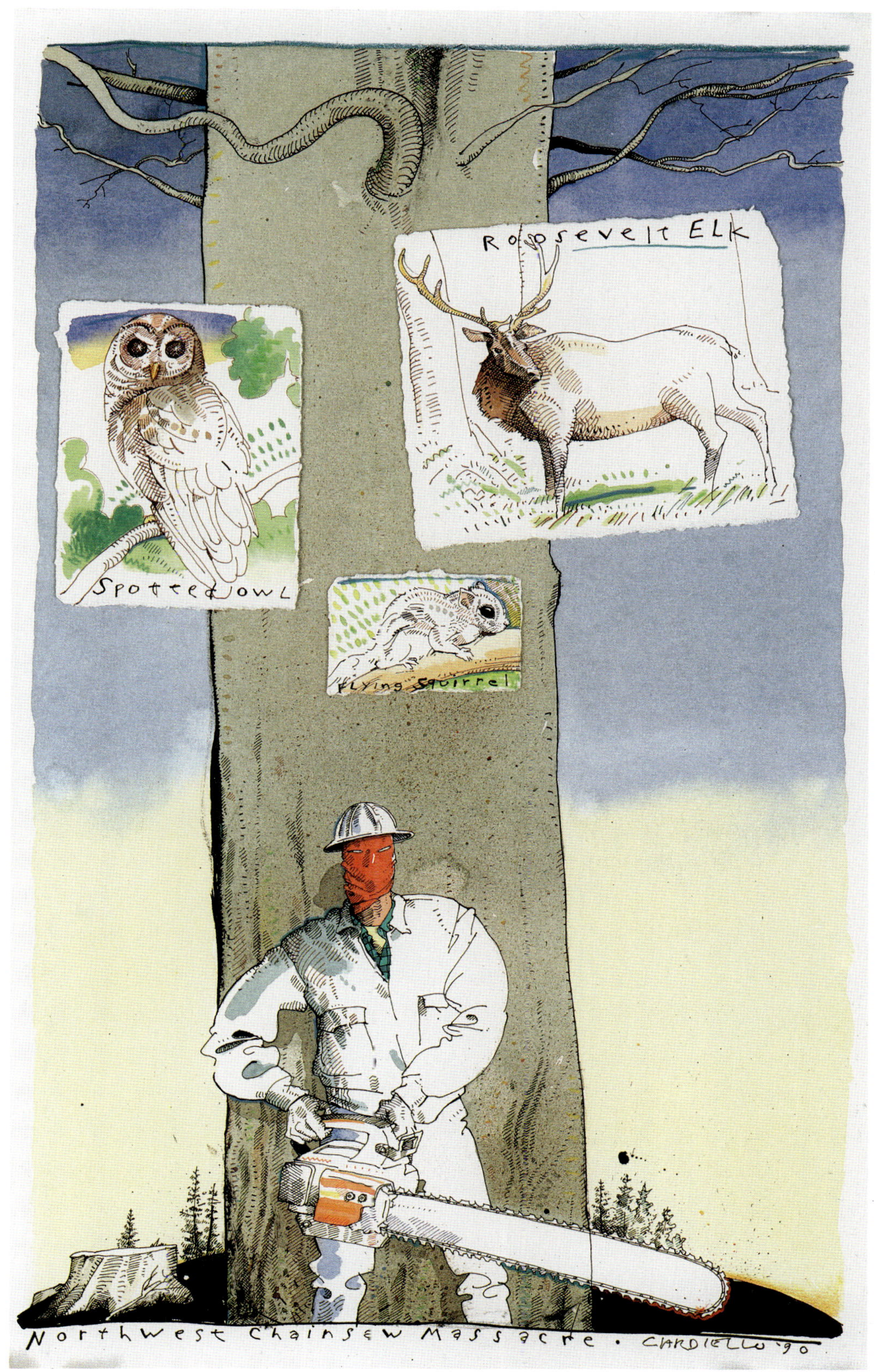


**THE NORTHWEST CHAINSAW MASSACRE**

Joe Ciardello

*Gouache and airbrush*

"Our consumption of timber threatens the survival of the ancient timber forests of the Pacific northwest, as well as many species of animals that inhabit them."

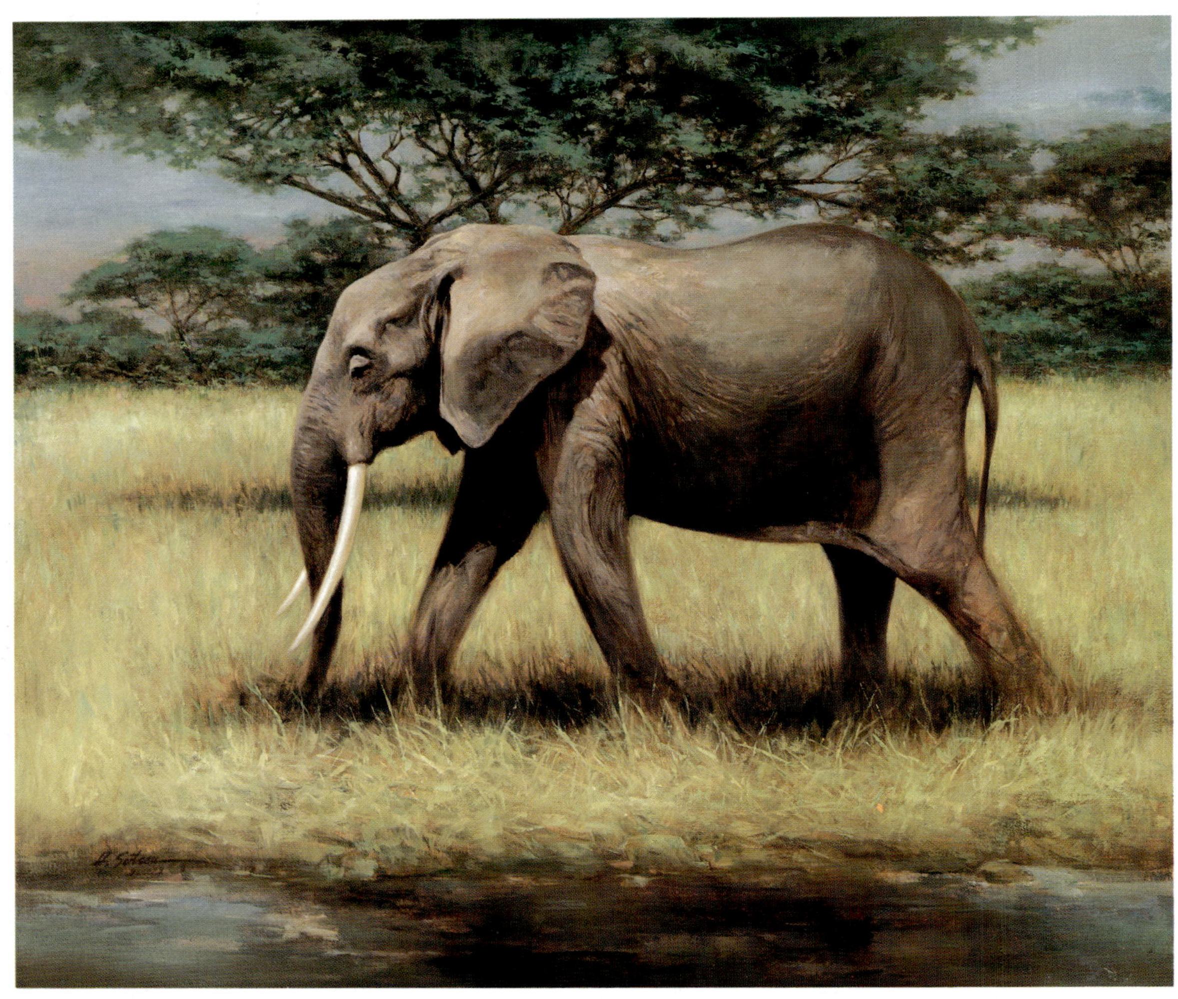

**AFRICAN ELEPHANT**

HODGES SOILEAU

*OIL ON CANVAS*

"THE AFRICAN ELEPHANT IS THE MOST INTERESTING PHYSICALLY OF THE ENDANGERED SPECIES—DECREASING HABITAT AND IVORY TUSKS HAVE THEM IN PERIL—HOPEFULLY THIS MIGHT BE CHANGED BEFORE IT IS TOO LATE."

AFRICA'S ELEPHANT POPULATION HAS DECREASED FROM 1.4 MILLION IN 1979 TO 750,000 TODAY. AT THIS RATE OF DECLINE—70,000 PER YEAR—THEY WILL VIRTUALLY DISAPPEAR BY THE TURN OF THE CENTURY.

..........................

DIE ZAHL DER AFRIKANISCHEN ELEFANTEN HAT SICH VON 1,4 MILLIONEN 1979 AUF HEUTE 750 000 REDUZIERT. WENN DER BESTAND WEITER IM GLEICHEN TEMPO ABNIMMT, WERDEN DIE ELEFANTEN ZUR JAHRHUNDERTWENDE AUSGESTORBEN SEIN.

..........................

EN AFRIQUE, LE NOMBRE D'ÉLÉPHANTS EST PASSÉ DE 1,4 MILLIONS EN 1979 À 750 000 AUJOURD'HUI. S'IL CONTINUE DE DIMINUER À CE RYTHME DE 70 000 PAR AN, ILS AURONT DISPARU À LA FIN DU SIÈCLE.

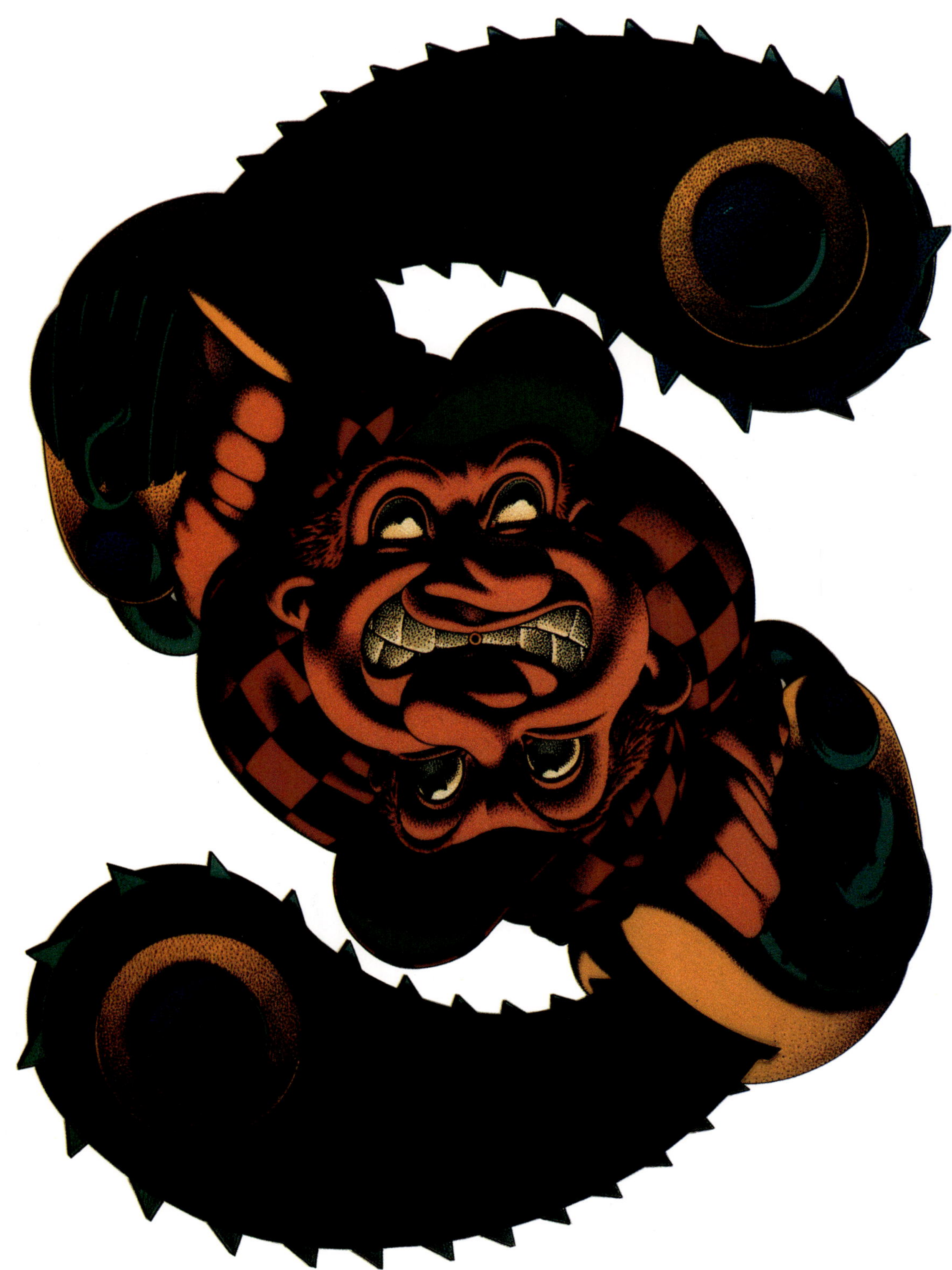

**PAUL BUNYAN'S PINWHEEL**

ALEX MURAWSKI

*INK, ACRYLIC, PAINT ON TREATED ACETATE, AND PHOTOGRAPHIC TRANSPARENCY*

"I HAVE ALWAYS BEEN INTERESTED IN MECHANICAL, WIND-DRIVEN TOYS LIKE WHIRIGIGS, PINWHEELS, WEATHER VANES, SAIL PLANES, AND ICE BOATS. SINCE TOYS REFLECT OUR HOPE AND EXPECTATIONS FOR BEHAVIOR IN SOCIETY, I BEGAN TO WONDER WHAT PAUL BUNYAN PLAYED WITH AS A CHILD THAT ENCOURAGED HIM TO BECOME AMERICA'S FIRST KING OF THE CLEARCUTTERS."

PRODUCING ONE TON OF PAPER FROM WASTE PAPER USES HALF AS MUCH ENERGY AND HALF AS MUCH WATER THAN PRODUCING IT FROM VIRGIN WOOD PULP.

........................

IN DEUTSCHLAND, DEN NIEDERLANDEN, DÄNEMARK UND SPANIEN GELTEN ÜBER 20 PROZENT DER VOGELARTEN UND ÜBER 40 PROZENT DER SÄUGETIERE ALS BEDROHT.

........................

PRODUIRE UNE TONNE DE PAPIER AVEC DES VIEUX JOURNAUX DEMANDE MOITIÉ MOINS D'ÉNERGIE ET D'EAU QUE DE LA FABRIQUER AVEC UNE NOUVELLE PÂTE À PAPIER.

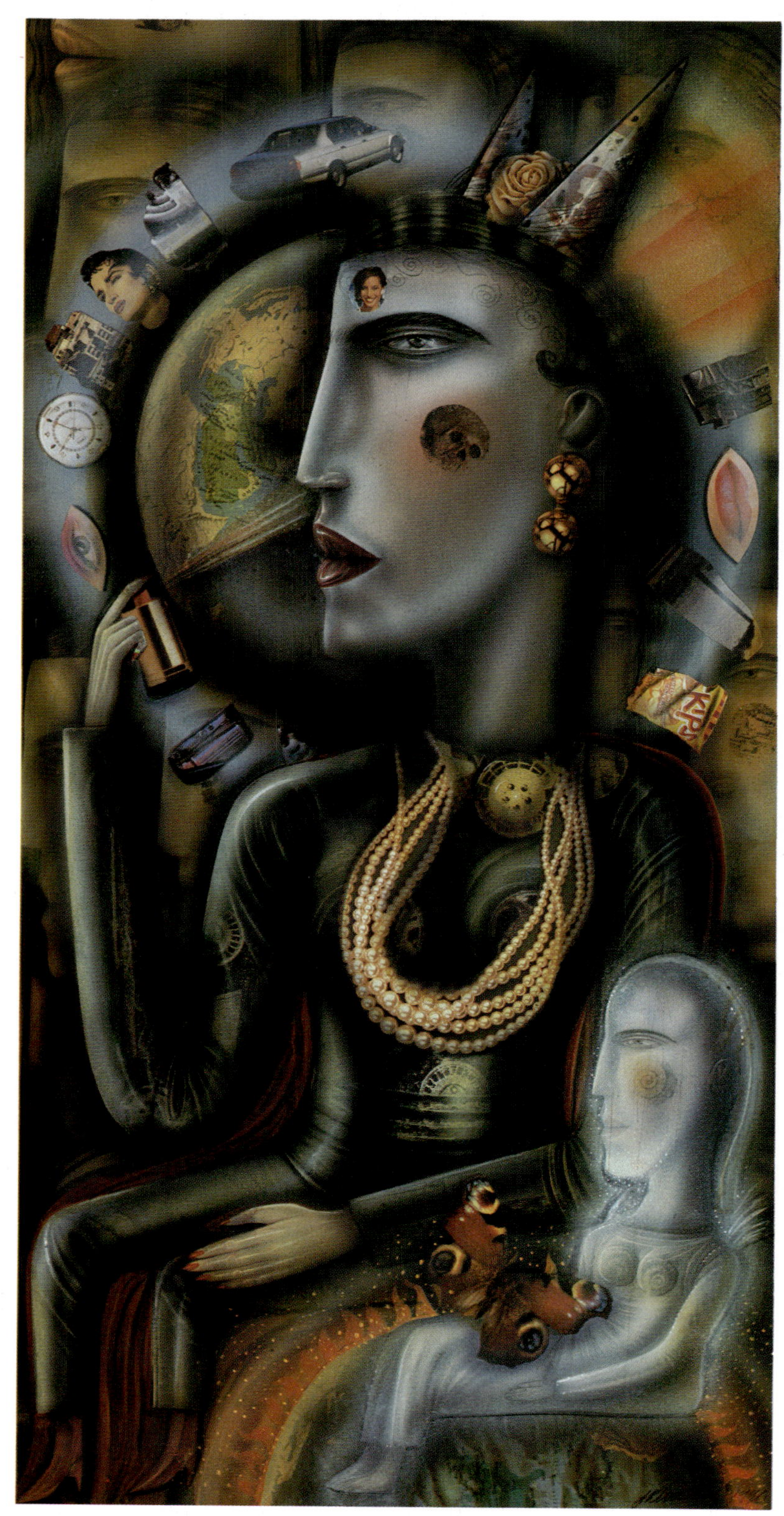

## BEAUTY AND THE BEAST

JANET WOOLLEY

*MIXED MEDIA*

"THE STORY OF A SUPPOSEDLY MORAL AND CARING HUMAN BEING WHO, DUE TO VANITY AND CONDITIONING, FAILS TO APPRECIATE THE BEAUTY AND QUALITIES OF THE BEAST UNTIL IT IS NEARLY TOO LATE, THUS POSING THE QUESTION, 'WHO IS THE BEAST?'"

EVIDENCE INDICATES THAT
AIR-BORNE POLLUTION FROM THE
INDUSTRIAL WORLD IS NOW
THREATENING THE HEALTH OF INUIT
PEOPLE LIVING IN THE
ARCTIC REGION.

..........................

DIE DURCH DIE INDUSTRIELÄNDER
VERURSACHTE LUFTVERSCHMUTZUNG
BEDROHT JETZT NACHWEISLICH DIE
GESUNDHEIT DES INUIT-STAMMES
IN DER ARKTISCHEN REGION.

..........................

IL EST PROUVÉ QUE LA
POLLUTION DE L'AIR CAUSÉE PAR
LES PAYS INDUSTRIALISÉS MENACE
ACTUELLEMENT LA SANTÉ DES
INUIT QUI VIVENT DANS LES
RÉGIONS ARCTIQUES.

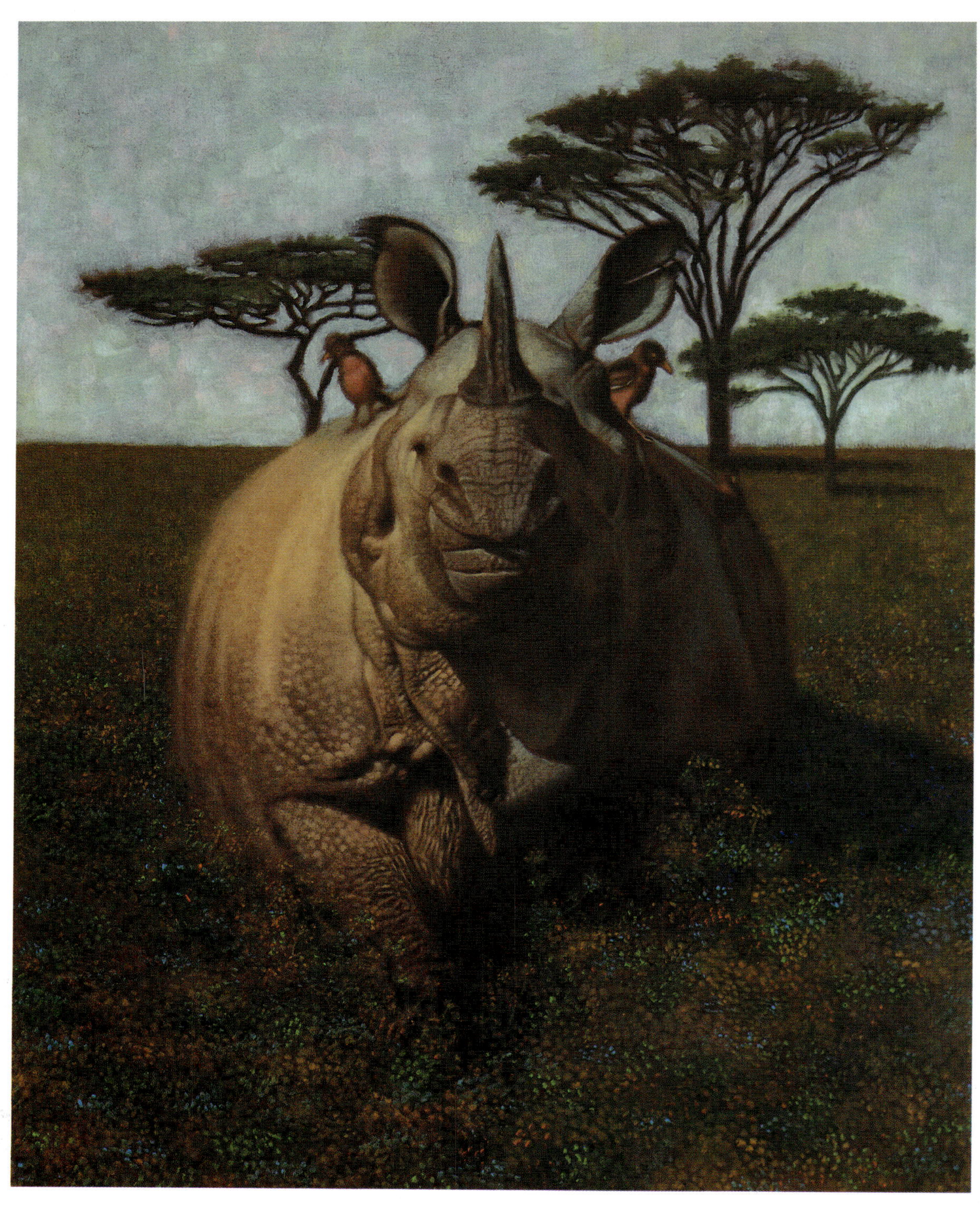

**UNTITLED**

M. JOHN ENGLISH

IN 1985 THERE WERE ONLY
7,500 AFRICAN RHINOS LEFT.
SINCE THERE IS NO ADEQUATE WAY
TO CONTROL THE POACHERS, WHO
KNOWS HOW MANY REMAIN?

...........................

1985 GAB ES NUR NOCH
7500 AFRIKANISCHE NASHÖRNER.
WEIL ES KEINE MÖGLICHKEIT GIBT,
DEN WILDERERN EINHALT ZU
GEBIETEN, FRAGT SICH,
WIEVIELE ÜBRIG BLEIBEN.

...........................

EN 1985, IL NE RESTAIT
QUE 7500 RHINOCÉROS AFRICAINS.
COMME ON NE CONTRÔLE PAS
VRAIMENT LE BRACONNAGE,
ON PEUT SE DEMANDER COMBIEN
ILS SONT AUJOURD'HUI.

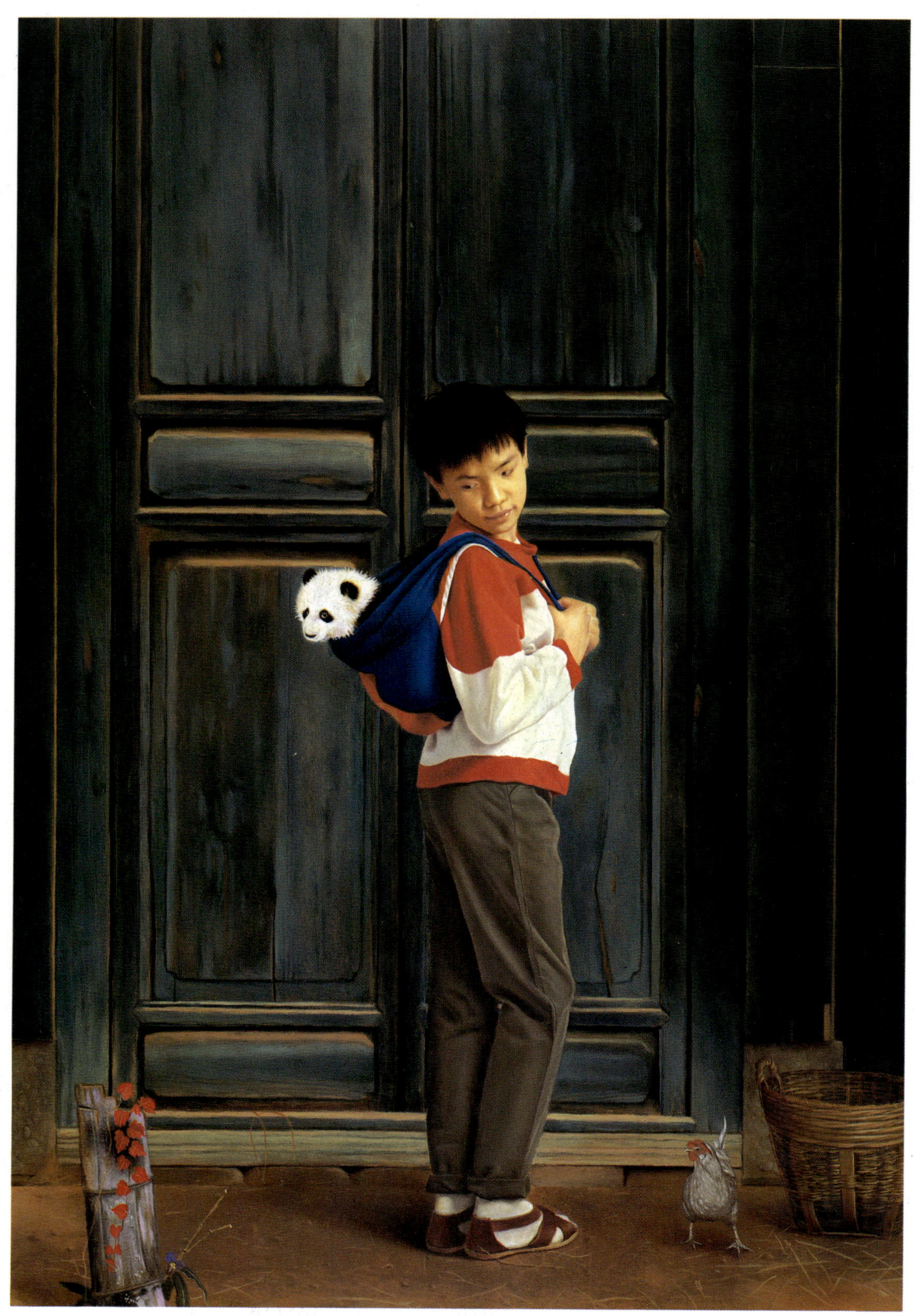

**THE YEAR OF THE PANDA**

Kam Mak

*Oil on panel*

"The increasing human population is threatening to destroy many animal habitats on earth. When all the animals disappear, what will be next?"

IT HAS BEEN ESTIMATED THAT WE COULD LOSE MORE THAN 25 PERCENT OF THE WORLD'S SPECIES IN THE NEXT COUPLE OF DECADES. THIS WOULD AMOUNT TO THE GREATEST BIOLOGICAL DEBACLE SINCE THE DINOSAURS DISAPPEARED 65 MILLION YEARS AGO.

..........................

WIR WERDEN MÖGLICHERWEISE ÜBER 25% ALLER ARTEN IN DEN NÄCHSTEN JAHRZEHNTEN VERLIEREN. DAS WÄRE DAS GRÖSSTE BIOLOGISCHE DEBAKEL, SEIT DIE DINOSAURIER VOR 65 MILLIONEN JAHREN VON DER ERDE VERSCHWANDEN.

..........................

25% DES ESPÈCES DEVRAIENT DISPARAÎTRE DANS LES 20 PROCHAINES ANNÉES. CE SERAIT LE PLUS GRAND DÉSASTRE BIOLOGIQUE DEPUIS L'EXTINCTION DES DINOSAURES IL Y A 65 MILLIONS D'ANNÉES.

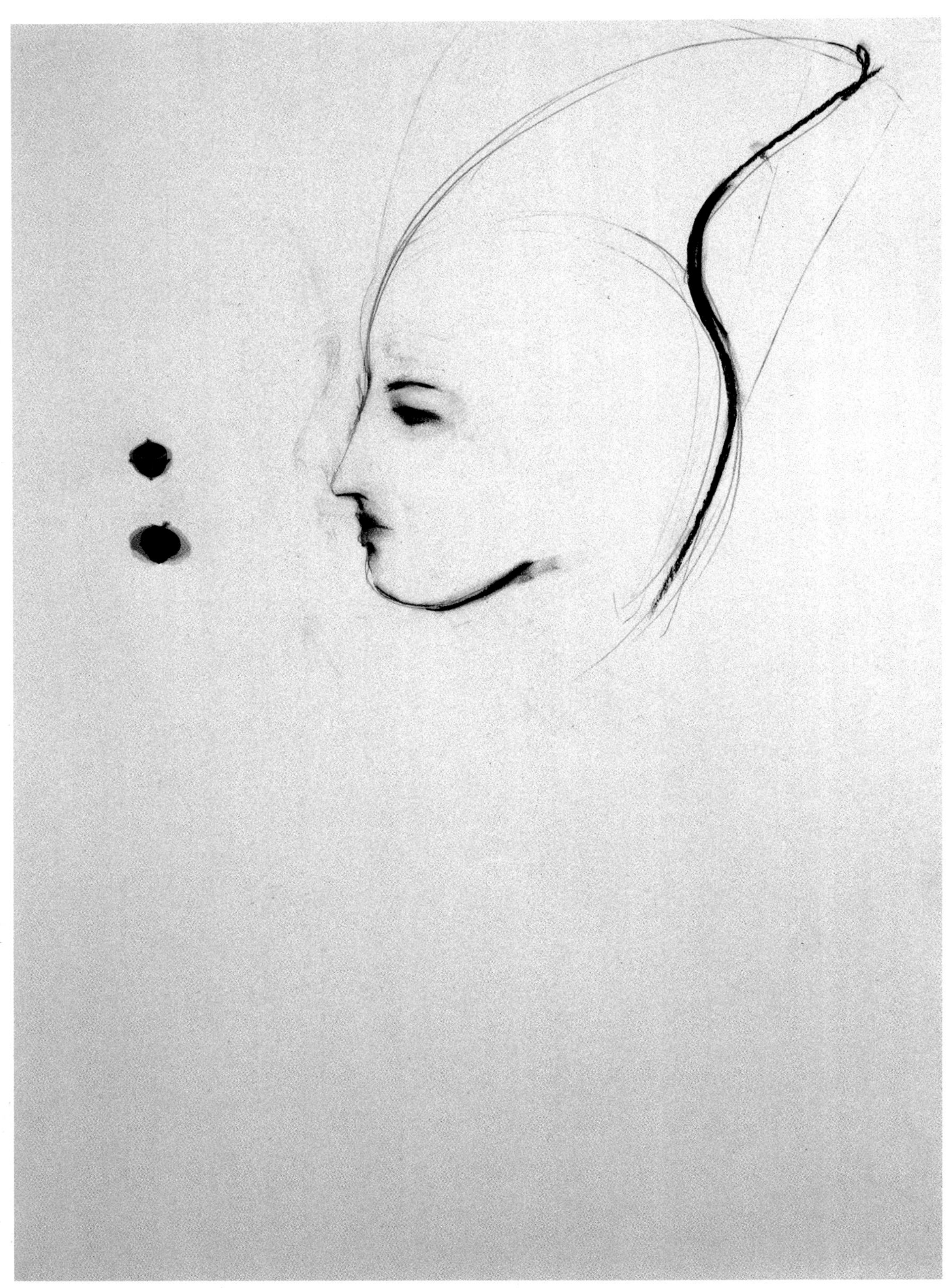

**ROCK AND EUCALYPTUS NUT**

DAGMAR FRINTA

*CHARCOAL AND FOUND OBJECTS ON PAPER*

"I FOUND THIS ROCK ON THE BEACH. THE NUT I FOUND ON AN ISLAND NEAR A MONASTERY. THERE IS SO MUCH BEAUTY AND MYSTERY IN NATURE. IF WE CAN STOP AND SEE IT, PERHAPS WE WOULDN'T BE SO DRIVEN AND FEELING SO EMPTY AND HUNGRY FOR SOMETHING MAGICAL."

IN MAY, 1989, THE UNITED NATIONS ENVIRONMENTAL PROGRAMME (UNEP), REPRESENTING THE WORLD'S GOVERNMENTS AND WITH 103 IN ATTENDANCE, APPROVED AN AGENDA OF EIGHT PRIORITY AREAS IN WHICH IT PLANS TO ALLOCATE AT LEAST 70 PERCENT OF ITS RESOURCES.

..........................

IM MAI 1989 STIMMTE DAS UNITED NATIONS ENVIRONMENT PROGRAM, DAS DIE REGIERUNGEN DER WELT VERTRITT, BEI ANWESENHEIT VON 103 MITGLIEDERN EINER LISTE VON ACHT GEBIETEN ZU, DENEN WENIGSTENS 70 PROZENT DER UNEP-GELDMITTEL ZUKOMMEN SOLLEN.

..........................

EN MAI 1989, LE UNITED NATIONS ENVIRONMENT PROGRAM (UNEP), QUI REPRÉSENTE LES GOUVERNEMENTS DU MONDE ENTIER, A DÉSIGNÉ EN PRÉSENCE DE 103 MEMBRES LES HUIT ZONES PRIORITAIRES QUI RECEVRONT 70% DES AIDES FINANCIÈRES DE L'UNEP.

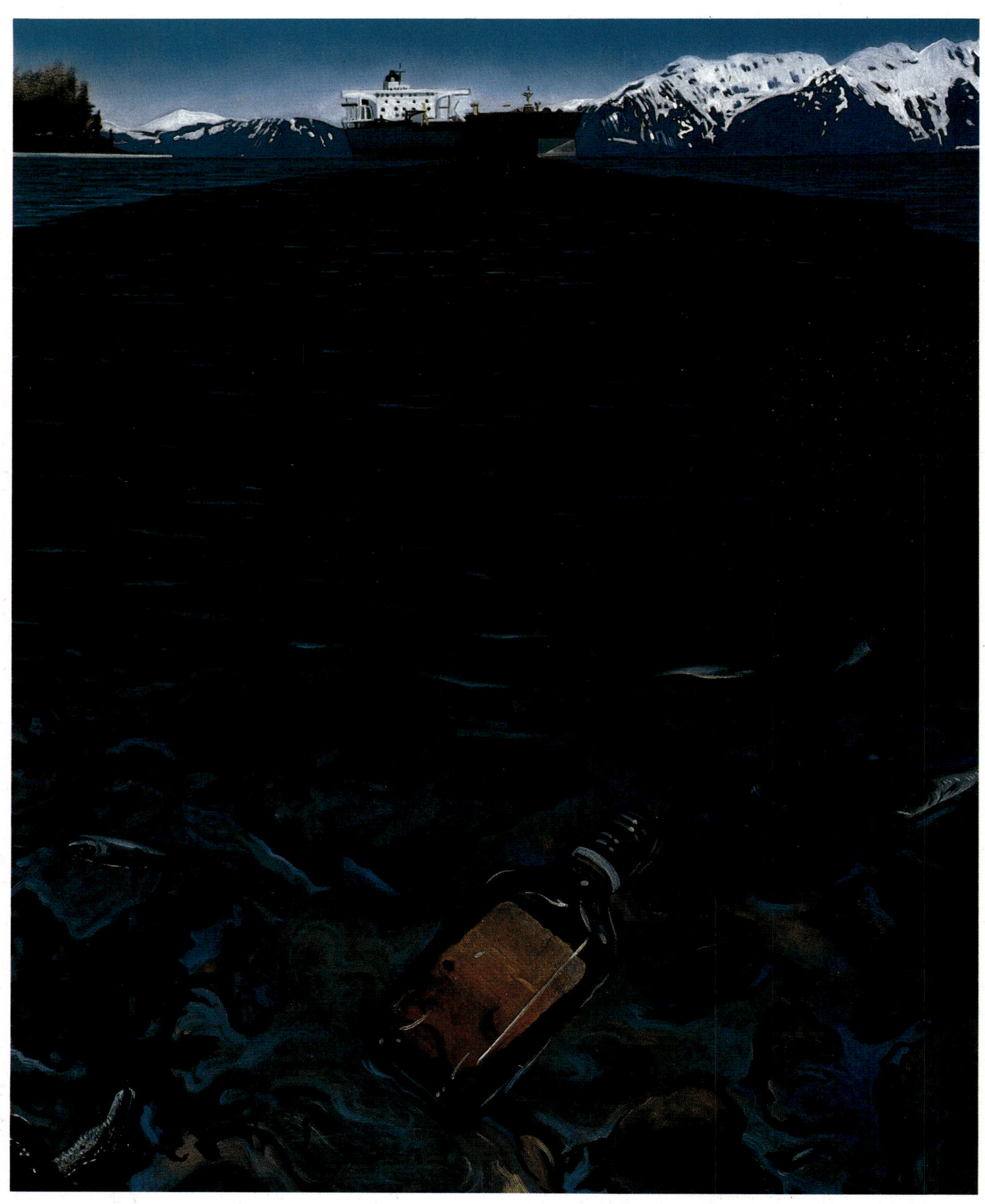

**ON THE ROCKS**

JULIAN ALLEN

*OIL*

"I WANTED TO FOCUS ON THE DEVASTATING EFFECT THAT THE ABUSE OF ALCOHOL AND DRUGS HAS HAD ON HUMAN BEHAVIOR. UNDER THEIR INFLUENCE, PEOPLE TAKE RISKS THEY WOULD NOT NORMALLY TAKE. THE GROUNDING OF THE VALDEZ WAS ALLEGEDLY THE RESULT OF HEAVY DRINKING ON BEHALF OF THE CAPTAIN. MY PAINTING IS AN ATTEMPT TO PRESENT THIS BEHAVIOR AS A METAPHOR FOR A GROWING, CLUMSY DISREGARD FOR THE WORLD."

THE EXXON VALDEZ
OIL SPILL IN ALASKA'S PRINCE
WILLIAM SOUND COVERED 7,800
SQUARE KILOMETERS AND
CONTAMINATED 650 KILOMETERS
OF SHORELINE. MORE THAN
20,000 DEAD BIRDS AND 725
DEAD SEA OTTERS HAVE
BEEN RECOVERED.

..........................

DER DURCH DIE EXXON-VALDEZ-
ÖLKATASTROPHE IN ALASKAS
PRINCE WILLIAM SUND
ENTSTANDENE ÖLTEPPICH WAR
7800 QUADRATKILOMETER GROSS
UND VERSEUCHTE EINEN
KÜSTENSTREIFEN VON 650 KM.
MEHR ALS 20 000 VÖGEL UND 725
MEEROTTER FANDEN DEN TOD.

..........................

LA NAPPE DE PÉTROLE QUI
S'EST ÉCHAPPÉE DES SOUTES DU
EXXON VALDEZ LORS DE
L'ACCIDENT DE PRINCE WILLIAM EN
ALASKA S'ÉTENDAIT SUR 7'800
KILOMÈTRES CARRÉS. ELLE A
SOUILLÉ 650 KILOMÈTRES DE CÔTE.
PLUS DE 20 000 OISEAUX ET 725
LOUTRES DE MER TROUVÈRENT
LA MORT.

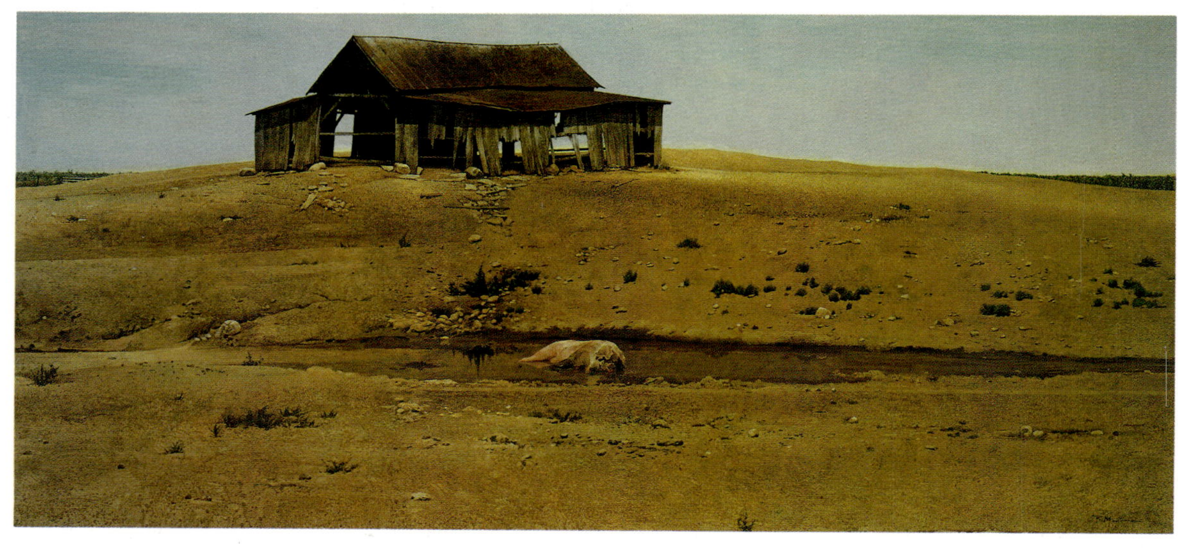

**THE HOG'S LOT**

ROBERT E. McGINNIS

*EGG TEMPERA*

"OBLIVIOUS TO APPROACHING DOOM, HE SLEEPS ON IN BLISSFUL REPOSE... REAL HOGS DON'T KNOW ANY BETTER—OTHERS SHOULD."

DUE IN PART TO THE INTENSE USE OF TOXINS IN THE UNITED STATES, THE RATE OF CANCER IS RISING BY 2 PERCENT EACH YEAR.

.........................

DER INTENSIVE GEBRAUCH VON GIFTSTOFFEN IN DEN USA WIRD ALS EIN GRUND FÜR DIE ERHÖHUNG DER KREBS-ERKRANKUNGEN UM ZWEI PROZENT PRO JAHR GENANNT.

.........................

AUX ÉTATS-UNIS, LE TAUX DE CANCERS, DUS EN GRANDE PARTIE À L'UTILISATION DE PRODUITS TOXIQUES, AUGMENTE DE DEUX POUR CENT CHAQUE ANNÉE.

IN A LIFETIME, ONE COULD GENERATE 600 TIMES ONE'S OWN WEIGHT IN SOLID WASTE.

........................

EIN MENSCH KANN IN SEINEM LEBEN DAS 600FACHE SEINES KÖRPERGEWICHTS AN FESTEN ABFALLSTOFFEN PRODUZIEREN.

........................

L'HOMME PEUT PRODUIRE AU COURS DE SA VIE 600 FOIS SON PROPRE POIDS DE DÉCHETS SOLIDES.

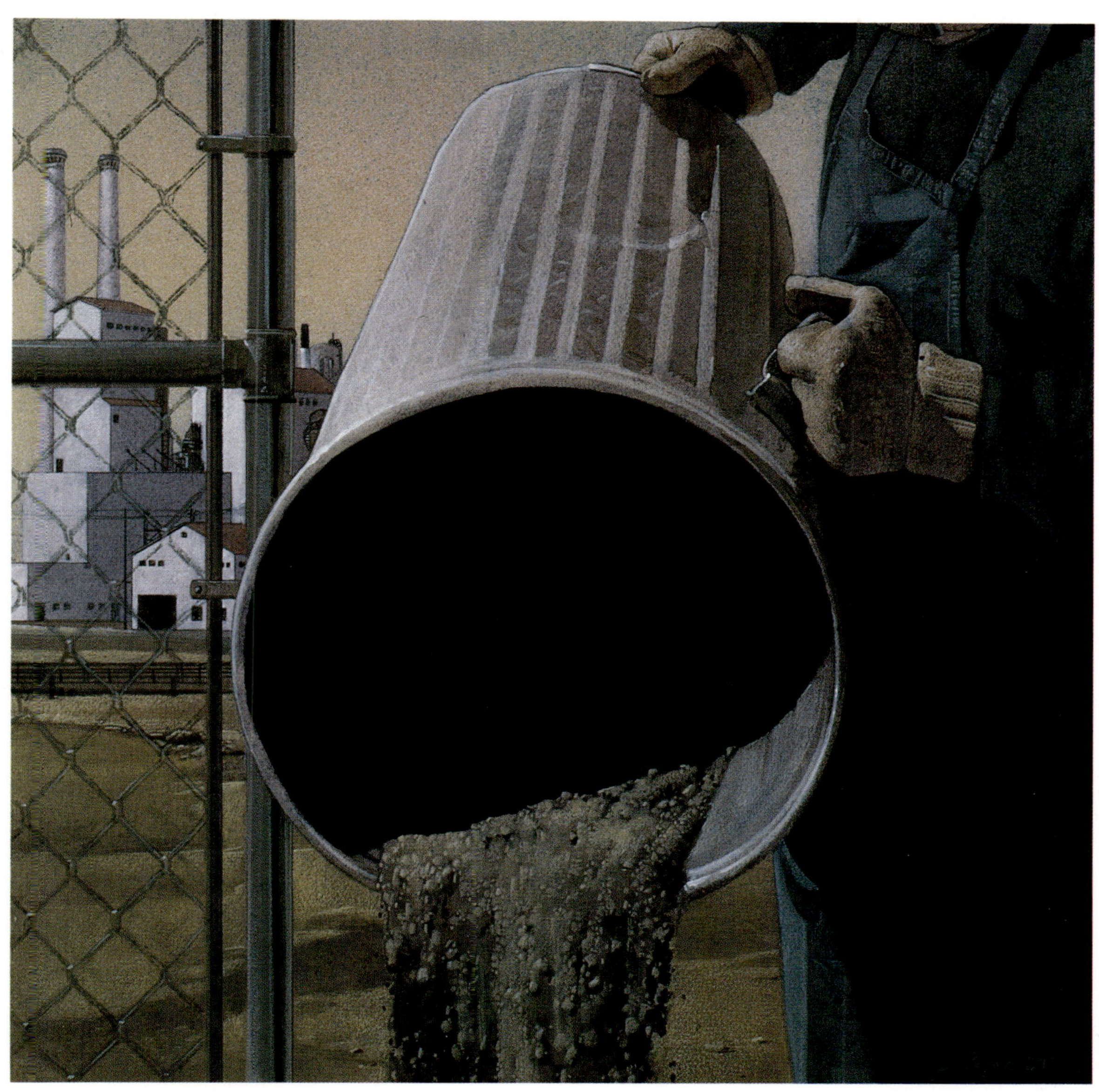

**WHERE DO TOXIC WASTE PLANTS PUT THEIR GARBAGE?**

C. F. Payne

*Mixed media*

THE BURNING OF FORESTS INTRODUCES MILLIONS OF TONS OF GREENHOUSE GASES AND POLLUTANTS INTO OUR AIR.

. . . . . . . . . . . . . . . . . . . . . . . . .

DIE TROPISCHEN WÄLDER HALTEN DIE SCHÄDEN VON NATÜRLICHEN STÜRMEN IN GRENZEN, INDEM SIE WIND ABSORBIEREN UND DIE KÜSTENSTREIFEN VOR EROSION SCHÜTZEN. JEDES JAHR WERDEN

. . . . . . . . . . . . . . . . . . . . . . . . .

LA DESTRUCTION DES FORÊTS PAR LE FEU EST SOURCE DE POLLUTION ATMOSPHÉRIQUE ET ACCENTUE L'EFFET DE SERRE.

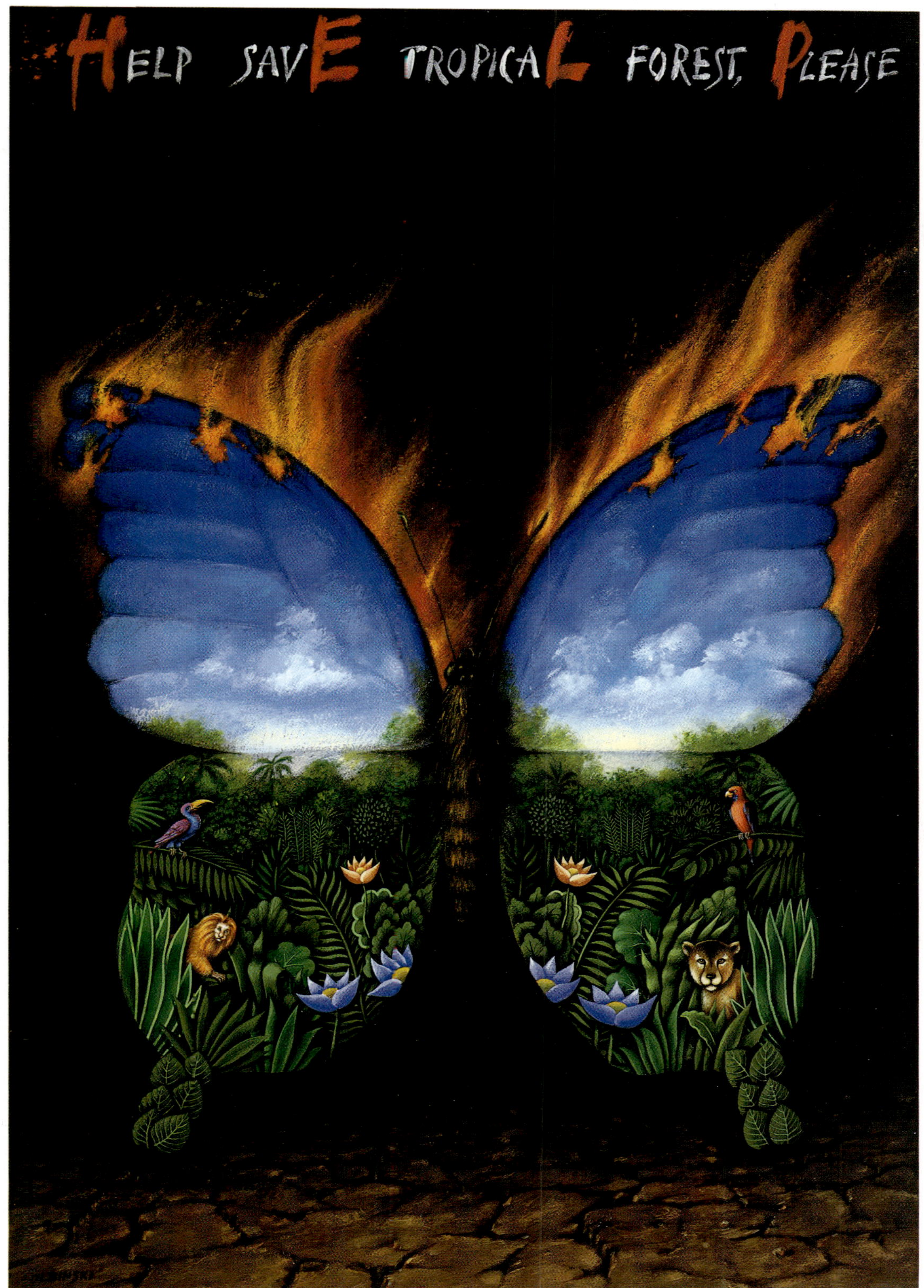


**HELP SAVE THE TROPICAL FOREST**

J. Rafal Olbinski

*Acrylic*

"The artwork was created with the intention to protect against the burning of tropical rainforest and, in a broader sense, the destruction of the fragile beauty of our planet by the greed and ignorance of its inhabitants."

OF THE MORE THAN 48,000 CHEMICALS LISTED BY THE EPA, NEXT TO NOTHINGIS KNOWN ABOUT THE TOXICEFFECTS OF ALMOST 38,000. FEWER THAN 1,000 HAVE BEEN TESTED FOR ACUTE EFFECTS AND ONLY ABOUT 500 FOR THEIR CANCER-CAUSING, REPRODUCTIVE OR MUTAGENIC EFFECTS.

..........................

BEI FAST 38 000 DER ÜBER 48 000 VON DER UMWELTBEHÖRDE GELISTETEN CHEMIKALIEN WEISS MAN SO GUT WIE NICHTS ÜBER DIE SCHÄDLICHEN AUSWIRKUNGEN.

..........................

PARMI LES QUELQUES 40 000 PRODUITS CHIMIQUES ENREGISTRÉS AUX USA, ON NE SAIT QUASIMENT RIEN DES EFFETS TOXIQUES DE 38 000 D'ENTRE EUX.

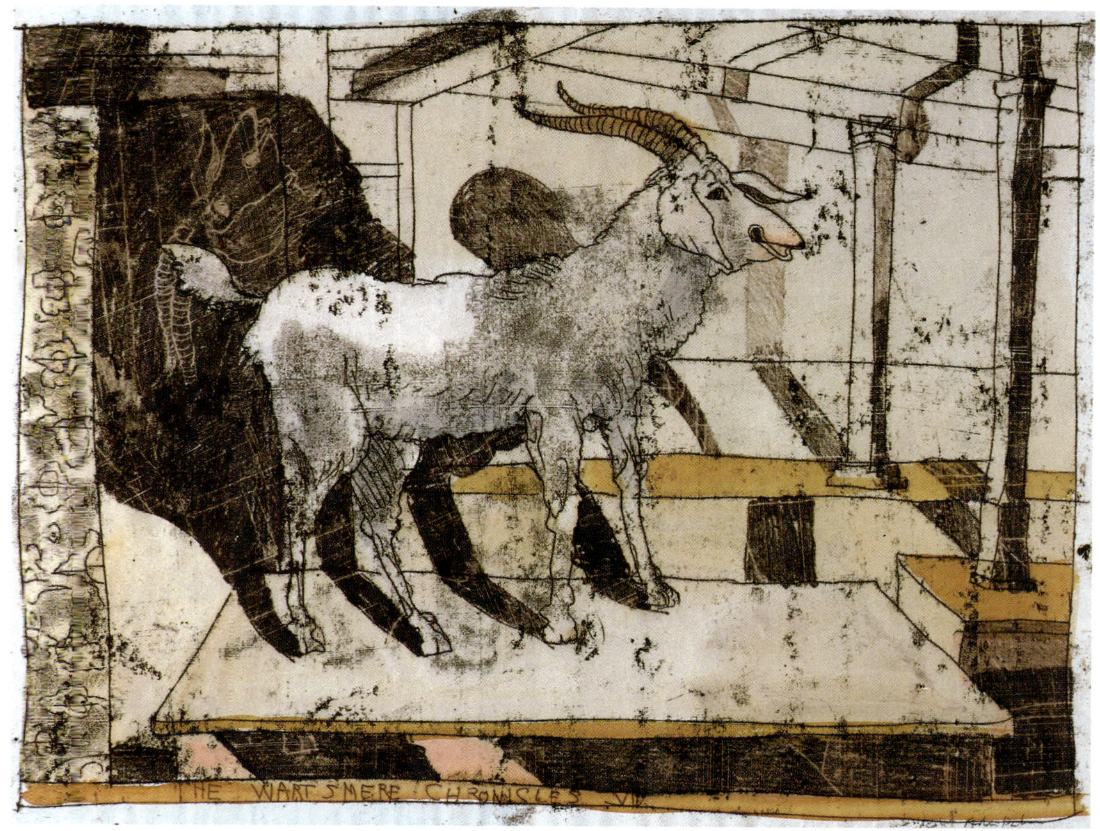



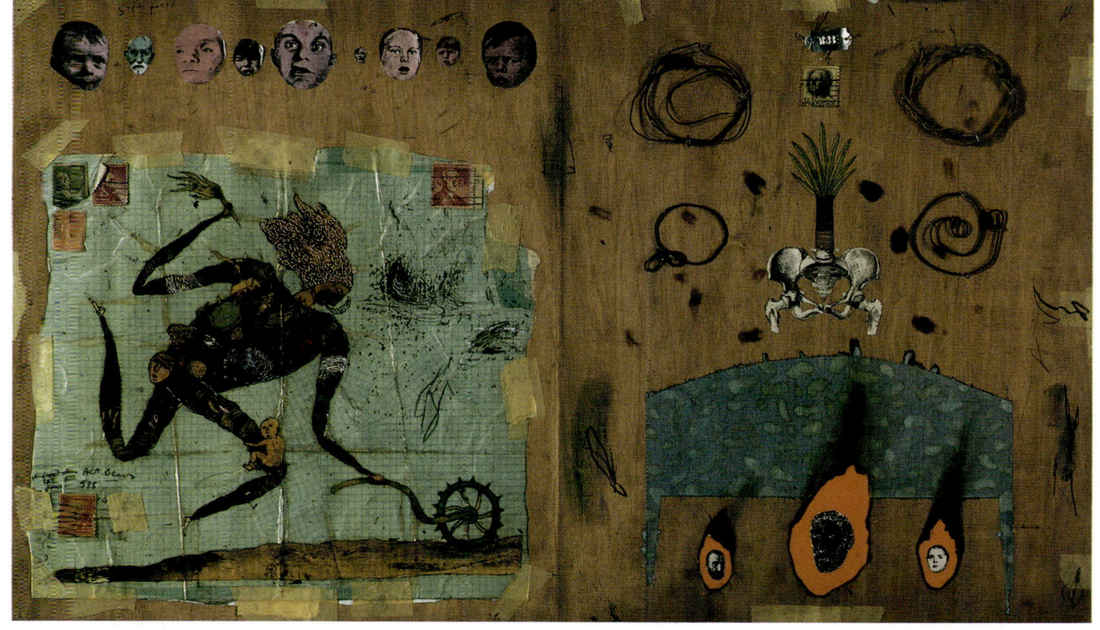

**UNTITLED**

Robert Andrew Parker

*Monoprint*

**RAKE & RAPE**

Henrik Drescher

*Mixed media*

"A notebook page about the environment."

AT LEAST 12 PERCENT OF
THE BIRD SPECIES IN THE AMAZON
BASIN AS WELL AS 15 PERCENT OF
THE PLANTS IN CENTRAL
AND SOUTH AMERICA CAN BE
COUNTED AMONG WHAT BIOLOGIST
DAVID JANZEN CALLS THE
"LIVING DEAD."

..........................

MINDESTENS 12
PROZENT DER IM AMAZONASBECKEN
HEIMISCHEN VÖGEL UND 15
PROZENT DER PFLANZEN IN MITTEL-
UND SÜDAMERIKA GEHÖREN ZU DEN
«LEBENDEN TOTEN», WIE DER
BIOLOGE DAVID JANZEN ES NENNT.

..........................

AU MOINS 12% DES
OISEAUX DU BASSIN DE
L'AMAZONE, AINSI QUE 15% DES
PLANTES D'AMÉRIQUE CENTRALE ET
D'AMÉRIQUE DU SUD SONT, SELON
L'EXPRESSION DU BIOLOGISTE
DAVID JANSEN, DES «MORTS
VIVANTS».

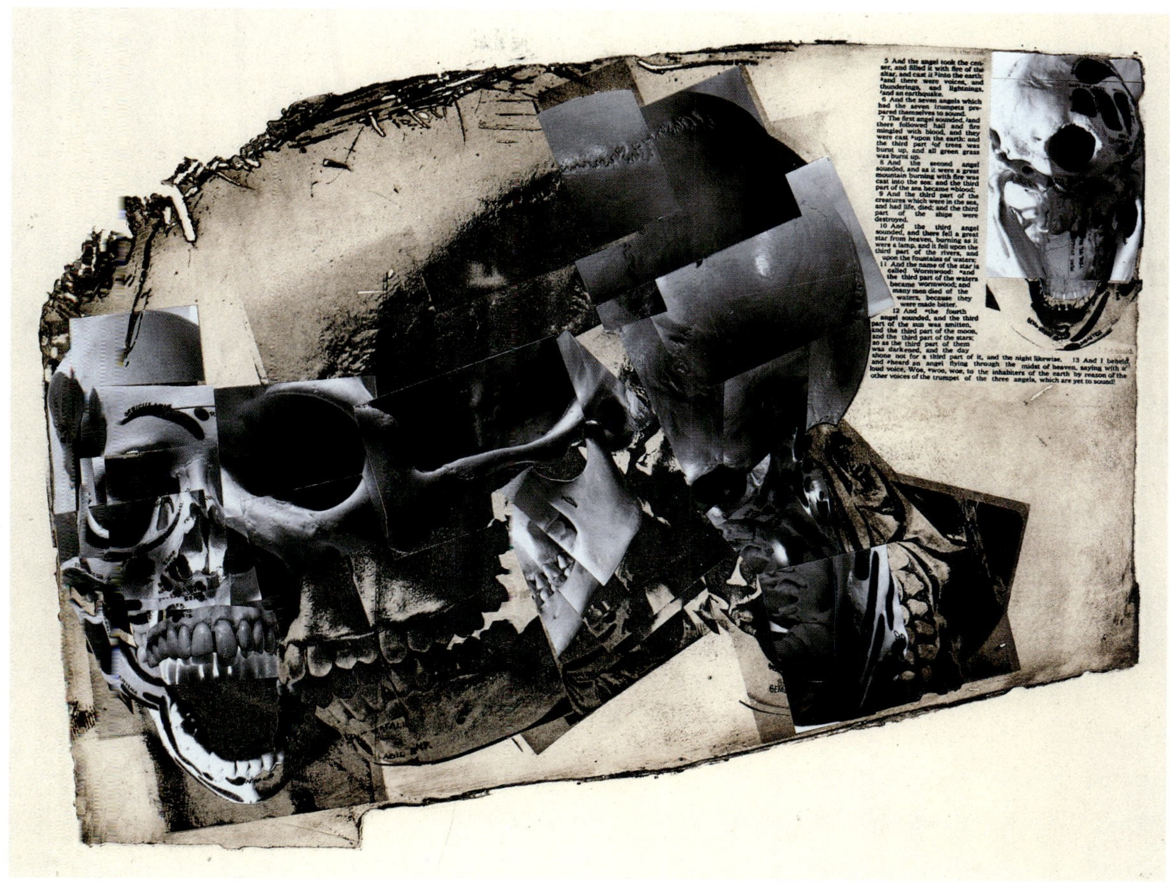


**ENDANGERED SPECIES**

JOHN RUSH

*LITHOGRAPH/ETCHING/PHOTO COLLAGE*

WASTE RECYCLING SAVES ENERGY AND MATERIALS AND REDUCES POLLUTION. THE U.S. RECYCLES ONLY 11 PERCENT OF ITS WASTE. WESTERN EUROPE RECOVERS 30 PERCENT, WHILE JAPAN RECOVERS 50 PERCENT.

..........................

IN DEN USA WERDEN NUR 11 PROZENT DER ABFÄLLE WIEDERVERWERTET. IN WESTEUROPA SIND ES 30 PROZENT, IN JAPAN 50 PROZENT.

..........................

LES ÉTATS-UNIS RECYCLENT SEULEMENT 11 POUR CENT DE LEURS DÉCHETS, L'EUROPE DE L'OUEST, 30 POUR CENT, LE JAPON, 50 POUR CENT.

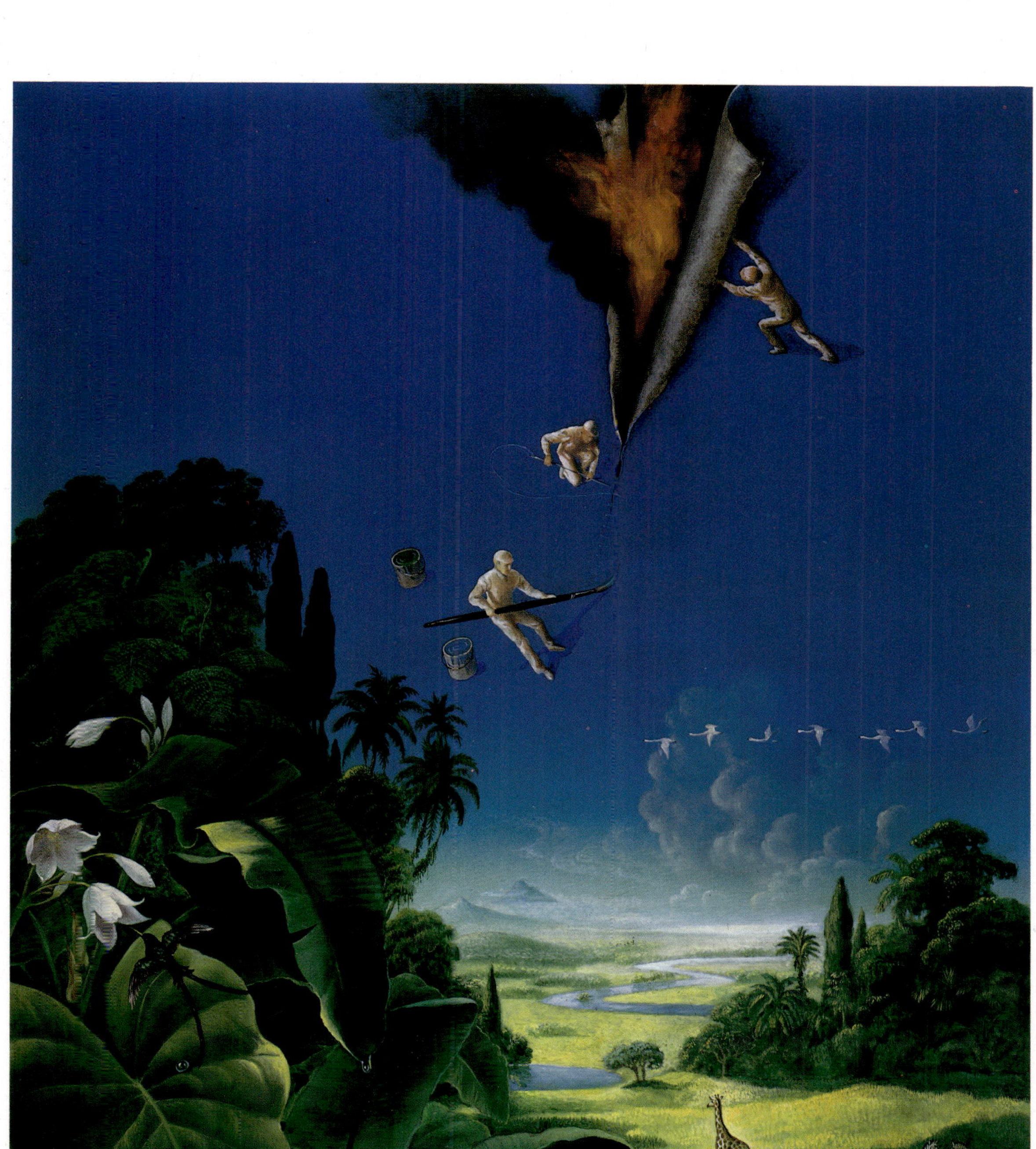

**THE MENDING OF THE ENVIRONMENT**

KINUKO Y. CRAFT

*OIL ON CANVAS*

"THE IMAGE ILLUSTRATED AN ARTICLE ABOUT IDEAS FOR ALL OF US TO USE FOR THE GOOD OF THE ENVIRONMENT IN *CREATIVE LIVING MAGAZINE*."

CLOSED AND OPEN FORESTS,
SHRUBLANDS, AND FOREST
REGROWTH COVER ABOUT 40
PERCENT OF THE WORLD'S LAND.

.........................

GROSSE UND KLEINE WALDGEBIETE,
BUSCHLAND UND GEBIETE, DIE
AUFGEFORSTET WERDEN, MACHEN
40 PROZENT DER LANDFLÄCHE
DER ERDE AUS.

.........................

LES FORÊTS DENSES, LES BOIS,
LE BOCAGE, LA BROUSSE ET
LES ESPACES REBOISÉS COUVRENT
ENVIRON 40% DE LA
SURFACE DU GLOBE.

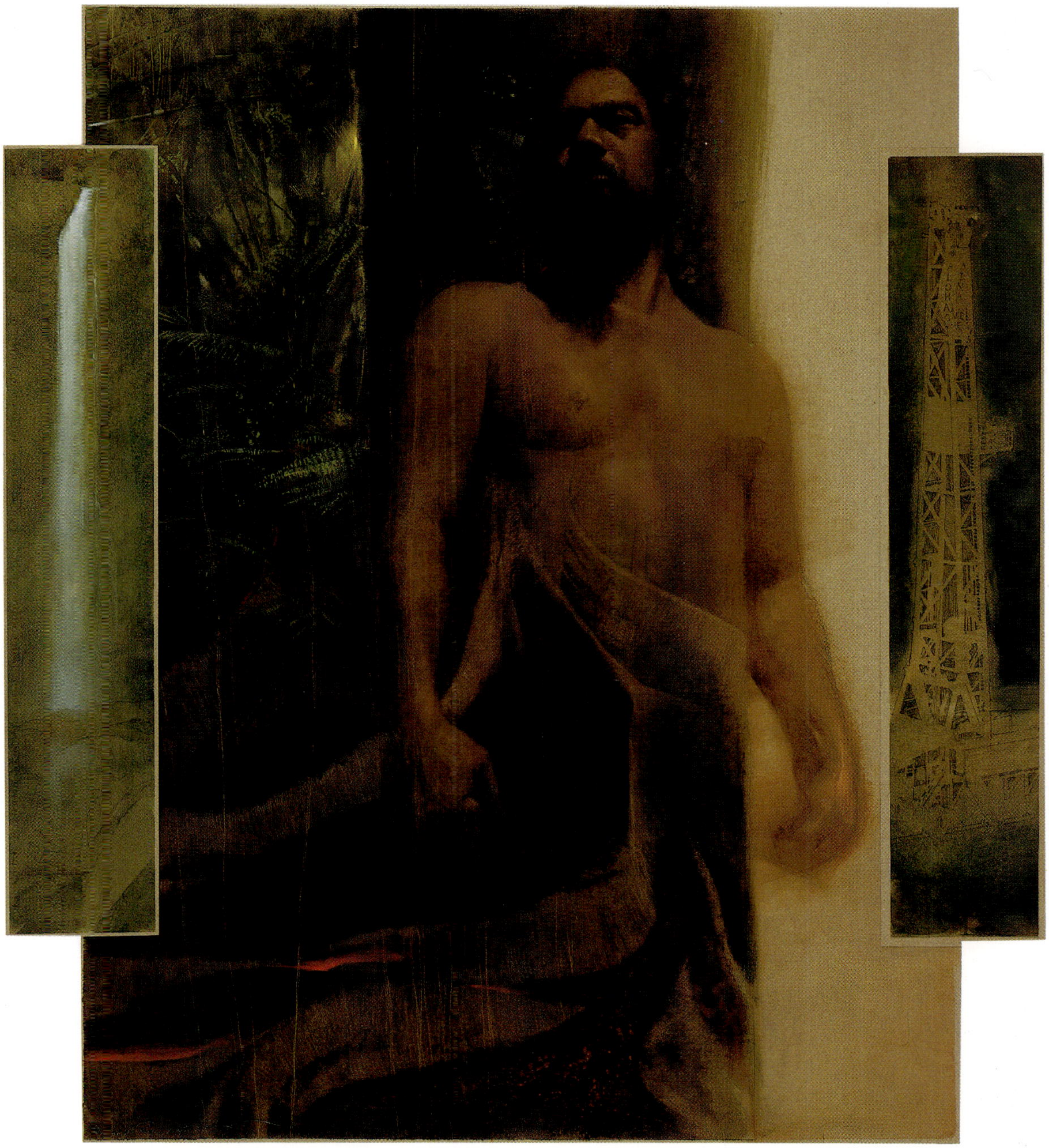

**PELE'S APPEAL**

Robert Hunt

*Oil on canvas*

"The slopes of the Kiluaea volcano on the island of Hawaii, where a 500-megawatt geothermal power station is under development, is the only lowland tropical rainforest in the U.S. Besides the damage to the forest ecosystem from construction, drilling into the volcano is an affront to the religious beliefs of many native Hawaiians. The wells will never replace Hawaii's current oil use, and at best will contribute to uncontrolled development."

REFORESTING 130 MILLION HECTARES WOULD CUT THE RELEASE OF CARBON FROM ALL HUMAN ACTIVITIES BY 8 TO 11 PERCENT.

........................

DIE AUFFORSTUNG VON 130 MILLIONEN HEKTAREN WÜRDE DIE DURCH DEN MENSCHEN VERURSACHTE FREISETZUNG VON KOHLENWASSERSTOFF UM 8-11 PROZENT VERRINGERN.

........................

LE REBOISEMENT DE 130 MILLIONS D'HECTARES POURRAIT FAIRE DIMINUER LES REJETS DE CARBONE PROVENANT DE TOUTES LES ACTIVITÉS HUMAINES DE 8 À 11%.

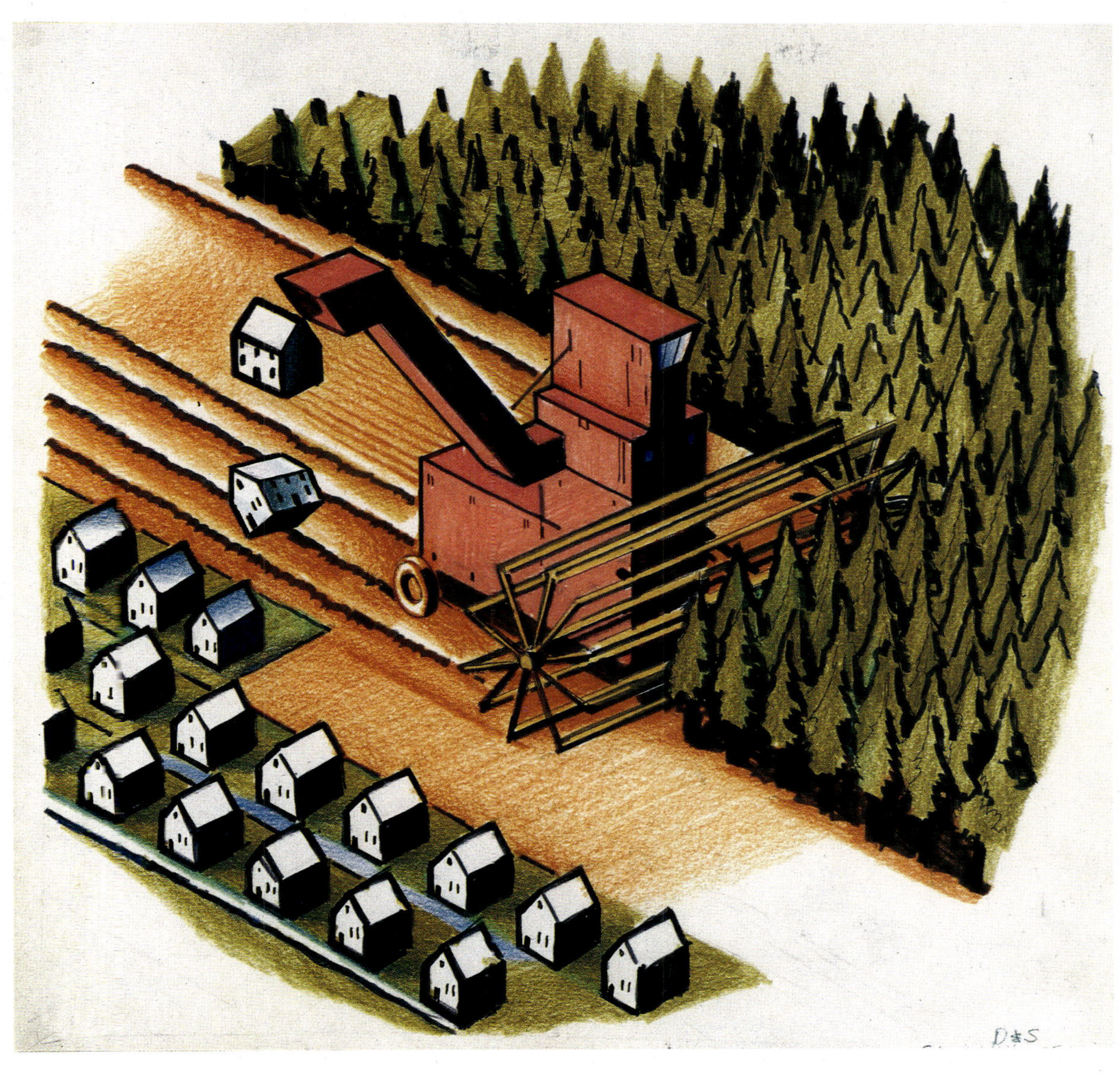

**DE FORESTATION**

David Suter

"Human habitation competes with the earth's regenerative processes."

IN DEVELOPED NATIONS, CHLORINE HAS BEEN ADDED TO THE PUBLIC WATER SUPPLY TO REMOVE PATHOGENS THAT ARE STILL HARMFUL TO POPULATIONS IN DEVELOPING NATIONS. FRESH WATER IN INDUSTRIAL NATIONS IS CONTAMINATED BY INDUSTRIAL AND AGRICULTURAL POLLUTANTS.

..........................

IN DEN ENTWICKLUNGSLÄNDERN WURDE DEM LEITUNGSWASSER CHLOR BEIGESETZT, UM KRANKHEITSERREGER ABZUTÖTEN, DIE FÜR DIE BEVÖLKERUNG DIESER LÄNDER NOCH EINE BEDROHUNG DARSTELLEN. FRISCHWASSER IN DEN INDUSTRIENATIONEN WIRD DURCH INDUSTRIE- UND LANDWIRTSCHAFTLICHE SCHADSTOFFE VERSCHMUTZT.

..........................

DANS LES PAYS EN VOIE DE DÉVELOPPEMENT, L'EAU DU ROBINET EST ADDITIONNÉE DE CHLORE AFIN DE LA PURIFIER DES AGENTS PATHOGÈNES QUI MENACENT PARTICULIÈREMENT LES POPULATIONS. DANS LES PAYS INDUSTRIALISÉS, L'EAU POTABLE EST CONTAMINÉE PAR DES POLLUANTS INDUSTRIELS OU AGRICOLES.

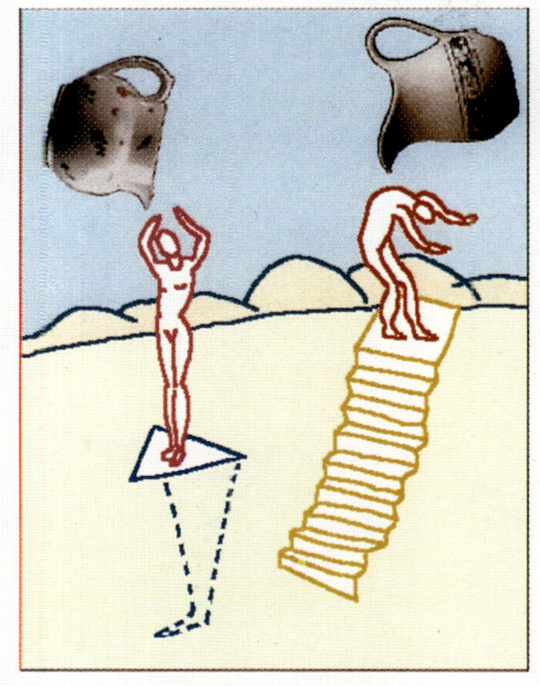

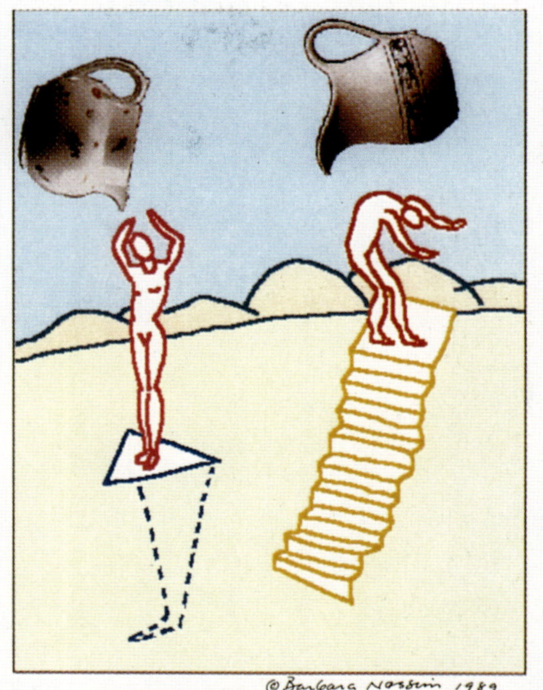


## WATER, WATER, EVERYWHERE;
## NOT A DROP TO DRINK

BARBARA NESSIM

*COMPUTER PAINTING*

"OUR LACK OF RESPECT FOR THE ENVIRONMENT HAS GREATLY DIMINISHED OUR NATURAL RESOURCES. I FOCUS ON WATER BECAUSE IT IS ONE OF EARTH'S MOST PRECIOUS ELEMENTS. IN MY CREATION OF THE SURREAL 3-D ENVIRONMENT, THE PLACEMENT OF THE FIGURES AND EMPTY PITCHER UNDERSCORES THE PARADOX OF OUR DISTANT PROXIMITY WITH NATURE."

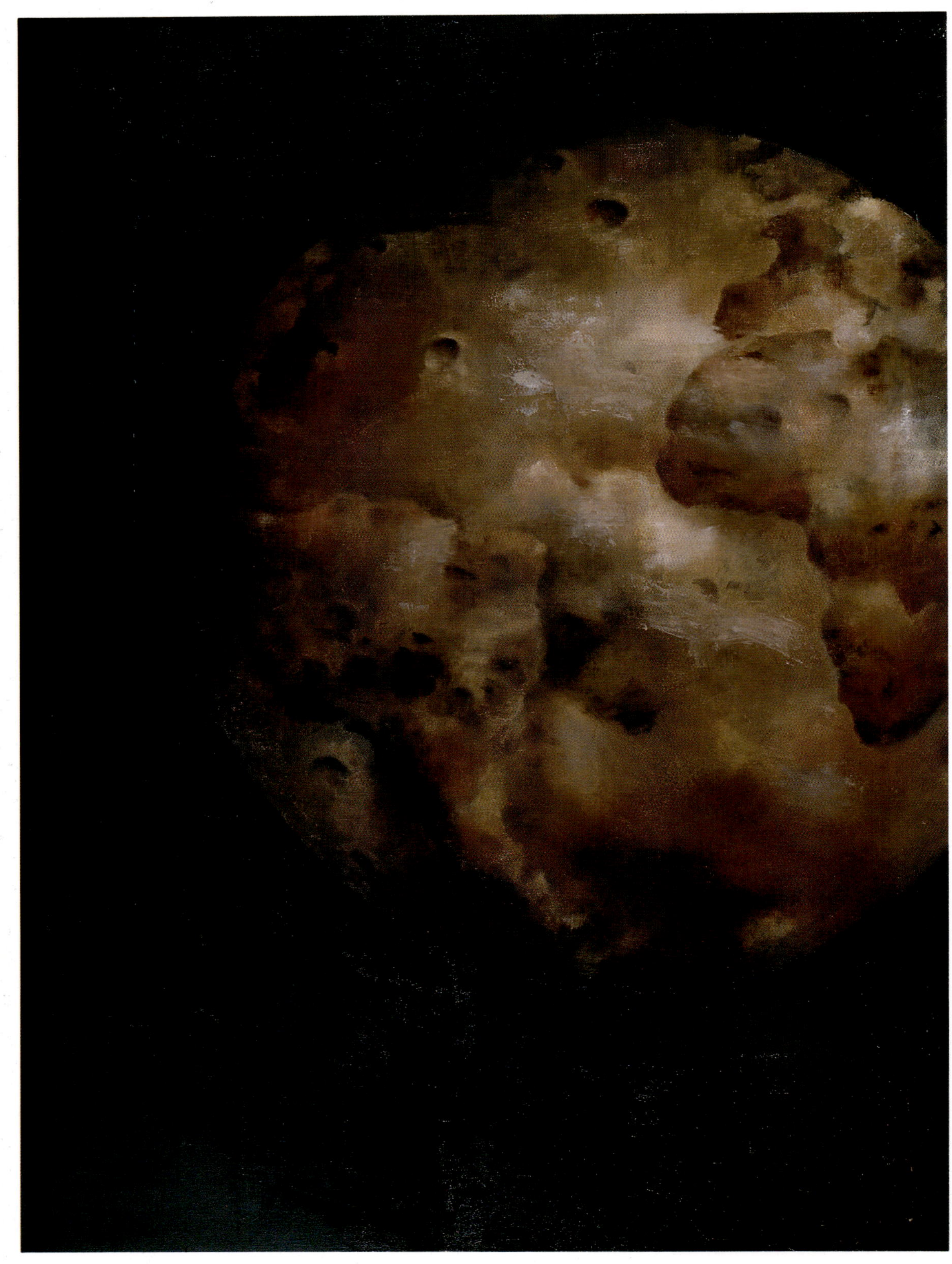

**THE FALL FROM GRACE**

Brad Holland

*Oil on canvas*

THE ENVIRONMENTAL DEFENSE FUND AND THE NATURAL RESOURCES DEFENSE COUNCIL REGULATE AND LITIGATE AGAINST THE GOVERNMENT AND THE ENVIRONMENTAL PROTECTION AGENCY IN FAVOR OF THE ENVIRONMENT.

..........................

DER ENVIRONMENTAL DEFENSE FUND UND DER NATURAL RESOURCES DEFENSE COUNCIL SETZEN SICH GEGENÜBER DER REGIERUNG UND DER STAATLICHEN UMWELTBEHÖRDE AUCH AUF DEM GERICHTSWEG FÜR DIE UMWELT EIN.

..........................

POUR DÉFENDRE LA NATURE, LE ENVIRONMENTAL DEFENSE FUND ET LE NATURAL RESOURCES DEFENSE COUNCIL S'OPPOSENT JURIDIQUEMENT AU GOUVERNEMENT ET AUX RESPONSABLES OFFICIELS DE L'ENVIRONNEMENT.

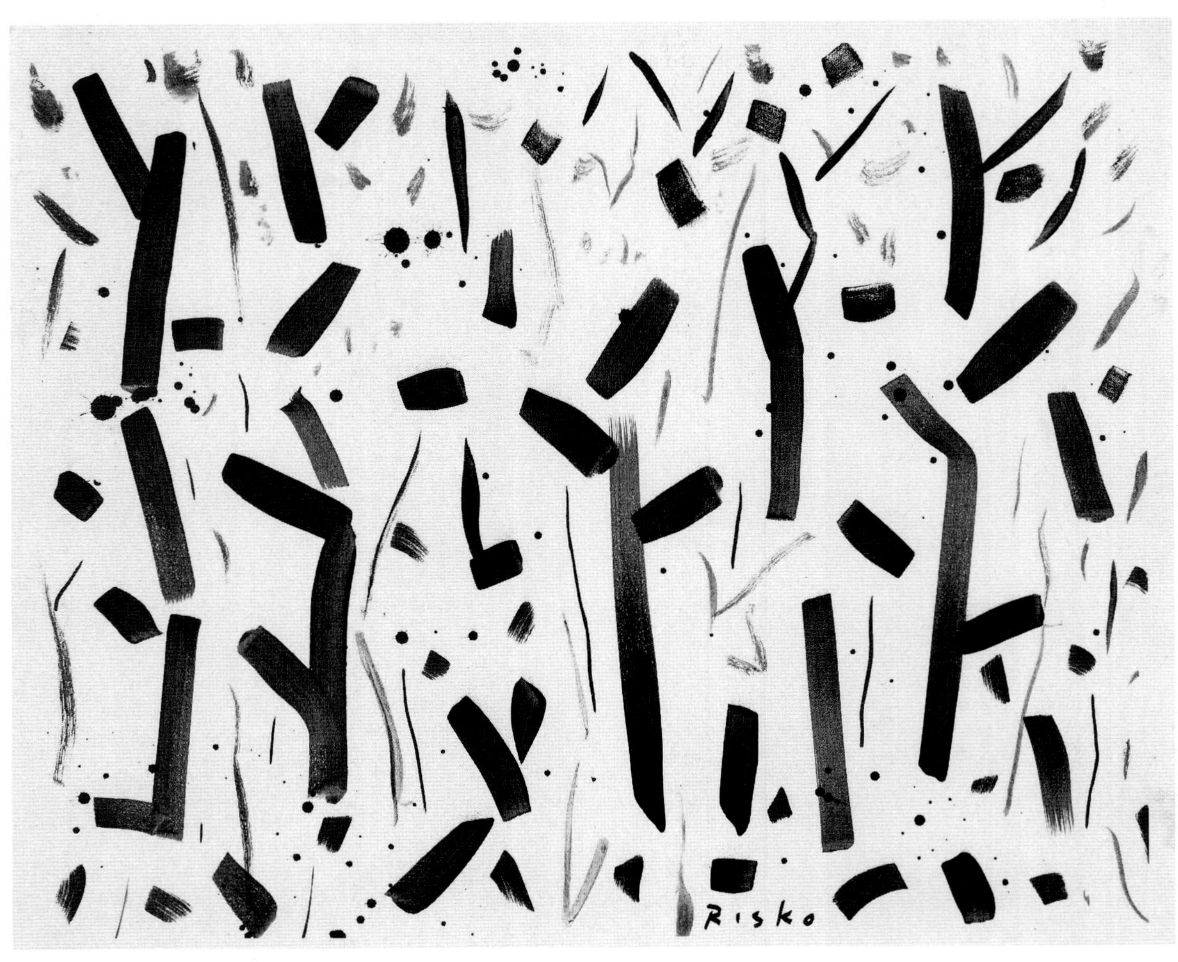


**ACID RAIN**

ROBERT RISKO

*ACRYLIC ON CANVAS*

"THE BLEAK AND COLORLESS FUTURE OF A POLLUTED WORLD."

ELECTRIC UTILITIES IN THE UNITED STATES ARE RESPONSIBLE FOR EMITTING 65 PERCENT OF OUR ATMOSPHERE'S SULPHUR DIOXIDE, A PRIMARY COMPONENT OF ACID RAIN.

...........................

DIE ELEKTRISCHEN GERÄTE IN DEN USA VERURSACHEN 65% DES SCHWEFELDIOXIDGEHALTS IN UNSERER ATMOSPHÄRE, EINE HAUPTURSACHE FÜR DEN SAUREN REGEN.

...........................

AUX ÉTATS-UNIS, LES APPAREILS ÉLECTRIQUES ÉMETTENT DANS L'ATMOSPHÈRE 65% DU DIOXYDE DE SOUFRE, UN DES COMPOSANTS DE BASE DES PLUIES ACIDES.

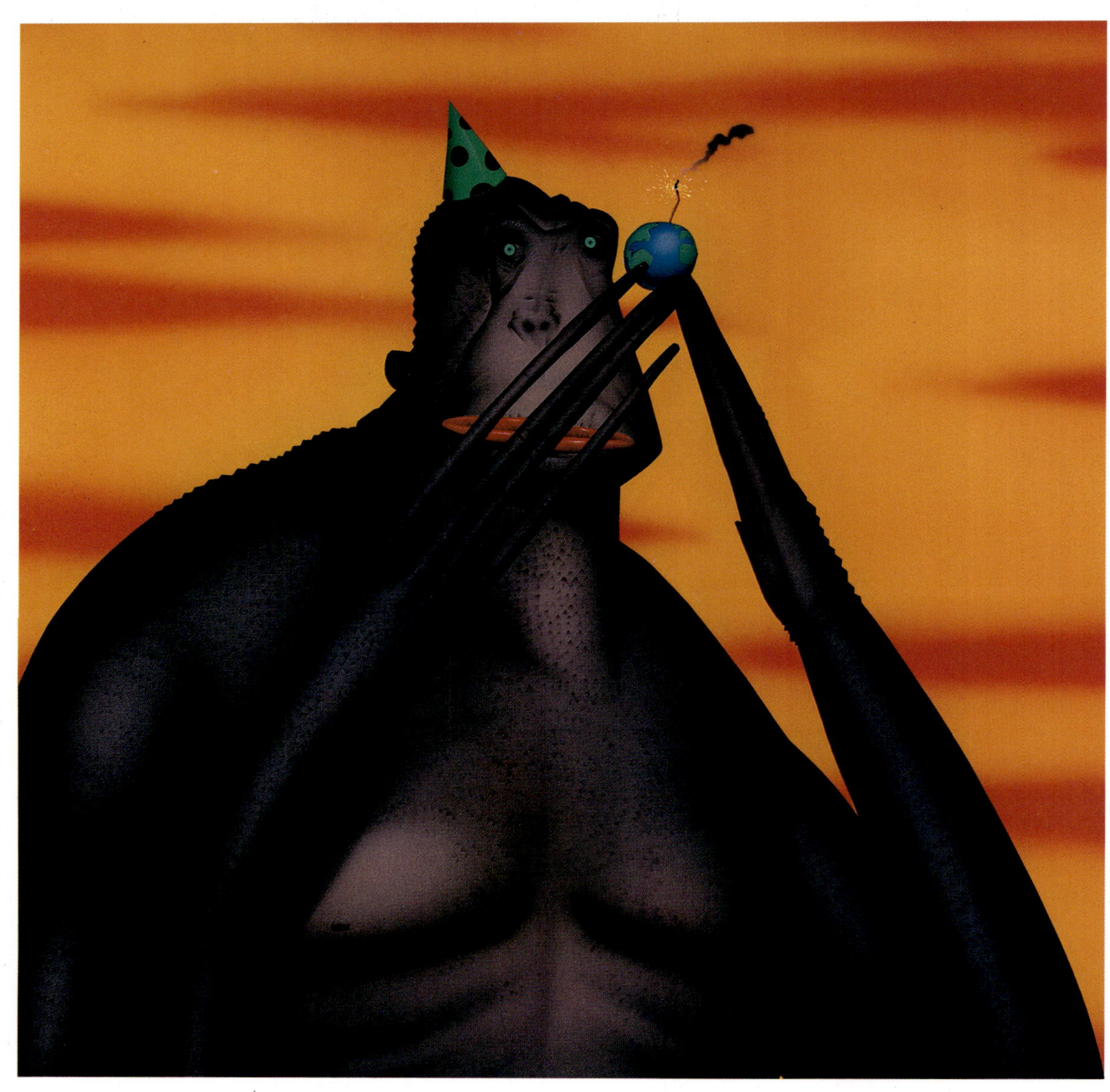

**MONKEY WITH THE EARTH BOMB**

BILL MAYER

*AIRBRUSH, GOUACHE, AND DYES*

"SUDDEN REALIZATION OF WHAT LITTLE TIME IS LEFT WILL BRING US ALL BACK TO THE ORIGINS OF OUR PROBLEMS."

WHILE THE POPULATION OF
ECONOMICALLY DEVELOPED
COUNTRIES WILL DOUBLE IN 120
YEARS, THE POPULATION OF THE
THIRD WORLD, REPRESENTING
THREE-QUARTERS OF THE WORLD
POPULATION, WILL DOUBLE IN
ABOUT 33 YEARS.

..........................

DIE BEVÖLKERUNG DER
INDUSTRIELÄNDER WIRD SICH IN
120 JAHREN VERDOPPELN.
IN DER DRITTEN WELT, DIE
DREIVIERTEL DER GESAMTEN
WELTBEVÖLKERUNG
DARSTELLT, WIRD SIE SICH IN CA.
33 JAHREN VERDOPPELN.

..........................

ALORS QUE LA POPULATION
DES PAYS INDUSTRIELS DEVRAIT
DOUBLER DANS 120 ANS,
CELLE DES PAYS DU TIERS MONDE,
QUI REPRÉSENTE LES TROIS QUART
DE LA POPULATION MONDIALE,
AURA DOUBLÉ DANS ENVIRON
33 ANS.

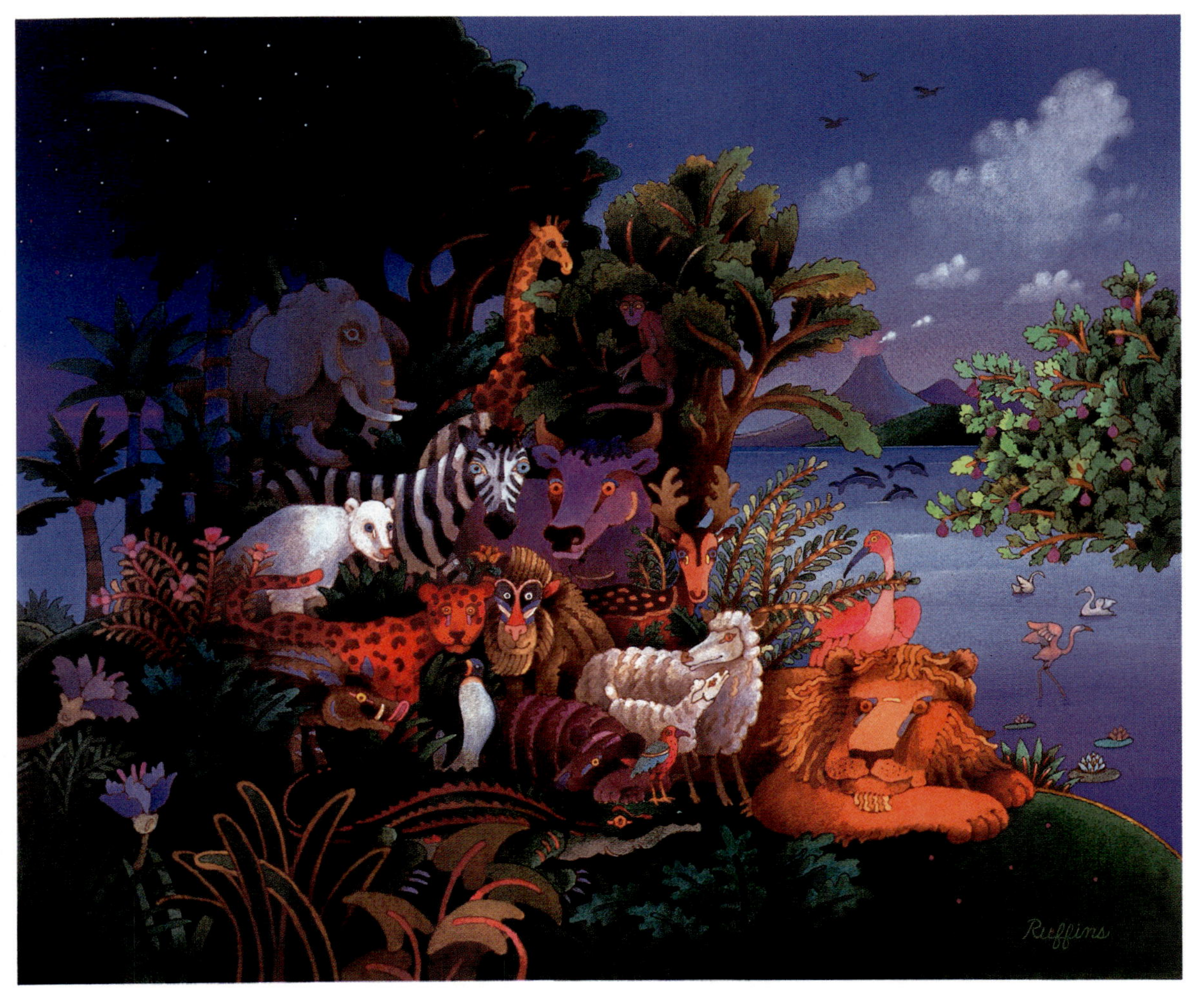

**PEACEABLE KINGDOM**

REYNOLD RUFFINS

*ACRYLIC*

"THE IMAGE OF CREATURES OF VARIED APPETITES PEACEFULLY COEXISTING SYMBOLIZES A PLANET IN ORDER AND AT PEACE. THE PUBLISHER FOR WHOM THIS WAS DONE WAS PROMOTING A NUMBER OF BOOKS ALL DEALING WITH NATURE. THIS SOLUTION WORKED TO TIE THE TITLES TOGETHER."

A STUDY OF A 10-SQUARE-MILE AREA IN THE AMAZON HAS IDENTIFIED 320 SPECIES OF BIRDS, 800 SPECIES OF TREES, AND 460 SPECIES OF BUTTERFLIES.

........................

DIE UNTERSUCHUNG EINER 15 KM2 GROSSEN ZONE IM AMAZONASGEBIET ERBRACHTE 320 VOGELARTEN, 800 BAUMARTEN UND 460 SCHMETTERLINGSARTEN.

........................

UNE ÉTUDE PORTANT SUR UNE SURFACE DE 15 KM2 EN AMAZONIE A PERMIS D'IDENTIFIER 320 ESPÈCES D'OISEAUX, 800 ESPÈCES D'ARBRES ET 460 ESPÈCES DE PAPILLONS.

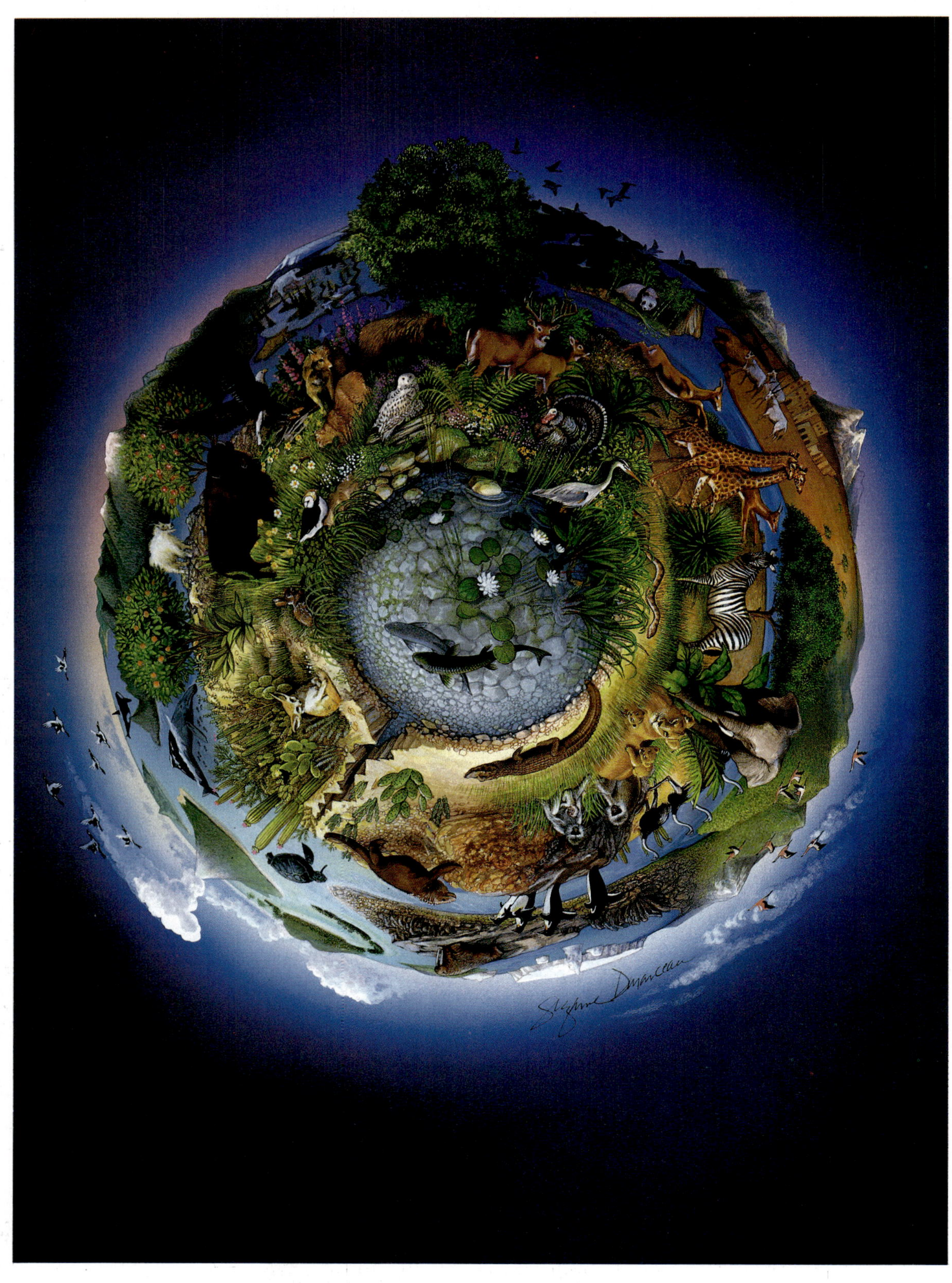

**TRILOGY OF THE EARTH**

SUZANNE DURANCEAU

*ACRYLIC ON ILLUSTRATION BOARD*

"PART OF A TFILOGY OF THE EARTH—PAST, PRESENT, AND FUTURE. THIS PAINTING PRESENTS THE PAST."

THE ENVIRONMENT LIAISON CENTER INTERNATIONAL IN NAIROBI MAINTAINS A REGISTRY OF 7,000 NONGOVERNMENTAL ORGANIZATIONS WORLDWIDE DEALING WITH THE ENVIRONMENT.

..........................

7000 NICHTSTAATLICHE ORGANISATIONEN BEFASSEN SICH WELTWEIT MIT DEN UMWELTPROBLEMEN.

..........................

7000 ORGANISATIONS NON GOUVERNEMENTALES DANS LE MONDE SE PRÉOCCUPENT DE L'ENVIRONNEMENT.

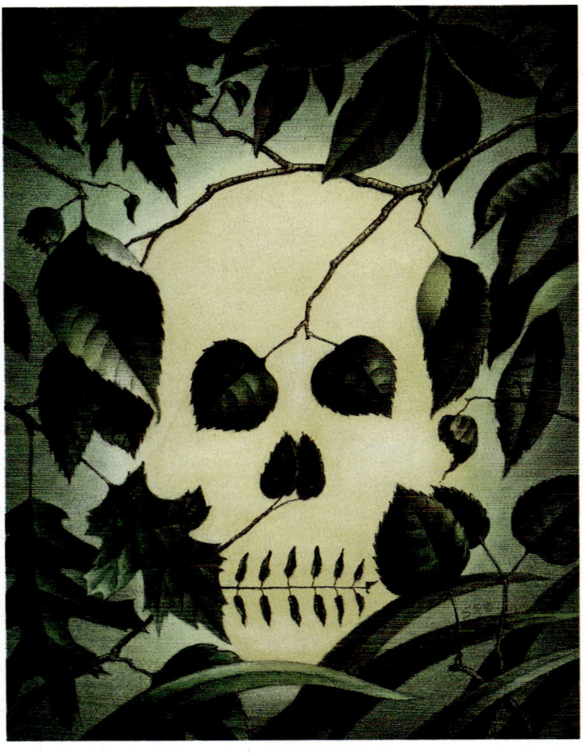

**YOU CAN SEE THE AIR**

Vivienne Flesher

*Pastel*

**FOREST DEATH**

Scott Reynolds

*Pastel*

"Acid rain is causing forests to spontaneously defoliate."

EVEN VARIOUS ORGANIC SOLVENTS THAT CAN BE FOUND IN OIL-BASED PAINTS, FURNITURE OILS, AND DEGREASERS WILL EVAPORATE INTO THE AIR AND CAUSE SERIOUS HEALTH EFFECTS WHEN INHALED.

...........................

SOGAR EINIGE ORGANISCHE LÖSUNGSMITTEL IN FARBEN AUF ÖLBASIS, MÖBELPOLITUREN UND FETTENTFERNERN VERDUNSTEN UND VERURSACHEN ERNSTHAFTE GESUNDHEITLICHE SCHÄDEN, WENN SIE EINGEATMET WERDEN.

...........................

MÊMES LES SOLVANTS ORGANIQUES CONTENUS DANS LES COULEURS À L'HUILE, LES VERNIS POUR BOIS ET LES DÉGRAISSANTS S'ÉVAPORENT ET PROVOQUENT DES TROUBLES GRAVES POUR LA SANTÉ LORSQU'ILS SONT INHALÉS.

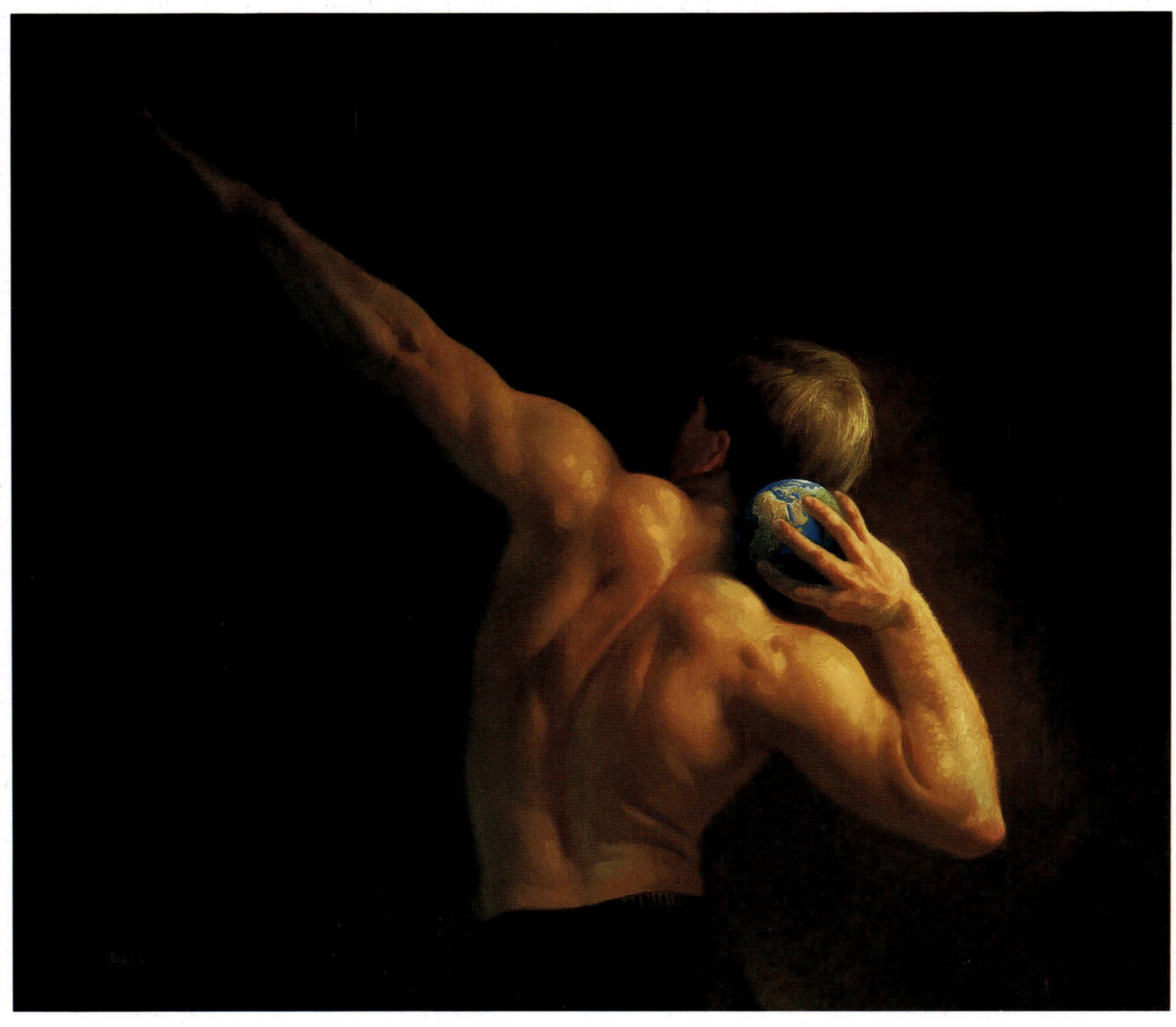

## MOMENT OF DECISION

JAMES E. TENNISON

*OIL ON CANVAS*

"THE EARTH HAS BEEN ENTRUSTED TO MANKIND.
MAN'S PROGRESS, ALTHOUGH NOT BAD IN ITSELF, HAS TAKEN ITS
TOLL ON THE ENVIRONMENT. HAVING BECOME AWARE OF THIS
DANGEROUS SITUATION, IS MANKIND WILLING TO DO WHAT IT
TAKES TO SAVE THE EARTH, OR WILL WE
'THROW IT ALL AWAY'?"

THE U.S. NATIONAL CANCER INSTITUTE HAS IDENTIFIED 3,000 PLANTS AS HAVING ANTI-CANCER PROPERTIES; OF THESE, 70 PERCENT ARE FROM THE RAINFOREST, INCLUDING THE ROSY PERIWINKLE, WHICH PRODUCES A SUBSTANCE USED TO COUNTERACT LEUKEMIA IN CHILDREN.

. . . . . . . . . . . . . . . . . . . . . . . . .

DAS US-KREBSINSTITUT HAT HERAUSGEFUNDEN, DASS 3000 PFLANZEN KREBSVERHINDERNDE EIGENSCHAFTEN HABEN; 70% DAVON STAMMEN AUS DEM REGENWALD, DARUNTER DAS ROSAROTE IMMERGRÜN, DAS EINE SUBSTANZ PRODUZIERT, DIE GEGEN LEUKÄMIE BEI KINDERN EINGESETZT WIRD.

. . . . . . . . . . . . . . . . . . . . . . . . .

L'INSTITUT AMÉRICAIN DE RECHERCHE POUR LE CANCER A IDENTIFIE 3000 PLANTES AYANT DES PROPRIÉTÉS ANTI-CANCÉREUSES. 70% POUSSENT DANS LA FORÊT TROPICALE, NOTAMMENT LA PERVENCHE QUI PRODUIT UNE SUBSTANCE UTILISÉE POUR COMBATTRE LA LEUCÉMIE CHEZ LES ENFANTS.

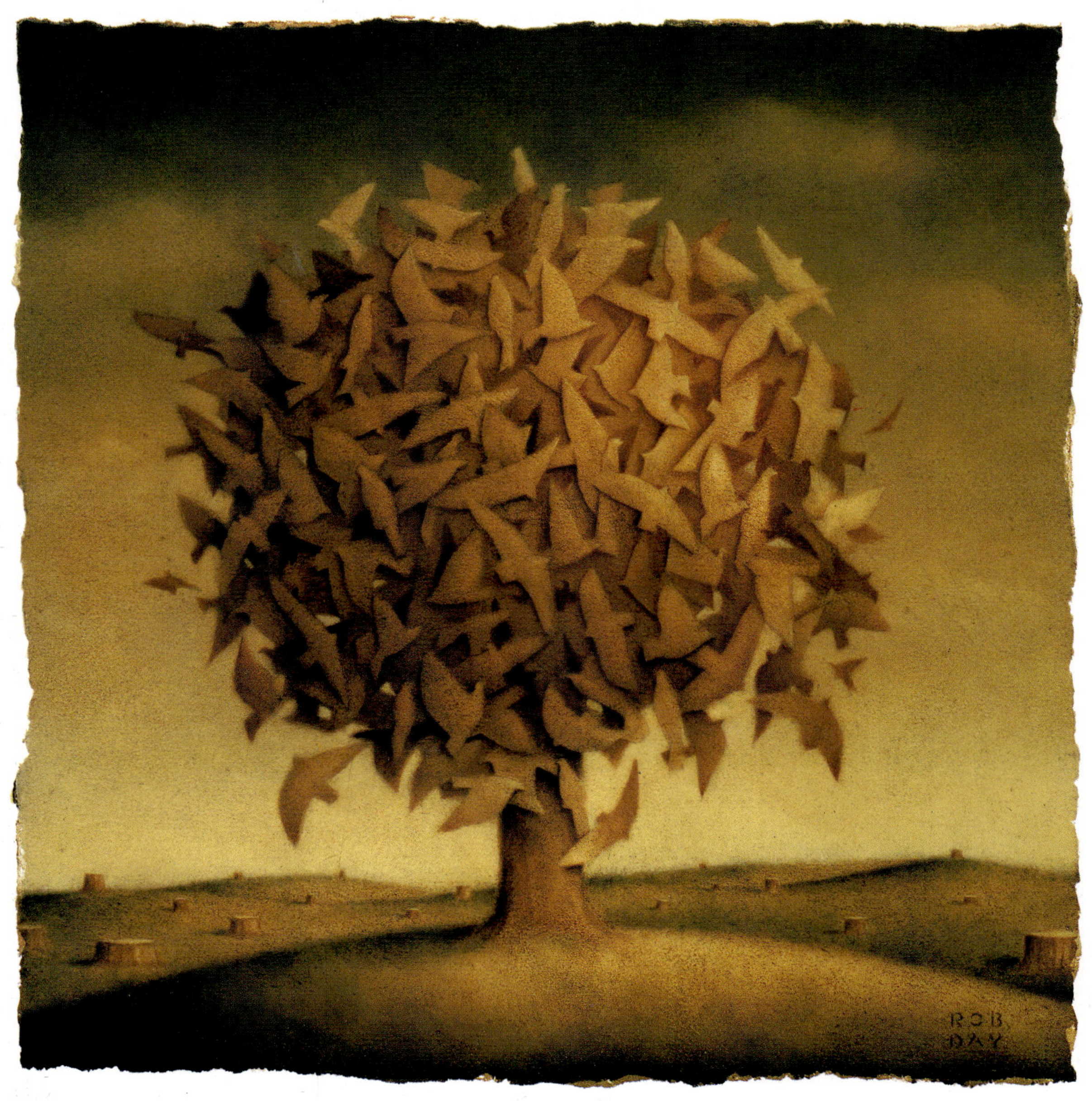


**TREEHOUSE**

Rob Day

*Oil on paper*

"The survival of wildlife and the endangered species rely on the preservation of their habitat."

SCIENTISTS ESTIMATE THAT 17,000 SPECIES PER YEAR ARE MADE EXTINCT AS TROPICAL RAINFORESTS ARE DESTROYED.

.........................

NACH SCHÄTZUNGEN VERSCHWINDEN PRO JAHR 17 000 ARTEN DURCH DIE ZERSTÖRUNG DER REGENWÄLDER.

.........................

ON ESTIME QUE 17 000 ESPÈCES PAR AN DISPARAISSENT À CAUSE DE LA DESTRUCTION DE LA FORÊT TROPICALE.

THE AVERAGE U.S. CITIZEN DISCARDS ABOUT 3.5 POUNDS OF WASTE PER DAY. IN A WORLDWIDE SURVEY OF WASTE GENERATION IN INDUSTRIAL CITIES, NEW YORK CITY TOPPED THE LIST, AVERAGING 4 POUNDS PER PERSON PER DAY, ONE POUND MORE THAN TOKYO, JAPAN.

........................

IN EINER ERHEBUNG ÜBER DIE ABFALLPRODUKTION ALLER INDUSTRIESTÄDTE STEHT NEW YORK MIT DURCHSCHNITTLICH 2 KILO PRO PERSON UND TAG AN DER SPITZE; DAS SIND FAST 500 GRAMM MEHR ALS IN TOKIO.

........................

DANS UNE ENQUÊTE SUR LA QUANTITÉ D'ORDURES PRODUITE PAR LES GRANDES VILLES INDUSTRIELLES, NEW YORK A ÉTÉ CLASSÉE EN TÊTE, AVEC UNE MOYENNE DE 2 KILOS PAR PERSONNE ET PAR JOUR, SOIT 500 G DE PLUS QU'À TOKYO.

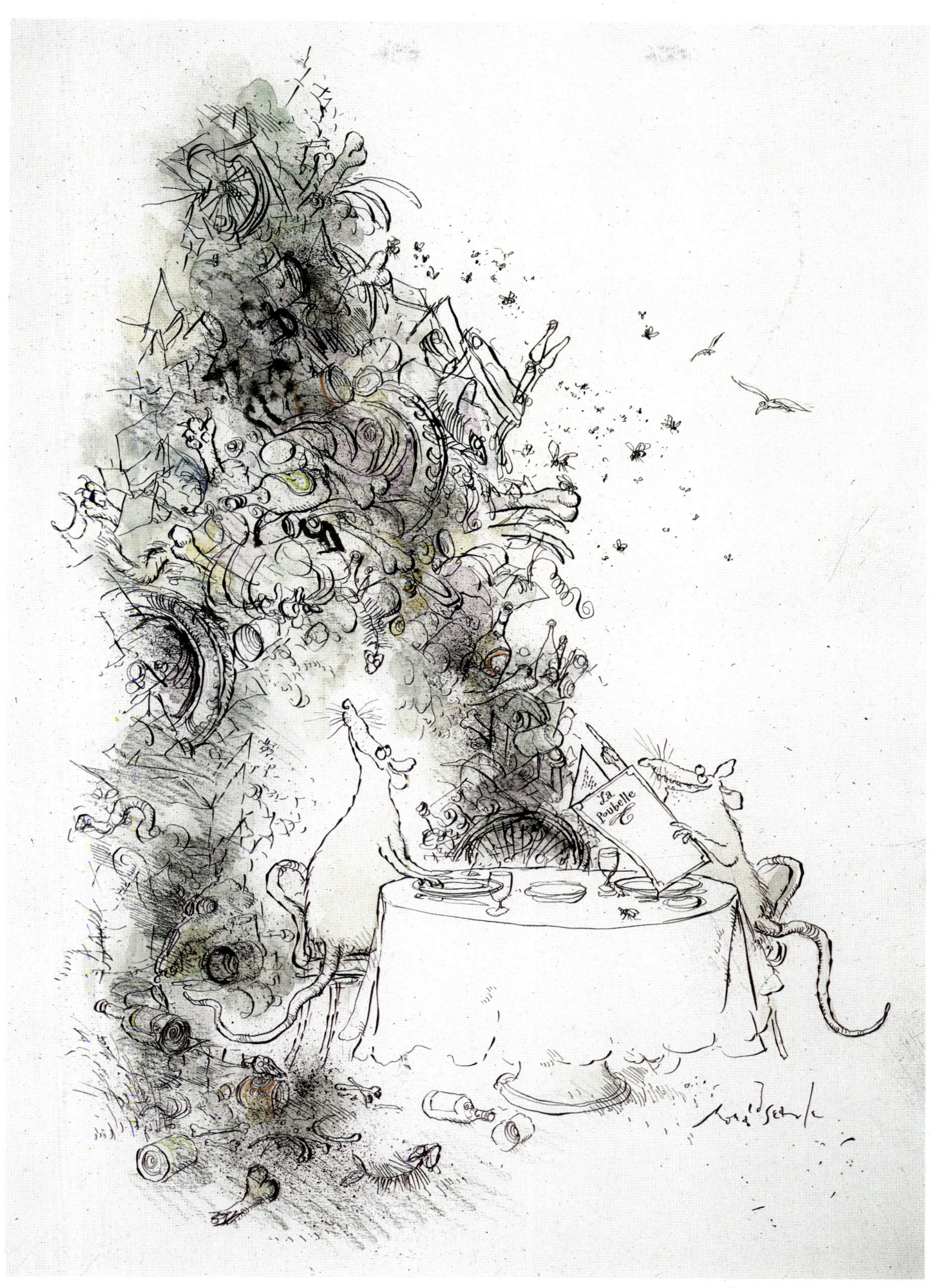


**LA CUISINE POUBELLE**

RONALD SEARLE

*PEN AND WATERCOLOR DRAWING*

"OUR GREEDY CONSUMER SOCIETY RISKS SMOTHERING ITSELF WITH ITS OWN GARBAGE. BUT AT LEAST THE DISCRIMINATING RAT BENEFITS."

REMOVING ENDANGERED SPECIES FROM THE WILD PROPOGATES THE LOSS OF THAT SPECIES'GENETIC DIVERSITY, MAKING IT MORE VULNERABLE TO EXTINCTION.

........................

DIE ENTFERNUNG BEDROHTER TIERARTEN AUS IHREM LEBENSRAUM VERRINGERT DIE CHANCEN FÜR DEN FORTBESTAND DER ART.

........................

EN ÉLOIGNANT LES ANIMAUX MENACÉS DE LEUR MILIEU NATUREL, ON ACCROÎT LES RISQUES D'EXTINCTION DE L'ESPÈCE.

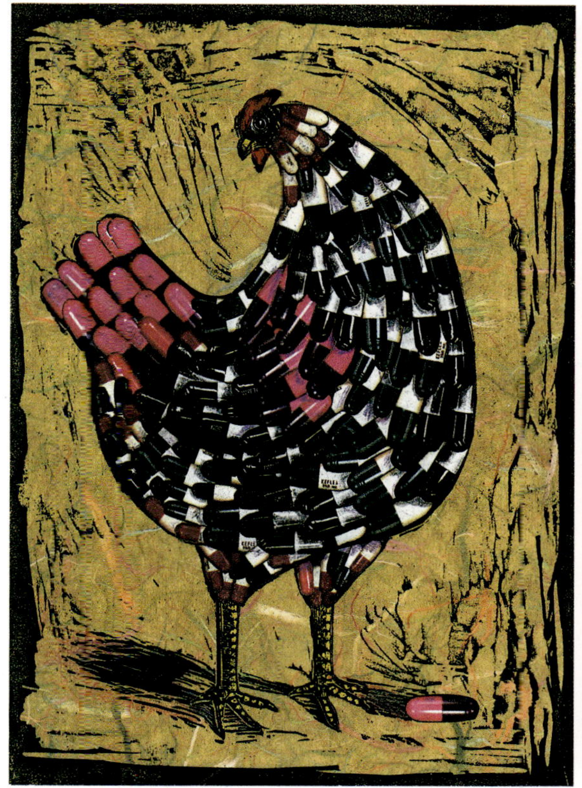

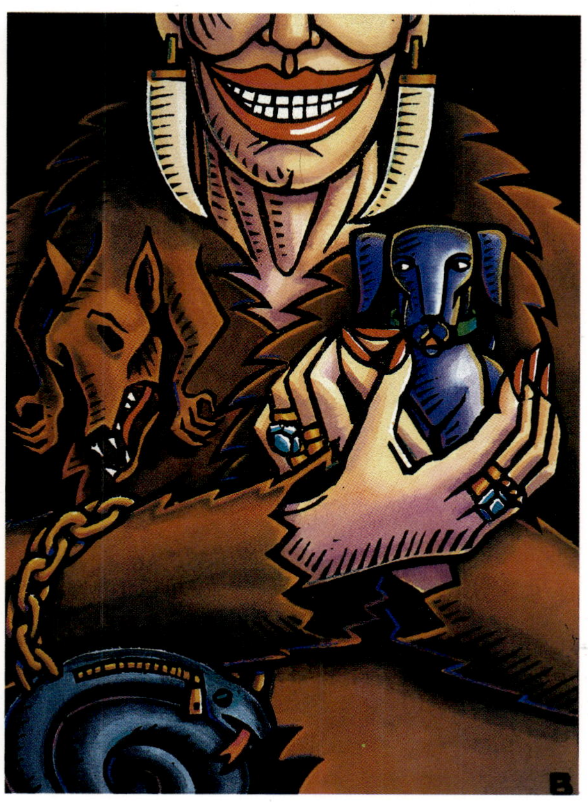

## ANTIBIOTIC CHICKEN

FRANCES JETTER

*LINOLEUM CUT AND COLLAGE*

"THIS IS AN ASPECT OF MODERN FARMING DANGEROUS TO HUMAN HEALTH. IF ANTIBIOTICS ARE USED AGAIN AND AGAIN IN ANIMALS, THE BACTERIA WILL PRODUCE A RESISTANT GENE. THESE BACTERIA SPREAD THROUGHOUT OUR ENVIRONMENT. IT MAY SOON BECOME IMPOSSIBLE TO FIGHT DISEASE WITH SPREADING ANTIBIOTIC RESISTANCE."

## THE ANIMAL LOVER

BASCOVE

*LINOCUT WITH WATERCOLOR AND PENCIL*

"THE ANIMAL RIGHTS ISSUE IS CENTRAL TO ANY DISCUSSION OF THE ENVIRONMENT. THIS PIECE WAS ORIGINALLY DONE FOR AN EXHIBITION AT THE GALERIE LUC QUEYREL, CALLED *PROPOSITIONS POUR UNE BASTILLE A PRENDRE*."

U.S. AGRICULTURAL
LAND MAY BE LOSING MORE THAN
3 BILLION TONS OF TOPSOIL
EVERY YEAR.

........................

IN DEN USA KÖNNTE DEM
AGRARLAND JÄHRLICH MEHR ALS 3
MILLIARDEN TONNEN ACKERKRUME
VERLORENGEHEN.

........................

PLUS DE 3 MILLIARDS DE
TONNES DE TERRES CULTIVABLES
POURRAIENT ÊTRE PERDUES
CHAQUE ANNÉE.

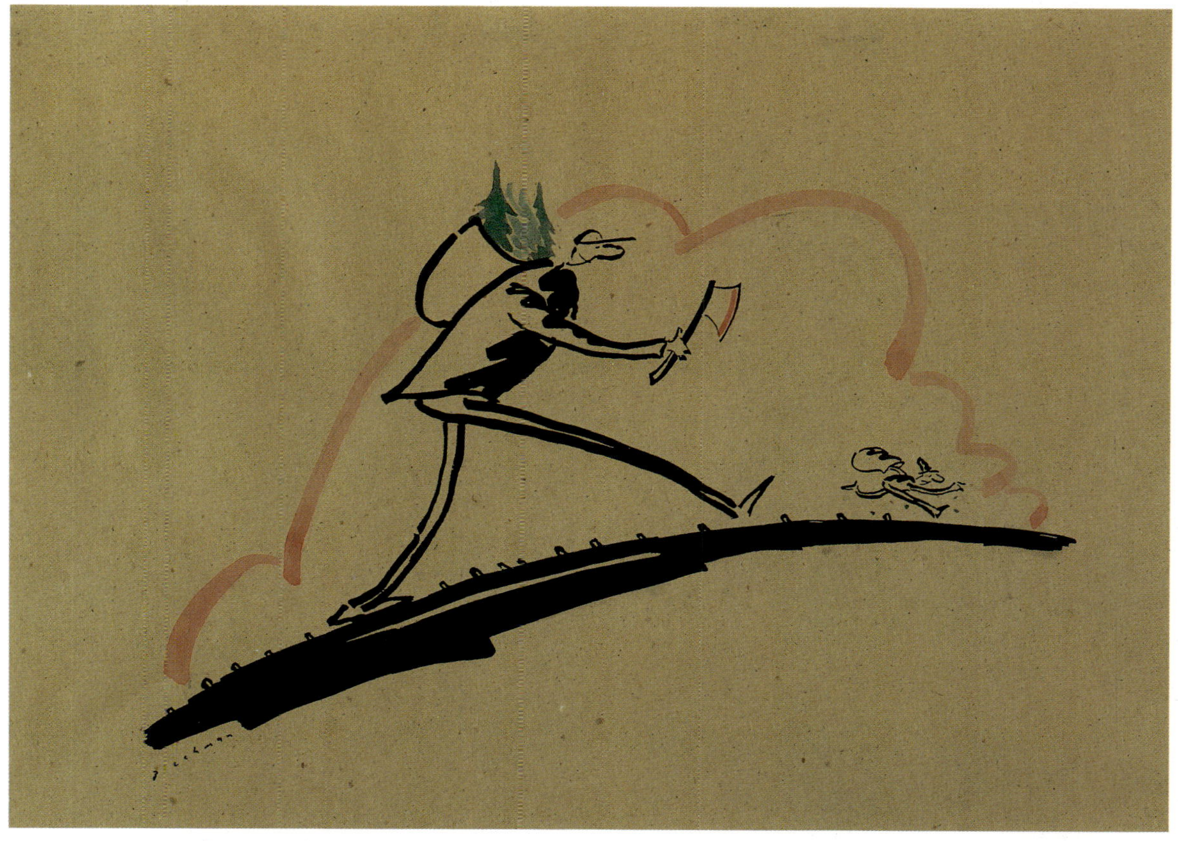

**PAUL BUNYAN AND JOHNNY APPLESEED**

R. O. Blechman

*India ink and watercolor*

"I used two mythic American characters, Paul Bunyan and Johnny Appleseed, to illustrate the race between the destruction and renewal of the environment."

OUR INDUSTRIES HAVE
DEFORESTED THE EARTH BY
25 PERCENT IN THE
LAST 30 YEARS.

..........................

UNSERE INDUSTRIE HAT
IN DEN LETZTEN 30 JAHREN 25
PROZENT DER WÄLDER ABGEHOLZT.

..........................

L'INDUSTRIE A CONTRIBUÉ
À 25% DE LA DÉFORESTATION
AU COURS DES TRENTE
DERNIÈRES ANNÉES.

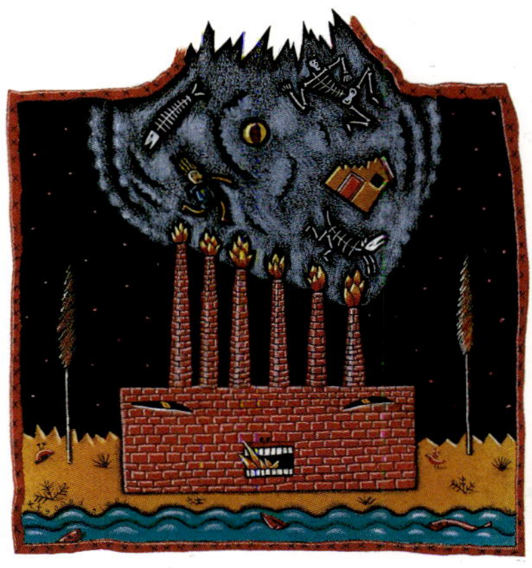

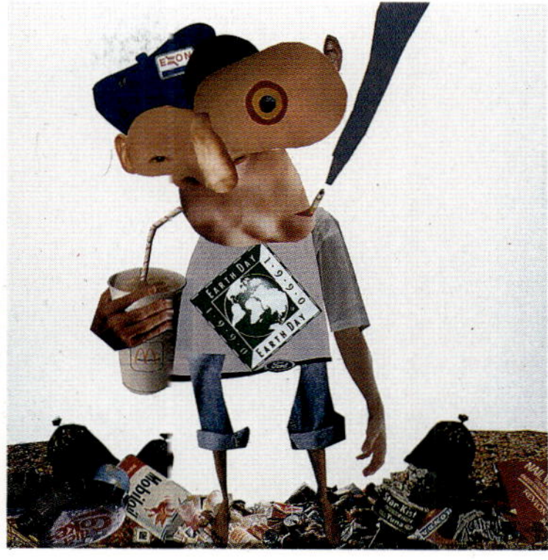

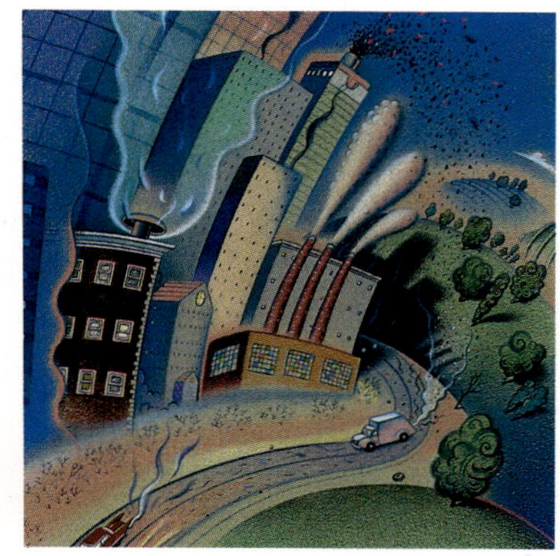

## INCINERATOR

JAMIE BENNETT

*DYES AND PRISMACOLOR*

"THIS WAS MY RESPONSE TO A PROPOSAL FOR AN INCINERATOR ON THE WATERFRONT OF LAKE ONTARIO, CLOSE TO A RESIDENTIAL AREA. IT'S A DEPICTION OF THE INCINERATOR'S ADVERSE EFFECTS ON THE ENVIRONMENT, ANIMALS, AND HUMANS."

## UNTITLED

STEPHEN KRONINGER

*COLLAGE*

## UNTITLED

DAVE CALVER

*COLORED PENCIL*

"THIS PIECE WAS CREATED AS AN ILLUSTRATION FOR A BASIC ECONOMICS TEXTBOOK, IN A CHAPTER ENTITLED 'ENVIRONMENT: ECONOMICS AND MARKET FAILURE.' THE POINT WAS SIMPLY TO SHOW URBAN AMERICA ENCROACHING UPON AND CONSUMING FARMLAND AND OTHER NATURAL ENVIRONMENTS."

GROUNDWATER IN THE U.S., WHICH PROVIDES 60 PERCENT OF THE POPULATION WITH DRINKING WATER, HAS BECOME CONTAMINATED BY SEEPAGE FROM UNDERGROUND CHEMICAL STORAGE TANKS AND LANDFILLS.

..........................

DAS GRUNDWASSER IN DEN USA WURDE DURCH UNDICHTE UNTERWASSERBEHÄLTER MIT CHEMISCHEN ABFÄLLEN UND DURCH ERDDEPONIEN VERSEUCHT.

..........................

AUX USA, LA NAPPE PHRÉATIQUE A ÉTÉ CONTAMINÉE PAR DES FUITES PROVENANT DE FÛTS DE DÉCHETS CHIMIQUES ENTREPREPOSÉS SOUS L'EAU OU DANS DES DÉCHARGES.

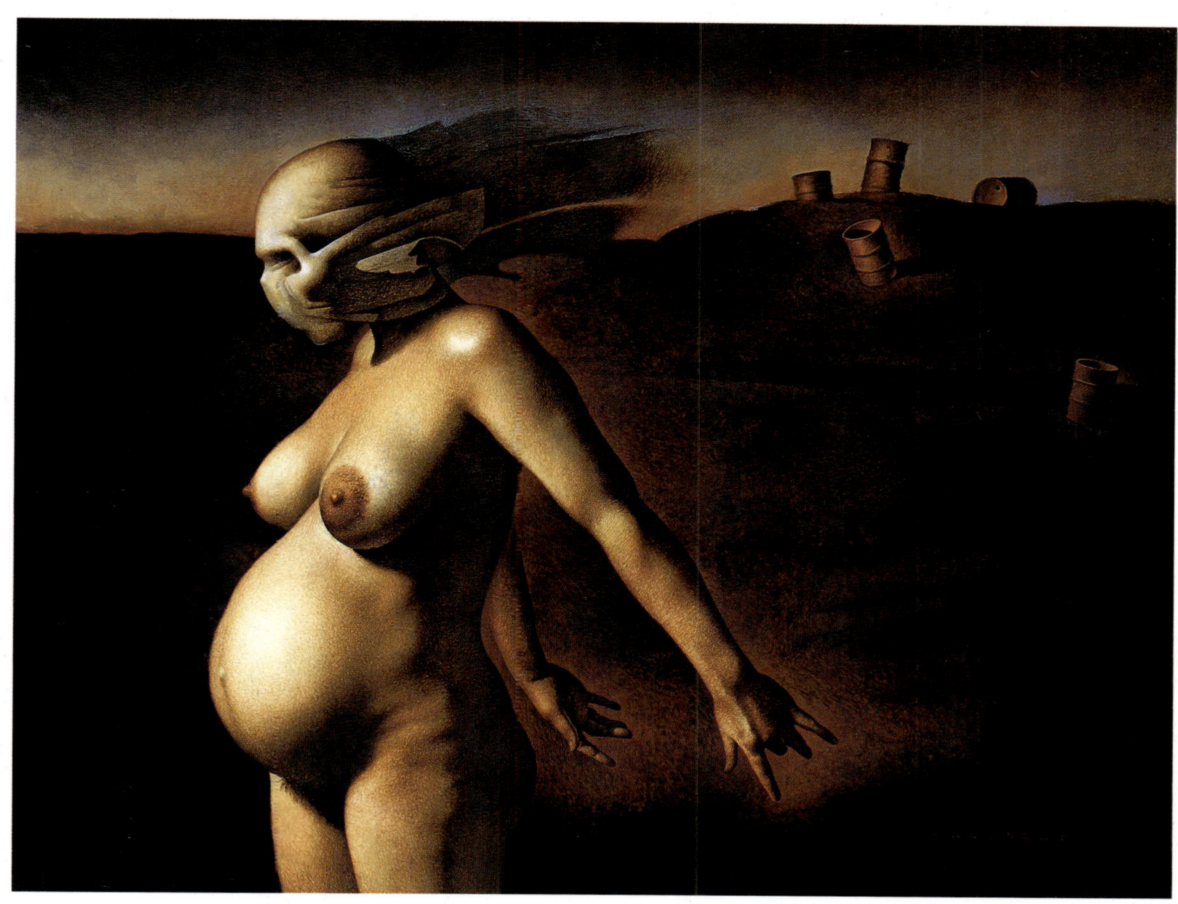

**GROUNDWATER**

John Jude Palencar

*Watercolor and acrylic*

"Industrial toxins adversely effect two worlds: the earth and the nner world of the unborn."

THE EARTH IS ESTIMATED TO BE 4.5 BILLION YEARS OLD AND HUMANS HAVE INHABITED IT FOR ONLY 2 OR 3 MILLION YEARS. ONLY IN THE PAST 200 YEARS HAVE WE BEGUN TO AFFECT OUR ENVIRONMENT WITH A SERIOUS IMPACT.

..........................

MAN SCHÄTZT, DASS DIE ERDE 4,5 MILLIARDEN JAHRE ALT IST. DEN MENSCHEN GIBT ES SEIT 2 BIS 3 MILLIONEN JAHREN, UND ERST IN DEN LETZTEN 200 JAHREN HABEN WIR BEGONNEN, DER UMWELT ERNSTHAFTE SCHÄDEN ZUZUFÜGEN.

..........................

ON ESTIME QUE LA TERRE A 4,5 MILLIARDS D'ANNÉES; L'HOMME Y HABITE SEULEMENT DEPUIS 2 OU 3 MILLIONS D'ANNÉES. C'EST AU COURS DES 200 DERNIÈRES ANNÉES QUE NOUS AVONS COMMENCÉ À DÉTRUIRE L'ENVIRONNEMENT.

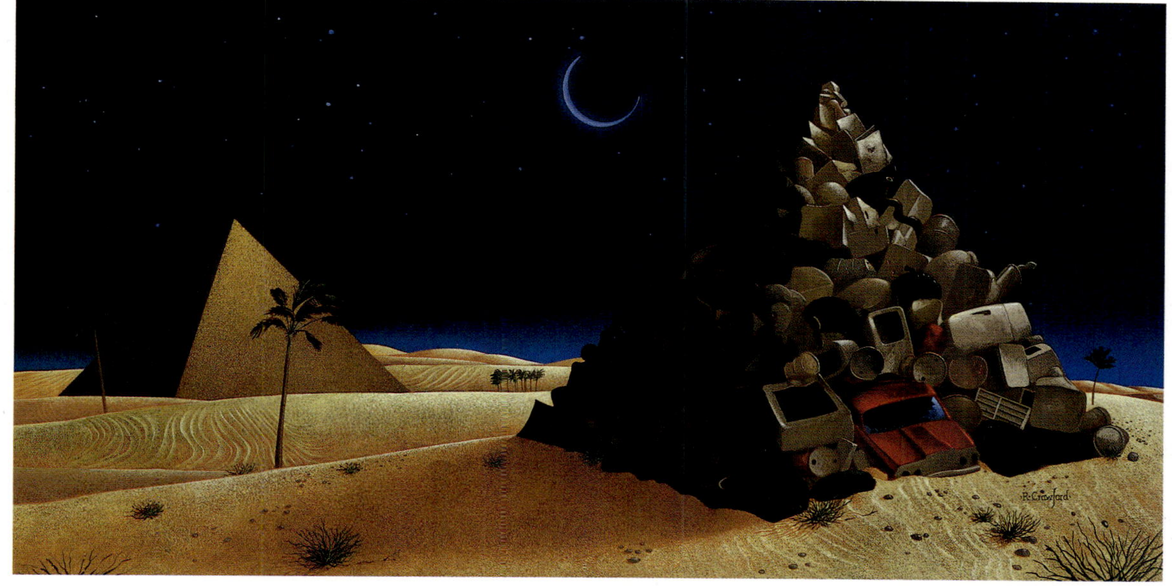

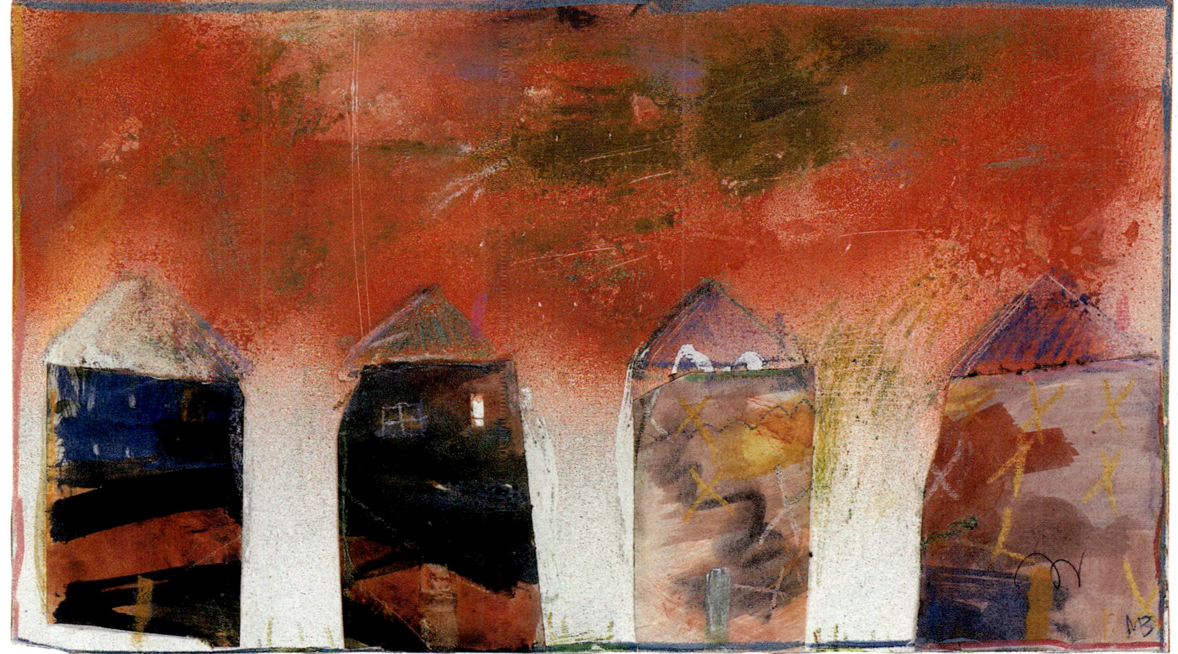

**LANDMARK**

Robert Crawford

*Acrylic on canvas*

"The pyramid serves as a symbol of beauty and continuation. Our new monuments have become the piles of trash seen everywhere throughout the world."

**CLOSE TO HOME**

Michelle Barnes

*Watercolor, crayon, collage*

"This piece shows the menacing effects of toxic contamination getting closer and closer to home in the form of toxic spills, radiation, and chemical pollutants."

IN 1983, NEGLIGENT LOGGING PRACTICES IN BORNEO CONTRIBUTED TO A FIRE THAT BURNED FOR FOUR MONTHS, DEVASTATING AN AREA LARGER THAN MASSACHUSETTS AND CONNECTICUT AND DESTROYING TIMBER WORTH $6 BILLION.

..........................

1983 FÜHRTEN NACHLÄSSIGKEITEN BEIM HOLZFÄLLEN IN BORNEO ZU EINEM FEUER, DAS VIER MONATE ANDAUERTE UND EINE FLÄCHE GRÖSSER ALS MASSACHUSETTS UND CONNECTICUT VERWÜSTETE. GLEICHZEITIG WURDE BRENNHOLZ IM WERT VON 6 MILLIARDEN DOLLAR VERNICHTET.

..........................

EN 1983, LA NÉGLIGENCE DES BÛCHERONS DE BORNÉO A ÉTÉ LA CAUSE D'UN INCENDIE QUI A DURÉ 4 MOIS, DÉVASTANT UN TERRITOIRE PLUS ÉTENDU QUE LE MASSACHUSETTS ET LE CONNECTICUT, ET DÉTRUISANT DU BOIS DE CHAUFFAGE POUR UNE VALEUR DE 6 MILLIARDS DE DOLLARS.

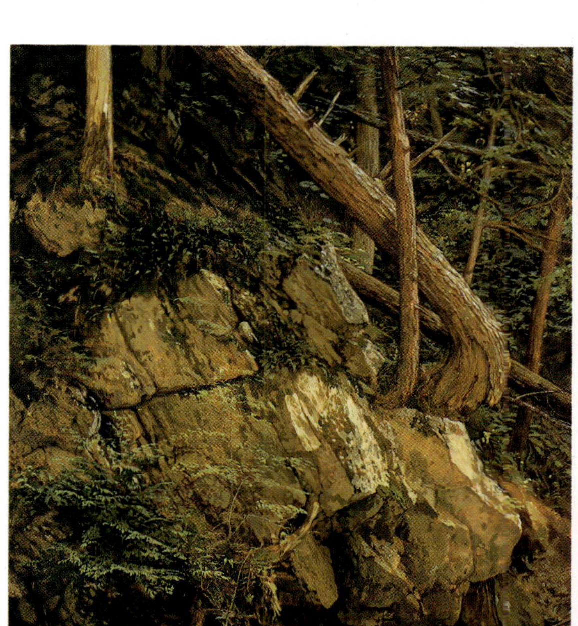

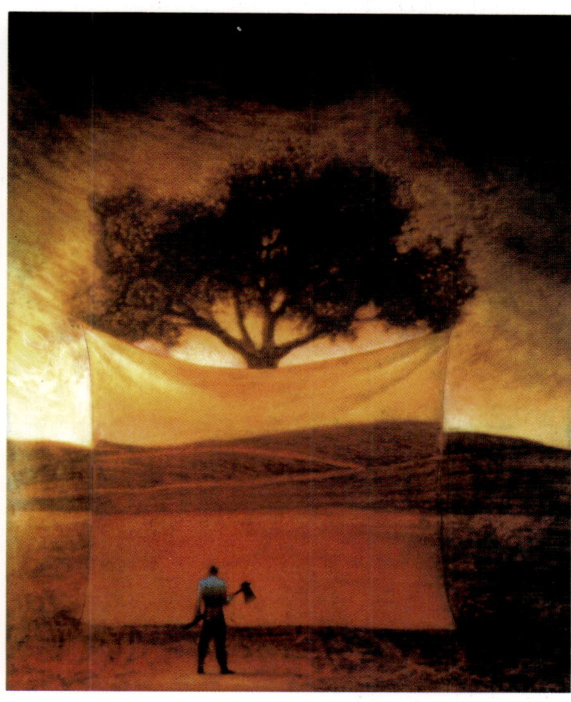

## RAVINE

John M. Thompson

*Acrylic on ragboard*

"This ravine is on the edge of the Cathedral Pines in Cornwall, Connecticut. A vertical landscape full of diagonals was being formed by the natural hazards of the forest. A week later a tornado hit the forest, knocking down 80 percent of the trees. This spot was spared."

## THE LESSON

Greg Spalenka

*Mixed media*

"If trees could communicate with us, I think their message would be clear enough."

WISCONSIN, ILLINOIS, FLORIDA, MINNESOTA, AND NEW JERSEY ARE INITIATING PROGRAMS REFUSING YARD WASTE IN LANDFILLS TO ENCOURAGE RECYCLING. LEAVES, BRUSH, AND GRASS CLIPPINGS COMPRISE ONE-FIFTH OF ALL WASTE IN MUNICIPAL LANDFILLS.

.........................

WISCONSIN, ILLINOIS, FLORIDA, MINNESOTA UND NEW JERSEY FÜHREN EIN VERBOT GEGEN ORGANISCHE ABFÄLLE IN DEPONIEN EIN, UM DAS KOMPOSTIEREN ZU FÖRDERN. 1/5 DES ABFALLS IN DEN STÄDTISCHEN DEPONIEN BESTEHT AUS BLÄTTERN, GESTRÜPP UND GRAS.

.........................

LE WISCONSIN, L'ILLINOIS, LA FLORIDE, LE MINNESOTA ET LE NEW JERSEY VIENNENT D'INTERDIRE LA COLLECTE DES DÉCHETS ORGANIQUES AFIN D'ENCOURAGER LE COMPOSTAGE. 1/5 DES DÉCHETS DES DÉCHARGES PUBLIQUES SONT COMPOSÉS DE FEUILLES, DE BROUSSAILLES ET D'HERBE.

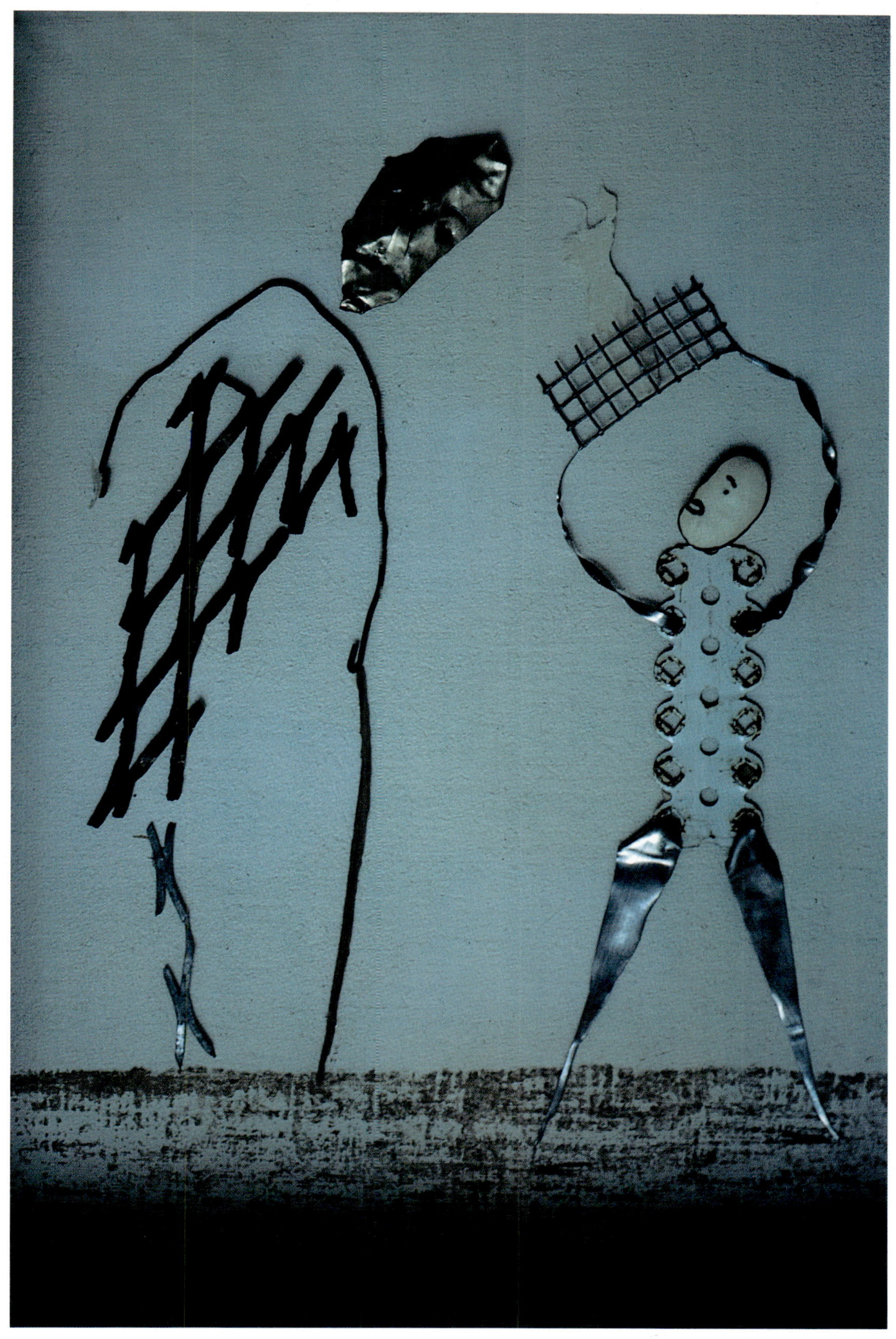

**RECYCLE**

Alexa Grace

*Found objects*

"It's a good thing to do."

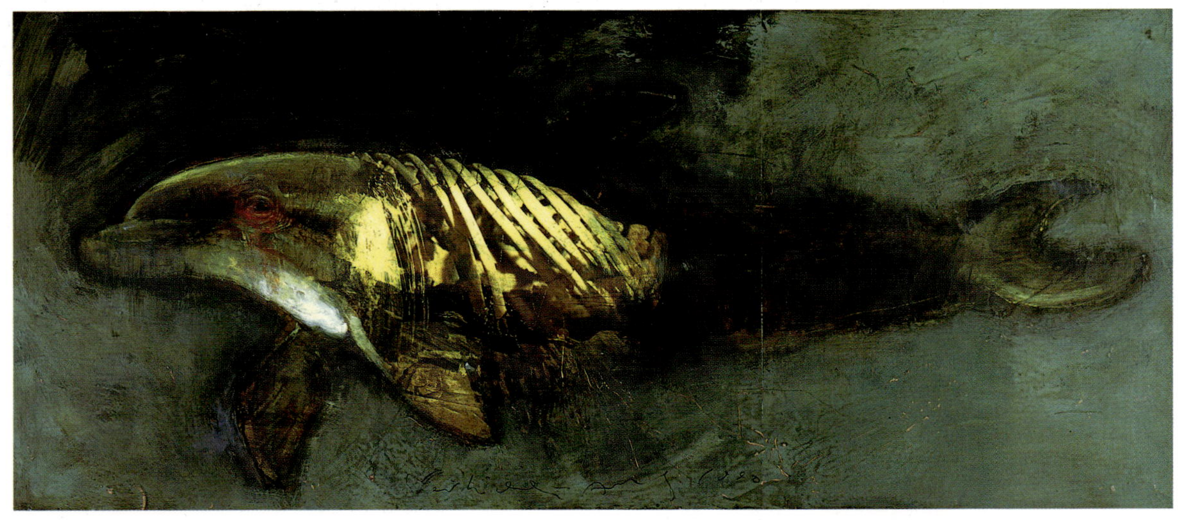

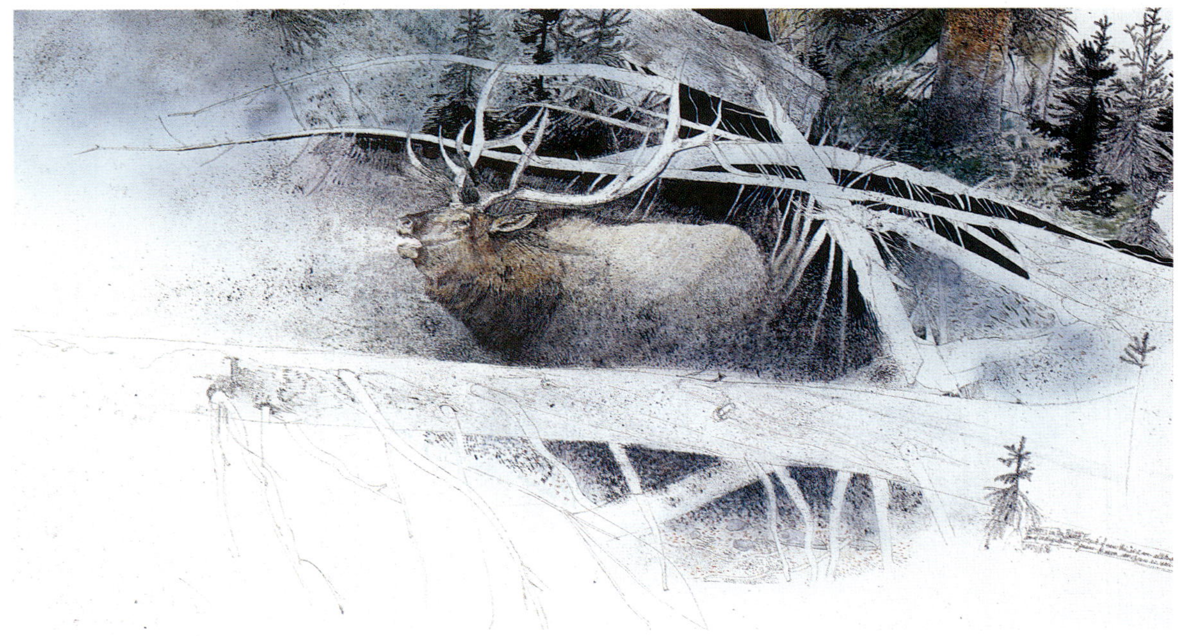

**UNTITLED**

KENT WILLIAMS

*MIXED MEDIA*

**BLACK FOREST VISION**

JACK UNRUH

*INK AND WATERCOLOR*

"PRESERVATION OF OUR WILDERNESS."

THE 1987 WORLDWATCH
"STATE OF THE WORLD REPORT"
MAINTAINED THAT HUMAN USE OF
NATURAL RESOURCES IS PUSHING
THE EARTH BEYOND THE
"THRESHOLDS" FOR CAUSING
PERMANENT DAMAGE.

..........................

DIE AUSBEUTUNG DER
NATÜRLICHEN RESSOURCEN DURCH
DEN MENSCHEN WIRD
SO VORANGETRIEBEN, DASS
PERMANENTE SCHÄDEN DER NATUR
DIE FOLGE SEIN WERDEN.

..........................

L'EXPLOITATION INTENSIVE
DES RESSOURCES NATURELLES DE
LA TERRE EST TELLE
QU'ELLE ENTRAÎNE DES DOMMAGES
IRRÉVERSIBLES POUR
L'ENVIRONNEMENT.

## UNTITLED

Jeff Seaver

*Pen and ink with colored pencil*

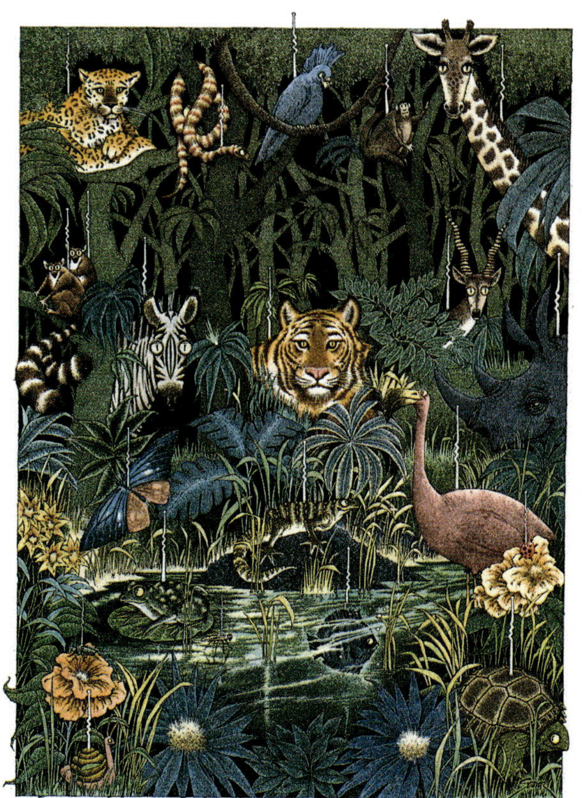

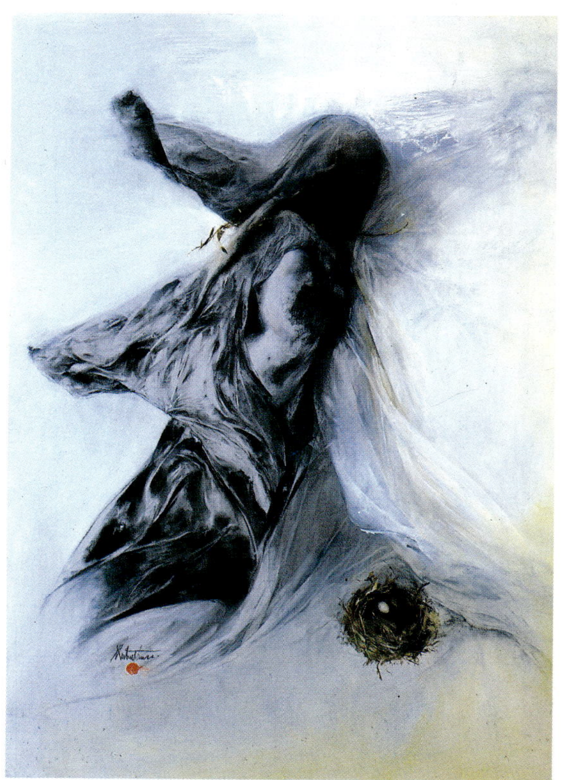

## BIRD'S NEST

Herbert Tauss

*Charcoal and oils*

"This is really a warning piece—of giving birth to death, if we continue to abuse our environmental concerns."

ONE PERUVIAN WILDLIFE PRESERVE CONTAINS MORE BIRD SPECIES THAN CAN BE FOUND IN THE ENTIRE UNITED STATES. SOME OF THOSE SPECIES ARE KNOWN ONLY TO THAT TROPICAL AREA AND COULD BECOME ENDANGERED DUE TO THE DESTRUCTION OF THE RAINFORESTS.

...........................

EIN NATURSCHUTZGEBIET IN PERU BEHEIMATET MEHR VOGELARTEN ALS DIE GESAMTEN VEREINIGTEN STAATEN. EINIGE DIESER ARTEN KOMMEN NUR IN DIESER TROPISCHEN GEGEND VOR UND WÄREN BEI ANHALTENDER ZERSTÖRUNG DER REGENWÄLDER IN IHREM FORTBESTAND BEDROHT.

...........................

AU PÉROU, UNE RÉSERVE NATURELLE RENFERME PLUS D'ESPÈCES D'OISEAUX QU'ON EN TROUVE SUR LE TERRITOIRE DES ÉTATS-UNIS. CERTAINES NE SONT CONNUES QUE DANS CES RÉGIONS TROPICALES ET POURRAIENT ÊTRE MENACÉES PAR LA DESTRUCTION DE LA FORÊT VIERGE.

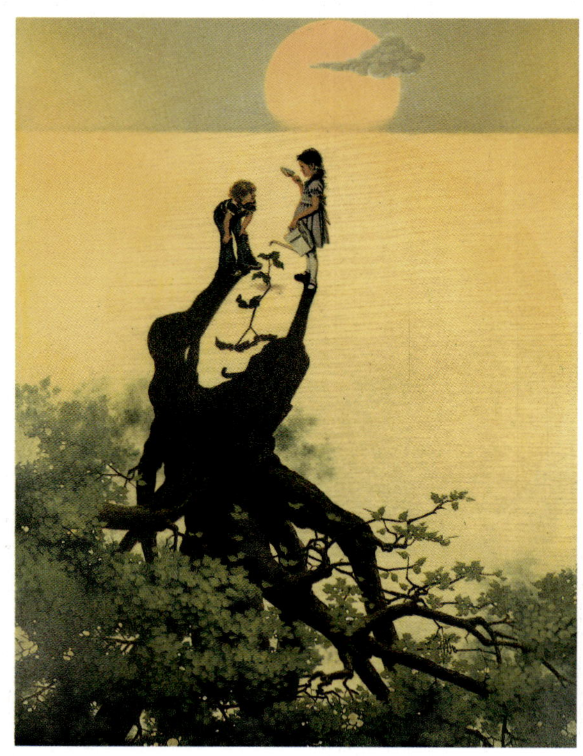

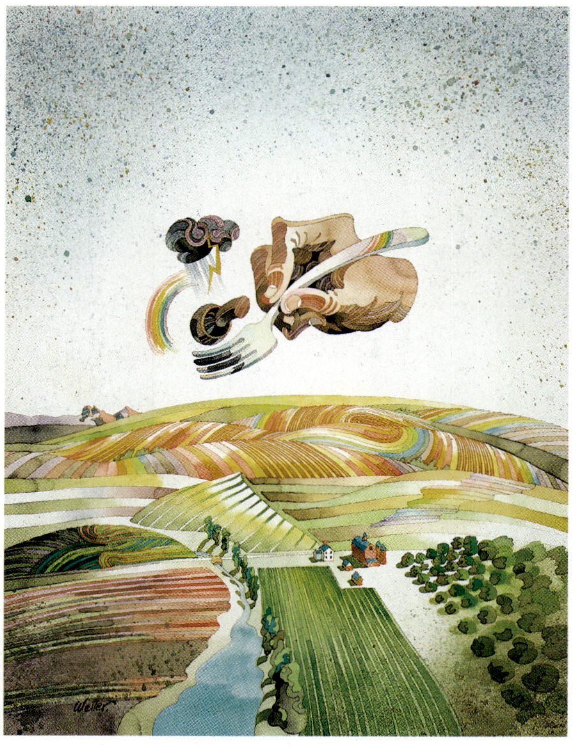

**UNTITLED**

Kunio Hagio

*Gouache*

**BOUNTIFUL HARVEST**

Don Weller

*Watercolor*

"As we manipulate and use our environment for our purposes, we must be careful not to deplete or abuse it. Our bountiful harvest can only continue if we return nutrients to the soil and preserve the purity of our air and water."

6,000 TREES HAVE BEEN PLANTED ALONG BALTIMORE'S THREE MAIN STREAMS IN ORDER TO PREVENT FURTHER POLLUTION OF THE CHESAPEAKE BAY BY REDUCING SOIL RUN OFF CONTAINING PHOSPHORS AND NITROGEN.

..........................

6000 BÄUME WURDEN ENTLANG DER HAUPTFLÜSSE BALTIMORES GEPFLANZT, UM EINE WEITERE VERSCHMUTZUNG DER CHESAPEAKE BAY DURCH REDUZIERUNG DER MIT PHOSPHOR UND STICKSTOFF VERSEUCHTEN ABWÄSSER ZU VERHINDERN.

..........................

6000 ARBRES ONT ÉTÉ PLANTÉS LE LONG DU PRINCIPAL COURS D'EAU DE BALTIMORE POUR EMPÊCHER UNE NOUVELLE POLLUTION DE LA BAIE DE CHESAPEAKE EN DIMINUANT LES INFILTRATIONS DE PHOSPHORE ET DE PRODUITS AZOTÉS.

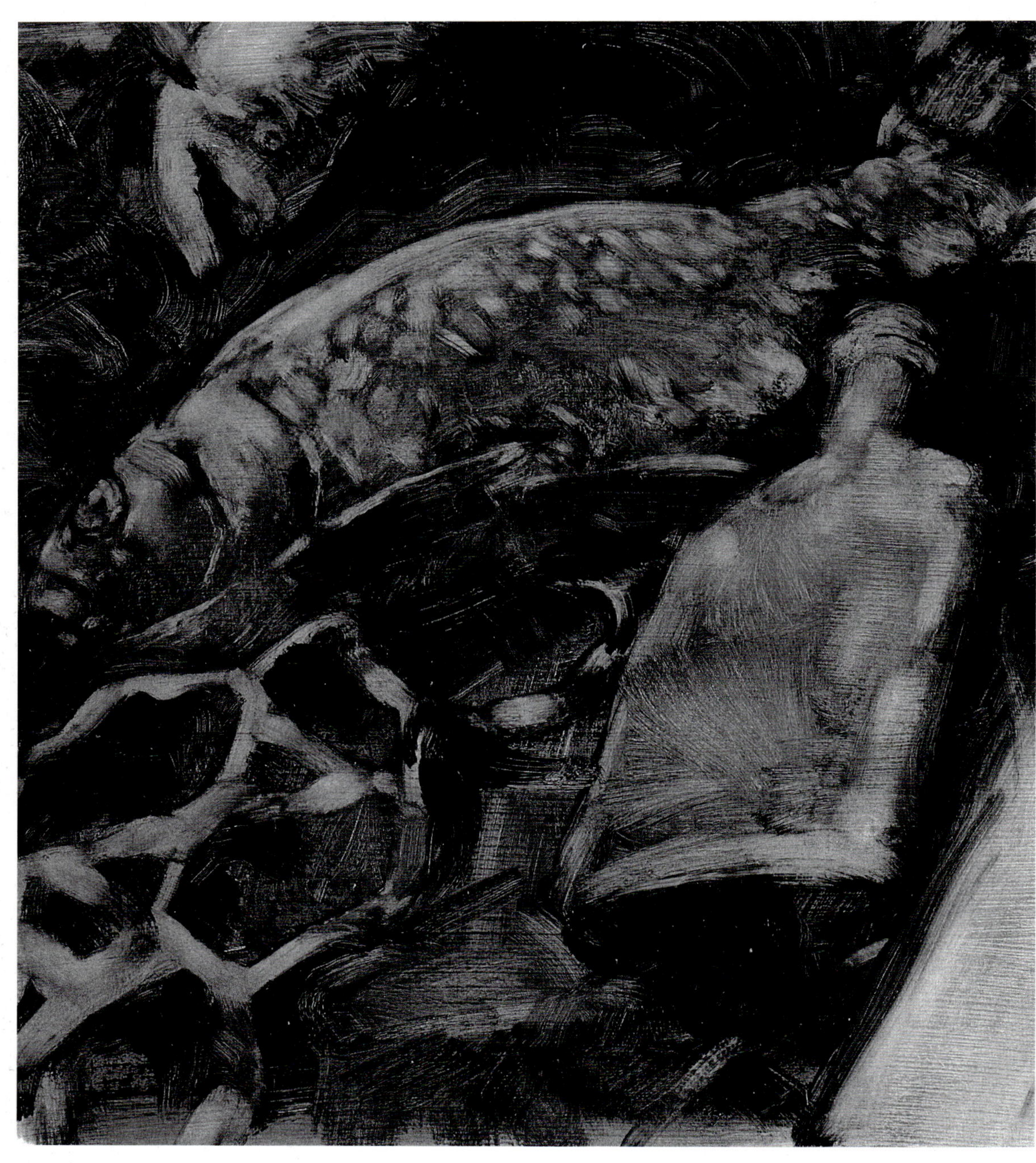

**POLLUTION**

Richard Sparks

*Oil on prepared surface*

"The artwork was originally done in conjunction with an article on polluted fishing waters. I thought it was a very strong statement—a visual comment—and deserved to be in the exhibit."

PRIMARY POLLUTANTS SUCH AS SULPHUR DIOXIDE, NITROGEN OXIDES, AND CARBON DIOXIDE REACT WITH MOISTURE AND EACH OTHER TO FORM SECONDARY POLLUTANTS SUCH AS NITRIC ACID, PHOTOCHEMICAL OXIDENTS AND OZONE—A MAJOR CONTRIBUTOR TO SMOG.

..........................

UMWELTSCHADSTOFFE WIE SCHWEFELDIOXID UND KOHLENDIOXID VERBINDEN SICH BEI FEUCHTIGKEIT ZU SEKUNDÄREN SCHADSTOFFEN WIE STICKOXID, PHOTOCHEMISCHE OXIDE UND OZON - DIE HAUPTURSACHEN FÜR SMOG.

..........................

LES POLLUANTS TELS QUE LE DIOXYDE DE SOUFRE, LES OXYDES D'AZOTE ET LE DIOXYDE DE CARBONE RÉAGISSENT À L'HUMIDITÉ EN PRODUISANT DES POLLUANTS SECONDAIRES COMME L'ACIDE NITRIQUE, LES OXYDANTS PHOTOCHIMIQUES ET L'OZONE — DIRECTEMENT RESPONSABLES DU SMOG.

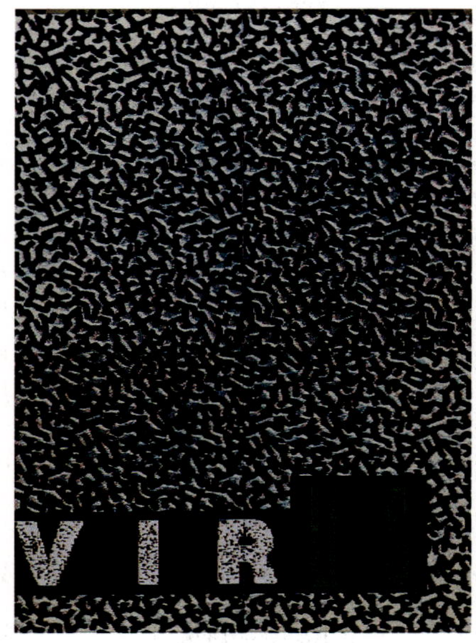


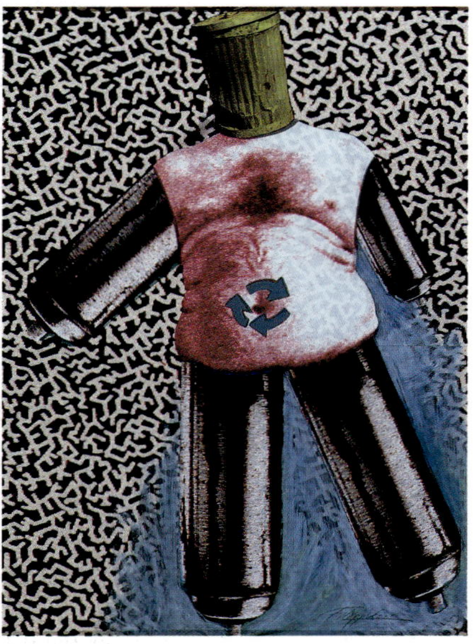

## VIRUS

Sandra Fillipucci

*Hand-rendered in Digital Monotype*

"This is a 'raw' image because there is nothing attractive about garbage, trash, waste, refuse, debris—there is nothing abstract about it no matter what you chose to call it. We breathe it and our children are forced to live in it."

## ARE WE ALONE?

Etienne Delessert

*Watercolor*

"Our planet is getting overpopulated, and perhaps other planets are as well."

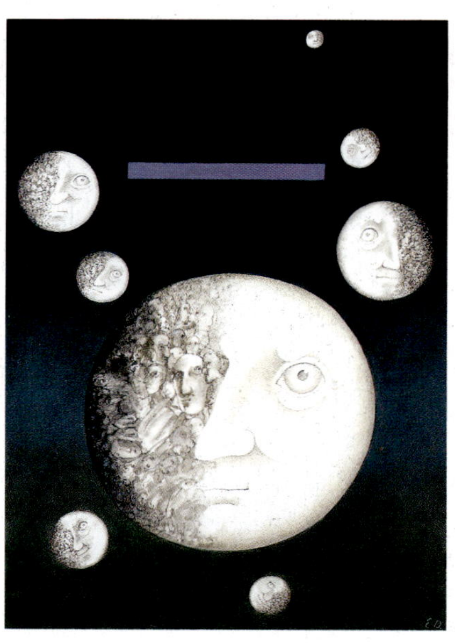

COUNTRIES WITH RAPID POPULATION GROWTH RATES RANK LOW ON THE MEASURE OF PHYSICAL QUALITY OF LIFE AND HIGH ON MEASURE OF HUMAN SUFFERING. RAPID GROWTH IS OFTEN ACCOMPANIED BY SEVERE ENVIRONMENTAL DEGRADATION, INCLUDING DEFORESTATION, DESERTIFICATION, AND SOIL EROSION.

...........................

SCHNELLES ANWACHSEN DER BEVÖLKERUNG GEHT OFT MIT SCHWEREN UMWELTSCHÄDEN EINHER, WIE ENTWALDUNG, VERWÜSTUNG UND EROSION DES BODENS.

...........................

LA CROISSANCE RAPIDE DE LA POPULATION S'ACCOMPAGNE SOUVENT D'UNE DÉGRADATION DE L'ENVIRONNEMENT, NOTAMMENT LA DÉFORESTATION ET L'ÉROSION DES SOLS.

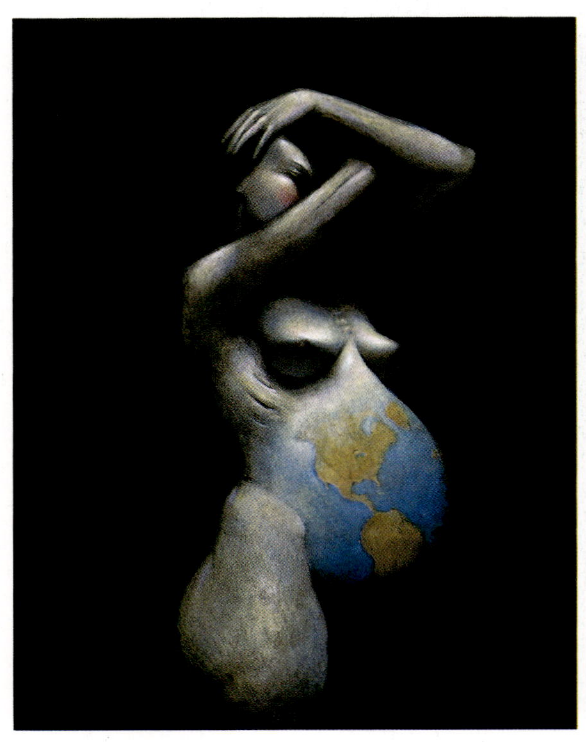

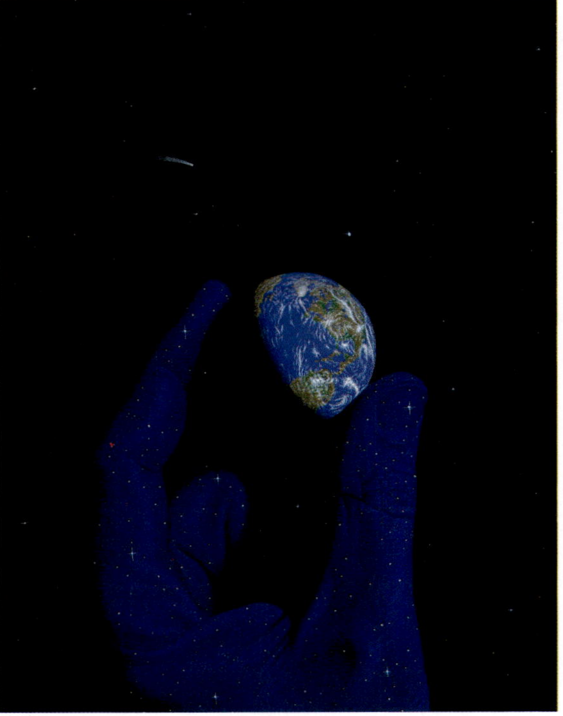

### MOTHER

David Shannon

*Acrylic*

"My intention was to portray the reciprocal and fragile relationship between earth and humanity."

### THE ENDANGERED EARTH

Marvin Mattelson

*Acrylic on 100-percent ragboard*

"The fate of the earth, quite simply, is in the hands of man."

EVERY DAY ONE SPECIES OUT OF THE WORLD'S 5-10 MILLION BECOMES EXTINCT. THIS RATE MAY BE INCREASING TO ONE AN HOUR. ONE MILLION SPECIES MAY HAVE VANISHED BY THE YEAR 2000.

.........................

JEDEN TAG WIRD EINE DER 5-10 MILLIONEN ARTEN DER WELT AUSGELÖSCHT. DIESE RATE KÖNNTE AUF EINE SPEZIES PRO STUNDE STEIGEN. IM JAHR 2000 SIND MÖGLICHERWEISE EINE MILLION ARTEN AUSGESTORBEN.

.........................

CHAQUE JOUR, L'UNE DES 5 À 10 MILLIONS D'ESPÈCES D'ANIMAUX VIVANT SUR LA PLANÈTE DISPARAÎT. LA CADENCE DEVRAIT S'ACCÉLÉRER À UNE PAR HEURE. UN MILLION D'ESPÈCES POURRAIENT AVOIR DISPARU D'ICI L'AN 2000.

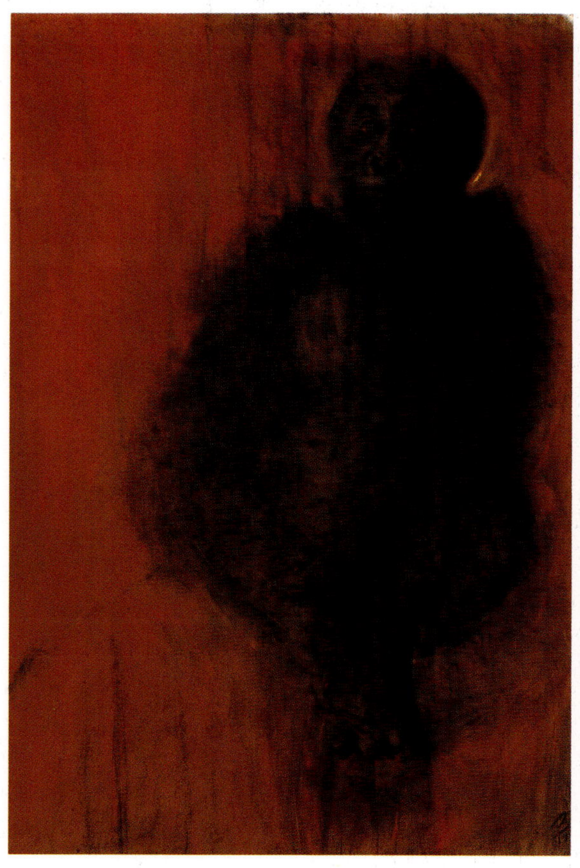

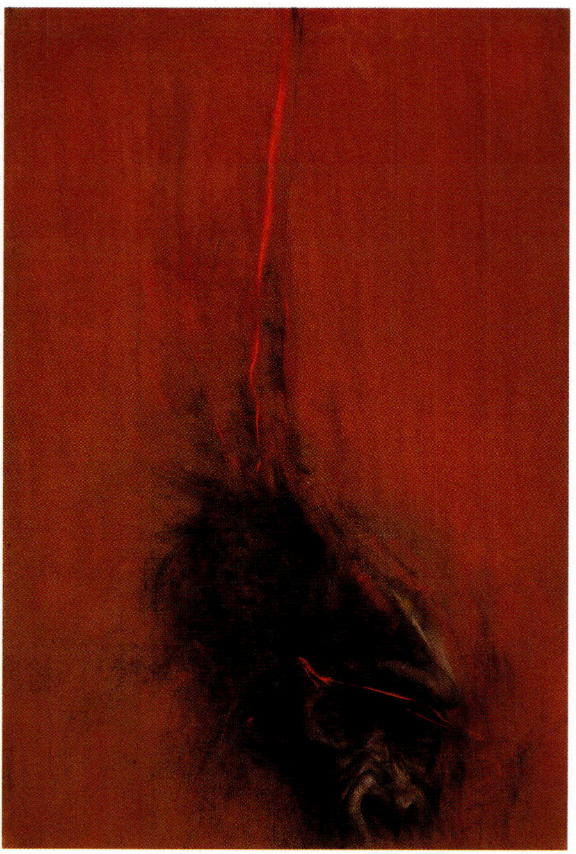

**THEN THERE IS ONE...**
**AND THEN THERE ARE NONE**

Bob Ziering

*Pastel*

"The mountain gorilla in the wild is seriously threatened and critically diminished by poaching. Extinction of species is forever. We are the only species with the ability to wipe out another—or prevent it. For the last four years, the gorilla has been the image of my metaphor for saying so."

*TIME* MAGAZINE REPORTS
THAT, SINCE LESS THAN 5 PERCENT
OF THE WORLD'S TROPICAL
RAINFORESTS RECEIVE
ANY PROTECTION, THE STAGE
IS SET FOR MASS EXTINCTION.

.........................

*TIME* BEHAUPTET, DASS EINE
MASSENVERNICHTUNG BEVORSTEHT,
WEIL WENIGER ALS FÜNF PROZENT
DER TROPISCHEN REGENWÄLDER
GESCHÜTZT WERDEN.

.........................

LE MAGAZINE *TIME*
AFFIRME QU'UNE DESTRUCTION
MASSIVE DE L'ENVIRONNEMENT EST
INÉLUCTABLE, ÉTANT DONNÉ QUE
MOINS DE 5% DES FORÊTS
TROPICALES SONT PROTÉGÉES.

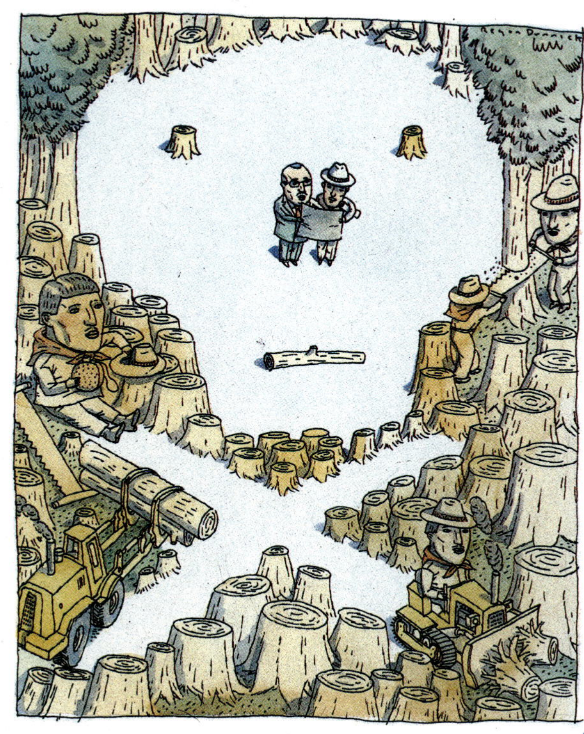

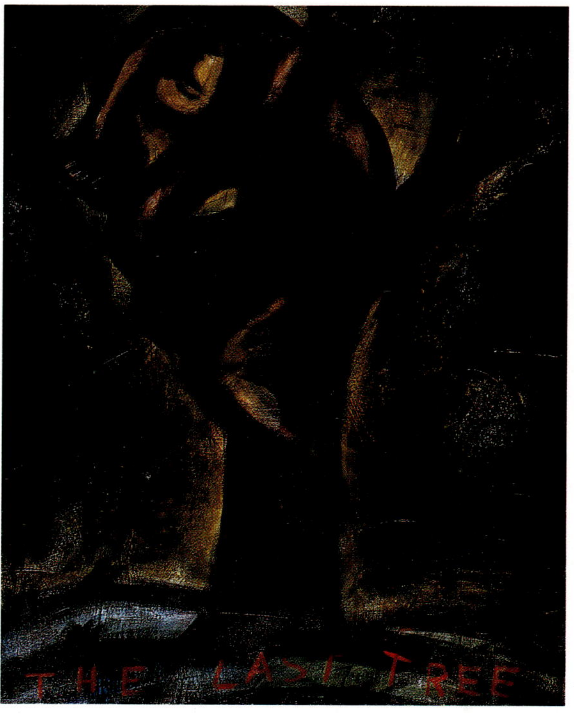


**RAINFOREST**

Regan Dunnick

"We need to bring more attention to the destruction."

**THE LAST TREE**

Anthony Russo

*Acrylics*

"Man's fate is tied in with nature."

TROPICAL FORESTS
HELP TO ABSORB DAMAGING
EFFECTS OF NATURAL STORMS BY
PREVENTING SHORELINE EROSION
AND ABSORBING STRONG WINDS.
EACH YEAR TROPICAL STORMS KILL
AT LEAST 20,000 PEOPLE AND
CAUSE $800 BILLION IN DAMAGE.
THE PRACTICE OF DEFORESTATION
WILL ALLOW THE STORMS TO
WREAK MORE HAVOC
IN THE FUTURE.

..........................

DIE TROPISCHEN
WÄLDER HALTEN DIE SCHÄDEN VON
NATÜRLICHEN STÜRMEN IN
GRENZEN, INDEM SIE WIND
ABSORBIEREN UND DIE
KÜSTENSTREIFEN VOR EROSION
SCHÜTZEN. JEDES JAHR
WERDEN DURCH TROPISCHE STÜRME
20 000 MENSCHEN GETÖTET UND
SCHÄDEN IN HÖHE VON $ 800
MILLIARDEN ANGERICHTET.
WEITERE ABHOLZUNGEN HÄTTEN
VERHEERENDE FOLGEN.

..........................

LES FORÊTS TROPICALES
PERMETTENT DE LIMITER LES
EFFETS DÉVASTATEURS DES
CYCLONES EN FREINANT LES VENTS
VIOLENTS ET EN PROTÉGEANT LES
CÔTES DE L'ÉROSION. CHAQUE
ANNÉE, LES ORAGES TROPICAUX
TUENT 20 000 PERSONNES ET
CAUSENT 800 MILLIARDS DE
DOLLARS DE DÉGÂTS. SI L'ON
CONTINUE À DÉBOISER CES FORÊTS,
LES CYCLONES SERONT ENCORE
PLUS CATASTROPHIQUES.

500 MILLION PEOPLE
WORLDWIDE ARE EXPOSED TO
TOXIC FUMES FROM BURNING
WOOD, DUNG, AND COAL INDOORS
FOR COOKING AND HEATING.

.........................

500 MILLIONEN MENSCHEN
SIND WELTWEIT VERSCHMUTZTER
LUFT AUSGESETZT, VERURSACHT
DURCH DIE VERBRENNUNG VON
HOLZ, MIST UND KOHLE ZUM
KOCHEN UND HEIZEN.

.........................

500 MILLIONS DE GENS
DANS LE MONDE SONT EXPOSÉS
AUX FUMÉES TOXIQUES PROVENANT
DE LA COMBUSTION DE BOIS,
FUMIER OU CHARBON POUR LA
CUISINE ET LE CHAUFFAGE.

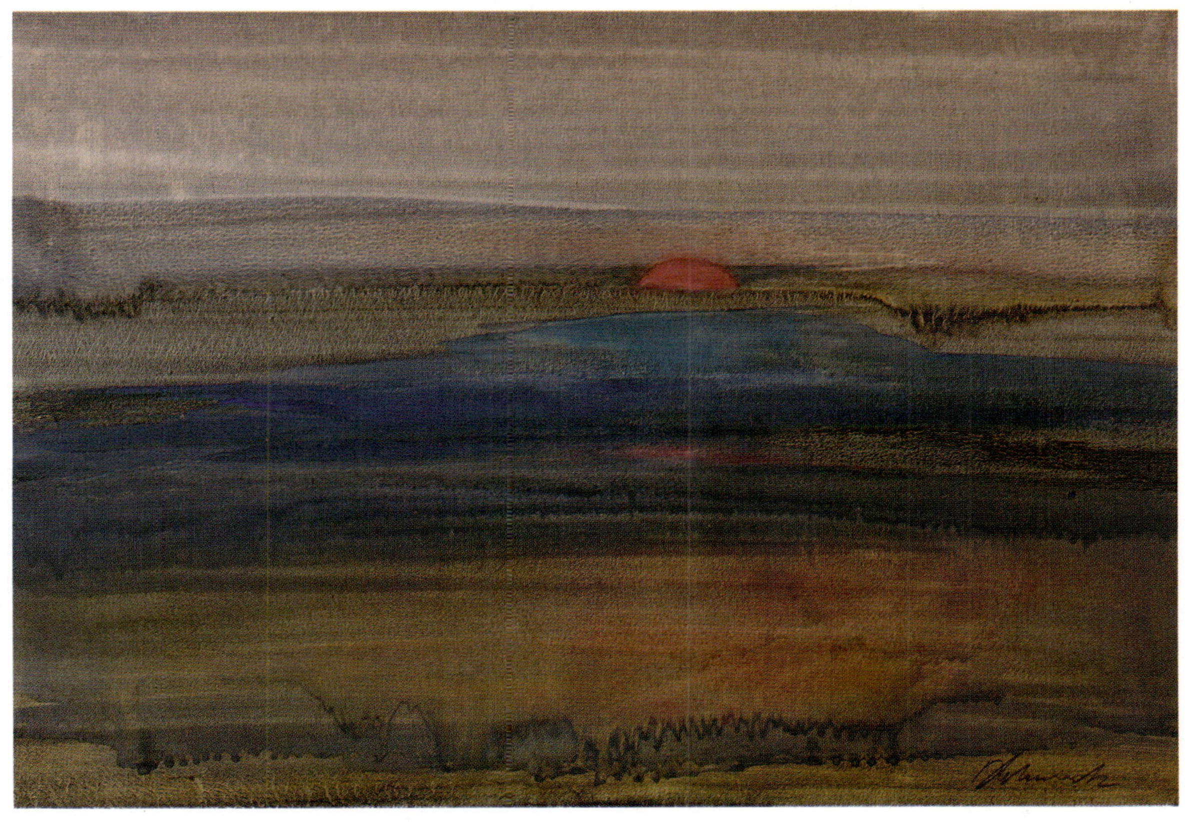

**SUNSET IN THE YEAR 2001**

DANIEL SCHWARTZ

*WATERCOLOR*

"SIMPLY STATED, IF THE POLLUTION OF OUR AIR CONTINUES AT ITS PRESENT PACE, I BELIEVE THAT WE WILL NEVER AGAIN SEE A CLEAR AND NATURAL SUNSET. THE SUN WILL BE SEEN AS A FADING BEACON SINKING INTO A HORIZON OF EVERLASTING FOG."

50,000 SQUARE KILOMETERS OF CLOSED TROPICAL RAINFORESTS ARE LOGGED ANNUALLY. LOGGERS TAKE ON 5 PERCENT OF THE TREES BUT LEAVE ONE-THIRD OF THE LAND OPEN TO EROSION, PERMANENTLY DAMAGED BY THE MACHINERY AND THE FALLING TREES.

........................

50 000 KM2 GESCHLOSSENEN TROPISCHEN REGENWALDES WERDEN JÄHRLICH ZERSTÖRT. DABEI WERDEN NUR 5 PROZENT DER BÄUME GEFÄLLT, ABER EIN DRITTEL DES BODENS WIRD DER EROSION UND BLEIBENDEN SCHÄDEN DURCH DIE MASCHINEN UND FALLENDEN BÄUME AUSGESETZT.

........................

CHAQUE ANNÉE, ON DÉTRUIT 50 000 KM2 DE FORÊTS TROPICALES DENSES. LES BÛCHERONS N'ABATTENT QUE 5% DES ARBRES, MAIS UN TIERS DE LA SURFACE EST EXPOSÉE À L'ÉROSION ET LES DOMMAGES CAUSÉS PAR LES MACHINES ET LES ARBRES ABATTUS SONT IRRÉVERSIBLES.

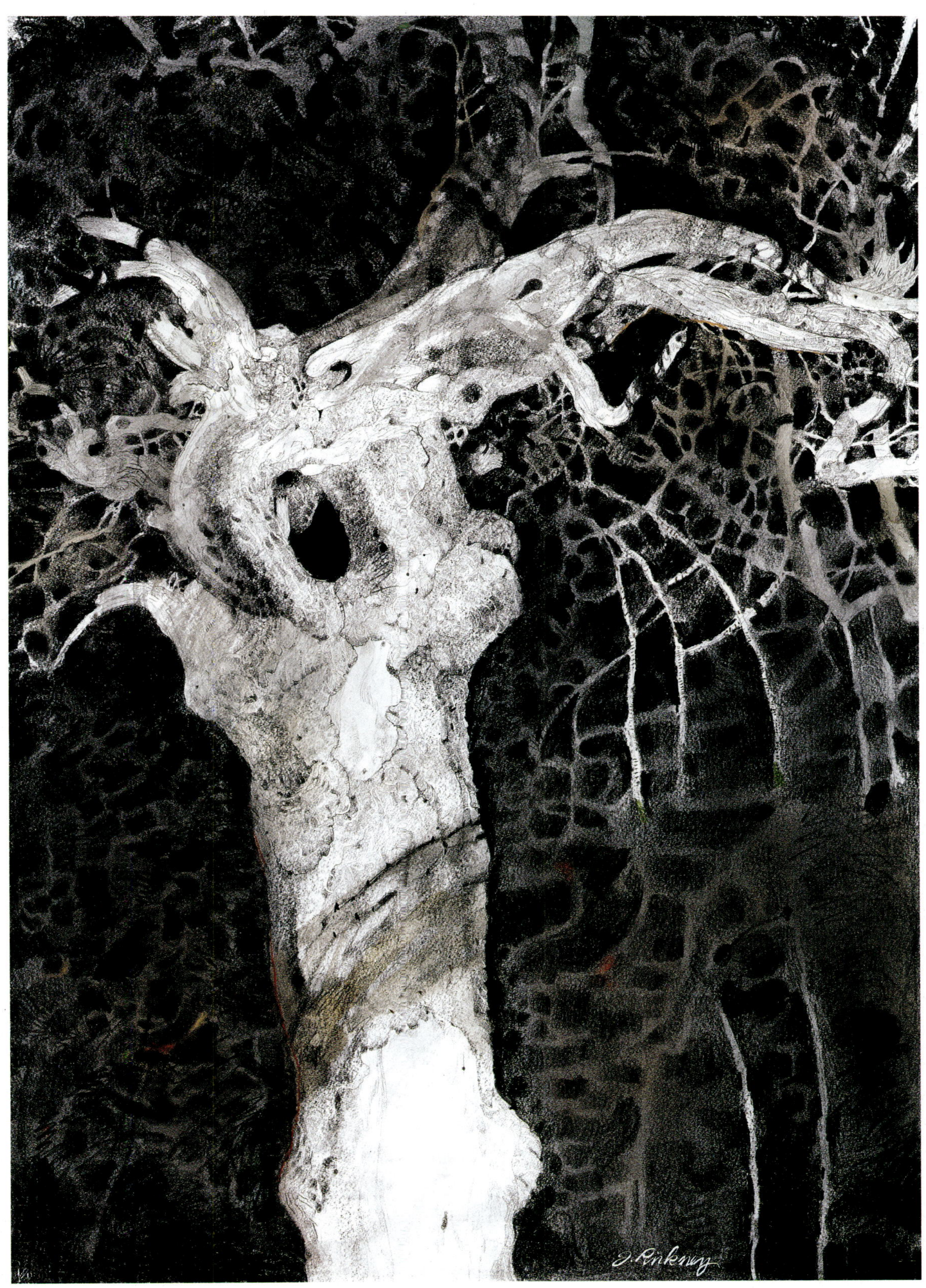

**DRAWING IN BLACK AND GREEN**

JERRY PINKNEY

*PENCIL AND WATERCOLOR ON PAPER*

"THE TORTURED APPEARANCE OF THIS TREE SYMBOLIZES MY FEAR FOR THE ENVIRONMENT."

THE WORLD BANK AND THE INTERNATIONAL MONETARY FUND ARE FUNDING DEVELOPMENT PROGRAMS IN BRAZIL: ONE PLACES A HIGHWAY THROUGH A RAINFOREST REGION TO PROMOTE RESETTLEMENT FROM CROWDED AREAS, AND THE OTHER PROMOTES MINING AND MINERAL DEVELOPMENT. THE RESETTLEMENT PROGRAM IS RESPONSIBLE FOR THE MOST RAPID DEFORESTATION IN BRAZIL. THE MINING PROJECT HAS ALREADY DESTROYED TWO-THIRDS OF THE TREES IN THE STATE OF MINAS GERAIS.

..........................

DIE WELTBANK UND DER INTERNATIONALE WÄHRUNGSFOND UNTERSTÜTZEN ENTWICKLUNGSPROJEKTE IN BRASILIEN: EINES FÖRDERT SIEDLUNGSBAU, EIN ANDERES BERGBAU UND DEN ABBAU VON MINERALIEN. DAS SIEDLUNGSPROGRAMM HAT ZUR RAPIDESTEN ABHOLZUNG DES REGENWALDES GEFÜHRT, DEM BERGBAUPROJEKT SIND BEREITS ZWEI DRITTEL DER BÄUME IN DER BETROFFENEN REGION ZUM OPFER GEFALLEN.

..........................

LA BANQUE MONDIALE ET LE FONDS MONÉTAIRE INTERNATIONAL FINANCENT DES PROGRAMMES DE DÉVELOPPEMENT AU BRÉSIL, NOTAMMENT L'ÉTABLISSEMENT DE COLONIES, LE DÉVELOPPEMENT DE L'INDUSTRIE MINIÈRE ET L'EXPLOITATION DES MINÉRAUX. LE PREMIER PROJET ENTRAÎNE LA DESTRUCTION DE LA FORÊT AMAZONIENNE. DEUX TIERS DES ARBRES ONT ÉTÉ SACRIFIÉS AU PROJET MINIER.

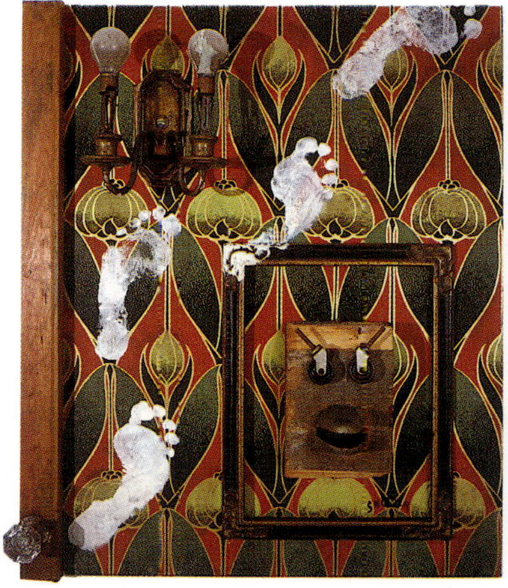

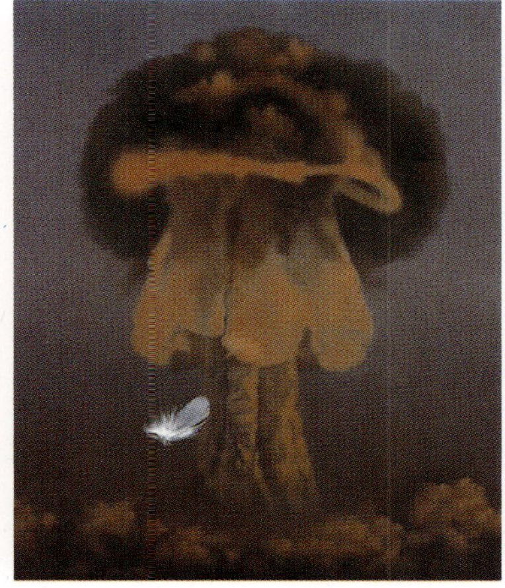

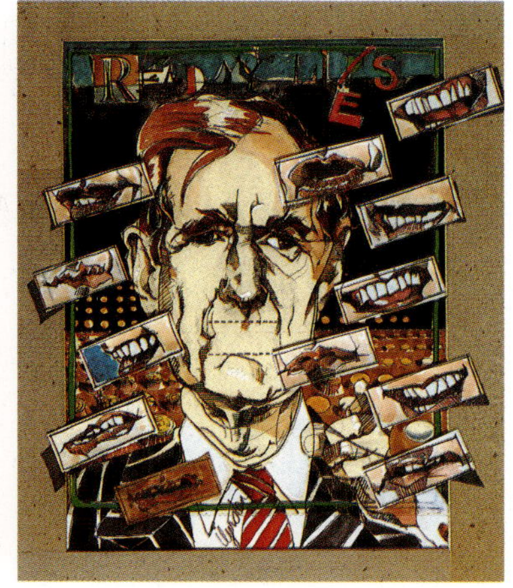

## WHAT ARE WE DOING?

Isadore Seltzer

*Mixed assemblage: paint, wood, glass, metal, paper*

"This piece depicts the destruction of animal life through the framed decapitated animal head; the destruction of plant life through the human footprints obliterating the flora; and the destruction of energy resources through the defunct electrical fixture. The doorknob offers our last chance through a choice by action."

## THE BEAUTY AND THE BEAST

Ben Verkaaik

*Oil on wood*

"Symbolizing a world where the ultimate vulnerability and the ultimate violence seem to be in a constant battle of balance."

## READ MY...

Gerry Gersten

*Pencil, dyes, and gouache on vellum*

"Environmental controls are manifested from the 'top' down. Our chief executive has tantalized us with environmental 'ideas' and has subsequently lied."

DEFORESTATION SIGNIFICANTLY REDUCES RAINFALL AND INCREASES SURFACE TEMPERATURES IN THE RAINFOREST. THIS CAUSES A GENERAL DRYING TREND THAT COULD HAVE BROADER REPERCUSSIONS.

........................

ENTWALDUNG REDUZIERT DIE REGENFÄLLE UND ERHÖHT DIE TEMPERATUREN IM REGENWALD. DIES VERURSACHT EIN ALLGEMEINES AUSTROCKNEN UND KÖNNTE WEITERREICHENDE AUSWIRKUNGEN HABEN.

........................

LA DÉFORESTATION FAIT DIMINUER LES CHUTES DE PLUIE, ENTRAÎNANT L'AUGMENTATION DE LA TEMPÉRATURE DANS LES FORÊTS TROPICALES. IL S'ENSUIT UN DESSÈCHEMENT GÉNÉRAL QUI POURRAIT AVOIR DES CONSÉQUENCES ÉNORMES.

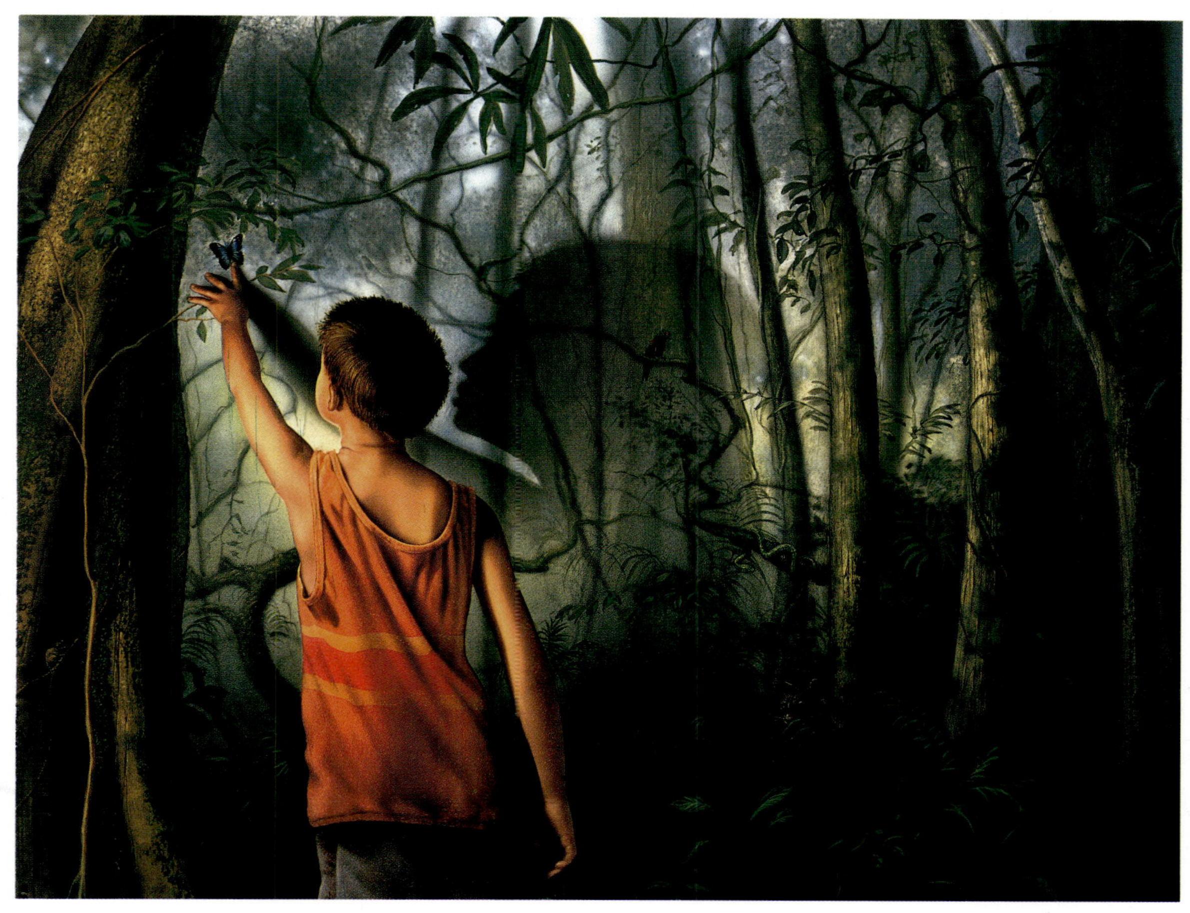

**UNTITLED**

Mark Frederickson

*Acrylic*

"The boy is real. The forest is a painting."

WE HAVE INCREASED THE AMOUNT OF CARBON DIOXIDE IN THE AIR BY ABOUT 25 PERCENT IN THE LAST CENTURY AND WILL ALMOST CERTAINLY DOUBLE IT IN THE NEXT; WE HAVE MORE THAN DOUBLED THE AMOUNT OF METHANE.

..........................

IM VERGANGENEN JAHRHUNDERT IST DER ANTEIL AN KOHLENDIOXID IN DER LUFT UM 25 PROZENT GESTIEGEN.

..........................

AU COURS DE CE SIÈCLE, LES ÉMISSIONS DE DIOXYDE DE SOUFRE DANS L'ATMOSPHÈRE ONT AUGMENTÉ DE 25%.

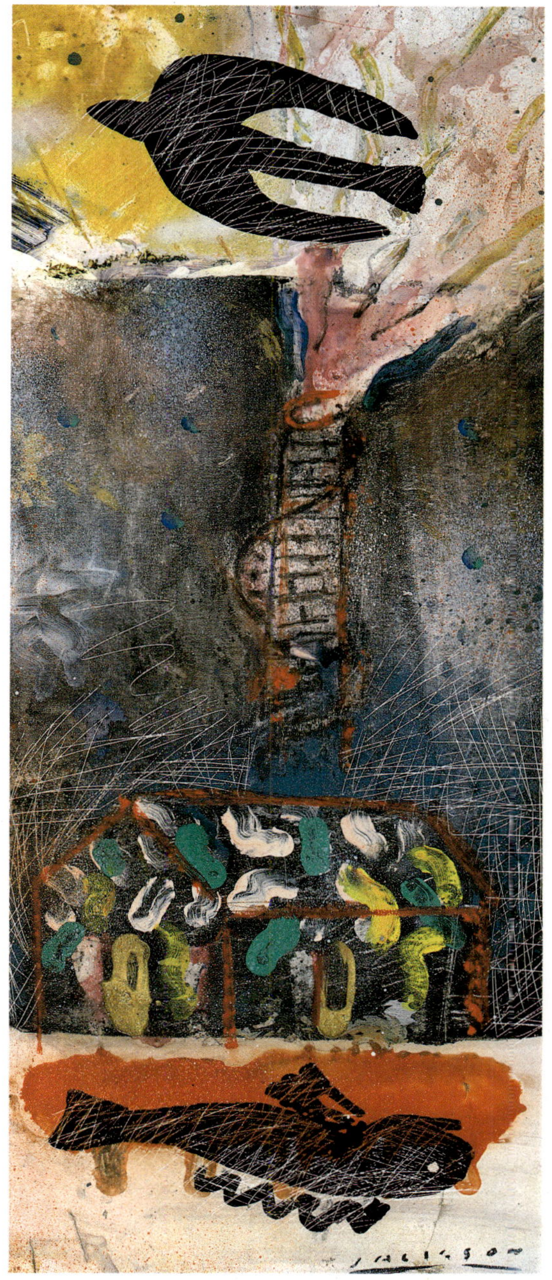

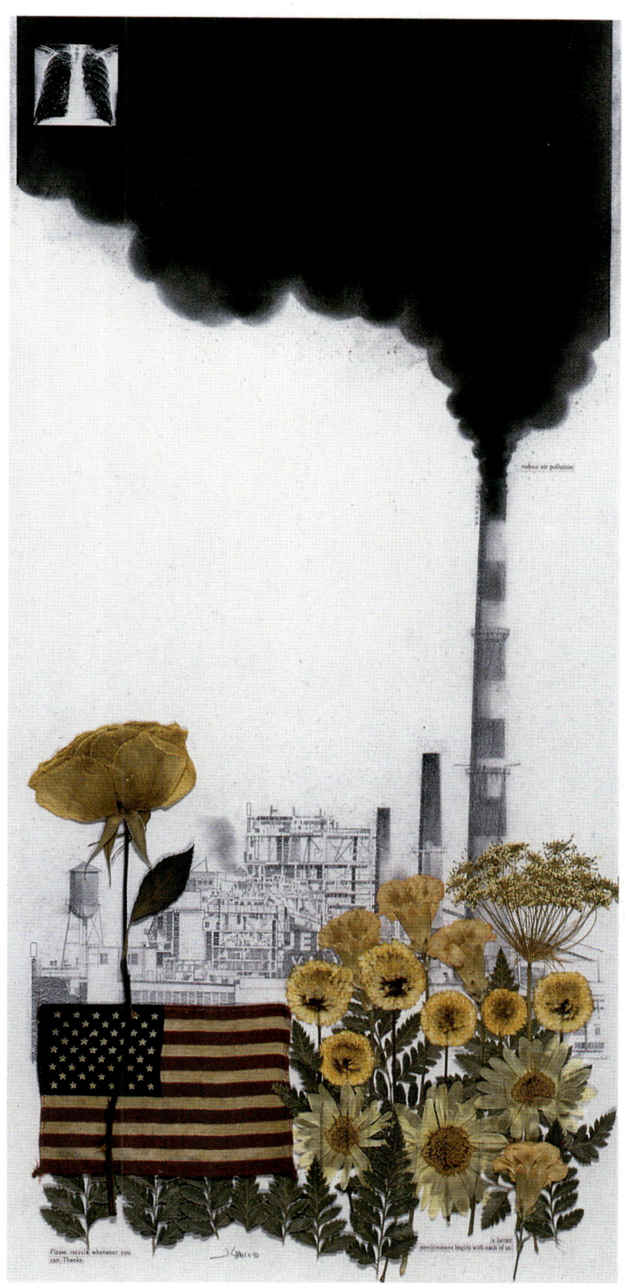


**ABOVE AND BELOW**

JEFF JACKSON

*MIXED MEDIA*

"AROUND US IS A FRAGILE ENVIRONMENT, GROWING WEAKER BY THE DAY. MAY THE 'GREENING' OF THE PLANET TURN BACK THIS DOWNWARD SPIRAL."

**IT'S IN OUR BACKYARD**

JEFF CORNELL

*MIXED MEDIA*

"POLLUTION IS IN OUR BACKYARDS. PEOPLE ARE DYING IN OUR OWN BACKYARDS BECAUSE OF POLLUTION, AND IF WE DON'T CLEAN UP THINGS, WE WILL NOT HAVE A GARDEN IN IT. AND IF YOU LOVE AMERICA, YOU'LL DO SOMETHING ABOUT IT."

2.4 BILLION POUNDS
OF DANGEROUS POLLUTANTS
ARE RELEASED INTO THE
AIR EACH YEAR.

........................

MEHR ALS 1 MILLION
TONNEN GEFÄHRLICHER
STOFFE WERDEN JÄHRLICH IN DIE
LUFT GELASSEN.

........................

PLUS D'UN MILLION DE
TONNES DE POLLUANTS DANGEREUX
SONT REJETÉS DANS L'ATMOSPHÈRE
CHAQUE ANNÉE.

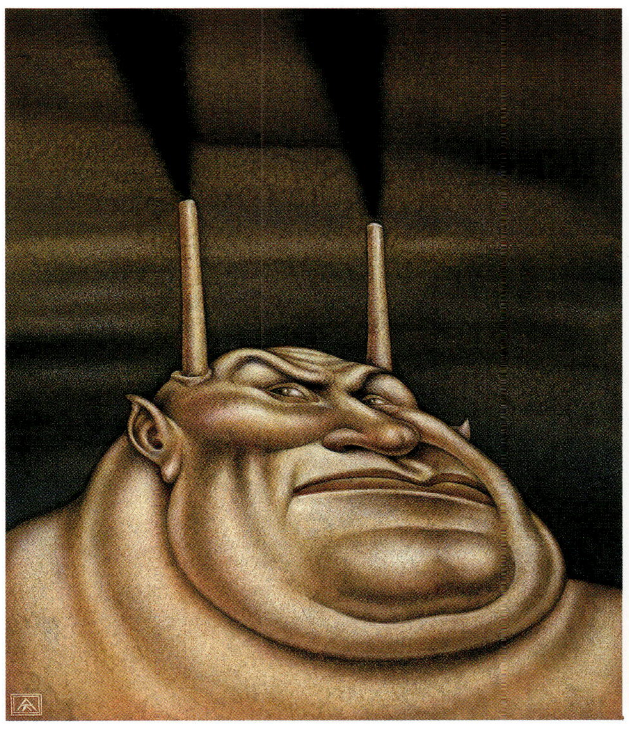

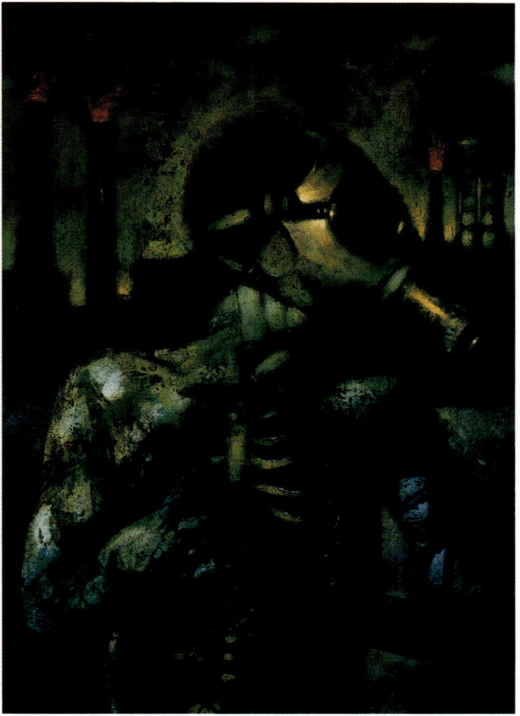

**PIG**

Anita Kunz

*Watercolor*

**THE SKY IS A POISONOUS GARDEN**

Eric Dinyer

*Oil on canvas*

"Starting in mid-August, 1990, in Jacksonville, Arkansas, a state contractor plans to burn 28,500 barrels of toxic waste at an abandoned pesticide plant in the middle of a residential neighborhood. Opponents fear that the burning could release deadly chemicals."

THE ATMOSPHERE IS NOT
A PERFUME—IT HAS NO TASTE
OF THE DISTILLATION—
IT IS ODORLESS;
IT IS FOR MY MOUTH FOREVER—
I AM IN LOVE WITH IT;
I WILL GO TO THE BANK BY
THE WOOD, AND BECOME
UNDISGUISED AND NAKED;
I AM MAD FOR IT TO
BE IN CONTACT WITH ME.
—WALT WHITMAN,
*LEAVES OF GRASS*

.........................

ICH WERDE ZU DER
BANKBEIM WALD GEHEN UND
UNGETARNT UND NACKT SEIN;
ICH SEHNE MICH NACH DER
BERÜHRUNG DER ATMOSPHÄRE.
WALT WHITMAN,
*LEAVES OF GRASS*.

.........................

«J'IRAI SUR LA RIVE PAR
LES BOIS, JE LAISSERAI TOMBER LE
MASQUE ET JE SERAI NU;
J'AI LA NOSTALGIE DE CETTE
ATMOSPHÈRE.
WALT WHITMAN,
*LEAVES OF GRASS*.

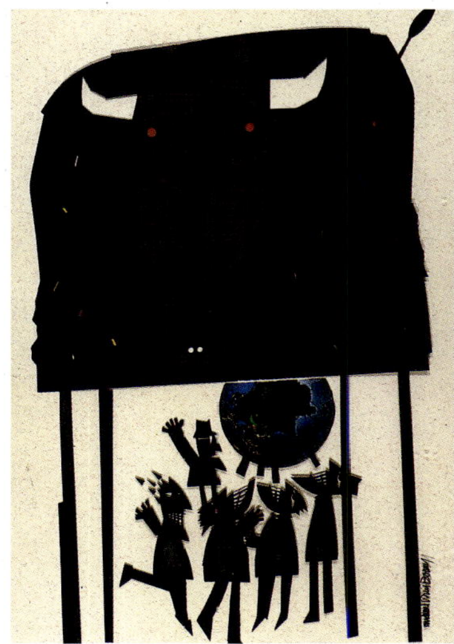

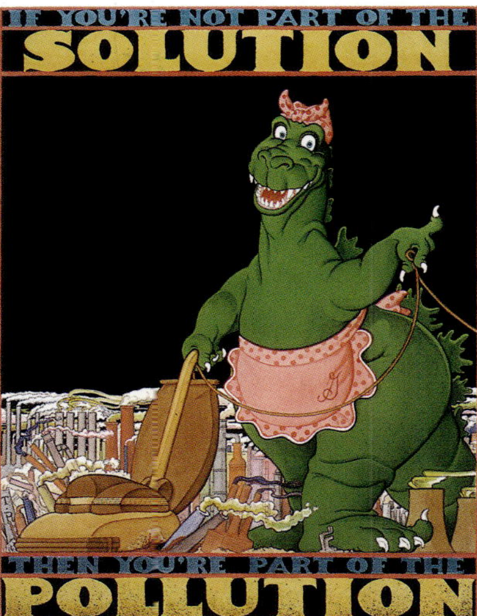



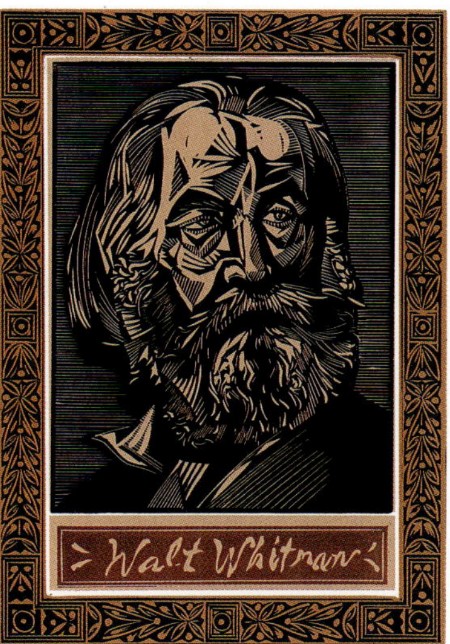



### MOTHER EARTH

Michael David Brown

*Collage*

"The piece simply symbolizes the drain mankind is exerting on earth's resources."

### SOLUTION/POLLUTION

Timothy C. Raglin

*Ink*

"I hope to demonstrate that we can apply a sense of humor to this serious situation."

### HOMAGE TO WALT WHITMAN

Stephen Alcorn

*Five-color linocut*

"With this portrait, which is one of an ongoing series, I would like to pay homage to a great poet whose jubilant and mystifying verses so eloquently express mankind's potential to be fascinated and moved by the wonders of nature."

THE WORLD COMMUNITY HAS DEDICATED SUCCESSIVE DECADES TO DEVELOPMENT. YET IN 1987, DEVELOPING COUNTRIES WITH 77 PERCENT OF OUR POPULATION AVERAGED A YEARLY INCOME OF ONLY $670 PER PERSON, WHILE THE AVERAGE INCOME IN INDUSTRIAL NATIONS WAS $12,070.

........................

DIE NATIONEN DER WELT HABEN IHRER ENTWICKLUNG VIELE JAHRZEHNTE GEWIDMET, DOCH 1987 LAG DAS JÄHRLICHE DURCHSCHNITTSEINKOMMEN IN DEN ENTWICKLUNGSLÄNDERN, D.H. VON 77% DER WELTBEVÖLKERUNG, BEI $ 670 PRO KOPF, IN DEN INDUSTRIENATIONEN DAGEGEN BEI $ 12 070.

........................

MALGRÉ LES EFFORTS DE LA COMMUNAUTÉ MONDIALE, EN 1987, LE REVENU MOYEN ANNUEL DES PAYS EN VOIE DE DÉVELOPPEMENT, SOIT 77% DE LA POPULATION MONDIALE, N'ÉTAIT QUE DE $ 670 PAR PERSONNE, CELUI DES PAYS INDUSTRIALISÉS DE $ 12'070.

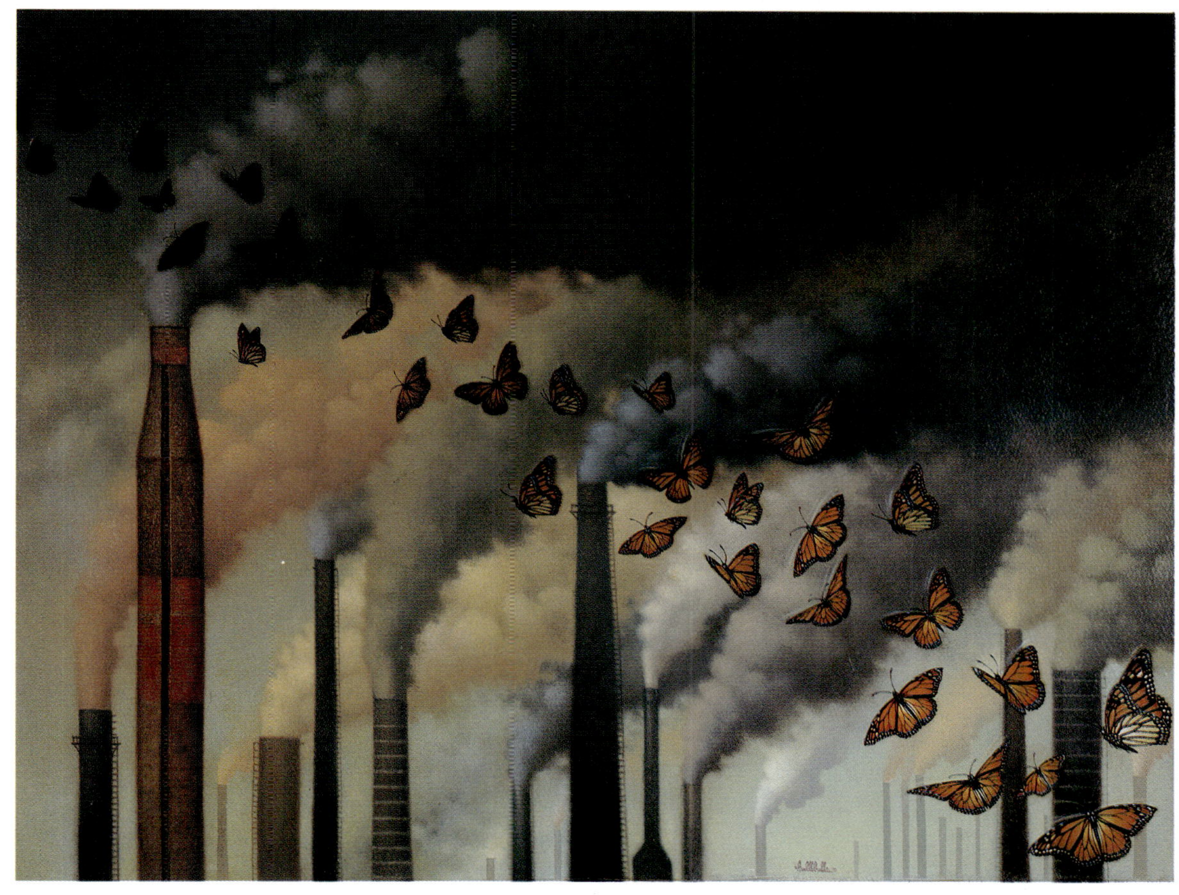

**MONARCHY OF DEATH**

Braldt Bralds

*Oil on paper*

**UNTITLED**

Seymour Chwast

*Oil on paper*

"Our earth is the unwitting victim of sloppy, nefarious greed in the name of progress."

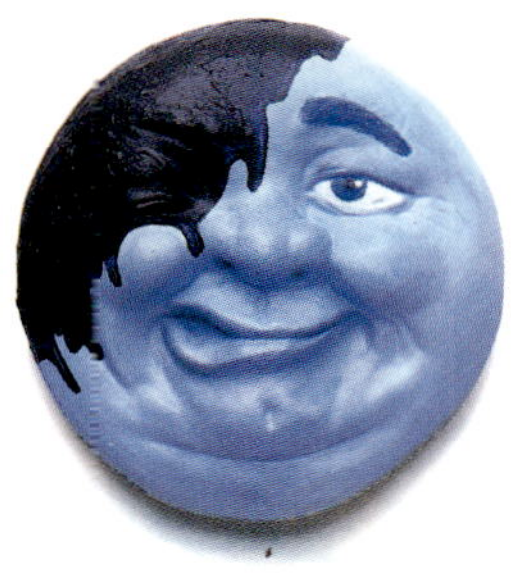

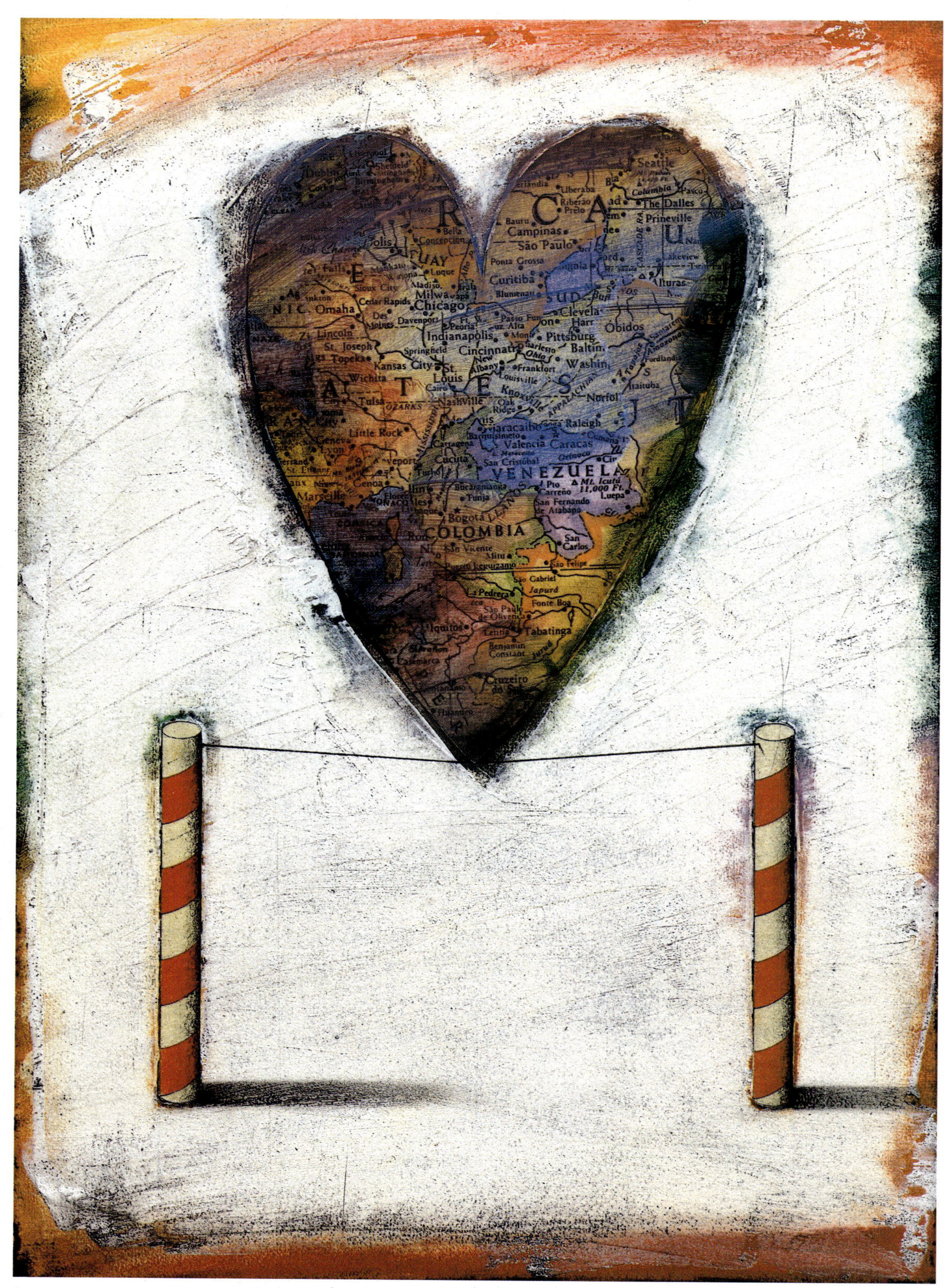


**BALANCE**

DAVID LESH

*MIXED MEDIA*

"THE IDEA OF THE WORLD BALANCED ON A TIGHTROPE REALLY PLAYS UP THE PRECARIOUS POSITION OF OUR PLANET TODAY. THIS TENSION OF 'IN BALANCE—OUT OF BALANCE' DEMANDS A SOLUTION BEFORE THE IRREVERSIBLE FALL TAKES PLACE."

THE MAIN CAUSE OF
ANIMAL EXTINCTION IS HABITAT
DESTRUCTION, ESPECIALLY IN
TROPICAL FORESTS WHERE RAPIDLY
INCREASING NUMBERS OF PEOPLE
MUST CLEAR MORE LAND FOR
AGRICULTURAL DEVELOPMENT,
FUEL WOOD, CATTLE
GRAZING, SETTLEMENT,
AND TROPICAL LUMBER.

..........................

HAUPTURSACHE FÜR
DAS AUSSTERBEN VON TIERARTEN
IST DIE ZERSTÖRUNG DES
LEBENSRAUMS DURCH RODUNGEN
DER TROPISCHEN WÄLDER ZUR
GEWINNUNG VON ACKER-, WEIDE-
UND BAULAND, BRENNHOLZ
UND TROPISCHER HÖLZER.

..........................

L'EXTINCTION D'ESPÈCES
ANIMALES PROVIENT DE LA
DESTRUCTION DE L'ESPACE VITAL,
SURTOUT DE L'ESSARTAGE DES
FORÊTS TROPICALES POUR
DÉVELOPPER L'AGRICULTURE ET
L'ÉLEVAGE, LA CONSTRUCTION,
LA PRODUCTION DE BOIS DE
CHAUFFAGE ET D'ESSENCES
TROPICALES.

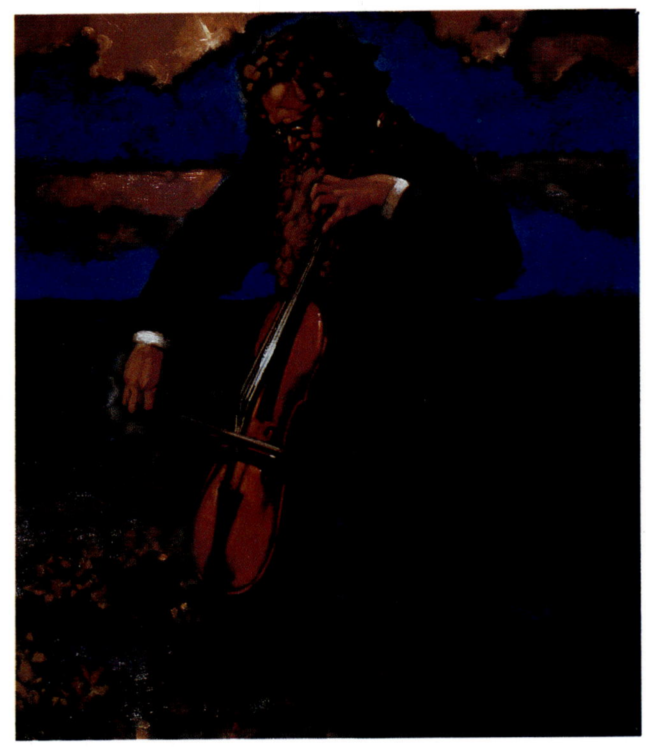

## THE ARTIST AND THE ENVIRONMENT

RICK McCOLLUM

*OIL ON LINEN BOARD*

"THE ENVIRONMENT GREATLY EFFECTS THE ARTIST AND HIS CREATIVITY. ALL THAT IS FELT, EXPERIENCED, AND INTERPRETED IS EXPRESSED THROUGH THE ARTS. AS THE ENVIRONMENT IS TAKEN AWAY OR LIMITED, SO IS THE ARTIST'S VISION. THE ARTIST IS HIS ENVIRONMENT."

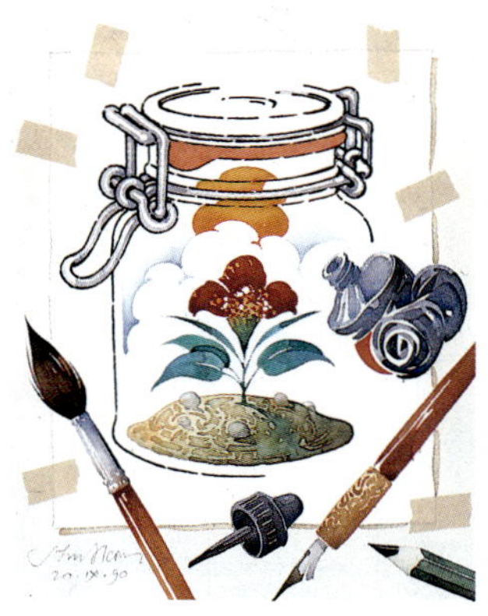

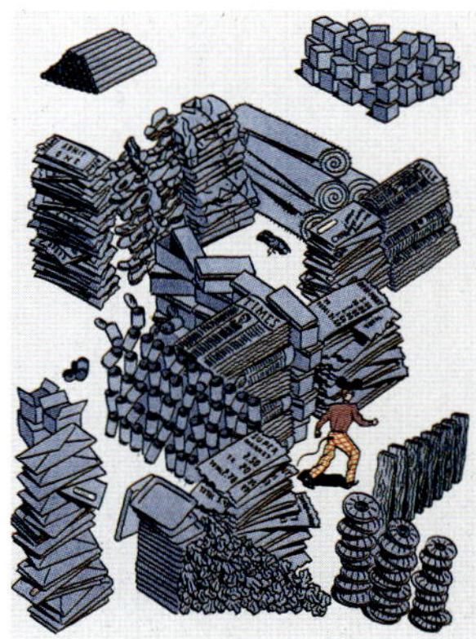

## PRESERVATION

JOHN ALCORN

*WATERCOLOR*

## PACKRAT

STEVEN GUARNACCIA

*PEN AND INK WITH WATERCOLOR*

ECOSYSTEMS, POLLUTION, AND ECONOMIC FACTORS DO NOT RESPECT NATURAL BORDERS, MAKING INTERNATIONAL COMMUNICATION AND COOPERATION CRITICAL TO GLOBAL RESTORATION AND SUSTAINABLE DEVELOPMENT.

........................

ÖKOSYSTEME, UMWELTVERSCHMUTZUNG UND WIRTSCHAFTLICHE FAKTOREN SIND GRENZÜBERSCHREITEND, SO DASS INTERNATIONALE KOMMUNIKATION UND ZUSAMMENARBEIT VORAUSSETZUNG FÜR WIRKSAME MASSNAHMEN SIND.

........................

LES ÉCOSYSTÈMES, LA POLLUTION ET LES FACTEURS ÉCONOMIQUES NE CONNAISSENT PAS DE FRONTIÈRES, AUSSI UNE COLLABORATION INTERNATIONALE EST-ELLE NÉCESSAIRE POUR UNE INTERVENTION EFFICACE.

## COMING TO OUR SENSES

LEO AND DIANE DILLON

*PASTEL AND WATERCOLOR*

"THE CONTRAST BETWEEN THE INSENSITIVE, MECHANIZED, INDUSTRIAL, PROFIT-ORIENTED MENTALITY, VERSUS THE CONCERNED, ENVIRONMENTAL, AND NATURE-ORIENTED MIND."

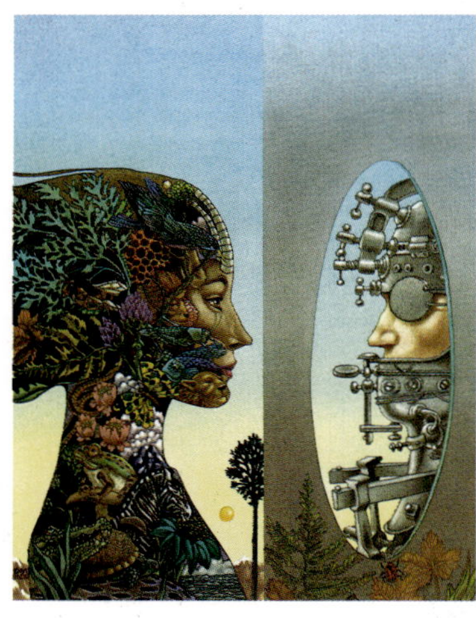

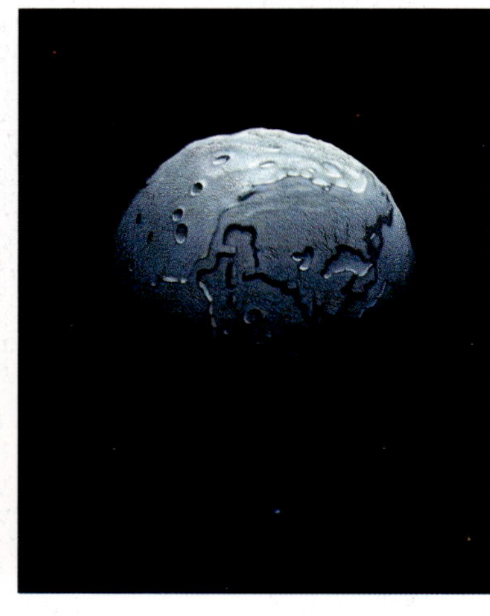

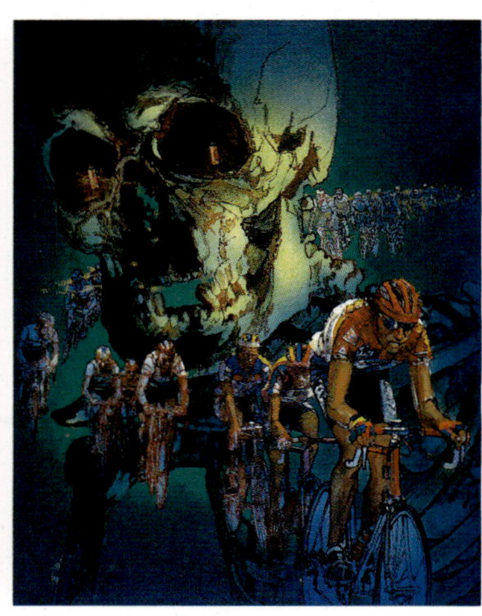

## DEAD PLANET

M. CHRISTOPHER ZACHAROW

*ACRYLIC ON BOARD*

"IF WE DON'T START CARING FOR THE EARTH, WE WILL END UP WITH A DEAD PLANET."

## THE RACE IS ON

JAMES SHARPE

*OIL AND ACRYLICS ON CANVAS*

"ATMOSPHERIC POLLUTION IS GRADUALLY GAINING ON EFFORTS TO CONTAIN IT. WE ARE IN A LIFE-AND-DEATH RACE FOR CLEAN AIR."

DURING THE LATTER HALF OF THE 1970S AND THE EARLY 1980S, THE OZONE CONCENTRATION IN JAPAN AND EUROPE WAS 75 PERCENT HIGHER THAN LEVELS CONSIDERED SAFE; AUSTRALIA AND AMERICA EXCEEDED LIMITS BY 400 PERCENT.

..........................

IN DER ZWEITEN HÄLFTE DER 70ER JAHRE UND IN DEN FRÜHEN 80ERN LAGEN DIE OZONWERTE IN JAPAN UND EUROPA 75 PROZENT ÜBER DEN AKZEPTABLEN GRENZWERTEN, IN AUSTRALIEN UND AMERIKA WURDEN DIE GRENZWERTE UM 400 PROZENT ÜBERSCHRITTEN.

..........................

PENDANT LA DEUXIÈME MOITIÉ DES ANNÉES 70 ET AU DÉBUT DES ANNÉES 80, LA CONCENTRATION D'OZONE AU JAPON ET EN EUROPE ÉTAIT 75% PLUS ÉLEVÉE QUE LES NIVEAUX ADMISSIBLES. EN AUSTRALIE ET EN AMÉRIQUE, CES VALEURS LIMITES AVAIENT ÉTÉ DÉPASSÉES DE 400%.

## LET'S WATCH WHALES

Simms Taback

*Pen, ink, watercolor, and airbrush*

"Whales are threatened species. This piece was commissioned by Scholastic, Inc., to help children identify whales."

## HUSK

Alan Magee

*Monotype collage*

"In 1984 I began a series of paintings and collages which addressed my concerns about the troubling direction being taken by my country. The standing figure in *Husk* represents these unwholesome values followed to their logical conclusion. The trappings of power remain intact, while the flesh has fallen away and the marvelous earth has become a wasteland."

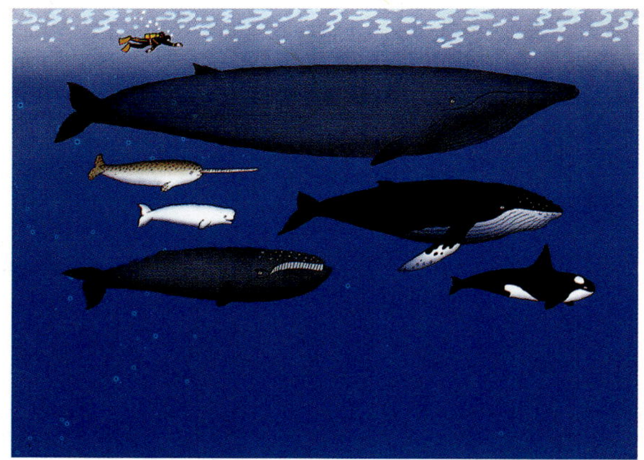

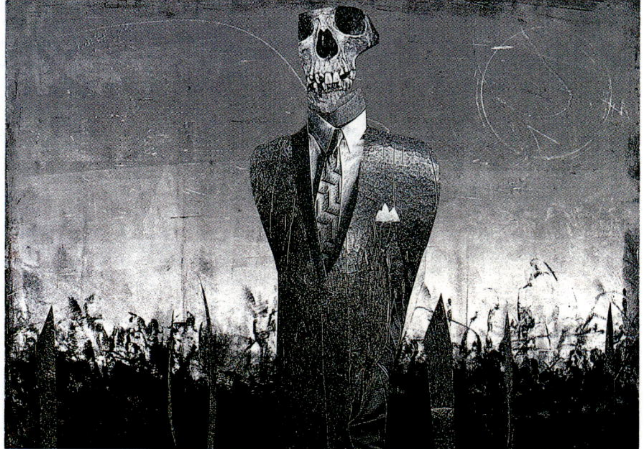

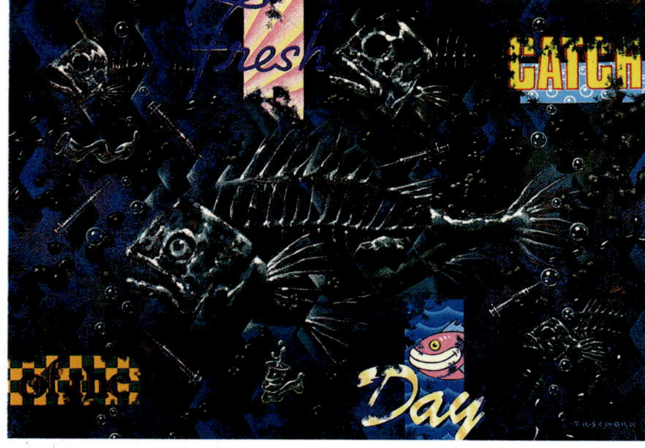


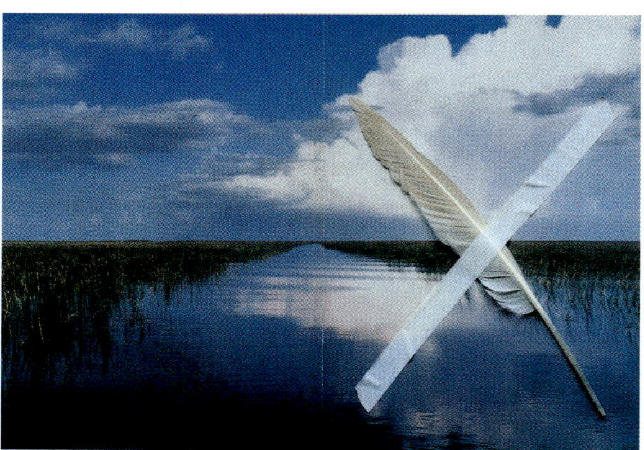

## FRESH CATCH OF THE DAY

Todd Schorr

*Acrylic on Arches watercolor paper*

"There is a tendency in our society to not want to truly confront some of the grimmer aspects of reality but to gloss over them or pay lip service to them until they hopefully go away, as is seen in this image of upbeat advertising slogans hiding a graver truth below the surface."

## CALIFORNIA'S VANISHING WETLANDS

Ivan Chermayeff

*Assemblage on color photograph*

THE WORLD'S POPULATION
OF BLUE WHALES AND HUMPBACKS,
ORIGINALLY NUMBERING 200,000
AND 50,000 RESPECTIVELY, NOW
NUMBER ONLY 15,000 AND 3,000.

. . . . . . . . . . . . . . . . . . . . . . . . . . .

DIE GESAMTE ANZAHL DER
BLAUWALE UND BUCKELWALE IST
VON URSPRÜNGLICH 200 000 BZW.
50 000 AUF NUR 15 000 BZW.
3000 ZURÜCKGEGANGEN.

. . . . . . . . . . . . . . . . . . . . . . . . . . .

LE NOMBRE DE BALEINES
BLEUES ET DE BALEINES NOIRES
DANS LE MONDE, ALORS QU'IL
S'ÉLEVAIT À 200 000 ET 50 000
AUTREFOIS, N'EST PLUS QUE
DE 15 000 ET 3000.

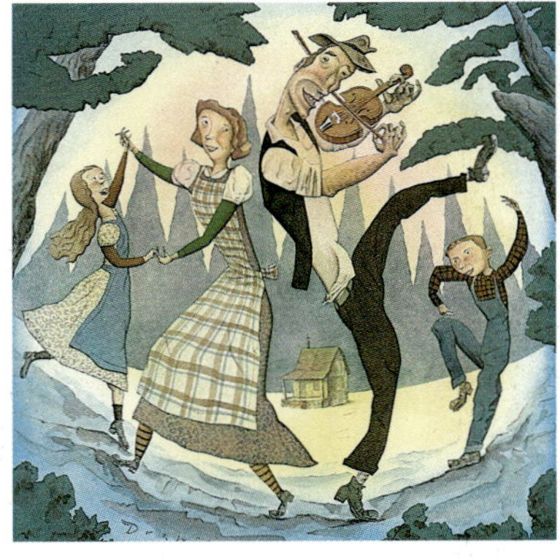

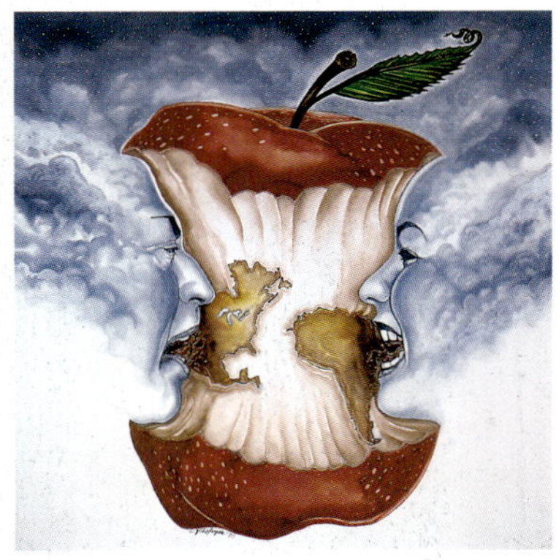

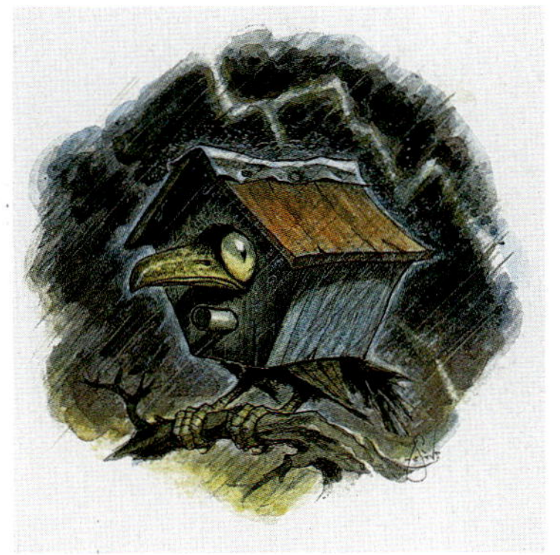

## TALL TIMBER MUSIC

BLAIR DRAWSON

*WATERCOLOR*

"IN THESE DARK DAYS OF THE WORLD'S HISTORY, OCCUPIED AS WE ARE NOW WITH OUR TROUBLES, WE SOMETIMES FORGET TO PLAY. I AM THEREFORE DEPICTING A FAMILY PLAYING MUSIC, DANCING, ALL THE WHILE SURROUNDED BY MIGHTY NATURE. THIS IS NOT A VISION OF APOCALYPSE, BUT OF HARMONY."

## THE BITTEN APPLE

GARY VISKUPIC

*WATERCOLOR DYES AND COLORED PENCIL*

"THE IMAGE OF THE EARTH AS AN APPLE BEING DEVOURED BY GLUTTONOUS HUMANKIND. THE FACES, BY DEPLETING THE EARTH, ARE ALSO ASSURING THEIR OWN DISAPPEARANCE— THEY ARE DISSOLVING INTO THE MIST. EATING THE FORBIDDEN FRUIT (OUR EARTH) MAY BANISH US FROM THE GARDEN OF EDEN FOREVER."

## BYE, BYE, BIRDIE

PETER DE SEVE

*WATERCOLOR AND INK*

"THIS ILLUSTRATION IS ABOUT THE SHRINKING REFUGE FOR WILDLIFE."

IN THE TROPICS, 10 TREES ARE BEING CUT FOR EVERY ONE PLANTED; IN AFRICA THE RATE IS 29 TO ONE.

........................

IN DEN TROPEN WERDEN FÜR JEDEN NEU GEPFLANZTEN BAUM 10 GEFÄLLT, IN AFRIKA IST DAS VERHÄLTNIS 29:1.

........................

DANS LES TROPIQUES, 10 ARBRES SONT COUPÉS POUR UN SEUL DE PLANTÉ; EN AFRIQUE, 29 POUR UN.

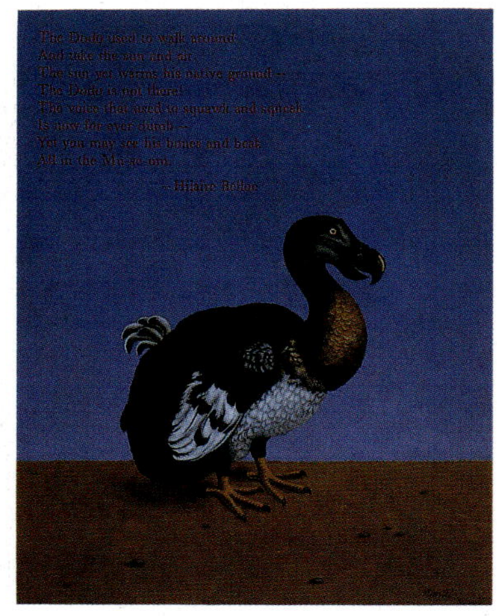

## THE DODO BIRD

Richard Mantel

*Acrylic*

"This flightless bird was discovered by explorers on the island of Mauritius in the sixteenth century and was hunted and haunted out of existence. This was the first documented extinction of a species brought about solely by man's brutal intrusion. The tragedy of this strange bird is a reminder of our responsibility to our fellow creatures."

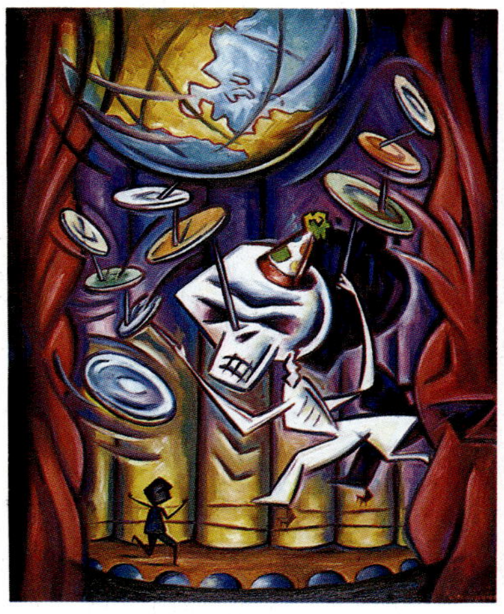

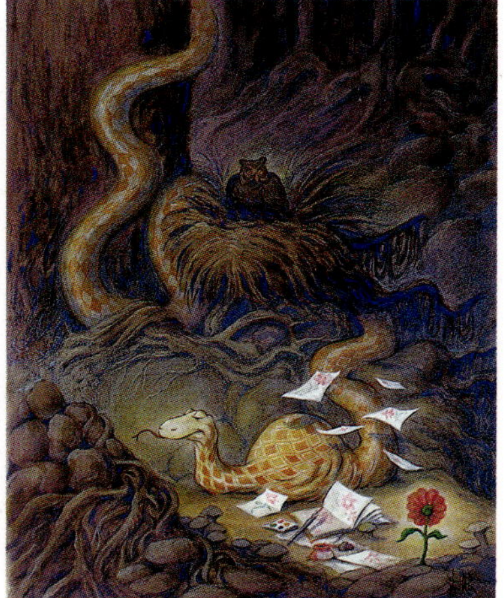

## A DELICATE BALANCE

Kathy Staico Schorr

*Oil on canvas*

"I wanted to focus on how serious it is for us to foolishly tamper with the balance of our fragile earth, the consequences of which are deadly and irreparable."

## SKETCHING IN THE RAINFOREST

Brian Ajhar

*Watercolor, ink, Prismacolor*

"The art was completed with the environment in mind. My approach to what is happening with the environment is by no means making light of such a serious matter. It shows how a lack of awareness can sneak up on those who appreciate the beautiful things in life."

A TEMPERATURE RISE OF
3 DEGREES CELSIUS DUE TO
GLOBAL WARMING COULD RESULT
IN A SEA LEVEL RISE OF UP TO
2 METERS BY THE END OF THE NEXT
CENTURY, FLOODING COASTAL
SETTLEMENTS AND ISLANDS.

..........................

EINE GLOBALE ERWÄRMUNG
UM 3 GRAD C KÖNNTE ENDE DES
NÄCHSTEN JAHRHUNDERTS EINE
ERHÖHUNG DES MEERESSPIEGELS
UM ZWEI METER UND DAMIT
DIE ÜBERFLUTUNG VON
KÜSTENSIEDLUNGEN UND INSELN
ZUR FOLGE HABEN.

..........................

UN RÉCHAUFFEMENT GLOBAL DE
LA TEMPÉRATURE DE 3 DEGRÉS
CELSIUS POURRAIT FAIRE MONTER
LE NIVEAU DES MERS DE DEUX
MÈTRES D'ICI LA FIN DU SIÈCLE
SUIVANT, INONDANT LES RÉGIONS
CÔTIÈRES ET LES ÎLES.

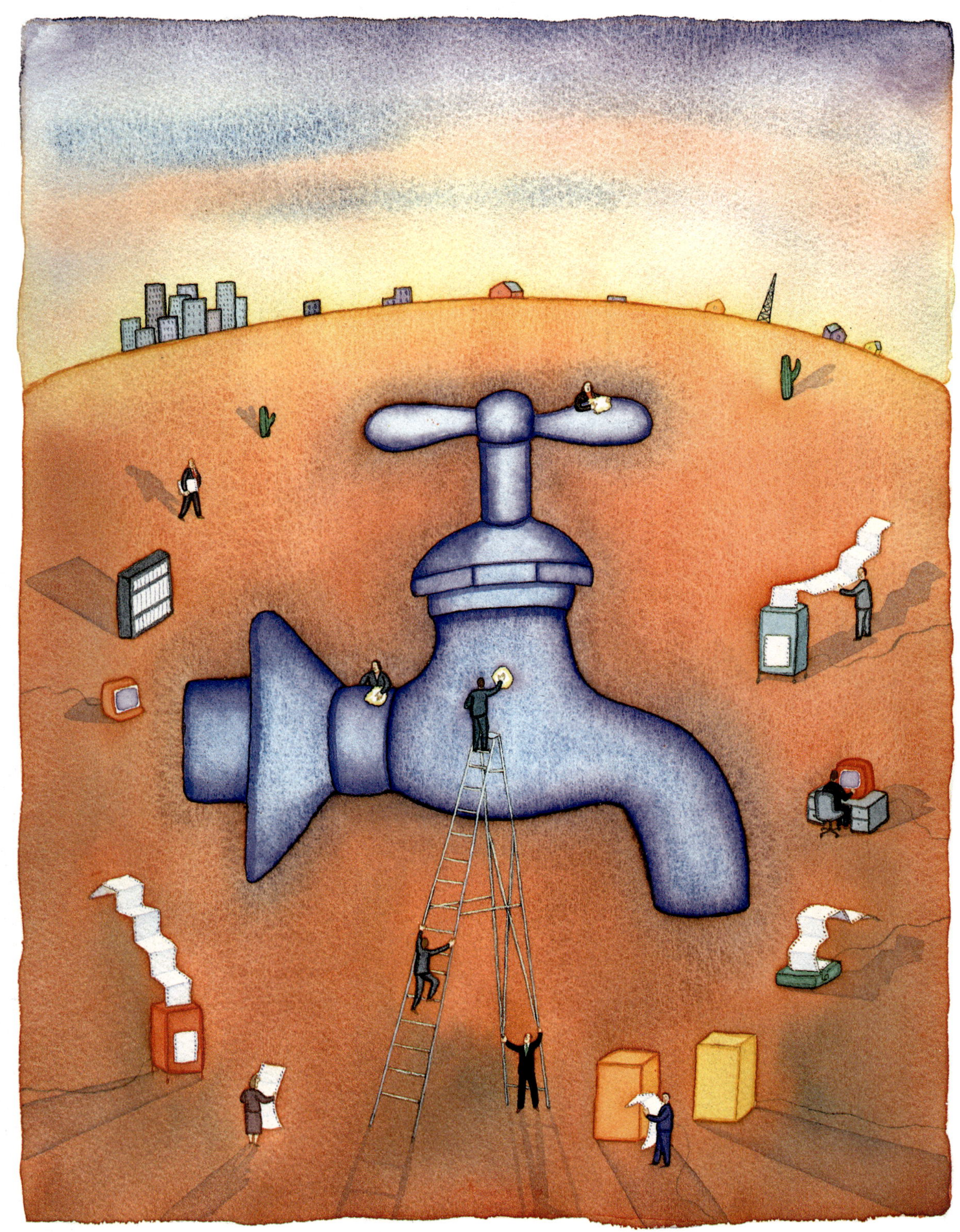

**DALLAS WATER UTILITY UNCLOGS THE INFORMATION PIPELINE (TAPWATER)**

LONNIE SUE JOHNSON

*WATERCOLOR*

"THE LIFESOURCE THAT IS TAKEN FOR GRANTED, WASTED, AND POLLUTED."

MORE THAN 700 CHEMICALS
HAVE BEEN DETECTED IN U.S.
DRINKING WATER, 129 OF WHICH
THE EPA CALLS DANGEROUS. ONLY
40 HAVE BEEN REGULATED.

............................

ÜBER 700 CHEMIKALIEN
WURDEN IM TRINKWASSER DER USA
GEFUNDEN, WOVON 129 GEMÄSS
UMWELTBEHÖRDE ALS GEFÄHRLICH
GELTEN. NUR 40 WURDEN
ABGESCHWÄCHT.

............................

AUX USA, ON A DÉTECTÉ
DANS L'EAU POTABLE PLUS DE 700
SUBSTANCES CHIMIQUES, DONT
129 CONSIDÉRÉES COMME
DANGEREUSES. 40 D'ENTRE
ELLES ONT ÉTÉ NEUTRALISÉES.

INDEX

VERZEICHNIS

INDEX

GRAPHIS SUBSCRIPTION AND BOOK ORDER INFORMATION

ABONNEMENT DER ZEITSCHRIFT GRAPHIS UND BUCHBESTELLUNGEN

ABONNEMENT POUR LA REVUE GRAPHIS ET COMMANDE DES LIVRES

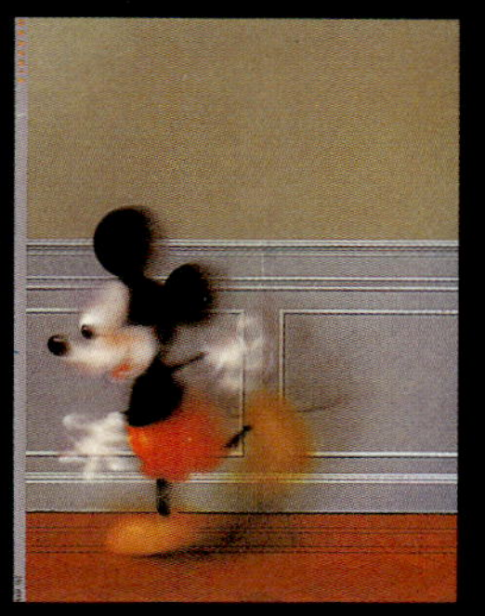
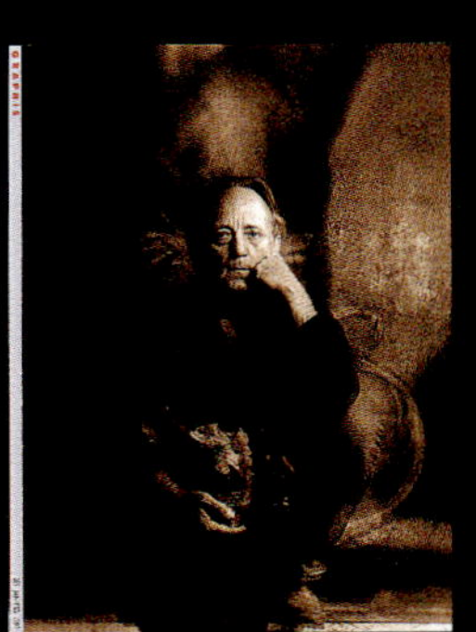
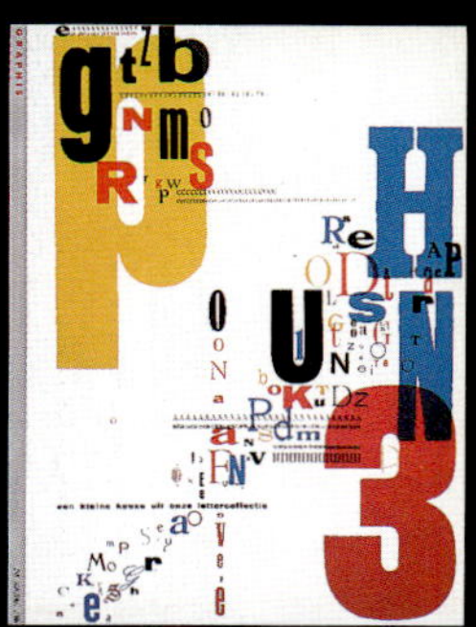
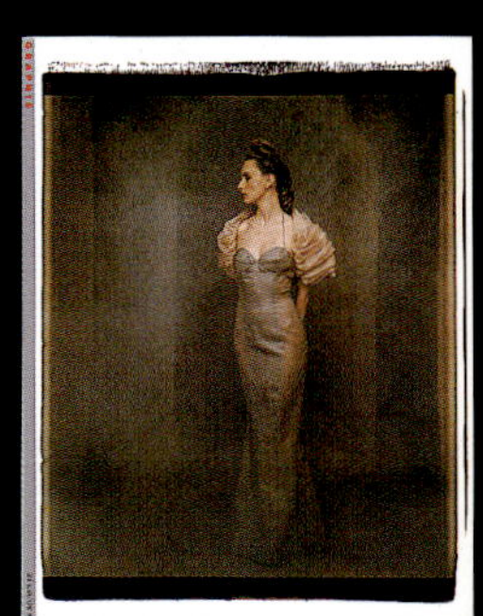
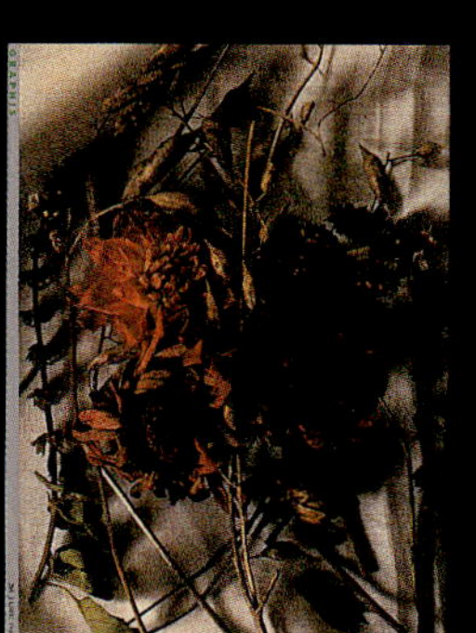
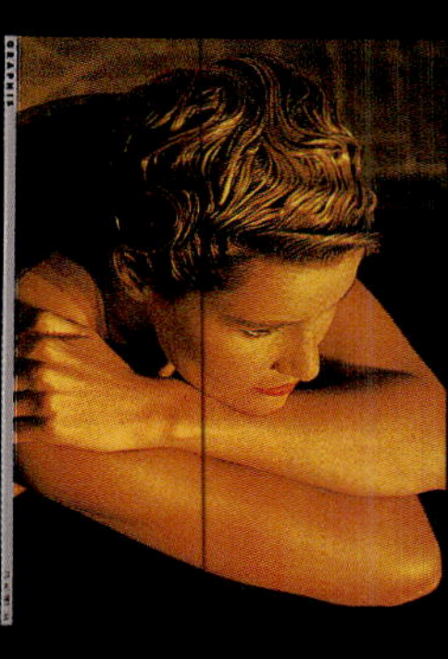

## SUBSCRIBE TO GRAPHIS: USA AND CANADA

| MAGAZINE | USA | CANADA |
|---|---|---|
| ☐ NEW ☐ RENEW | | |
| ☐ TWO YEARS (12 ISSUES) | US$149.00 | US$166.00 |
| ☐ ONE YEAR (6 ISSUES) | US$ 79.00 | US$ 88.00 |

☐ 25% DISCOUNT FOR STUDENTS WITH COPY OF VALID, DATED STUDENT ID AND PAYMENT WITH ORDER

FOR CREDIT CARD PAYMENT:

☐ VISA ☐ MASTERCARD

**ACCT. NO** **EXP. DATE**

**SIGNATURE**

☐ CHECK ENCLOSED ☐ BILL ME

CHECK THE LANGUAGE VERSION DESIRED:

☐ ENGLISH ☐ GERMAN ☐ FRENCH

PLEASE PRINT

**NAME** **DATE**

**TITLE**

**COMPANY**

**ADDRESS**

**CITY** **POSTAL CODE**

**STATE/PROVINCE**

**COUNTRY**

**PLEASE SEND ORDER FORM AND MAKE CHECK PAYABLE TO:**

GRAPHIS US, INC.,

P.O. BOX 3063 SOUTHEASTERN, PA 19398-3063

SERVICE WILL BEGIN WITH ISSUE THAT IS CURRENT WHEN ORDER IS PROCESSED (LETTERHEAD 1)

**REQUEST FOR CALL FOR ENTRIES**

PLEASE PUT ME ON THE "CALL FOR ENTRIES" LIST FOR THE FOLLOWING TITLES:

☐ GRAPHIS DESIGN
☐ GRAPHIS DIAGRAM
☐ GRAPHIS POSTER
☐ GRAPHIS PACKAGING
☐ GRAPHIS LOGO
☐ GRAPHIS ANNUAL REPORTS
☐ GRAPHIS CORPORATE IDENTITY
☐ GRAPHIS PHOTO
☐ GRAPHIS LETTERHEAD

SUBMITTING MATERIAL TO ANY OF THE ABOVE TITLES, QUALIFIES SENDER FOR A 25% DISCOUNT TOWARD PURCHASE OF THAT TITLE.

## SUBSCRIBE TO GRAPHIS: EUROPE AND WORLD

| MAGAZINE | BRD | WORLD | U.K. |
|---|---|---|---|
| ☐ NEW ☐ RENEW | | | |
| ☐ TWO YEARS (12 ISSUES) | DM305,- | SFR262.- | £102.00 |
| ☐ ONE YEAR (6 ISSUES) | DM162,- | SFR140.- | £ 54.00 |

☐ 25% DISCOUNT FOR STUDENTS WITH COPY OF VALID, DATED STUDENT ID AND PAYMENT WITH ORDER

SUBSCRIPTION FEES INCLUDE POSTAGE TO ANY PART OF THE WORLD. AIRMAIL AVAILABLE EVERYWHERE EXCEPT EUROPE AND NORTH AMERICA.

☐ AIRMAIL SURCHARGE (6 ISSUES) SFR 58.-

FOR CREDIT CARD PAYMENT:

(ALL CARDS DEBITED IN SWISS FRANCS):

☐ AMERICAN EXPRESS ☐ DINER'S CLUB ☐ EURO/MASTERCARD

☐ VISA/BARCLAY/CARTE BLEUE

**ACCT. NO** **EXP. DATE**

**SIGNATURE** **CARDHOLDER NAME**

☐ CHECK ENCLOSED ☐ BILL ME

CHECK THE LANGUAGE VERSION DESIRED:

☐ ENGLISH ☐ GERMAN ☐ FRENCH

PLEASE PRINT

**NAME** **DATE**

**TITLE**

**COMPANY**

**ADDRESS**

**CITY** **POSTAL CODE**

**STATE/PROVINCE**

**COUNTRY**

**PLEASE SEND ORDER FORM AND MAKE CHECK PAYABLE TO:**

GRAPHIS PRESS CORP.,

DUFOURSTRASSE 107 CH-8008 ZÜRICH, SWITZERLAND

SERVICE WILL BEGIN WITH ISSUE THAT IS CURRENT WHEN ORDER IS PROCESSED (LETTERHEAD 1)

**REQUEST FOR CALL FOR ENTRIES**

PLEASE PUT ME ON THE "CALL FOR ENTRIES" LIST FOR THE FOLLOWING TITLES:

☐ GRAPHIS DESIGN
☐ GRAPHIS DIAGRAM
☐ GRAPHIS POSTER
☐ GRAPHIS PACKAGING
☐ GRAPHIS LOGO
☐ GRAPHIS ANNUAL REPORTS
☐ GRAPHIS CORPORATE IDENTITY
☐ GRAPHIS PHOTO
☐ GRAPHIS LETTERHEAD

SUBMITTING MATERIAL TO ANY OF THE ABOVE TITLES, QUALIFIES SENDER FOR A 25% DISCOUNT TOWARD PURCHASE OF THAT TITLE.

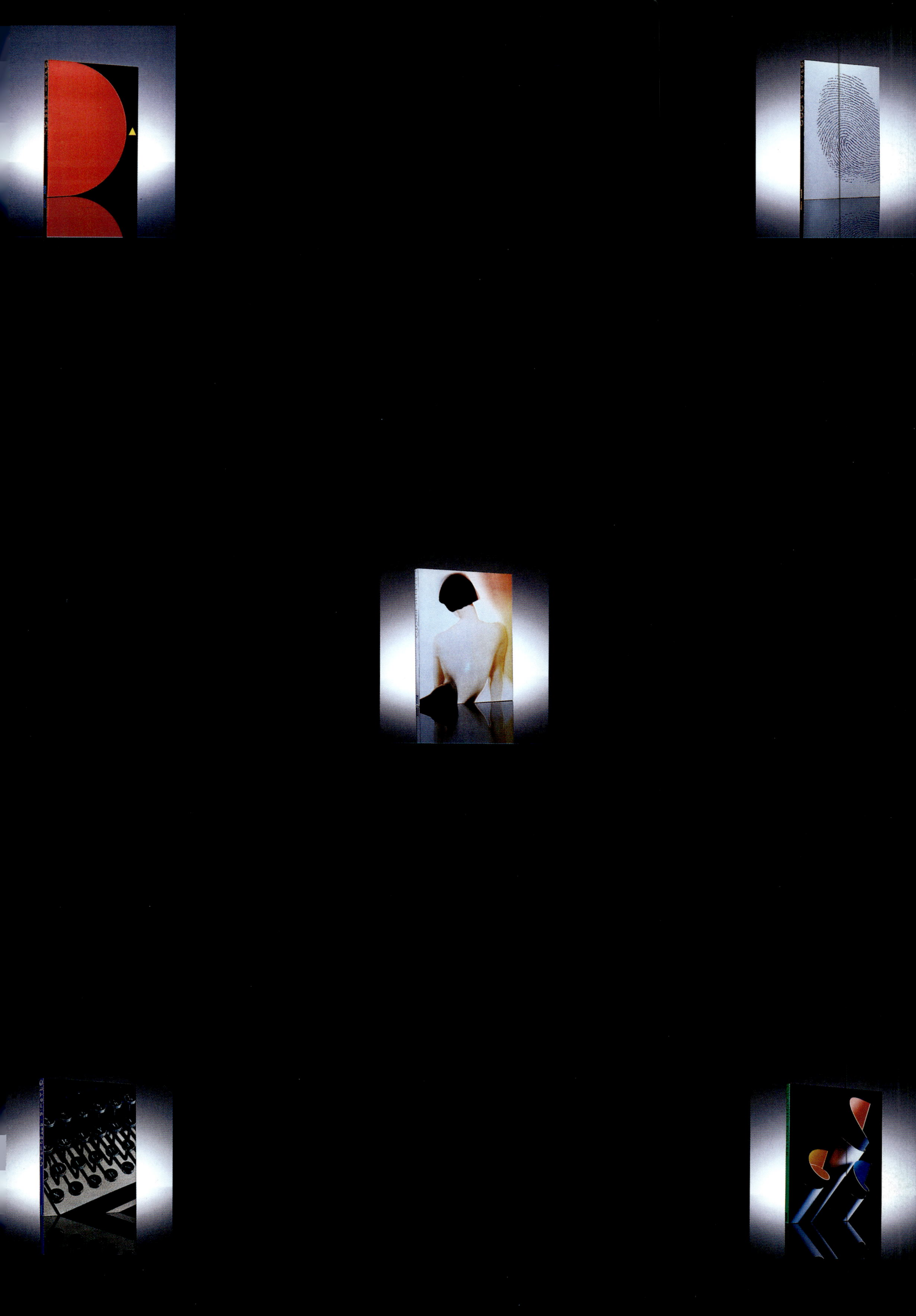

## BOOK ORDER FORM: USA AND CANADA

| BOOKS | USA | CANADA |
|---|---|---|
| □ GRAPHIS PHOTO 91 | US$69 | US$ 94 |
| □ GRAPHIS POSTER 91 | US$69 | US$ 94 |
| □ GRAPHIS DESIGN 91 | US$69 | US$ 94 |
| □ GRAPHIS PUBLICATION 1 | US$75 | US$100 |
| □ GRAPHIS ANNUAL REPORTS 3 | US$75 | US$100 |
| □ ART FOR SURVIVAL: THE ILLUSTRATOR AND THE ENVIRONMENT | US$40 | US$ 60 |
| □ GRAPHIS LETTERHEAD 1 | US$69 | US$ 94 |
| □ GRAPHIS LOGO 1 | US$50 | US$ 70 |
| □ THE GRAPHIC DESIGNERS GREEN BOOK | US$25 | US$ 41 |
| □ GRAPHIS PHOTO 90 | US$69 | US$ 94 |
| □ GRAPHIS POSTER 90 | US$69 | US$ 94 |
| □ GRAPHIS CORPORATE IDENTITY 1 | US$75 | US$100 |
| □ GRAPHIS PACKAGING 5 | US$75 | US$100 |
| □ GRAPHIS DIAGRAM 1 | US$65 | US$ 91 |

□ CHECK ENCLOSED (GRAPHIS AGREES TO PAY MAILING COSTS)

□ BILL ME (MAILING COSTS IN ADDITION TO ABOVE BOOK PRICE WILL BE CHARGED. BOOK(S) WILL BE SENT WHEN PAYMENT IS RECEIVED)

PLEASE PRINT

**NAME** **DATE**

**TITLE**

**COMPANY**

**ADDRESS**

**CITY**

**POSTAL CODE**

**STATE/PROVINCE**

**COUNTRY**

**SIGNATURE** **DATE**

**PLEASE SEND ORDER FORM AND MAKE CHECK PAYABLE TO:**

GRAPHIS US, INC.

141 LEXINGTON AVENUE, NEW YORK, NY 10016 USA

### REQUEST FOR CALL FOR ENTRIES

PLEASE PUT ME ON THE "CALL FOR ENTRIES" LIST FOR THE FOLLOWING TITLES:

□ GRAPHIS DESIGN
□ GRAPHIS DIAGRAM
□ GRAPHIS POSTER
□ GRAPHIS PACKAGING
□ GRAPHIS LOGO
□ GRAPHIS ANNUAL REPORTS
□ GRAPHIS CORPORATE IDENTITY
□ GRAPHIS PHOTO
□ GRAPHIS LETTERHEAD
□ GRAPHIS TYPOGRAPHY

SUBMITTING MATERIAL TO ANY OF THE ABOVE TITLES QUALIFIES SENDER FOR A 25% DISCOUNT TOWARD PURCHASE OF THAT TITLE.

## BOOK ORDER FORM: EUROPE AND WORLD

| BOOKS | BRD | WORLD | U.K. |
|---|---|---|---|
| □ GRAPHIS PHOTO 91 | DM 149,- | SFR.123.- | £49.00 |
| □ GRAPHIS POSTER 91 | DM 149,- | SFR 123.- | £49.00 |
| □ GRAPHIS DESIGN 91 | DM 149,- | SFR 123.- | £49.00 |
| □ GRAPHIS PUBLICATION 1 | DM 162,- | SFR.137.- | £52.00 |
| □ GRAPHIS ANNUAL REPORTS 3 | DM 162,- | SFR.137.- | £52.00 |
| □ ART FOR SURVIVAL: THE ILLUSTRATOR AND THE ENVIRONMENT | DM 86,- | SFR.73.- | £28.00 |
| □ GRAPHIS LETTERHEAD 1 | DM 149,- | SFR.123.- | £49.00 |
| □ GRAPHIS LOGO 1 | DM 108,- | SFR.92.- | £36.00 |
| □ THE GRAPHIC DESIGNER'S GREEN BOOK | DM 54,- | SFR.46.- | £18.00 |
| □ GRAPHIS PHOTO 90 | DM 149,- | SFR.123.- | £49.00 |
| □ GRAPHIS POSTER 90 | DM 149,- | SFR.123.- | £49.00 |
| □ GRAPHIS CORPORATE IDENTITY 1 | DM 160,- | SFR.132.- | £48.00 |
| □ GRAPHIS PACKAGING 5 | DM 160,- | SFR.132.- | £48.00 |
| □ GRAPHIS DIAGRAM 1 | DM 138,- | SFR.112.- | £45.00 |

□ CHECK ENCLOSED (FOR EUROPE, PLEASE MAKE SFR. CHECKS PAYABLE TO A SWISS BANK)

□ AMOUNT PAID INTO GRAPHIS ACCOUNT AT THE UNION BANK OF SWITZERLAND, ACCOUNT NO 3620063 IN ZÜRICH.

□ AMOUNT PAID TO POSTAL CHEQUE ACCOUNT ZÜRICH 80-23071-9 (THROUGH YOUR LOCAL POST OFFICE)

□ PLEASE BILL ME (MAILING COSTS IN ADDITION TO ABOVE BOOK PRICE WILL BE CHARGED. BOOK(S) WILL BE SENT WHEN PAYMENT IS RECEIVED)

PLEASE PRINT

**NAME** **DATE**

**TITLE**

**COMPANY**

**ADDRESS**

**CITY**

**POSTAL CODE**

**STATE/PROVINCE**

**COUNTRY**

**SIGNATURE** **DATE**

**PLEASE SEND ORDER FORM AND MAKE CHECK PAYABLE TO:**

GRAPHIS PRESS CORP., DUFOURSTRASSE 107, CH-8008 ZÜRICH, SWITZERLAND

### REQUEST FOR CALL FOR ENTRIES

PLEASE PUT ME ON THE "CALL FOR ENTRIES" LIST FOR THE FOLLOWING TITLES:

□ GRAPHIS DESIGN
□ GRAPHIS DIAGRAM
□ GRAPHIS POSTER
□ GRAPHIS PACKAGING
□ GRAPHIS LOGO
□ GRAPHIS ANNUAL REPORTS
□ GRAPHIS CORPORATE IDENTITY
□ GRAPHIS PHOTO
□ GRAPHIS LETTERHEAD
□ GRAPHIS TYPOGRAPHY

SUBMITTING MATERIAL TO ANY OF THE ABOVE TITLES QUALIFIES SENDER FOR A 25% DISCOUNT TOWARD PURCHASE OF THAT TITLE.